PLANET X

X

THE SIGN OF THE SON OF MAN

AND THE END OF THE AGE

PLANET X

THE SIGN OF THE SON OF MAN
AND THE END OF THE AGE
Planet X at the Creation, Nativity & Second Coming

©2010 Douglas A. Elwell
All Rights Reserved

Planet X, the Sign of the Son of Man, and the End of the Age:
Planet X at the Creation, Nativity & Second Coming

Defender
Crane, Missouri 65633

©2010 Douglas A. Elwell
All Rights Reserved. Published 2010.

Printed in the United States of America

ISBN 13: 9780984630011

A CIP catalog record of this book is available from
the Library of Congress.

All Scripture quotations, unless otherwise noted, are from the
(Authorized) King James Version (KJV)

"Elwell's Law" and
"The Elwell Progression" theory of planetary formation
© 2010 Douglas A. Elwell. All rights reserved.

All retranslations of Genesis, the Psalms, Isaiah, Job,
and all other Scriptures
© 2010 Douglas A. Elwell. All rights reserved.

All rights reserved. No part of this manuscript may be reproduced in any form without express written consent from the author, except for brief quotations in books or critical reviews.

Cover illustration and design by Doug Elwell, Inc.

CONTENTS

INTRODUCTION 1

I. GOD'S CONFLICT WITH THE DRAGON IN THE SEA 5
THE CREATION AS A "DIVINE CONFLICT" 6
THE "DIVINE CONFLICT" CREATION THEME
IN THE ANCIENT NEAR EAST 14
THE ANCIENT CREATION TRADITION 27
THE ANCIENT CREATION TRADITION IN THE OLD TESTAMENT 46
THE ANCIENT CREATION TRADITION IN THE NEW TESTAMENT 77
CHAPTER I: PRELIMINARY CONCLUSIONS 83

II. THE ASTRONOMICAL RELIGIONS
OF THE ANCIENT NEAR EAST 87
THE TOWER OF BABEL IN THE BIBLE 88
THE TOWER OF BABEL IN BABYLONIAN MYTH 92
PLANETARY DEITIES IN ANCIENT NEAR EASTERN RELIGION 101
THE RISE AND DEVELOPMENT OF SCIENTIFIC ASTRONOMY 108
THE MAGI:
THE INHERITORS OF THE ANCIENT CREATION TRADITION 115

III. THE STAR OF BETHLEHEM: A TENTH PLANET? 125
THE MAGI AND THE STAR OF BETHLEHEM 126
A NEW THEORY ON THE STAR OF BETHLEHEM:
A TENTH PLANET 131
PLANET X: THE EVIDENCE 152
CONCLUSION 208

IV. "WHEN ON HIGH": THE ASTRONOMICAL
INTERPRETATION OF THE ENUMA ELISH 211
ENUMA ELISH REINTERPRETED 213
ENUMA ELISH:
AN ACCOUNT OF THE CREATION OF OUR SOLAR SYSTEM 220
TABLET I: A GENERAL OVERVIEW
OF THE CREATION OF OUR SOLAR SYSTEM 229
TABLET IV: PLANET X AND THE GIANT IMPACT 249
TABLET V: MORE RESULTS OF THE GIANT IMPACT 261
TABLET VI:
THE CREATION OF MAN AND THE TOWER OF BABEL 273
TABLET VII: PLANET X: THE STAR OF THE CROSSING 278
SUMMARY 279

V. "IN THE BEGINNING": THE BIBLICAL CREATION MATERIAL REINTERPRETED 283
THESIS: GOD USED PLANET X TO CREATE HEAVEN AND EARTH 284
GENESIS 1:
GOD USES PLANET X TO (RE)CREATE HEAVEN AND EARTH 289
REFERENCES TO THE CREATION OF THE EARTH REINTERPRETED 303
REFERENCES TO THE CREATION
OF THE HEAVENS REINTERPRETED 310
REFERENCES TO GOD'S "THRONE" IN HEAVEN REINTERPRETED 320

VI. JOB: THE HEBREW CREATION EPIC 341
THE RETURN OF PLANET X: 2000 B.C. 343
JOB: THE MAN IN THE MOON 354
JOB'S COMPANIONS, THE COMETS 362
ECHOES OF THE DIVINE CONFLICT IN JOB 368
THE THEOPHANY OF GOD:
THE DIVINE CONFLICT REMEMBERED 374
CONCLUSIONS 402

VII. PLANET X, THE SIGN OF THE SON OF MAN, AND THE END OF THE AGE 405
THE "STAR" OF THE MESSIAH: THE BIBLICAL EVIDENCE 406
REVELATION: THE RETURN OF THE DRAGON 426
THE SIGN OF THE SON OF MAN AND THE END OF THE AGE 428
FINAL CONCLUSIONS 453

INTRODUCTION

Planet X, The Sign of the Son of Man, and the End of the Age is essentially a thorough analysis of the heavenly sign that preceded Christ's birth within the context of the Bible, ancient Near Eastern religion, and modern astronomy. This analysis is intended to serve as a well illuminated background to help us understand the true nature of the heavenly "Sign" that Jesus said would immediately precede His Second Coming (Matt. 24:30), and the implications that this Sign's existence has upon our understanding of human history and religion — particularly that period of time described in the Bible as the "End Times" — which will be discussed in the final chapter of this book. By studying the Bible, ancient Near Eastern religion, and modern astronomy together, we will find that they have much more in common than can be seen at first glance. We will also find that the "Sign" that will herald Christ's Second Coming has a history that stretches all the way back to the creation of the world. This is why *Planet X, The Sign of the Son of Man, and the End of the Age* is subtitled, "Planet X at the Creation, Nativity, and Second Coming" — both the Creation, the Nativity, and the Second Coming of Christ are inextricably linked by the mysterious "Planet X", the true nature and relevance of which will be revealed throughout the pages of this book.

My interest in this subject was originally inspired by an enigmatic passage in the Book of Matthew, typically referred to as "The Olivet Discourse," where Jesus describes to His disciples the conditions that will precede His Second Coming. At the climax of this discourse, Christ highlights the central importance of a heavenly "Sign" that will immediately precede His return in glory:

> And as he sat upon the mount of Olives, the disciples came unto him privately, saying, Tell us, when shall these things be? and what shall be the sign of thy coming, and of the end of the world? And Jesus answered and said unto them, Take heed that no man deceive you.... For as the lightning cometh out of the east, and shineth even unto the west; so shall also the coming of the Son of man be. For wheresoever the carcase is, there will the eagles be gathered together. Immediately after the tribulation of those days shall the Sun be darkened, and the Moon shall not give her light, and the stars shall fall from heaven, and the powers of the heavens shall be shaken: *And then shall appear the sign of the Son of man in heaven*:

and then shall all the tribes of the earth mourn, and they shall see the Son of man coming in the clouds of heaven with power and great glory. And he shall send his angels with a great sound of a trumpet, and they shall gather together his elect from the four winds, from one end of heaven to the other. (Matt. 24:3-4, 27-31, KJV, emphasis mine)

The exact nature of this mysterious "Sign" has eluded commentators to this day. However, as we shall see in this book, the answer to this mystery is actually quite logical, and neatly explains many of the more enigmatic passages in the Bible, particularly those having to do with the Creation, Nativity, and Second Coming. The history of this heavenly Sign stretches all the way back to the creation of Earth. It also held a central role in ancient Near Eastern religion, served as the central focus of the Book of Job, made a crucial appearance as the "Star of Bethlehem" event described in the Book of Matthew, and will make its final appearance as the Sign of the Son of Man and the end of the age.

Planet X, The Sign of the Son of Man and the End of the Age is divided into seven chapters, each of which deals with the various concepts that the reader needs to understand in order to fully comprehend what exactly "the Sign of the Son of Man" is. Though individually these concepts are so broad in scope that one could easily devote an entire volume to each, a thorough understanding of all of these concepts together, in the same work, is crucial to a complete understanding of the true nature of the Sign of the Son of Man. These concepts are divided up among seven chapters. The first six chapters assimilate the evidence, and the final, seventh chapter draws it all together in order to answer the question that lies in the heart of every true believer: "what will be the Sign of your coming, and of the end of the age?"

Douglas A. Elwell

October 10, 2010

I

GOD'S CONFLICT WITH THE DRAGON IN THE SEA

In that day the L<small>ORD</small> with his sore and great and strong sword
shall punish leviathan the piercing serpent,
even leviathan that crooked serpent;
and he shall slay the dragon that is in the sea.
(Isaiah. 27:1)

Penetrating to the core of the Bible, we find that the dominant theme throughout the whole canon is that of God as the Divine Warrior. Regardless of the situation, throughout salvation history God has constantly warred — and won — against the forces of evil that have sought to defeat His plans for His people.

This conflict can be found throughout the Bible. It can be found both in the open war God waged against the dragon at the Creation and in the fierce inner struggle Christ endured in the Garden. It can be found both in Paul's endurance of trials for his confession of Christ and in Michael's casting down of the dragon from heaven in the end-times. The Bible is all about conflict — about struggle, about drawing distinctions between right and wrong, between good and evil. And though these distinctions may range from subtle to clear, all are based on the same underlying conflict: God's conflict with the dragon in the sea.

"The Destruction of Leviathan" by Gustave Doré (1865), inspired by the prophecy of Isaiah 27:1, wherein God promises in the End Times to finish the job He began at the Creation. Thus both the Creation and the End Times are inextricably linked.

THE CREATION AS A "DIVINE CONFLICT"

God creating the solar system, from "Creation of the Sun, Moon, and Planets" by Michelangelo Buonarroti (1511).

The majority of the Creation references in the Old Testament portray the Creation not as a peaceful act, but as the result of a "divine conflict" in heaven. In this "divine conflict" Creation scenario, Earth is seen as having been created as the result of some sort of heavenly cataclysm, symbolized in the Bible as a battle between God and a "dragon." In other words, the Israelites actually believed that, in the beginning, God had defeated this "dragon," and created the heavens and Earth from its dead body.

Some biblical scholars have argued that this belief actually formed the very foundation of Israelite worship. As Frank Moore Cross, Jr. explains, "The central or constitutive movement in the early cultus was the celebration of the enthronement of Yahweh as King and Creator of cosmos by virtue of His victory over His enemy or enemies in a cosmogonic struggle."[1] This "cosmogonic struggle," as described

---

[1] Frank Moore Cross, Jr., "The Divine Warrior in Israel's Early Cult," in *Biblical Motifs*, ed. Alexander Altmann (Cambridge, MA: Harvard University Press, 1966), 11.

in such passages as Psalm 74:12-17, Isaiah 51:9-15, and Job 9:6-13, refers to a conflict between God and a dragon that is closely linked with the Creation in the Old Testament. And even in Genesis 1, where "the dragon" is not directly mentioned, echoes of the divine conflict can be clearly seen under closer examination.

This "divine conflict" theme resurfaces in the New Testament, in the Book of Revelation (Rev. 12–13; 20), where war between God and the dragon similarly defines the scenario surrounding the Second Coming of Christ. Isaiah confirms this, explaining that the Creation battle with the dragon will be repeated in the end-times, when God will crush the dragon forever (Isa. 27:1). Thus, a study of the Creation material in the Bible presents us with foundational material critical to a complete understanding of the end-times, as the events surrounding both the Creation and the end-times appear to be inextricably linked.

God Is a Warrior

All together, the numerous references to the divine Creation conflict in the Old Testament, combined with the prominent heavenly conflict imagery in the Book of Revelation, form the foundation of a theme that runs throughout and binds together the Old and New Testaments: God the Divine Warrior, Creator of the heavens and Earth, and Defeater of the dragon. Tremper and Longman explain in their seminal book, *God Is a Warrior,*

> On the surface, the Bible is a diverse collection of writings, a veritable anthology of different literary works.... In the midst of diversity, however, the careful reader is drawn into the organic unity of the Bible. Though it is often difficult to explain, the Bible's message coheres on a profound level. This message cuts across time and genres, so that not only is the Bible composed of many different stories, we may also say that it tells a single story.... The present study focuses on one of the most pervasive of all biblical themes: the divine warrior.[2]

---

[2]Tremper Longman III and Daniel G. Reid, *God Is a Warrior,* Studies in Old Testament Biblical Theology (Grand Rapids: Zondervan, 1995), 13. See also Millard C. Lind, *Yahweh*

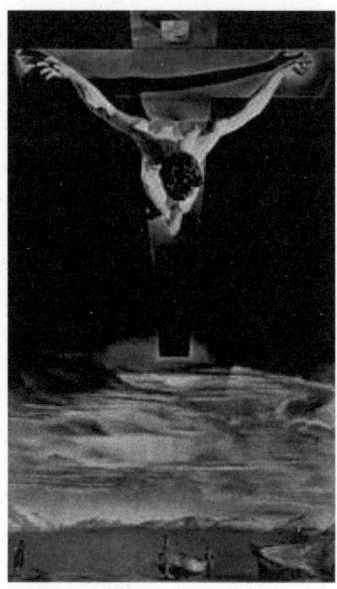

"Christ of St. John of the Cross" by Salvador Dali (1951).

Though Tremper and Longman claim that it is only *one* of the most pervasive of all biblical themes, I believe they have actually hit upon the theme that is by far *the most* dominant throughout the entire Bible. Though there are numerous thematic similarities between the Old and New Testaments, particularly the theme of the saving grace of God, the primary themes of the Old and New Testaments are basically dissimilar. Whereas the primary theme of the Old Testament is the foundation and history of the nation of Israel as God's chosen people, the New Testament's primary theme instead focuses on the birth, crucifixion, and resurrection of Jesus Christ, and upon the foundation and early history of His Church.

Based upon this comparison, there might appear to be, at first glance, little to compare between the Old and New Testaments. However, though the Old Testament focuses on God's acting in history to create the nation of Israel, and the New Testament focuses on God's acting in history to send His Son to die on the Cross for the sins of the world, the common theme between the two is *God's acting in history*. This is the "profound level" where the message of the Bible coheres, as Tremper and Longman argue. And how does God act in history? In retrospect it is clear that the God of Moses is in fact an excellent General, always making the perfect tactical decisions throughout history to achieve the strategic goals that He had set out to accomplish from the beginning. He divided the Red Sea just long enough to allow the Israelites to cross safely, and then allowed it to drown the pursuing Egyptians. He brought the nation of Israel back out of captivity so His Son could be born in Bethlehem, to become the saviour of the world at the appointed time. And in the end He will send His Son back to Earth

Is a Warrior: The Theology of Warfare in Ancient Israel (Scottsdale, AZ: Herald Press, 1980).

to claim His rightful throne. All history was foreordained by God from before the foundation of the world to accomplish His one goal: to rule the universe forever. But in order to accomplish this goal, God first had to fight and defeat His enemy: the Dragon.

God's Enemy the Dragon

Every warrior must have an enemy, and God's enemy is the dragon — a being who is the living embodiment of chaos and evil, of everything that stands in opposition to God's perfect rule over Earth. This being takes various forms thoughout the Bible: as a serpent (Hebrew נָחָשׁ, *naḥash*), as a dragon (תַּנִּין, *tannin*; Greek δράκων, *drakon*) and as a "sea dragon." As a sea dragon, God's enemy usually has a personal name such as Rahab (רַהַב, *rahav*, lit., "storm" or "arrogance"), or Leviathan (לִוְיָתָן, *liv'yathan*).

The political enemies of Israel are also often portrayed in the Bible as dragons or associated with serpents, which appear to have been used in the ancient Near East as universal symbols of evil (cf. Deut. 32:32-33; Jer. 51:34; Ezek. 29:3-4). As Nicholas Kiessling explains in his seminal article, "Antecedents of the Medieval Dragon in Sacred History," "The most fearsome dragons of the OT, tannin, Leviathan, and Rahab, are the horrible but vague incarnations of evil, darkly outlined opponents of both God and man. They inhabit the depths of the seas and are often employed as apt metaphors of heathen kings hostile to the children of Israel."[3] Though there are many and varied instances of conflict between God and serpentine creatures in the Bible, in this book we will be focusing primarily on those passages which deal with God's conflict with the sea dragons tannin, Leviathan, and Rahab.

---

[3]Nicolas K. Kiessling, "Antecedents of the Medieval Dragon in Sacred History," *Journal of Biblical Literature* 89 (1970): 167.

✟ *Tannin*. The most common of the three names of the dragon, this generic term is also the most ambiguous. Various Bible versions have translated tannin as different types of creatures, depending upon the context in which the word appears — from the standard translation of "dragon," to "monster," "whale," or even "jackal."

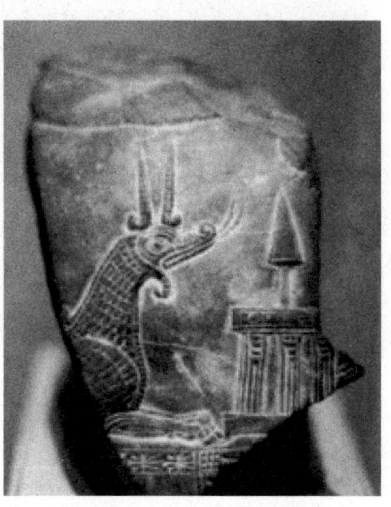

A stone fragment showing the head of the dragon-goddess Tiamat as she was typically depicted in ancient Near Eastern art and architecture.

Tannin generally means "dragon," but it is often translated differently by modern scholars because "dragons" *per se* are not accounted for in the archaeological record of the biblical period. For example, in Genesis 1:21, God is described as having created "great *whales,* and every living creature that moveth, which the waters brought forth abundantly" (KJV). The word that is translated "whales" here is actually *tannin*. Other ambiguous usages of *tannin* occur many times throughout the Bible, but although the *King James Version* tends to translate most of these references as "dragon," the *New International Version* prefers either "jackal" (Neh. 2:13; Job 30:29; Ps. 44:19; Isa. 13:22; 34:13; 35:7; 43:20; Jer. 9:11; 10:22; 49:33; 51:37; Lam. 4:3; Micah 1:8), "serpent" or "snake" (Ex. 7:9-12; Deut. 32:33; Ps. 91:13; Jer. 51:34), "monster" (Job 7:12; Ps. 74:13; Isa. 27:1; 51:9; Ezek. 29:3), or "sea creature" (Ps. 148:7).

In fact, it appears that the NIV translators made a concerted effort to erase *all* the references to dragons found throughout the Old Testament. This is part of a dangerous trend toward demythologizing the Bible that that has walked hand in hand in recent decades with the progressive liberalization of biblical interpretation and the abandonment of correct, contextual interpretations in favor of popular, "politically correct" ones. This subversive trend is ably illustrated by the replacement of "dragon" with "monster" in some of the most well-known dragon references in the Old Testament: Psalm 74:13 and

Isaiah 27:1. As a result, the NIV translators have actually eliminated the word "dragon" entirely from the Old Testament.

Though the *King James* translation's frequent use of "dragon" should be retained in most cases, some of the references, such as Lam. 4:3 and Micah 1:8, are problematic. For example, the NIV's translation of *tannin* as "jackals" in Micah 1:8 is probably the best. In 1:8 Micah says he will "howl like a *tannin* and moan like an owl." The NIV translates *tannin* here as "jackal," mainly because jackals are one of the few desert creatures that howl. Since "dragons," or reptiles of any kind, are not known for howling, "jackals" is probably the best translation here.

Kiessling illustrates this dilemma, pointing out the numerous ways *tannin* has been and can be translated:

> In Psalm 74:13, Isaiah 27:1 and 51:9, it denotes a monster in the sea which God has destroyed or will destroy. In Psalm 148:7, Genesis 1:21, and Job 7:12, *tannin* refers to "sea monsters" in general. On three occasions it is used metaphorically to connote the malign nature of foreign rulers. In Jeremiah 51:34, God tells the children of Israel that Nebuchadrezzar 'has swallowed me like a dragon,' and in Ezekiel 29:3 and 32:2, the prophet Ezekiel is to tell Pharaoh—that 'great dragon lying in the midst of his streams'—of God's coming judgment. On four occasions the *tannin* is more like a land serpent. It is the serpent-dragon whom God will trample under his feet in Psalm 91:13, and in Exodus 7 *tannin* once names the serpents that magically appear when the priests of Egypt throw down their staffs (7:12) and twice refers to the serpent that will appear when Aaron throws down his staff (7:9-10). A final occurrence, in Lamentations 4:3, is ambiguous—"Even the *tannin*...give(s) the breast and suckle(s) their (her) young." It may refer to sea beasts—whales suckle their young. Thus, *tannin* consistently refers to some pernicious beast, generally the opponent of God and man, whether it is a sea or land monster.[4]

It appears, then, that *tannin* is a generic word that can be used to designate any large, dangerous creature, a word similar in use to the English word "monster." As such, its translation will depend on the

---

[4]Kiessling, "Antecedents of the Medieval Dragon," 167-68.

context in which it occurs. However, as we shall see, the most basic meaning of *tannin* is "dragon."

- Leviathan. "Leviathan" is used several times in the Old Testament as the name of a powerful sea dragon that fought God at the Creation, and will do so again in the end-times. The passage that most clearly describes the creation battle between God and Leviathan is Psalm 74:12-17. Two other references, Job 3:8 (KJV)[5] and Job 41 refer to Leviathan as a great dragon of antiquity, but do not directly refer to the Creation battle.[6] Leviathan appears twice in one passage in Isaiah, where it is prophesied that God will fight Leviathan again when He returns to Earth in the end-times (Isa. 27:1). The sixth and last occurrence of Leviathan, however, in Psalm 104:26, refers to Leviathan simply as a sea creature, with no reference to the creation, or to conflict of any kind. Kiessling explains, "לִוְיָתָן [Leviathan], used six times in all, thrice refers in unmistakable terms to the great God-dragon combat, Isaiah 27:1 (twice) and Psalm 74:14. In two other passages, Job 3:8 and 40:25 (41:1), references to this combat are also evident but oblique.... Psalm 104:26, on the contrary, tells of a milder Leviathan, one which plays in the sea."[7]

Unlike *tannin*, Leviathan is used as a proper name in all but one passage (Psalm 104), and it is used much more consistently overall than is *tannin*. Also unlike *tannin*, Leviathan almost always refers to a specific being, variously described as a "dragon" or "serpent," that lives in the sea. For example, Leviathan is described as a "serpent" in Isaiah 27:1 and as both a "serpent" and as a "dragon" *(tannin)* in Psalm 74:13-14 and Isaiah 27:1. Leviathan is also described as having multiple heads (Ps. 74:13), as being huge and menacing (Job 3:8; 41), and as living in the sea (Job 41; Isa. 27:1; Pss. 74:13-14; 104:26). Clearly then, "Leviathan," "dragon," and "serpent" can be used

---

[5] This passage is translated as "their mourning" in the KJV, but the actual text says "Leviathan", the same dragon that is the subject of Job 41. Other translations, such as the NIV and NASB, also have "Leviathan".

[6] A more thorough translation of Job 41 actually shows clear divine conflict imagery similar to that used in *Enuma Elish*.

[7] Kiessling, "Antecedents of the Medieval Dragon," 168.

interchangeably to refer to a being that is the enemy of God, a being who opposed Him at the Creation of Earth and who will oppose Him again upon His return.

✢ *Rahab.* The name "Rahab," which occurs seven times in the Old Testament, also clearly designates a sea dragon that God fought at the Creation. Kiessling explains, "רָהַב [Rahab] clearly denotes some evil monster at war with God.... Four times Rahab is used in connection with the God-dragon combat — Isaiah 51:9, 'Was it not thou...that didst cut Rahab, that didst pierce the dragon? (*tannin*)'; Psalm 89:11, 'Thou hast broken Rahab in pieces'; Job 9:13, 'God will not turn back his anger, beneath him bowed the helpers of Rahab'; and Job 26:12, 'By His power He stilled the sea, by His understanding He smote Rahab.' "[8] Rahab was also occasionally used as a generic term, in this case referring to enemies of the nation of Israel. "Elsewhere Rahab refers to opponents of God, either to those who do not obey Him as in Psalm 40:5, or to those nations that oppose Israel, and therefore God, as in Psalm 87:4 and Isaiah 30:7."[9]

The similarities between Rahab and Leviathan make it clear that Rahab, Leviathan, and "the dragon" *tannin* are all designations for the same evil entity that fought against God at the Creation. As Graves and Patai explain, "Leviathan cannot be easily distinguished from Rahab, Tannin, Nahash, or any other mystical creatures that personify water."[10] As He had with Leviathan, God had fought against the dragon Rahab at the Creation: "piercing it" (Isa. 51:9), breaking it "in pieces" (Ps. 89:11), and defeating its "helpers" (Job 9:13; Ps.

A stone fragment showing the head of the dragon-goddess Tiamat as she was typically depicted in ancient Near Eastern art and architecture.

---

[8]Kiessling, "Antecedents of the Medieval Dragon," 168.

[9]*Ibid.*," 168.

[10]Robert Graves and Raphael Patai, *Hebrew Myths: The Book of Genesis* (Garden City, NY: Doubleday & Company, 1964), 31.

89:10). Like Leviathan, Rahab is also closely associated with the sea (Ps. 89:9-10; Isa. 51:9-10) and is described as being both a "dragon" *(tannin)* and a "serpent" (Job 26:12-13).

All together, the references to Rahab, Leviathan, and "the dragon" clearly support the conclusion that the Hebrews conceived of the Creation not as a peaceful act, but as an act that involved a conflict between two warring entities: God and a dragon. This theme, the "divine conflict" creation theme, appears consistently throughout the Old Testament and even in the New Testament, in the Book of Revelation, where the dragon makes a prominent reappearance (Rev. 12-13; 16:30; 20:2). The divine conflict creation theme is also present in other important ancient Near Eastern creation stories, many of which closely parallel the Hebrew creation story in many respects. As such, by studying the divine conflict creation theme in the Old Testament and relating it to similar ancient Near Eastern conceptions of the Creation, we can arrive at an understanding of the Hebrew concept of Creation that is both biblically and contextually accurate.

THE "DIVINE CONFLICT" CREATION THEME IN THE ANCIENT NEAR EAST

A depiction of the battle between the Babylonian god Marduk and the dragon-goddess Tiamat from the Babylonian Epic of Creation. In the myth, the chief god of Babylon, Marduk, was believed to have defeated Tiamat and created the heavens and the Earth from her dead body.

Understanding the context in which the Bible was written is crucial to accurate interpretation. Textual studies are only half the battle. Without using the correct interpretational procedure, grammatical historical criticism (a method of interpretation in which a text is studied both according to strict grammatical rules *and* according to the philosophical and cultural context of the period in which it was written), it is impossible to arrive at a truly accurate understanding of what the Bible was intended to communicate. Gordon Wenham explains this ably in his commentary on Genesis:

> Modern man makes assumptions about the world that are completely different from those of the second millennium B.C. Consequently when we read Genesis, we tend to grab hold of points that were of quite peripheral interest to the author of Genesis and we overlook points that are fundamental. By looking at the oriental background and the place of Genesis 1–11 within the whole book, we hope to escape this particular pitfall and understand Genesis [and the Bible as a whole] as it was originally intended.[11]

The Old Testament was written using a literary style that was intended to reach an audience that lived in a period of history very different from our own. Thus, in order to translate the Bible properly into our modern context, we must first understand the ancient concepts and assumptions that the writers of the Old Testament employed when they did their writing. The question becomes then, what concepts would these Godly writers have used to communicate what God had revealed to them concerning the Creation? They would have employed commonly known Creation concepts that people who lived at that time would have easily understood.

But was there a common Creation theme in ancient Near Eastern thought? In fact, even a brief survey of ancient creation stories, particularly Mesopotamian creation stories, makes it clear that the belief that Earth had been created from the body of a dragon by a warrior deity was the dominant creation theme during that period.

This was especially true of the ancient Babylonians, whose creation myth, *Enuma Elish*, describes the Creation as the result of a battle between the supreme god of their pantheon, Marduk, and an evil dragon-goddess named Tiamat. In the *Enuma Elish,* more generally known as The Babylonian Creation Epic, Marduk defeats Tiamat and then cuts her body into pieces, using these pieces as raw material to create heaven and Earth. Like the Hebrews, the Babylonians saw the Creation as a sort of "divine conflict," where a supreme deity representing the forces of law and good defeats a lesser, rebellious deity representing the forces of chaos and evil.

Though the relationship between *Enuma Elish* and the Creation material in Genesis 1 is not immediately clear to the untrained eye,

---

[11]Gordon J. Wenham, *Word Biblical Commentary Vol. 1: Genesis 1–15* (Dallas: Word Books, 1987), *xlv.*

closer examination of the original Hebrew text, translated within the context of ancient Near Eastern thought, reveals clear parallels not only between *Enuma Elish* and Genesis 1, but also with many other biblical references to the Creation scattered throughout the Psalms, Isaiah, and Job. In fact, many scholars, including such notables as Gerhard Von Rad, R.K. Harrison, and Cyrus Gordon, believe these similarities are due to a common Mesopotamian literary background that the biblical writers drew upon as a rich, familiar source for descriptive imagery. As Gordon explains, "The Hebrew accounts of creation, though later in date, drew (as a rule indirectly), upon the earlier traditions of other people including the Mesopotamians."[12] These scholars believe *Enuma Elish* was a particularly influential source for many of the biblical writers. They also point out that few if any of the references to the Creation scattered throughout the Old Testament describe the Creation as a peaceful act; rather, most, if not all, references to the Creation describe it using the same "divine conflict" imagery found in *Enuma Elish*. For example, both the biblical creation accounts and *Enuma Elish* use the imagery of a warrior deity defeating a dragon, both describe the dragon as having allies in its struggle against the warrior deity, and both are based upon the idea that Earth was made from the dead body of this dragon – specifically, its head.

This theory, that the Hebrews and the Babylonians had both conceived of the Creation as being the result of a "divine conflict," has been gaining more and more adherents since it was first proposed by the prominent German theologian, Hermann Gunkel, around the turn of the century. John Day explains in his excellent monograph, *God's Conflict with the Dragon and the Sea,*

> The effective beginning of the study of this theme...came about with the publication of the book by H. Gunkel entitled *Schopfung und Chaos in Urzeit und Endzeit* [Creation and Chaos in the Beginning and in the End-Times].... He recognized the mythical character of the various passages in the Old Testament which speak of a conflict between Yahweh and the sea and a dragon or dragons, variously called Leviathan, Rahab, etc., and saw these as being an Israelite appropriation of the Babylonian myth of Marduk's victory over Tiamat at the time of creation recounted in

---

[12]Cyrus H. Gordon, *The Ancient Near East* (New York: W.W. Norton & Company, 1965), 45.

Enuma Elish, a work sometimes called "the Babylonian Creation Epic."[13]

Figure 1.1. A map of the ancient Near East during the time of Abraham, and of the Babylonian Creation Epic (ca. 2000 B.C.). This was the world of the Old Testament. Babylon arose around the 17th Century B.C to fill the power vacuum left by the Sumerian Empire, and would become one of the dominant players in Mesopotamia.

Gunkel's work sparked a trend in biblical studies which is still strong today. Even those skeptical of Babylonian influence upon the biblical writers are forced to recognize the numerous similarities between the biblical and ancient Near Eastern Creation stories, particularly those from Mesopotamia, a geographic region in which Babylon was for a time one of the most powerful countries. (See Figure 1.1.) This trend has left a trail of numerous excellent studies on the subject, most of which are centered on one ancient text: *Enuma Elish,* or "the Babylonian Creation Epic." A careful study of this important text should be revealing as to the Creation concepts prevalent in the ancient Near East during the biblical period.

---

[13]John Day, *God's Conflict with the Dragon and the Sea: Echoes of a Canaanite Myth in the Old Testament* (Cambridge: Cambridge University Press, 1988), 1–2. It is important to note that Gunkel was dealing with both the Creation *and* the end-times (Urzeit *and* Endzeit), as they are linked together in the Bible.

The Babylonian Creation Epic

The Babylonian Creation Epic is, like the Hebrew creation account in Genesis 1, basically a description of how the heavens and Earth were created. However, unlike Genesis 1, *Enuma Elish* is written in the form of a story, complete with a cast of mythical/symbolic "god" characters, a plotline, and a climax. This story is divided into seven tablets:

I. Tablet I describes how the Babylonian "gods" first came into being. Apsu, the father of the gods, along with Mother Tiamat and their adviser, Mummu, are shown as having existed from the beginning, floating in the heavenly "waters." Father Apsu and Mother Tiamat then give birth to six more gods: Lahmu, Lahamu, Anshar, Kishar, Anu, and Ea. However, Apsu and Tiamat, disturbed by the noise and commotion made by their newborn children, suddenly change their minds and decide to destroy them. Overhearing their plot, their son Ea attacks them. He kills Apsu, and imprisons Mummu, their adviser, but is unable to kill his mother, Tiamat. To finish her off, Ea and his wife Damkina (whose origin is not explained) give birth to a son, Marduk, whom they prepare as a warrior to fight for them against Tiamat. Tiamat, seeing their plan, gives birth to twelve monstrous serpents to help her defend herself against Marduk, making the largest of them, Kingu, the head of her newborn army. Tiamat then gives Kingu a "tablet of destinies," a symbol of authority that symbolizes his leadership over the army of twelve. By doing so, Tiamat has effectively made Kingu a god, since, according to the epic, only the gods can have "destinies."

II. The description of Tiamat's preparations for battle against Marduk is repeated. Anshar sends his brother Anu to try to defeat Tiamat, but Anu is unable to do so. Anshar then calls upon Ea's son Marduk to fight against Tiamat. Ea consents, and sends Marduk forth to Anshar, who heaps praise and encouragement upon him.

III. Anshar sends his adviser, Gaga, to inform his brothers Lahmu and Lahamu of the upcoming conflict between Marduk and Tiamat. Shocked, Lahmu and Lahamu agree to travel with Gaga to the assembly of the gods, their brothers, where they feast together in fellowship in their assembly hall.

IV. The gods erect a throne for Marduk in their assembly hall, and crown him as their king and defender against Tiamat. Marduk then makes ready his armor and various exotic weapons including, among other things, a bow and arrows, a mace, lightning, flaming armor and helm, a net to capture and entangle Tiamat, seven "winds," and his chariot, "the flood storm," which is drawn by a "team-of-four." Marduk then approaches Tiamat in the climactic scene of the story. They exchange words and then struggle briefly but furiously. Tiamat opens her mouth to devour Marduk, but Marduk sends one of his "winds" into Tiamat's open mouth, followed by an arrow from his bow, which pierces her heart. Marduk then defeats and imprisons her army of helpers and takes the "tablet of destinies" away from Kingu, keeping it for himself. (With his own tablet of destiny, Marduk now officially becomes one of the gods.) Marduk then cuts Tiamat's dead body in half, using her lower half to create heaven, the "firmament"[14] and her upper half to create Earth.

V. Marduk creates Earth from Tiamat's upper half, or "head." He then determines the motion of the stars (relative to the newly created Earth) in the heavens, dividing them into constellations and using the stars and constellations as a calendar to mark the seasons, months, and days of the year. He then sets the motion of the Sun and Moon in like manner. Next, Marduk forms

---

[14] The Hebrew word translated as "firmament" in Genesis 1:6-8, רָקִיעַ *raqiya*, comes from the root רָקַע *raqa*, "to beat, strike, hammer and/or spread out". The Akkadian equivalent translated as "firmament" in *Enuma Elish, rakkis,* has the same meaning and is linguistically closely related to *raqiya*.

the clouds, rain, seas, and rivers from Tiamat's "spittle," the mountains from her "udders," and twists her tail to form the *Durmah* — "the great band"[15] — in heaven. Finally, Marduk rounds up Tiamat's army and imprisons them, bringing them to his father Ea's house where he sets them up as "statues" to commemorate his victory over Tiamat. (He retains Kingu, the chief of Tiamat's army, for other purposes.) The gods, his fathers then praise him for his handiwork and seat him on his throne, proclaiming him their king.

VI. Marduk continues his creative activity. First he kills Kingu, the chief of Tiamat's defeated army, and creates mankind from his blood. Then he organizes the greater and lesser gods into various heavenly and earthly orders. In gratitude, the gods build Babylon for him as a place of rest, and a stage-tower in Babylon (not unlike the one mentioned in Genesis 6) as the center of his worship on Earth. Lastly, they proclaim the first nine of Marduk's "fifty names," fifty different appellations which describe different aspects of his character and achievements.

VII. The remaining forty-one names of Marduk are listed, number forty-nine being, interestingly enough, a description of Marduk as "the star which in the skies is brilliant" (VII:126).

Enuma Elish was the liturgy for a religious ceremony that the Babylonians performed during the height of their "akitu festival," an annual religious festival that was held at the beginning of their New Year. Alexander Heidel, a recognized authority in the field of Babylonian religion, explains in *The Babylonian Genesis,*

> At the end of the fourth day of the New Year's celebration in Babylon, which lasted from the first to the eleventh of Nisan [late March], *Enuma Elish* was recited in its entirety by the high priest before the statue of Marduk. Then in the course of the festival, on

---

[15] See above note – the *Durmah* is the same as the *rakkis*, something that has been hammered into pieces and stretched out into a circle in heaven.

an undetermined day, *Enuma Elish* was again recited, or chanted. Parts of the epic may even have been dramatized, the king and the priests playing the roles of Marduk, Tiamat, Kingu, and other figures in the story.[16]

During the Akitu Festival, it is widely believed, the king and priests of Babylon acted out the roles of the various characters in *Enuma Elish*. The climax of the Epic, the battle scene in Tablet IV, where Marduk defeats Tiamat, was also reenacted. As Lambert explains, "a battle was conceived to take place annually between Tiamat and Marduk in the akitu rites of Babylon under the Late Babylonian kings."[17] This battle formed the very basis of Babylonian religion, as it was believed that heaven and Earth had been created as a result of the battle between Marduk and Tiamat. The Babylonians actually believed that Earth was made of the upper part, or "head," of the dragon Tiamat, and that the heavens were made from Tiamat's lower half, her "body," which Marduk had crushed into pieces and spread out into a "great circle" in heaven (Akk. *Durmah,* "great band").[18] Acting out the combat was a form of worship and reverence, both of worshiping their god Marduk and of remembering and revering the day of the creation of Earth. It also helped them to remember all of the details of their Creation story and to keep that knowledge alive.

---

[16]Alexander Heidel, *The Babylonian Genesis*, 2d ed. (Chicago: University of Chicago Press, 1963), 16.

[17]W.G. Lambert, "The Great Battle of the Mesopotamian Religious Year: The Conflict in the Akitu House," *Iraq* 25 (1963): 189.

[18]For a more detailed discussion of the Babylonian Creation Epic and its astronomical implications, see chapter IV.

The use of a pantomime dragon in religious festivals began with the ancient Mesopotamians, and continues to this day in various cultures, including the Chinese.

E.C. Krupp summarizes the rituals and importance of the Babylonian Akitu Festival in *Beyond the Blue Horizon: Myths & Legends of the Sun, Moon, Stars, and Planets,*

> At Babylon, *Enuma Elish* was staged as a sacred drama in a New Year's festival that lasted twelve days. Ceremonial reading of the creation myth was the same as reenacting it, and so each year the world was symbolically created all over again. Creation in the *Enuma Elish* did not, however, mean manufacturing the components of the cosmos. It meant the establishment of order. The *akitu* ceremony annually mirrored the original creation, or establishment of cosmic order, by re-establishing the terrestrial order. That was accomplished through ritual renewal of the authority of the king at the spring equinox, which coincided with New Year's at Babylon.... The *akitu* ceremony authorized the mandate of the king and linked his office to the maintenance of order and renewal of life in the land he ruled. Through a ritual battle with wooden representations of Tiamat and her monstrous brood, the king won the Tablets of Destiny, which recorded new

proclamations, laws, appointments, promotions, and goals for the coming year.[19]

The Babylonian version of the ancient creation epic that we now possess was written shortly after the rise of the First Dynasty of Babylon, which took place around 1900 B.C.[20] *Enuma Elish*, in fact, was only the most recent version of the liturgy for a Mesopotamian New Year's festival that was "an old established custom,"[21] a custom that had been around for many centuries before the Babylonians took over the region. Because of this, scholars generally agree that *Enuma Elish* is not an entirely original Babylonian composition. Instead, they argue, it was actually an adaptation and consolidation of one or more older creation stories borrowed from the Sumerians and their Semitic neighbors, the Akkadians, the two major people groups who had dominated Mesopotamia prior to the Babylonian conquest. They believe that the Babylonians had conquered the Sumerians and Akkadians and, instead of maintaining their own creation myths, simply borrowed the creation myths of their conquered foes and rewrote them so that the chief god of Babylon, Marduk, was glorified as creator of the heavens and Earth instead of the Sumerian/Akkadian deity Enlil. As Svend Aage Pallis, a noted authority on Babylonian myth and ritual, explains, "The priesthood of Babylon sought throughout to give Marduk the place of the formerly powerful deities. Thus he superseded Enlil and Ea in the hymns."[22] Heidel elaborates,

> It is generally admitted that *Enuma Elish*, though it is one of the literary masterpieces of the Babylonian Semites, is undoubtedly based on the cosmology of the Sumerians and that the central figure of the Sumerian story was Enlil, the most important god in

---

[19]E.C. Krupp, *Beyond the Blue Horizon: Myths & Legends of the Sun, Moon, Stars, & Planets* (New York: Oxford University Press, 1991), 140-141. For a more detailed discussion of the relationship between astronomy and *Enuma Elish*, see chapters II and IV.

[20]Heidel, *The Babylonian Genesis*, 14. The tablets of *Enuma Elish* now in our possession are actually from the libraries of the Assyrian King Ashurbanipal in Nineveh, who reigned during the seventh century B.C. These copies of copies of the originals witness to the longevity of the ancient Mesopotamian creation tradition, a tradition that had lasted over twelve centuries since the original writing of *Enuma Elish* by the Babylonians. And *Enuma Elish*, of course, was largely derived from traditions that were even more ancient. (Krupp, *Beyond the Blue Horizon,* 140.)

[21]Svend Aage Pallis, *The Babylonian Akitu Festival* (Copenhagen: Bianco Lunos Bogtrykkeri, 1926), 140.

[22]Pallis, *The Babylonian Akitu Festival,* 188.

Babylonia until Marduk's rise to supremacy. For not only do all the gods, with the exception of Tiamat, appear to have Sumerian names but some of the gods themselves, such as Apsu, Anu, and Enlil, are admittedly Sumerian.... Even man himself is called by a Sumerian term, *lullu,* which is immediately translated by the Semitic *amelu....* Another important point to be considered in this connection is the fact that the Semites in Babylonia became in general the heirs of the Sumerians, and as such they took over, with certain modifications, their script and literature, their religion, their culture and civilization.[23]

The Babylonians, then, altered the Sumerian creation myths so that they now favored Marduk, the patron deity of Babylon. "As it is, there can be no doubt that, in its present form, *Enuma Elish* is first and foremost a literary monument in honor of Marduk as the champion of the gods and the creator of the Earth."[24] The rest of *Enuma Elish,* however, was without a doubt inherited from the Sumerians.

Sumer: The Foundation of Ancient Near Eastern Civilization
The Sumerians are perhaps the oldest recorded culture in human history, rivaled in antiquity only by the ancient Egyptians. According to C. Leonard Wooley, the founder and recognized scholar of Sumerology, the Sumerians had flourished as early as 3500 B.C. in the delta of the Persian Gulf between the Tigris and Euphrates rivers.[25] (See Figure 1.1.) Though they had been conquered by a Semitic people known as the Akkadians around 2400 B.C., the warlike, less sophisticated Akkadians gradually assimilated into Sumerian culture, to the point where the kings of Mesopotamia soon began referring to themselves as "king of Sumer and Akkad." This mixed Sumerian/Akkadian race disappeared as a coherent culture around 2000 B.C., however, when the city of Ur and many parts of Sumer were apparently destroyed by some sort of powerful wind or storm from heaven. But despite the widespread destruction, much of their written records have survived, including accounts of the unusually violent storm that had destroyed them. According to their accounts,

---

[23]Heidel, *The Babylonian Genesis,* 12.
[24]*Ibid.,* 11.
[25]C. Leonard Wooley, *The Sumerians* (New York: The Norton Library, 1965), 1–9. The Babylonians later supplanted the Sumerians as the rulers of the land between the rivers.

this storm, which had been accompanied by earthquakes and "fire from heaven," was so utterly devastating that the Sumerians believed it had been purposely sent by their god Enlil, and the assembly of the "gods" in heaven, to punish them.[26]

Shortly after this disaster, seeing that Sumer's time had finally come, the Sumerian scribes began to write down extensive records of their history and culture for posterity. Wooley explains, "About 2000 B.C., after the fall of the Third Dynasty of Ur, Sumerian scribes took it in hand to record the glories

The famous "Standard of Ur" discovered near Baghdad in the 1920s by the famed Sumerologist Sir Leonard Wooley. Dating back to around 2500 B.C., its two sides show scenes of daily life in ancient Sumer, both in peace and in war. It is believed by some to have been used possibly as a battle standard, a musical instrument, or both. The ancient Sumerians invented many of the things that form the foundations of civilization to this day, and their civilization represented a high water mark in ancient human history.

of the great days that had passed away. They must have had at their disposal a mass of documentary evidence, and from this they compiled on the one hand the political history and on the other the religious traditions of the land."[27] This body of literature was then the root and inspiration for all the post-Sumerian civilizations of ancient Mesopotamia.

All Mesopotamian religion and culture was borrowed from the Sumerians. The first to do so were their Semitic conquerors, the Akkadians, followed later by the Babylonians and Assyrians and, to some extent, the Persians. "The Akkadians had borrowed the whole of their material civilization from their more advanced neighbors; what is curious is the degree to which they assimilated the religion of the Sumerians, taking over *in toto* their pantheon, their cosmology and their legends, and seldom even attempting to engraft anything Semitic

---

[26]Samuel Noah Kramer, trans., "Lamentation over the Destruction of Ur," and "Lamentation over the Destruction of Sumer and Ur," in *Ancient Near Eastern Texts Relating to the Old Testament,* ed. James B. Pritchard (Princeton, NJ: Princeton University Press, 1969), 455–63, 611-19.

[27]Wooley, *The Sumerians,* 27.

onto the borrowed stock."[28] Their myths, their legal codes, everything in their culture was based on Sumerian concepts, with the exception that the Semitic adaptations of the legal codes, such as the code of Hammurabi, tended to exact harsher penalties than the Sumerian originals.[29] The consensus in the field of ancient Near Eastern studies is that Sumer, in fact, formed the technological and cultural foundation for most of the ancient world:

> In the course of this century's investigations, it has become clear that the other civilizations that developed in the ancient Near East were deeply influenced by that of the Sumerians, the earliest to achieve its apex of cultural development. Some of the many influences that emanated from early Sumer include writing, the city-state, the accumulation of capital, the wheel, the potter's wheel, monumental architecture (including various architectural features such as the arch, dome, and vault), the sexagesimal number system, written legal documents, schools, and the cylinder seal.[30]

A Sumerian cylinder sealing stone with its accompanying clay seal impression. Cylinder seals first came into use during the Uruk period of Sumerian history, ca. 4000 B.C., used for both religious, artistic and security purposes in order to both verify the identity of the sealer, as well as ensure the security of documents sealed by them.

After surveying Mesopotamian history, it becomes clear that the Sumerians had reached such great heights of intellectual achievement

---

[28]Wooley, 77.

[29]Wooley, 91-92.

[30]Walter R. Bodine, "Sumerians," in *Peoples of the Old Testament World*, Alfred J. Hoerth, Gerald L. Mattingly, and Edwin M. Yamauchi, eds. (Grand Rapids: Baker, 1994), 21.

in their time that their religion, philosophy, and science continued to dominate Mesopotamian thought for hundreds, even thousands of years after their downfall. But how is the history of Sumer relevant to a study of parallels between the Bible and the Babylonian Creation Epic? Sumer is critical to the study of similarities between the Hebrew and Babylonian creation stories mainly because the Sumerians had set the intellectual context from which both the Hebrew and Babylonian creation stories were derived. For example, our modern, linear, Western worldview is actually based in large part upon Greek and Roman philosophy. Although we might hesitate to admit it, we have to accept the fact that the philosophers and politicians of ancient Greece and Rome still have a dominant influence upon our philosophical beliefs, and that their teachings still form the foundations of our social and political systems. In much the same way, the Sumerians had also set the intellectual foundations upon which the Semitic peoples of Mesopotamia, including both the Hebrews and the Babylonians (among others), were able to build and maintain their own similar creation traditions. This is why the "divine conflict" theme appears in both the Hebrew and Babylonian accounts: both traditions were founded in the same intellectual context: that of the Sumerians. Just as Paul used Greek concepts to better communicate the Gospel to the Greeks, the Hebrews, who at that time lived primarily in Mesopotamia, maintained their Creation story by using the concept of the Creation dominant in Mesopotamia at that time: that of a conflict between God and a dragon.

But does this mean that the Creation passages in the Bible were merely "borrowed" from the Sumerians? Certainly not. Rather, the Sumerians were mainly a dominant voice in a sea of creation traditions, of which only one, the Hebrew Creation tradition, was totally accurate.

THE ANCIENT CREATION TRADITION

Behind the "divine conflict" motif, some believe, lays an unbroken chain of thousands of years of tradition, a tradition that started when God told Adam how He had created the heavens and Earth. This Creation tradition was then passed down from generation to generation, for thousands of years, and was carried on by Noah to the post-Flood world. Then, as the sons of Noah and their descendants spread out over the post-Flood Earth, they carried the ancient Creation tradition with them.

However, most of Noah's descendants began to forget the ancient tradition, and instead began to fall into superstition and idolatry. And though many of the ancient peoples of the world have clearly discernible echoes of this ancient tradition in their creation myths, only two people groups retained the ancient knowledge of the Creation with any real clarity: the Sumerians, who lived in southern Mesopotamia, and their neighbors in northern Mesopotamia, the Semites.

The Sons of Shem

The "Semites" of northern Mesopotamia, of which the Akkadians were just one group, were the descendants of Shem, the son of Noah (Gen. 6–10). Thus to be more accurate, they should probably be called "Shemites." The Israelites were also a Semitic people, descended from Shem through Abraham (Gen. 11:10-26). The Semitic Akkadians, who conquered and assimilated with the Sumerians around 2400 B.C., were thus distantly related to the Israelites. It is important to remember that the Israelites did not actually appear as a distinct tribal group until around 1800 B.C.

Records of other Semitic groups can also be found in the Sumerian chronicles of the destruction of Sumer that took place around 2000 B.C. In these chronicles, the Sumerians recorded the names of two other Semitic groups — the Elamites and the Subarians — who had followed the path of destruction left by the mysterious heavenly storm to plunder crippled Sumer (cf. also Job 1:13-19, "Chaldeans" and "Sabeans"). The conquest of ancient Sumer, begun around 2000 B.C., was finally completed by the Amorites under Hammurabi, who eventually completed the conquest of the weakened Sumerians around 1800 B.C. and supplanted them as the dominant power in Mesopotamia.[31]

Semitic tribes had actually dominated Mesopotamia from the earliest times. According to Genesis 10:30, after the Flood, the descendants of Shem had settled in the area stretching from "Mesha" to "Sephar," Sephar identified as "toward the eastern hill country" (NIV). Clues to the identity of these areas can be found by comparing the descendants of Shem with known Semitic peoples and the geographic areas in which they are known to have lived. (See Figure 1.1)

---

[31] Peter A. Piccione, "Chronology of Mesopotamia", http://spinner.cofc.edu/~piccione/graphics/mesop_chronol.html.

Shem's descendants included Elam, Ashur, Arpachshad, Lud, and Aram and their sons, as listed in Genesis 10:21-31:

- *Elam.* Elam was the father of the Elamites, a people whom Gordon Wenham describes as "The powerful eastern neighbor and rival of Mesopotamia from earliest times."[32] Semites lived in Elam since the late third millennium (3000–2500 B.C.).

- *Ashur.* Ashur was of course the father of the Assyrians, who lived in northwest Mesopotamia.

- *Arpachshad.* Arpachshad is not as easily placed. Some scholars believe that he is possibly the father of the Babylonians, but "The only supports for this notion are (a) the theory that the last three letters of Arpachshad, *ksd*, could spell *kasidim*, i.e., the Chaldaeans, and (b) the conviction that somewhere Babylon must appear among the sons of Shem."[33] This assumption is made because the Babylonians are generally recognized as having been a Semitic people. However, one thing that has not been considered is the fact that *arpa* may be related to the later Aramaic word *abba*, "father." If these words are in fact related, this would make Arpachshad literally, "the father of the Chaldeans" (*arpa kasad*), making Arpachshad fit well into the genealogy.

- *Lud.* Lud could be the father of the Lydians, but it is unclear, as historians tend to group the Lydians in with the Greeks, who were descendants of Japheth. Some feel that it was derived from the controversial King Gyges, who hailed from the region of Luddu, thus beginning the Luddu, or "Lydian" dynasty from which the name of the region was derived. This particular family may have been Semitic in origin, indicating a Semitic presence in that region.[34] Lydia emerged out of the western half of what was once the Hittite Empire around 1200 B.C.

---

[32] Wenham, *Genesis 1–15*, 228.
[33] Wenham, 228.
[34] See http://en.wikipedia.org/wiki/Lydia for a detailed article on Lydia and its people.

✤ *Aram.* Aram is easily identified, the Arameans being well attested from the third millennium onwards. The Arameans lived north of Elam and east of Assyria, in the eastern Tigris river valley in or near the foothills of the Zagros Mountains, which would explain the reference to "toward the eastern hill country" in Genesis 10:30. Arameans also show up in Syria at the end of the second millennium B.C.[35]

Thus, from the evidence, it appears that Shem's descendants occupied an area encompassing primarily northern, eastern, and central Mesopotamia and including areas as far north and east as Elam and the Zagros Mountains and possibly stretching around the Fertile Crescent as far west as Asia Minor. Sephar is thus easily identified, probably being "Sippar," the ancient city of the Sumerians in central Mesopotamia. This is not much of a reach, because most of Mesopotamia was apparently dominated by Semites from the earliest times. Thus, Sippar undoubtedly had a significant Semitic population. "The eastern hill country" probably refers to the Zagros Mountains, where the descendants of Aram settled. And it was into this Semite-dominated world, Mesopotamia ca. 2000 B.C., that Abram the Hebrew was born.[36]

---

[35]C.f. also Deuteronomy 26:5.

[36]Despite the attempts of liberal theologians (Julius Wellhausen, et al) to prove that Hebrew history, as described in the Pentateuch, was a "glorified mirage" that was "invented" by the Hebrews during the Babylonian dispersion (ca. 600-500 B.C.), more modern scholarship, using concrete archaeological evidence instead of guesswork, has proven that the Bible is, in fact, an ancient historical text, fitting well into the period in which it has traditionally been placed. For example, Kenneth Kitchen has proved in his article "The Patriarchal Age: Myth or History?" (*Biblical Archaeology Review* 21 n.2 (March-April 1995): 48-57, 88, 90, 92, 94-95) that Abraham, Isaac, and Jacob had actually lived in the early second millennium B.C., the same time period traditional scholarship had placed them all along. Kitchen had reached this conclusion by examining some seemingly minor clues in the text itself. Using evidence from the "Merneptah Stele," an ancient Egyptian war record recently unearthed by archaeologists, we can place Israel in the land of Canaan at least as early as 1300-1200 B.C. This is because the stele mentions "Israel" as one of the nations Pharaoh Merneptah had attacked during a campaign into Canaan, and we are fairly certain that Merneptah ruled during this period. Since we know that the Israelites were in Egypt for 400 years before the Exodus (Genesis 15:13), we can subtract 400 years from roughly 1300 B.C. and arrive at 1700 B.C. This places the birth of Joseph, who was probably around 30-40 years of age when Israel went down into Egypt, around 1740 B.C., if not sooner. If there were on average 40-year intervals between the births of Isaac, Jacob, and Joseph, this places the birth of Isaac at around 1860 B.C. or possibly earlier. Isaac, of course, was born just

Abraham: Bearer of the Ancient Creation Tradition

Abram, or "Abraham" as he was later called, was born in Ur, one of the chief cities in one of the largest and most sophisticated countries of his time: Sumer. According to Gen. 11:27-29, Abram's father Terah took Abram and several other family members and departed from a place called "Ur of the Chaldees." (See Figure 1.1) This is generally understood to be Ur, one of the largest cities in Sumer, though some scholars have disputed this claim.[37] Eugene Merrill explains in *Kingdom of Priests: A History of Old Testament Israel,*

> Terah lived in Ur of the Chaldees (v. 28), the famous Sumerian city located by the Euphrates River, about 150 miles northwest of the present coast of the Persian Gulf. The most satisfactory reconstruction of biblical chronology places the birth of Abram at 2166 B.C.... As just suggested, Ur was a Sumerian city, one of a great number of city-states populated by the highly cultured Sumerians from at least as early as the mid-fourth millennium. The Ur of Terah and Abram was, however, quite cosmopolitan, for non-Sumerians such as Abram's own Semitic ancestors lived there and mingled their intellectual and cultural traditions with those of the Sumerians. Since by that time Sargon (2371–2316) had created the Semite-dominated Akkadian Empire at Agade, nearly 200 miles northwest of Ur, Abram was almost certainly bilingual, commanding both the Sumerian and Akkadian languages.[38]

---

after Abraham had reached 90 years of age, placing the birth of Abraham well into the twentieth century B.C., if not earlier (I place his birth at around 2000 B.C.).

And there are many concrete reasons to believe this chronology. For one, Kitchen found that the price of a slave in the Laws of Hammurabi and in many ancient cities of that period (1850-1700 B.C.) was 20 silver shekels, up from 10 shekels around 2000 B.C., but less than the 30 shekels a slave would be worth in the fourteenth century B.C. This firmly sets Joseph in or around 1750 B.C., as that was exactly what his brothers had sold him for—20 shekels of silver (Gen. 37:28). Kitchen also points out that the kinds of oaths/treaties made by the patriarchs also clearly match prevailing patterns elsewhere in the ancient Near East during the period 2000-1800 B.C., whereas oath structures only a few centuries before or after that time were noticeably different. This evidence is further bolstered by the fact that oaths in the books of Exodus, Deuteronomy and Joshua are fairly similar in structure to Hittite treaties made during the period of 1500-1200 B.C., reinforcing the traditional period of the Exodus as being somewhere between 1450 and 1300 B.C. Kitchen also offers several more telling clues, too many to list here, but all of which are convincing.

[37]Cf. H.W.F. Saggs, "Ur of the Chaldees: A Problem of Identification," *Iraq* 22 (1960).

[38]Eugene H. Merrill, *Kingdom of Priests: A History of Old Testament Israel* (Grand Rapids: Baker, 1987), 25–26.

Scholars typically date Abraham anywhere from 2100 B.C. to 1800 B.C., but for our purposes we will assume that Abraham was born in or near Ur around 2000 B.C. Abraham was doubtless quite familiar with the history and customs of his Sumerian neighbors. And though it was originally a Sumerian city, Ur probably became known as "Ur of the Chaldees" in the Bible because the Chaldeans, or "Babylonians," had conquered and taken control of Sumer around 1900 B.C., around the same time Terah had fled Ur with Abram and the rest of his family. The Chaldeans were a Semitic tribe that came to power in Mesopotamia after the collapse of the Sumerian Empire. They derived the name "Babylonians" from the city of Babylon, which was apparently their central political power base, from which they eventually conquered the rest of Mesopotamia. As Saggs explains, "The term 'Chaldees' or 'Chaldeans' represents the Hebrew *kasdim,* Septuagint Χαλδαῖος, Akkadian *Kaldu.* The *Kaldu* were a people organized on a tribal basis, found in lower Babylonia from the end of the second millennium. Their territory at the beginning of this period extended roughly north and east from the city of Ur, in the region known as the Sealands, but rapidly extended up the Euphrates until it reached almost to Borsippa."[39]

So Abraham originally came from Mesopotamia, apparently fleeing the collapse of the Sumerian Empire and the subsequent chaos. However, the question remains, are the biblical creation accounts borrowed from Babylonian myths, or are both the Hebrew and Babylonian creation accounts simply similar stories both derived from an even older source? And how is the question of Abraham's nativity relevant? John Oswalt explains in his article, "The Myth of the Dragon and Old Testament Faith,"

> Ever since the first fragments of the Babylonian Creation Epic began to come to light it has been customary to see the biblical creation accounts as being in some sense derived from that story. At first, it was fashionable to see the biblical accounts as direct derivations. The implication was that Israel only has a creation account because of direct dependence upon the Mesopotamian myth. The passing of time has shown this to be, at best, a vast over-simplification. It can now be demonstrated that such a myth, in one form or another, was spread all over the ancient Near East,

---

[39] Saggs, "Ur of the Chaldees," p. 205.

including India and Greece. The Mesopotamian version was not the original, nor does it appear to have had any undue influence on the other versions.[40]

So, despite the close similarities between the Hebrew and Babylonian creation accounts, scholars are still undecided as to whether or not the creation passages in Genesis were in fact influenced by *Enuma Elish*, or perhaps by some other, even earlier tradition. John Walton, in his seminal work, *Ancient Israelite Literature in Its Cultural Context*, points out that there are in fact three basic schools of thought among those that accept the possibility of "borrowing" between the Israelite and Babylonian creation traditions:

- *Moses borrowed from the Babylonian account.* Though possible, there is enough dissimilarity between the two accounts to make this conclusion questionable.

- *The Babylonians borrowed from the Mosaic account.* Unlikely, because of the chronological differences. Even the traditional early dating of the Pentateuch, in the fifteenth century B.C., would have occurred a full three centuries after the generally accepted date of Hammurabi and the codification of Enuma Elish in its final form (eighteenth century B.C.).

- *Both borrowed from an even more ancient common source.* This is the most likely conclusion. Walton feels that the similarities and differences between the Mosaic and Babylonian accounts are due to a basic difference in worldview between the monotheistic Moses and the polytheistic Babylonians. It is this difference in worldview that caused Moses and the Babylonians to interpret the same source material two different ways. As Walton explains, "The similarities are conceptual, not specific.... The common source need not be a literary source or even a specific tradition. Common cultural roots could just as easily account for the similarities seen in the creation traditions.... We would

---

[40] John N. Oswalt, "The Myth of the Dragon and Old Testament Faith," *The Evangelical Quarterly* 49 n.3 (July-Sept. 1977): 163.

tentatively account for the similarities by acknowledging the cultural roots of the Israelites and the Babylonians and recognizing that this alone, or possibly a common tradition in the past of the roots that these two civilizations hold in common, could be the source from which the similarities are derived."[41]

Since the Hebrews and the Babylonians were both Semitic peoples who originated from Mesopotamia, and since both the Hebrew and Babylonian creation stories contain many similar themes, if they did not borrow from each other, then it must be that both the Hebrew and Babylonian traditions were based on another, even older tradition. This common past tradition, as we have seen, lies in the creation stories of Mesopotamia. Both Abraham and the Babylonians, therefore, must have derived their knowledge of the Creation from even older traditions, perhaps dating all the way back to Noah or even to the pre-Flood world.

The Hebrew version of the ancient Creation tradition is actually very similar to the Babylonian version. Besides the obvious fact that the Babylonian version is polytheistic whereas the Hebrew version is monotheistic, many of the Creation passages in the Bible are strikingly similar to parallel passages in the Babylonian Creation Epic. Thus the Hebrew and Babylonian Creation stories are not so much different in form than they are in attribution. In the beginning, according to the Hebrews, there was just one God, in distinct contrast to the many gods of the Babylonian Creation Epic. Obviously, the Hebrews and the Babylonians took the same source material but interpreted it in vastly different ways, explaining why their creation stories are so similar, yet so different. As Wooley explains,

> The stories of the Creation and the Flood were part of the cultural heritage that Abraham took with him from Ur, and...they had been familiar to the Hebrew people ever since that time.... The story of the Creation and the story of the Flood both originate in southern Mesopotamia, and we have texts of them that go back in date to before the time of the patriarch Abraham.... Both stories

---

[41]John H. Walton, *Ancient Israelite Literature in Its Cultural Context: A Survey of Parallels between Biblical and Ancient Near Eastern Texts,* Library of Biblical Interpretation, Regency Reference Library (Grand Rapids: Zondervan Publishing House, 1989), 37.

would have been known to Abraham if he lived (as he certainly did) at Ur, and one at least, probably both, would have been current at Haran in the patriarchal period. Both were adopted by the patriarchal family and were handed down as oral tradition, becoming part of the popular belief of the Hebrew people.... The old Sumerian (Babylonian) Creation myth was radically cut down so as to leave only that philosophical speculation which recognizes in God the Prime Cause.[42]

The best explanation for the similarities and differences between the Hebrew and Babylonian creation accounts is that they represented two main branches of an ancient creation tradition that had dominated Mesopotamian thought for millennia. This tradition, some believe, has roots stretching all the way back to Noah, and from him all the way back to Adam. In this scenario, God had told Adam of the Creation, and over the millennia that knowledge of the Creation was passed down from generation to generation, kept alive through the use of memory aids such as stories and symbolic imagery. The use of these "memory aids" caused the ancient creation tradition to gradually metamorphose into the "divine conflict" concept, where the creation of the heavens and Earth came to be symbolized as a heavenly conflict between God and a dragon.

Though we cannot prove that the ancient creation tradition had its origin with Adam, there is evidence to support its existence as far back as Noah, and through Noah to the world before the Flood. For example, despite the fact that all of the peoples of the ancient world had their own creation traditions, many of these variant traditions have been found to bear remarkable similarities to the Hebrew and Babylonian traditions—particularly in their use of the same "divine conflict" imagery to describe the Creation. Furthermore, these traditions come from widely scattered geographical regions—from as far east as India, and as far west as Greece. And the only explanation for such close similarities between these traditions from such distant lands is that they all had a common source: Noah.

---

[42]C. Leonard Wooley, "Stories of the Creation and the Flood," *Palestine Exploration Quarterly* 88 (Jan-Apr. 1956): 19, 21.

Echoes of the Ancient Creation Tradition

When the sons of Noah spread out over the face of Earth, they took the creation tradition that God had given to Adam with them. But not all of Noah's descendants were as true to the original story as were the Promised Line of the Hebrew Semites. As a result, over time, errors crept into these variant traditions until the original story was all but forgotten. Yet, there remained just enough of the original creation story in many of the creation myths of the ancient Near East to make the connection. Young explains,

> The facts of Creation, we have suggested, were probably handed down from father to son. And if among the promised line error may soon have been fused with truth before the truth was finally preserved through inscripturation, what may we say of the line of Cain? Certainly in this line error would have had free play. Superstition would soon have entered in and obscured the truth. This is the reason why among so many people we find accounts of creation bearing some relation to what is recorded in Genesis 1. Among the various nations and peoples of Earth the truth would indeed have been handed down, but it would have been grossly garbled truth, one encrusted with layers of superstition. Hence, in almost all cosmogonies there are certain elements of truth itself, namely, the formal resemblances which these cosmogonies sustain to the contents of Genesis 1.[43]

The clearest examples of this trend outside of the two main branches can be found in the creation stories of the Canaanites, the Egyptians, the Hittites and, of course, the Sumerians. Other interesting examples can be found in Greek and Vedic Indian myths.

The Canaanites. The Canaanites wrote many different epic poems about their gods Ba'al and Anath. In one of these lengthy poems, prominent mention is made of how the goddess Anath had defended her mate, Ba'al, against a seven-headed sea dragon. This dragon had

---

[43]Edward J. Young, "The Interpretation of Genesis 1:2," *Westminster Theological Journal* 23 (May 1961): 164. Obviously, Young meant to refer to those descendants of Noah who did not faithfully keep the knowledge of the Creation, as the line of Cain had been eliminated by the Flood—unless, of course, one of the wives of Shem, Ham and/or Japheth was of the line of Cain, which is doubtful.

many names, including "Yamm," "El's Flood Rabbim,"[44] "the Dragon," "the crooked serpent," and "Shalyat the seven-headed."

> *What enemy's ris[en] against Ba'al,*
> *What foe against the Rider of Clouds?*
> *Crushed I not El's beloved Yamm?*
> *Destroyed I not El's Flood Rabbim?*
> *Did I not, pray, muzzle the Dragon?*
> *I did crush the crooked serpent,*
> *Shalyat the seven-headed...*[45]

"Yamm," one of the pseudonyms of the dragon, literally means "the sea." The next name, "El's Flood Rabbim" means, literally, "God's Great Flood." Thus, like the Babylonian Tiamat and the Hebrew Leviathan, the dragon of the Canaanite creation story was also closely identified with the sea, to the point where it was actually considered a personification of the sea. The third and fourth names, "the Dragon," and "the Crooked Serpent" confirm this association.

An ancient Near Eastern deity doing battle with a seven-headed dragon. The seven-headed dragon makes an appearance in both Canaanite and Semitic literature, including Revelation 12, 13 and 20.

---

[44]El was the chief god of the Canaanite pantheon. Not coincidentally, "El" is also the Hebrew name for God (the word translated as "God" in the Bible is actually either אֵל, "El" or אֱלֹהִים, "Elohim"), a fact which has caused great interest among translators ever since the Ba'al epics were discovered around the turn of the century. Since then, many parallels have been drawn between Canaanite and Hebrew writings, although for the most part there are distinct differences between the two religions, particularly in the area of ethics and morality. The areas which do parallel are interesting, however, and point to the conclusion that the Canaanites may have also shared in the belief that Earth was created as the result of a conflict between God and a dragon.

[45]H.L. Ginsberg, trans., "Poems About Baal and Anath," in *Ancient Near Eastern Texts Related to the Old Testament,* 3d ed. with Supplement, ed. James B. Pritchard (Princeton, NJ: Princeton University Press, 1969), 137.

Other fragments of Canaanite poems have been discovered with similar imagery, possibly attributing the defeat of the dragon to Ba'al. The imagery in this fragment is remarkably like that of Isaiah 27:1:

> *If thou smite Lotan, the serpent slant,*
> *Destroy the serpent tortuous,*
> *Shalyat of the seven heads...*[46]

Interestingly, the name "Lotan" in the Canaanite myths, except for a slight difference in pronunciation, is essentially the same name for the dragon "Leviathan" that appears in the Bible. Scholars studying parallels between Ugaritic (the Canaanite language in which the Baal epics were written) and ancient Hebrew, have come to this conclusion based upon similarities in spelling and pronunciation between the two words. As J.A. Emerton explains, "It has been recognized for [over] half a century that the *ltn* [Lotan] mentioned in CTA 5.I.1 is the Ugaritic equivalent of Leviathan in the Old Testament. The resemblances between the Ugaritic passage and, in particular, Isaiah 27 put the identification beyond reasonable doubt."[47] This close linguistic similarity, combined with the parallels between these Canaanite poems and such passages as Isaiah 27:1, Job 26:13, and Psalm 29:10, make the connection clear. Though the Creation is not explicitly discussed in these poems, their clear connection with biblical Creation material, particularly with Isaiah 27:1, does make it likely that these passages are also echoes of the ancient creation myth.[48]

Other Baal myths show Baal in conflict with a monster called "Yamm," a name which, as we have seen, is a pseudonym for the dragon. The word *yamm*, like *Lotan*, actually appears in both the Canaanite and Hebrew languages, and in both languages Yamm means, literally, "the sea." This battle between Baal and the sea-god Yamm appears to be linked to Baal's battle with the dragon Lotan to

---

[46]Ginsberg, "Poems about Baal and Anath," 138.

[47]J.A. Emerton, "Leviathan and *Ltn*: The Vocalization of the Ugaritic Word for the Dragon," *Vetus Testamentum* XXXII no.3 (1982): 327–328. "CTA 5.I.1" is part of a numbering system used by interpreters to index the poems about Baal and Anath, similar to the chapter and verse designations used with the Bible. These poems are some of the many writings and fragments of writings found in this century in Ugarit, an ancient city of the Canaanites dating back to the Old Testament period.

[48]For a more in-depth discussion of this topic, see Loren R. Fisher, "Creation at Ugarit and the Old Testament," *Vetus Testamentum* 15 (1965): 313–24.

the point where, as is the case with Leviathan and the sea in the Bible, Lotan and the sea are so closely linked as to be almost indistinguishable.[49]

In the story of Baal's conflict with Yamm, Baal is attempting to dethrone the tyrant Yamm who, like Tiamat, rules over the gods with fear and terror. Like Marduk, Baal is also helped by his fellow gods; in this case another of the gods of Ugarit called "Kothar-wa-Khasis." Kothar-wa-Khasis encourages Baal to destroy Yamm the dragon, and provides him with weapons in order to help him do so. Baal agrees, using the weapons given to him by Kothar-wa-Khasis to defeat the monstrous Yamm, alias "Judge Nahar" (lit., "Judge River"):

> *Under the throne of Prince Yamm, quoth Khothar-wa-Khasis:*
> *"I tell thee Prince Baal, I declare, O Rider of the Clouds.*
> *Now thine enemy, O Baal, now thine enemy wilt thou smite,*
>   *now wilt thou cut off thine adversary.*
> *Thoul't take thine eternal kingdom, thine everlasting dominion."*
>   *Kothar brings down two clubs and gives them names.*
> *"Thou, thy name is Yagrush ('Chaser'). Yagrush, chase Yamm!*
> *Chase Yamm from his throne, Nahar from his seat of dominion....*
>   *Thou, thy name is Ayamur ('Driver'). Ayamur, drive Yamm!*
> *Drive Yamm from his throne, Nahar from his seat of dominion....*
>   *The club [Ayamur] swoops in the hand of Baal,*
>   *[like] an eagle between his fingers;*
>   *It strikes the pate of Prince [Yamm],*
>   *between the eyes of Judge Nahar.*
>   *Yamm collapses, he falls to the ground;*
>   *His joints bend, his frame breaks.*
>   *Baal would rend, would smash Yamm,*
>   *would annihilate Judge Nahar.*[50]

Besides numerous similarities with the biblical creation material, there are also several similarities between the Baal myth and *Enuma Elish*. As Gronbaek explains, "The Baal-Yam conflict ... approximates to *Enuma Elish*, since in both contexts the foe is a sea monster, a dragon, which represents the forces of chaos."[51] Moreover, in *Enuma Elish*, the

---

[49]Jakob H. Gronbaek, "Baal's Battle with Yam—A Canaanite Creation Fight," *Journal for the Study of the Old Testament* 33 (1985): 31.

[50]Ginsberg, "Poems about Baal and Anath," 130-131.

[51]Gronbaek, 30.

gods also encouraged Marduk and armed him with weapons to fight against the oppressive dragon Tiamat, just as Kothar-wa-Khasis encouraged and armed Baal. Gronbaek also mentions other parallels between the Baal-Yam conflict and *Enuma Elish,* such as the helplessness of the gods as contrasted with the determination of the young and active god, and similarities between the names of Baal's weapons and the frightful creatures which are harnessed to Marduk's chariot.[52]

The Egyptians. More echoes of the ancient creation tradition can be found in the creation myths of the Egyptians. For example, one Egyptian text, "The Repulsing of the Dragon at Creation," describes the Creation in terms of the repulsion of a dragon named "Apophis" by their chief god "Re." Here, Re describes how he accomplished the destruction of the dragon at the creation of Earth:

A depiction of the Egyptian god Re battling against the demon Aphophis. The Egyptians believed Re defeated Apophis at the creation of Earth, and had to re-defeat him every morning so that the Sun could rise again.

> I sent out these who came into being from my body to overthrow that evil enemy. He is one fallen to the flame, Apophis with a knife on his head. He cannot see, and his name is no more in this land. I have commanded that a curse be cast upon him; I have consumed his bones; I have annihilated his soul in the course of every day; I have cut his vertebrae at his neck, severed with a knife which hacked up his flesh and pierced into his hide....His soul, his corpse, his state of glory, his shadow, and his magic are not. His bones are not, and his skin is not. He is fallen and overthrown....[53]

---

[52]Gronbaek, 31–32. These creatures were named "the Killer, the Relentless, the Trampler, and the Swift." Two other weapons were called "the Smiter" and "the Combat" (IV:52–56).

[53]John A. Wilson, trans., "The Repulsing of the Dragon at Creation," in *Ancient Near Eastern Texts Related to the Old Testament,* 3d ed. with Supplement, ed. James B. Pritchard (Princeton, NJ: Princeton University Press, 1969), 6; cf also "The Repulsing of the Dragon," 11-12.

Again, there are many surprising similarities between *Enuma Elish* and this Egyptian creation text. For one, Re explains that the weapons he used to destroy the dragon Apophis he made from his own body—literally, "came into being from my body." This has a parallel in *Enuma Elish,* where Marduk created three of the seven divine "winds" he used against Tiamat from his own body: "He *brought forth* Imhullu, 'the Evil Wind,' the Whirlwind, the Hurricane" (*Enuma Elish* IV:45). In doing so, Marduk copied Anu, who had brought forth the first four of the seven winds from his own body and given them to Marduk: "Anu brought forth and begot the fourfold wind" (I:105). Tiamat also brought forth her weapons from her body: "Mother [Tiamat], she who fashions all things, added matchless weapons, bore monster serpents" (I:132–33). Furthermore, as Marduk had in *Enuma Elish,* Re decapitated the dragon, "cut his vertebrae at his neck," and used a weapon to divide the dragon's body into pieces. The savage imagery in the Egyptian myth is also reminiscent of Baal's desire to rend, smash, and annihilate Yamm after he had defeated him.

Yet another clear link with the ancient creation tradition can be found in an Egyptian proverb, wherein the teacher explains, "Well directed are men, the cattle of the god. He made heaven and Earth according to their desire, and he repelled the water-monster."[54] Again, the concept of a conflict between a creator-deity and a "water-monster" appears, clearly in the context of the creation of both heaven and Earth.

The Hittites. The Hittites had a myth involving a battle between a warrior deity and a dragon, called "The Myth of Illuyankas." In this myth, the Hittite storm god fights a sea dragon named Illuyankas. This myth has a variation on the theme in that the storm god fights the dragon twice. The first time the dragon wins, but the second time the storm god wins, and destroys the dragon forever. Interestingly, in the second, final battle, the storm god's son sacrifices himself so that the dragon Illuyankas could finally be defeated:

> When the Storm-god and the Dragon Illuyankas *came to grips* in Kiskilussa, the Dragon Illuyankas vanquished the storm god...and took (his) heart and (his) eyes away from him. The Storm-god [sought to revenge himself] upon him. He took the daughter of

---

[54] John A. Wilson, trans., "The Instruction of the Vizier Ptah-Hotep," in *Ancient Near Eastern Texts Related to the Old Testament,* 3d ed. with Supplement, ed. James B. Pritchard (Princeton, NJ: Princeton University Press, 1969), 417.

the poor man for his wife and begat a son. When [his son] grew up, he took the daughter of the Dragon Illuyankas in marriage. The Storm-god instructs his son: "When thou goest to the house of thy wife, ask them for (my) heart and (mine) eyes!"... He brought them to the Storm-god, his father. Thus the Storm-god got back his heart and eyes. When his frame had been restored to its old state, he left to the Sea for battle. When he had engaged the Dragon Illuyankas in battle, he came close to vanquishing him. But the son of the Storm-god, who was with Illuyankas, shouted up to heaven to his father: "Count me as with (him)! Spare me not!" So the Storm-god killed the Dragon Illuyankas and his son too. In this way the Storm-god got even with the Dragon Illuyankas.[55]

The Sumerians. As we have seen, *Enuma Elish* was basically a compilation of Sumerian and Babylonian creation stories that had been compiled into a single, complete unit. One of the Sumerian stories that was probably used as source material was a creation story called "The Feats and Exploits of Ninurta." Mary K. Wakeman explains in *God's Battle with the Monster: A Study in Biblical Imagery,* "Ninurta... is god of the stormy south wind. He is encouraged by his weapon, Shar-ur, to attack and destroy Asag, the demon ('of sickness and disease') whose abode is the Kur."[56] The "Kur" is a sort of "primeval mountain," which is apparently how the Sumerians conceived of Earth. By attacking Asag, in "the Kur," then, Ninurta is basically attacking Earth, which makes "The Feats and Exploits of Ninurta" a creation myth.

---

[55] Albrecht Goetze, trans., "The Myth of Illuyankas," in *Ancient Near Eastern Texts Related to the Old Testament,* 3d ed. with Supplement, ed. James B. Pritchard (Princeton, NJ: Princeton University Press, 1969), 125–26. Note the similarities between this story and the Gospel account of Jesus' birth and death. Like Jesus, the son of the Storm-god was born of a "daughter of [a] poor man," and also sacrificed himself so that his father could defeat his enemy, the dragon (or, "Satan"). This may point to the idea that the coming of Christ had also been known since the beginning, and had been retained as part of the ancient creation story. The Creation, Nativity, and Second Coming *do* seem to be graphically linked throughout the Bible. It could be that at one time, the belief that the son of God would be born of a poor virgin and sacrifice Himself so that His Father could triumph over His enemies was widely known, but had become buried under centuries of accreted myth and superstition, becoming only a passing reference in the myths of the nations until it was forgotten altogether.

[56] Mary K. Wakeman, *God's Battle with the Monster: A Study in Biblical Imagery,* (Leiden: E.J. Brill, 1973): 7.

Wakeman explains the myth in detail: "At first Ninurta runs in fear. Returning, he destroys Asag, but the result is that the primeval waters of the Kur flood the fields, preventing cultivation. Now Ninurta heaps up a wall of stones over the Kur to hold back the waters, and proceeds to gather the flood into a river."[57] Again, as in *Enuma Elish,* Ninurta's successful defeat of the demon Asag results in Earth bringing forth great floods of water. Ninurta also carefully channeled the floods that came forth from Earth after the conflict so that their destructive powers are neutralized. Likewise, both the Bible and *Enuma Elish* talk about how the primeval waters were separated by a "firmament," separated into "waters above" and "waters below."

One of the creation myths that inspired the Babylonian Creation Epic was the Sumerian epic, "The Feats and Exploits of Ninurta." In the story, Ninurta destroys various demons, including the demon Asag, who lives in the divine mountain of the beginning, which may represent the Earth, and/or an actual mountain on Earth. On the right is the demon Asag, and on the left is Ninurta, with armaments very similar to that of Marduk. The creature Ninurta rides may be cognate to the same sort of divine "cherub" or chariot that God is described as flying in in 2 Samuel 22:11.

Other Ancient Creation Traditions. And the parallels don't stop there. The Greeks had a myth about how their chief god Zeus had fought a many-headed serpent named Typhon, setting it afire and throwing it into hell (Gk., "Tartarus"). Another version of this myth actually resembles the Hittite myth of Illuyankas, in that it occurs in two stages: Zeus wrestles with Typhon, but the serpent wrestles Zeus' weapon, a sickle, out of his hands and uses it to cut off his hands and feet. Zeus, however, like the Hittite storm god, later recovers full use of his body and returns to defeat the serpent.[58] The Vedic Indians also had a story in their hymns where their chief god Indra fights against a demonic serpent named Vritra, destroying it with a weapon, a

---

[57]Wakeman, *God's Battle with the Monster,* 7.

[58]Wakeman, *God's Battle with the Monster,* 9.

lightning bolt, provided by Tvashtri the smith, one of the gods loyal to Indra. Indra splits open the snake with his weapon, the lightning bolt, and waters pour forth:

> *I will proclaim the manly deeds of Indra,*
> *The first that he performed, the lightning wielder.*
> *He slew the serpent, then discharged the waters...*[59]

Not only the Babylonians, but also the Canaanites, the Egyptians, the Hittites, the Greeks, the Vedic Indians and, of course, the Sumerians, had echoes of the divine conflict between a warrior deity and a dragon in their creation myths. These similarities, in such geographically distant countries, could only have been caused by a common root creation tradition passed down from a time before mankind had begun to spread out over Earth's surface. And the last time these conditions existed was in the time of Noah. Though this story had, since the time of Noah, become distorted to some extent with myth and speculation, the same root story of a combat between a warrior deity and a dragon had remained intact. Thus our interpretation of the creation material in the Bible should take into consideration not only all of the Creation material in the Bible besides that related in Genesis 1–2, but also other, parallel ancient Near Eastern creation stories that mirror in many ways the biblical view of the Creation.

The Ancient Creation Tradition in the Bible

The Creation material in the Bible represents the only branch of the ancient creation tradition that is 100 percent reliable and free of distortion. This is because God Himself wrote it, using Moses and the Prophets as His scribes to turn the old oral creation story of the Hebrews into a written form. Before Moses, the Scriptures of the Hebrews were oral traditions; that is, the patriarchs of the tribes told the story of the Creation and God's plan for mankind to their sons, and their sons told the stories to their sons. Because the stories were told again and again, the patriarchs had no trouble recalling them but, inevitably, small errors and misunderstandings no doubt began to creep into the oral traditions. Therefore, God decided that it was time to translate the Hebrew oral traditions into written form, before the distortions led to theological errors. He did this because written texts are much less

---

[59]Wakeman, *God's Battle with the Monster*, 9.

likely to be distorted over time than oral traditions are, as written texts are clearly written down in black and white and therefore much less subject to human error.

The man whom the LORD chose to translate the oral traditions into written form was Moses. It was for this purpose that Moses was raised up in the court of Egypt: that he might be exposed to the highest levels of learning that were available anywhere in the entire world at that time. In the Egyptian court, Moses was exposed to all of the writings of the ancient world, including the creation traditions that, as we have seen, had their roots even from the very beginning of mankind. Thus Moses was able to translate the old Hebrew oral traditions, helped out by his knowledge of the other, parallel traditions, into what we know as the Book of Genesis. Young explains,

"Moses Breaks the Tables of the Law" by Gustave Doré. Much of the story of the Exodus, including the breaking forth of the waters from the "divine mountain," may be the same as that described in the myths of Ninurta. The events at Sinai may have been a repeat of an ancient pattern. See our breakthrough article at <http://www.mysteriousworld.com/Journal/2008/Spring/Artifacts/> to learn more.

> If we come to the Bible with the presupposition that it is the trustworthy Word of God, we shall be inclined to take seriously what the Bible itself has to say about the entire account of creation. May it be that God spoke to Adam concerning the creation and that Adam taught the revealed truth on this subject to his children?...Oral transmission, however, is no guarantee of accurate transmittal. Even among the promised line, there would be the danger of corruption unless the tradition was somehow preserved and protected. Even in the line of promise there was the danger that the truth might be perverted and in time even become unrecognizable. It was necessary that the truth concerning creation should be written down that the church might possess that truth in an uncorrupted form. The man whom God chose to perform this task was, we believe, Moses. But how did Moses learn the truth which he expressed in Genesis 1? Obviously he

could not have learned it first-hand. But there were other means of learning this truth. It may be that Moses had access to written documents which were at his disposal. It may also be that he was acquainted with oral tradition.... That is to say God, in his providence, prepared by training and education the particular man whom he desired to write the first chapter of the Bible, and when that man set to the work of writing he was superintended by the Spirit of God with the result that what he wrote was what the Spirit of God desired him to write. If he did employ ancient documents he was protected and guided in his use of them so that he chose from them only what God desired him to employ.[60]

Moses was the ideal candidate to be the author of the Pentateuch. Not only was he from a priestly family, from the tribe of Levi, and therefore intimately familiar with the beliefs and traditions of the Hebrews, but he also had direct access to the scholars and libraries of Egypt.[61] With God's divine guidance, he assembled the Hebrew traditions, carefully modified with relevant information from parallel traditions, into the Book of Genesis. Moses committed the ancient oral creation traditions of the Hebrews to written form, but took great care to make sure that all mythological references were cut out of them so that the Israelites, having escaped 400 years of Egyptian idolatry, would not soon lapse back into it. Any references to "dragons" might have created a link with the Mesopotamian idolatry typified by the Babylonian accounts of creation. As a result, as Lambert explains it, "A battle between Yahweh and the sea, or sea monsters...had existed in Hebrew traditions of creation, but had been washed out of the monotheistic formulation of Genesis 1."[62]

THE ANCIENT CREATION TRADITION IN THE OLD TESTAMENT
Though the Genesis account of the Creation appears, at least on the surface, to have no apparent links with the Babylonian Creation Epic, the divine conflict creation tradition is actually quite strong both in Genesis and throughout the Old Testament. Many of the Old Tes-

---

[60]Young, "The Interpretation of Genesis 1:2," 162-163.

[61]Moses was set adrift in the waters of the Nile and found by the daughter of Pharaoh, but he was kept in close contact with his mother at least until he was weaned (Ex. 2:1-10). No doubt during his earlier years the traditions of the Hebrews were firmly ingrained in him.

[62]W.G. Lambert, "A New Look at the Babylonian Background of Genesis," *Journal of Theological Studies* 16 (Oct. 1965): 287-300.

tament prophets, psalmists, and even Job held to this belief, exalting YHWH as the defeater of the dragon and creator of the world. As Walther Eichrodt explains in his classic *Theology of the Old Testament,* "Occasional allusions have preserved statements about a battle of Yahweh against a sea and chaos monster called Rahab or Leviathan. Thus Isaiah 51:9 reads, 'Was it not thou who cut Rahab in pieces, that didst pierce the dragon?'; and Ps. 89:11: 'Thou didst crush Rahab like a carcass, thou didst scatter thy enemies with thy mighty arm.' It is not impossible that Israel, too, knew of a myth of Yahweh as the warrior against Chaos, analogous to that current in Babylonia."[63]

Echoes of the Divine Conflict in Genesis

All of the similarities between *Enuma Elish* and the Book of Genesis can be found in the first two chapters of Genesis. Unlike *Enuma Elish,* however, the Genesis account of creation is surprisingly brief, as if it were written merely as a short prologue for the rest of the book. Not only is it much shorter than *Enuma Elish,* it is also written in a completely different style. Closer examination, however, reveals numerous clues that, as a whole, clearly define a commonality of thought between *Enuma Elish* and Genesis 1–2:

✦ *Genesis 1:1-2:*
  ¹ In the beginning God created the heaven and the Earth.
  ² And the Earth was without form, and void; and darkness was upon the face of the deep. And the Spirit of God moved upon the face of the waters. (KJV)

There are two schools of thought on the evidence to be found in Genesis 1:1-2. The first is the traditional school, with which we are all familiar. According to the traditional school of thought, verse 1 describes how God created the entire universe, Earth in particular. The term "the heaven" refers to the entire created order: all of the stars and planets, solar systems, and galaxies throughout the entire universe. Verse 2 then explains that God created Earth in a chaotic condition, cloudy and formless, waiting for its Creator to shape it into its final form.

---

[63]Walther Eichrodt, *Theology of the Old Testament: Volume Two,* The Old Testament Library, trans. J.A. Baker (Philadelphia: The Westminster Press, 1967), 114.

The second major school of thought is largely the same, except for the belief that there was a gap of time between the events described in Genesis 1:1 and 1:2, during which time a catastrophe occurred that made Earth, formerly stable and orderly, "without form and void." This theory, that there was a "gap" of time between Genesis 1:1 and 1:2 is called, predictably, "the gap theory." As Arthur C. Custance explains in his *Without Form and Void*, "Essentially there are two possible interpretations of Genesis 1:2. Either it is a chaos (without form and void) which marks the first stage of God's creative activity, or it is a chaos which resulted from some catastrophic event marring what had formerly been an orderly and beautiful world."[64] Gap theorists like Custance begin their arguments with the assumption that God would not have created Earth as a chaotic place, but as an orderly one. Therefore, something must have happened to Earth in the primeval past to ruin God's good creation.

One of the major supports for the gap theory is a passage in Isaiah which uses some of the same terminology as Genesis 1:2. Gap theorists point out that the word תֹּהוּ, *tohu*, "without form," also shows up in Isaiah 45:18, where Isaiah uses it to describe how God did *not* create Earth "without form" (or, as the KJV translates it, "in vain"): "For thus saith the LORD that created the heavens; God himself that formed the Earth and made it; he hath established it, he created it not *in vain*, he formed it to be inhabited: I [am] the LORD; and [there is] none else" (Isa. 45:18, KJV, emphasis mine). The word here for "vain" is *tohu*, the same word used in Genesis 1:2 to describe the condition of Earth at its creation—"without form." Based on this, gap theorists argue that Isaiah is clearly saying that Earth was *not* originally created in a chaotic state. Therefore, something must have happened between Genesis 1:1 and 1:2 to cause it to be so.

Though both of these schools of thought have strong and persuasive arguments, I would like to suggest a third alternative: that Genesis 1:1 does not summarize the creation of the *universe* and Earth. Instead, it is actually discussing how the *asteroid belt* and Earth were created. God's creation of the universe is assumed; it is merely a background setting for a much more localized Creation event, restricted to our solar system, and focused on the specific circumstances leading up to the creation of Earth and the asteroid belt in their present form.

---

[64] Arthur C. Custance, *Without Form and Void* (Brookville, Canada: Arthur C. Custance, 1970), 2.

Strange as this theory may seem on the face of it, we shall see in the following chapters that there is significant evidence to support the conclusion that the asteroid belt and Earth were once part of a larger planetary body. This planet had been shattered, destroyed by a Giant Impact with a large object, an event not unlike the meteoric impact many now believe had caused the extinction of the dinosaurs, except on a much larger scale. Thus I agree with the gap theorists in that something *did* happen to Earth to cause it to be without form and void, but that this disaster is the subject of the entire chapter. As such, verse 1 is simply a summary statement for the rest of the chapter: "In the beginning, God created the asteroid belt and Earth." (Exactly *how* He accomplished this is the subject of chapters III and V of this book.)

Another important point of controversy in the text of Genesis 1:1-2 has caused some problems for interpreters. It is the Hebrew word תְּהוֹם, *tehom*, "deep water," a word that Moses uses in Genesis 1:2 to help describe the condition Earth was in after it had been reduced to a chaotic state: "and darkness was over the face of *tehom* ("the deep"). The controversy lies in the fact that the word *tehom* is actually closely related to the Babylonian word *tiam,* which also means "deep water." *Tiam* shows up as *Tiamat* in the Babylonian Creation Epic, the addition of the feminine pronoun suffix *-at* turning the word *tiam,* "deep water" into a feminine personal name: *Tiamat,* or "lady sea."[65] This is the same dragon that the Babylonian deity Marduk had defeated, creating heaven and Earth from its corpse. Thus, the character of *Tiamat* is the personification of deep water — a symbolic representation of Earth and its vast, deep oceans — and an excellent parallel to Genesis 1:2. Even more, the plural of the Hebrew word *tehom* is תְּהֹמוֹת *tehomot*, which is nearly identical to the Akkadian word *Tiamat*. That and the fact that the plural *tehomot* is of the feminine gender, and the fact that the dragon of the creation is not only consistently shown to be female in gender, but also to have a plurality of heads — 7 in total — makes this grammatical link between *tehomot* and *Tiamat* very strong indeed.[66]

Many scholars have come to the same conclusion. They also believe that the use of *tehom* in Genesis 1:2 is evidence Abraham brought with

---

[65] See David Marcus, *A Manual of Akkadian* (Lanham, MD: University Press of America, 1978), 18.

[66] Gesenius, W., & Tregelles, S. P. (2003). *Gesenius' Hebrew and Chaldee Lexicon to the Old Testament Scriptures* (857). Bellingham, WA: Logos Research Systems, Inc.

him from Mesopotamia a Creation tradition very similar to that of the Babylonians. As Morgenstern explains, "Unquestionably...the word is derived from the Babylonian *Tiamat*. And its early use in Hebrew attests early Israelite acquaintance with the Babylonian *Enuma Elish* epic, or at least with the Babylonian creation myth in some form or another."[67] The form of the creation myth with which they were familiar, as we have seen, was at least partly Sumerian in origin, which both Abram and the Babylonians had used as a source for their understanding of the creation; thus there are both distinct similarities and distinct differences.

A third important point of controversy is the prominent mention of the use of "winds" in the creation of Earth. In *Enuma Elish,* Marduk was armed with seven great "winds." He used one of these winds to defeat Tiamat, and another to divide Tiamat's dead body, creating Earth from the upper part of her body and moving it to a new location in heaven (IV:93-104, V:123-34). Similarly, in Genesis 1:2, the words רוּחַ אֱלֹהִים, *ruah elohim,* "the Spirit of God," can also be translated as "mighty wind" or "divine wind", strongly implying that God may have used a similar method to create the Earth in its present form and location.[68]

☥ Genesis 1:3-8:
> [3] And God said, Let there be light: and there was light.
> [4] And God saw the light, that it was good: and God divided the light from the darkness.
> [5] And God called the light Day, and the darkness he called Night. And the evening and the morning were the first day.
> [6] And God said, Let there be a firmament in the midst of the waters, and let it divide the waters from the waters.
> [7] And God made the firmament, and divided the waters which were under the firmament from the waters which were above the firmament: and it was so.
> [8] And God called the firmament Heaven. And the evening and the morning were the second day. (KJV)

---

[67] Julian Morgenstern, "The Sources of the Creation Story—Genesis 1:1–2:4," *The American Journal of Semitic Languages and Literatures* 36 no.3 (April 1920): 197.

[68] This concept will be covered in depth in Part V.

Another clear parallel between Genesis 1 and *Enuma Elish* is the creation of a "firmament" that divides the waters on Earth from the waters in the heavens. In *Enuma Elish* and other traditions, as we have seen, when the dragon was defeated, water came forth from her dead body. Some of this water remained with Earth, Tiamat's "head", but much of it remained, along with the shattered remnants of her body, as a ring, or "great band" in heaven. It is likely that some of this water is what comprises the "waters above" described in Genesis 1:7, which, like the firmament, remain somewhere in "heaven", or outer space, to this day. If so, then the "waters below" must describe Earth's hydrosphere — all of the water in Earth's atmosphere, oceans, lakes, rivers, and everywhere on and under the Earth's surface, as described in verses 9-10. The "firmament", Akkadian *esharra*[69], appears to be a more solid object that is somehow linked with the "waters above", a subject we shall discuss in more depth in Part V.

✢ Genesis 1:14-19:
[14] And God said, Let there be lights in the firmament of the heaven to divide the day from the night; and let them be for signs, and for seasons, and for days, and years:
[15] And let them be for lights in the firmament of the heaven to give light upon the earth: and it was so.
[16] And God made two great lights; the greater light to rule the day, and the lesser light to rule the night: he made the stars also.
[17] And God set them in the firmament of the heaven to give light upon the earth,
[18] And to rule over the day and over the night, and to divide the light from the darkness: and God saw that it was good.
[19] And the evening and the morning were the fourth day. (KJV)

Both creation accounts, of course, offer explanations for how and why the Sun, Moon and stars were created. However, unlike the Babylonian account, the Hebrew account is distinctly non-mythological to the point of being anti-mythological. Gerhard Hasel goes so far as to argue that Genesis was purposely written in such a way so that it is actually a polemic against idolatry.

---

[69] At the end of tablet IV, Marduk names the firmament that holds back the heavenly waters *Esharra*, which he set as a "house" in heaven.

> Against the background of the widespread astral worship the creation and function of the luminaries in Gen. 1:14-18 appears in a new light. In the biblical presentation the creatureliness of all creation, also that of the Sun, Moon, and stars, remains the fundamental and determining characteristic. Conversely, *Enuma Elish* depicts Marduk as the one who fixes the astral likenesses of the gods as their characteristics as constellations.... Genesis 1 avoids the names "Sun" and "Moon" undoubtedly because these common Semitic terms are at the same time names for deities. An inherent opposition to astral worship is thus apparent. The heavenly bodies appear in Genesis in the "degrading" status of "luminaries" whose function it is to "rule." As carriers of light they have the serving function "to give light" (vv. 15-18). The enigmatic Hebrew phrase "and the stars" in verse 16...emphasize[s] that the stars themselves are created things and nothing more. They share in the creatureliness of all creation and have no autonomous divine quality.[70]

Scholars are greatly divided on this issue as to whether or not the numerous similarities between Genesis 1–2 and *Enuma Elish* indicate a common root creation tradition. And though the connection is clear, even obvious, here is a summary of the similarities in parallel, for the reader to decide.

Genesis 1–2	Enuma Elish
(1:1) In the beginning God creates the heavens and Earth.	In the beginning, Marduk creates heaven and Earth from Tiamat's body (IV:93–140; V:59–65).

---

[70]Gerhard F. Hasel, "The Polemical Nature of the Genesis Cosmology," *The Evangelical Quarterly* 46 (1974): 89. See chapter II for a more in-depth study of astral worship in the ancient Near East.

Cataclysm resulting in creation of Earth (gap theory).	"Battle" resulting in creation of Earth (IV:93–140).
(1:2) Spirit or "mighty wind" (*ruah elohim*)[71] hovers over the waters.	Marduk uses the "Evil Wind" to defeat Tiamat[72] (IV:97–98).
(1:2) Primeval waters of Earth as *tehom*; *tehom* a feminine noun.	Primeval waters of Earth as *Tiamat*; Tiamat a feminine proper noun.
(1:6-8) Earth's waters divided into "waters above" and "waters below" by a "firmament."	Tiamat's waters divided into "waters above" and "waters below" by a "firmament" (IV:129–45).
(1:14) God creates the stars and sets them as signs to mark off the days, seasons, and years.	Marduk sets the stars as constellations and uses them to define the days, months, seasons, and years (V:1–5).
(1:15-18) God creates the Sun and Moon to light the Earth.	Marduk establishes the movements of the Sun and Moon (V:12–45).
(2:6) God uses a "mist" to water the ground.	Marduk brings forth a "mist" from Tiamat to water the ground (V:51).

---

[71] See Victor P. Hamilton, *The Book of Genesis: Chapters 1–17,* NICOT (Grand Rapids: William B. Eerdmans Publishing Company, 1990), 111-114 for an excellent discussion of this translation. Some scholars translate this as "mighty wind" or "awesome gale" rather than "Spirit of God" as is traditionally the case. Of these scholars, including such notables as Von Rad and Harrison, some do so in order to make the same links with *Enuma Elish* as do I. See also H.M. Orlinsky, "The Plain Meaning of *Ruah* in Gen. 1.2," *JQR* 48 (1957/58) 174–82 and R. Luyster, "Wind and Water: Cosmogonic Symbolism in the Old Testament," *ZAW* 93 (1981) 1–10.

[72] The use of the name "Evil Wind" in the Epic may be propagandistic in nature. The writers of the Babylonian version of the Creation Epic may have used the term to associate Sumer, their conquered enemy, with Tiamat who, like Sumer, had also been destroyed by an "evil wind." Thus the Babylonians, helped by their god Marduk, perceived themselves as having defeated the Sumerians, who to them represented the evil Tiamat.

(2:7-8, 15) God creates man to till His garden.	Marduk creates man to work for him (VI:1–8).
(Gen. 2:10-14) God creates four primary rivers, one of them the Euphrates.[73]	Marduk creates two primary rivers, one of them the Euphrates (V:55).

The above table makes it clear that there are in fact many similarities between *Enuma Elish* and the creation account in Genesis 1. This is strong evidence for an even older creation tradition, a "foundation text," that lies behind both accounts. This creation tradition shows up throughout the Old Testament where God is seen as being in conflict with a dragon and/or the sea. And the passages that most clearly reflect the divine conflict motif that is the basis of the Old Testament can be found primarily in the Psalms, Isaiah, and Job.

Echoes of the Divine Conflict in the Psalms
✟ Psalm 74:12-17:
[12] For God *is* my King of old, working salvation in the midst of the earth.
[13] Thou didst divide the sea by thy strength: Thou brakest the heads of the dragons in the waters.
[14] Thou brakest the heads of leviathan in pieces, *and* gavest him *to be* meat to the people inhabiting the wilderness.
[15] Thou didst cleave the fountain and the flood: Thou driedst up mighty rivers.
[16] The day *is* thine, the night also *is* thine: Thou hast prepared the light and the Sun.
[17] Thou hast set all the borders of the earth: Thou hast made summer and winter. (KJV)

---

[73] Though knowledge of the rivers "Pison" and "Gihon" have been lost to history by the time of the Babylonian Empire, satellite photos have recently discovered an ancient riverbed running through Saudi Arabia that once ran near the Euphrates. Whether this refers to Pison or Gihon is not clear, but it is more likely the Pison as commentators believe "Havilah" refers to the area now known as Saudi Arabia. The Gihon has yet to be found, however.

Perhaps the strongest example of the divine conflict creation motif to be found in the Bible outside of Genesis is Psalm 74, which describes God as having "split open the sea" and breaking the "heads of the monster in the waters", indicating that this single monster had multiple heads, as in the Canaanite and Sumerian creation stories (v. 13). "Leviathan" is then explicitly mentioned as the name of this monster (v. 14). Next, also as in *Enuma Elish*, it is explained that God crushed the heads of Leviathan, and from her heads streams of waters flowed (vv. 14-15).[74] God then also set Leviathan's crushed head (assumedly the largest of them) as the new Earth just as Marduk did Tiamat's, establishing its new relative position and motion in space so that, from Earth's perspective, the Sun and Moon now rose and set at different times (v.16). God also gave the new Earth a new axial tilt, so that there would be seasons to moderate the extremes of hot and cold typical of planets that do not have axial tilts. All in all this verse is almost a perfect cognate with *Enuma Elish* and related Near Eastern creation stories, as well as with modern science, though of course God is given the glory instead of pagan idols or random chance.

⁕ Psalm 89:8-11:
> [8] O LORD God of hosts, who *is* a strong LORD like unto thee? Or to thy faithfulness round about thee?
> [9] Thou rulest the raging of the sea: when the waves thereof arise, thou stillest them.
> [10] Thou hast broken Rahab in pieces, as one that is slain; thou hast scattered thine enemies with thy strong arm.
> [11] The heavens *are* thine, the earth also *is* thine: *as for* the world and the fulness thereof, thou hast founded them. (KJV)

Psalm 89, though less detailed and extensive than Psalm 74, also displays some clear examples of the divine conflict creation motif. God is once again seen here as King over the chaotic, tempestuous sea, which since the beginning of Creation has been a threat to divine order and civilization (v. 9). Then, in verse 10, the dragon is again mentioned in parallel with the chaotic, deep sea, this time with the name רַהַב "Rahab", which literally

---

[74] Psalm 74 also contains a clear allusion to the events of the Exodus in verse 14, where somehow the head of the dragon was turned into the manna and/or quail that was used to feed the Israelites. See our breakthrough article on the mysteries of the Exodus at http://www.mysteriousworld.com/Journal/2008/Spring/Artifacts/, and in the commentary on Isaiah 51 following page 60 of this book.

means "great one" or "haughty one" — an excellent description of the character and personality of Tiamat, whose greatness as the "queen of the gods" made her intolerably arrogant, power hungry, and tyrannical. The use of the generic term "Rahab" rather than "Tiamat" may have been, as it was in Genesis, used in order to avoid mentioning the name of a foreign deity, thereby giving that false idol credibility. God is then shown as the conquering King, who overthrew and destroyed the arrogant Rahab and her helpers, just as Marduk defeated Tiamat and the monstrous serpents she gave birth to in order to defend herself and her corrupt kingdom from Marduk. Finally, in verse 11, this reference to God's battle against the dragon Rahab is affirmed to be a reference to the great creation battle between God and the dragon, wherein God used Rahab's head to create the new Earth, and her tail to create the new heavens.

✟ Psalm 93:1-4
> [1] The LORD reigneth, he is clothed with majesty; the LORD is clothed with strength, *wherewith* he hath girded himself: The world also is stablished, that it cannot be moved.
> [2] Thy throne *is* established of old: Thou *art* from everlasting.
> [3] The floods have lifted up, O LORD, the floods have lifted up their voice; the floods lift up their waves.
> [4] The LORD on high *is* mightier than the noise of many waters, *yea, than* the mighty waves of the sea. (KJV)

John Day points out that "the dragon" is almost always described in close relation to the sea, to the point that the two are not always clearly distinguishable. In fact, some Creation references in the Bible actually forego any references to a "dragon" and talk directly about God's conflict with the primordial sea. Day explains,

> We do have other passages in which the creation is associated and causally connected with Yahweh's conflict with or control of the primordial sea, e.g. Ps. 104:6-9, Job 38:8-11, Prov. 8:29, and since elsewhere the sea is mentioned parallel with the dragon, with which it is closely associated (e.g. Isa. 51:9-10), we can only conclude that passages which refer to a conflict with the dragon in the context of creation similarly alluded to a struggle at that

time. Psalm 74:12-17 and 89:10-15 (ET 9-14), for example, certainly fall into this category.[75]

God's conflict with the sea should thus be considered the same as his conflict with the dragon, as both the dragon and the sea seem to be inseparably linked. In *Enuma Elish,* as we have seen, Tiamat is also closely linked with the primordial sea. In fact, according to the Babylonian account, the clouds and seas of Earth were actually made from Tiamat's "venom," and the heavens were made of the waters that Marduk had caused to come forth from Tiamat's womb (IV:136-40; V:57-62).

Echoes of the Divine Conflict in Isaiah

☥ Isaiah 26:20–27:1
[20] Come, my people, enter thou into thy chambers, and shut thy doors about thee: hide thyself as it were for a little moment, until the indignation be overpast.
[21] For, behold, the LORD cometh out of his place to punish the inhabitants of the Earth for their iniquity: the Earth also shall disclose her blood, and shall no more cover her slain.
[1] In that day the LORD with his sore and great and strong sword shall punish leviathan the piercing serpent, even leviathan that crooked serpent; and he shall slay the dragon that is in the sea.
(KJV)

Here, "in that day" is a reference to the end time, when God will battle Leviathan, the "sea dragon" that we also saw in Psalm 74. This links nicely with the end-time description of "the dragon" (Rev. 12:3–13:11; 16:13; 20:2), a being who is also in opposition to God. In 20:2, the dragon is equated with "that old serpent," "the devil," and "Satan," and is believed to be the same dragon mentioned throughout the Old Testament. At Armageddon, at the final battle between God and the forces of evil led by the dragon, Jesus attacks and annihilates his ancient enemy and his cohorts with a sword that comes out of his mouth (19:15, 21).

---

[75]Day, *God's Conflict with the Dragon and the Sea,* 3.

✟ Isaiah 51:9-10, 13, 15:
> ⁹Awake, awake, put on strength, O arm of the LORD; awake, as in the ancient days, in the generations of old. *Art* thou not it that hath cut Rahab, *and* wounded the dragon?
> ¹⁰ *Art* thou not it which hath dried the sea, the waters of the great Deep; That hath made the depths of the sea a way for the ransomed to pass over?
> ¹³ And forgettest the LORD thy maker, that hath stretched forth the heavens, and laid the foundations of the earth; and hast feared continually every day because of the fury of the oppressor, as if he were ready to destroy? And where *is* the fury of the oppressor?
> ¹⁵ But I *am* the LORD thy God, that divided the sea, whose waves roared: The LORD of hosts *is* his name. (KJV)

Next to Psalm 74, Isaiah 51 has the next most explicit reference to the divine conflict creation motif. Here again the creation of the heavens and the Earth are placed in the context of God's battle with a sea monster, using terminology very similar to that used in Psalm 74. And, just as in Psalm 89, Isaiah uses the more neutral name "Rahab" as the name of the dragon. In verse 13 the cosmic battle is once again related to the Creation of both the heavens and the Earth, verse 15 reiterating the concept of the "dividing of the sea" into waters above and waters below.

The terminology of this passage is even more reminiscent of the Exodus than that used in Psalm 74. Whereas in Psalm 74, the heads of the dragon were given as food to the "people inhabiting the wilderness", i.e., the children of Israel in the wilderness of Sinai, Isaiah 51 makes the connection with the Exodus even more explicit by inserting a clear reference to the crossing of the Red Sea, relating it to the division of the waters described in Genesis 1. As such, Isaiah and the psalmist may have been implying that the Exodus event was one of the major battles in God's ongoing war to finally subdue the dragon. This implies that God's victory over the dragon at the Creation of the Earth did not destroy the power of the dragon completely, but merely diminished its power to the point where the dragon could be subdued by the ongoing efforts of God's people, culminating in the final battle at the end of time when the dragon's power will be destroyed forever (Rev. 20:10).

Echoes of the Divine Conflict in Job

Job also contains numerous references to a sea dragon in the context of the creation. It is referred to alternatively as a generic monster that lives in the sea, or as a specific creature such as Leviathan or Rahab. A second being, a land monster named "Behemoth," is also mentioned, and may also have a parallel in *Enuma Elish* with "Kingu", the chief of Tiamat's army. These creatures are all without exception mentioned in the context of the Creation.

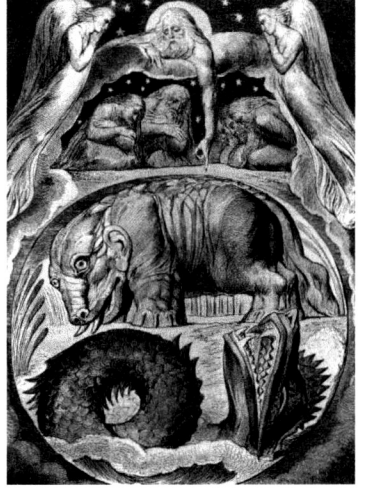

"Behemoth and Leviathan" from Illustrations to "The Book of Job" (1825) by William Blake. Here Behemoth is seen as the archetypal "earth monster", whereas Leviathan is seen as the archetypal "water monster", both created by God and controlled in "the circle of the Earth."

✢ Job 3:3-4, 8-9:
> ³Let the day perish wherein I was born, and the night *in which* it was said, There is a man child conceived.
> ⁴Let that day be darkness; let not God regard it from above, neither let the light shine upon it.
> ⁸ Let them curse it that curse the day, who are ready to raise up *Leviathan*.
> ⁹ Let the stars of the twilight thereof be dark; let it look for light, but *have* none; neither let it see the dawning of the day.
> (KJV)

This first example occurs immediately after the death of Job's sons and daughters and the destruction of all of Job's property. Here Job is lamenting the day he was born. Strangely, he mentions Leviathan, as if somehow his downfall and that of Leviathan's are somehow linked.[76]

---

[76] This is one of the major themes of the Book of Job, which will be discussed at length in Chapter VI.

✟ Job 7:12:
¹²Am I the sea or the *tannin* that thou settest a watch over me? (KJV)

In chapter 7, Job once again relates his fate to that of the "monster of the deep", in this case *tannin*, (translated as "whale" in the KJV) that God placed under guard to make sure that she does not rise again. Marduk is also said to have placed guards over Tiamat's body, so that her waters could not escape (IV: 140-141).

✟ Job 9:4-9, 13:
⁴ He is wise in heart, and mighty in strength: who hath hardened himself against him, and hath prospered?
⁵ Which removeth the mountains, and they know not: which overturneth them in his anger.
⁶ Which shaketh the earth out of her place, and the pillars thereof tremble.
⁷ Which commandeth the Sun, and it riseth not; and sealeth up the stars.
⁸ Which alone spreadeth out the heavens, and treadeth upon the waves of the sea.
⁹ Which maketh Arcturus, Orion, and Pleiades, and the chambers of the south.
¹⁰ He performs wonders that cannot be fathomed, miracles that cannot be counted.
¹³*If* God will not withdraw his anger, the proud helpers [of Rahab] do stoop under him. (KJV)

Though it is clearly alluded to in the previous verses we have cited, Job 9 contains the first direct reference in Job to the dragon in the context of the divine conflict creation scenario. Though the reference to the dragon remains hidden in the KJV, the name of the dragon "Rahab" is indeed there in verse 13, "the proud helpers" retranslated correctly in the NIV as "the cohorts of Rahab." This once again correlates perfectly with the combat between Marduk and Tiamat in Enuma Elish, where, after defeating Tiamat, Marduk then defeated her helpers and trampled them underfoot (*Enuma Elish* IV: 118). Further detail is given in Tablet V of *Enuma Elish* of the fate of the helpers of Tiamat: "The gods who had *done battle* (and) been scattered, he led bound into the presence of his fathers....the eleven creatures which

Tiamat had made, whose weapons he had shattered, [he] tied to his foot" (V:71–74). Rahab and her "helpers" are also mentioned in Psalm 89, where God is described as having "shattered" them (v. 10).

Verse 6 gives specific details regarding what happened to the Earth during the Creation process, starting with the fact that the Earth was literally moved from its place, assumedly to a new orbit closer to the Sun, as we saw in our analysis of Genesis 1:1 (הַמַּרְגִּיז אֶרֶץ מִמְּקוֹמָהּ) *ha-maregiyz eretz mi-meqowmah*, "the Earth was shaken from her place". The word *mimeqowmah*, "from her place" interestingly, is actually the feminine singular, so the Earth is seen by Job as a "her", just as Tiamat was also identified as a goddess rather than a god in *Enuma Elish*. The rest of verse 6, וְעַמּוּדֶיהָ יִתְפַלָּצוּן *ve-'amoowdeyha yitephalatsoown*, literally means "her pillar was broken". In the context of the Earth being moved to a new orbit, "her pillar" could only refer to Earth's rotational axis, which to this day is 23.44 degrees deviant from vertical.[77] Thus, this very pithy and highly informative verse describes with stunning scientific precision how Earth was moved into a new orbit and given an axial tilt.

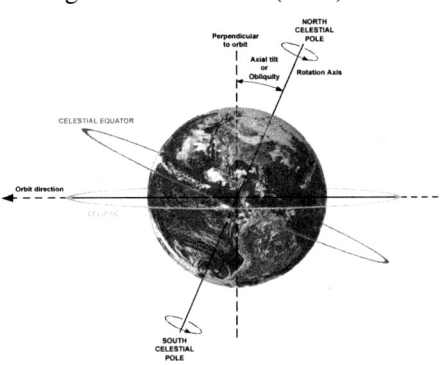

Earth has an axial tilt of over 23 degrees relative to its orbital plane of the ecliptic, and scientists to this day have not yet definitively determined the cause. Once again, the Bible appears to have the answer.

Verse 7 then goes into more detail regarding the results of the divine conflict between God and the dragon, describing how God then set events in motion so that the Sun and the stars were no longer visible from Earth. The only way to achieve this outcome, of course, was to have covered the face of the Earth with deep darkness so that nothing was visible, not even the Sun. This would be the natural outcome of a catastrophe so great that it caused Earth to be shattered and moved to an entirely new orbit closer to the Sun — massive amounts of dust and ashes would have been thrown up into the atmosphere, effectively "sealing up" the sky so that no light could come through for many hundreds, possibly thousands of years.

---

[77] http://en.wikipedia.org/wiki/Axial_tilt

Verse 8 then reiterates the concept of God "spreading out" the heavens, which are once again described as being a sort of "heavenly sea" through which God travels. The Hebrew text is literally בָּמֳתֵי יָם , *bamatay yam*, which literally translates as "the high places of the sea". The word *bamatay* is very similar to the name of the monster Behemoth who is the biblical cognate of Kingu, the monster whom Tiamat gave birth to in order to defend herself against Marduk. It may also be translated as "mountains", perhaps symbolically representing Rahab's "breasts" from which the waters of heaven flowed forth.[78] Thus the *bamatay yam* may be literally translated as the "breasts of Yamm", or "the breasts of the dragon", whose waters were used by God to created the heavens.

In verse 9, Job then speaks of God creating the constellations, which also has a clear parallel in *Enuma Elish* (V:1–4). Names of specific constellations are also given, including עָשׁ כְּסִיל וְכִימָה *'ash, kesil vekiymah*, "Ash, Kesil and Kimah", typically understood to be the constellations Ursa Major, Orion and the Pleiades, respectively, though the KJV retains the translation "Arcturus" for *Ash*.[79]

It is also possible that Ash, Kesil and Kimah are also names of some of the helpers of Leviathan/Tiamat, because in the following verse (10), God is literally described as עֹשֶׂה גְדֹלוֹת עַד־אֵין *oseh gedolowt ad-ayn*, "making the great ones as nothing forever." The remainder of verse 9 is a typical Hebrew parallel construct, חֵקֶר וְנִפְלָאוֹת עַד־אֵין מִסְפָּר *ḥaqer ve-niphela'owt ad-ayn mispar*, "they were cut into pieces and hidden forever, accounted as nothing." This would seem to apply most directly to the helpers of Rahab, described in verse 13, though further investigation in later chapters of this book should shed more light on this question.

---

[78] This was believed of the Egyptian goddess Hathor, the milk from whose breasts, it was believed, formed the Milky Way, and indeed powered the entire universe. See http://www.mysteriousworld.com/Journal/2008/Spring/Artifacts/ for a detailed explanation of Hathor and her role in the Exodus.

[79] For a solid biblical perspective on the constellations, consult the following books: Joseph A. Seiss, *The Gospel in the Stars* (Grand Rapids: Kregel, 1972 [reprint of Philadelphia: E. Claxton and Company, 1882]); E.W. Bullinger, *The Witness of the Stars* (Grand Rapids: Kregel, 1967 [reprint of 1897 edition]); Donald B. DeYoung, *Astronomy and the Bible: Questions and Answers* (Grand Rapids: Baker Book House, 1988); G. Shiaparelli, *Astronomy in the Old Testament* (Oxford: The Clarendon Press, 1905), 10. We will also be discussing astronomy in the Bible in Chapter II of this book.

✥ Job 26:6-14:

⁶Hell is naked before him, and destruction hath no covering.

⁷He stretcheth out the north over the empty place, and hangeth the earth upon nothing.

⁸He bindeth up the waters in his thick clouds; and the cloud is not rent under them.

⁹He holdeth back the face of his throne, and spreadeth his cloud upon it.

¹⁰He hath compassed the waters with bounds, until the day and night come to an end.

¹¹The pillars of heaven tremble and are astonished at his reproof.

¹²He divideth the sea with his power, and by his understanding he smiteth through the proud [Rahab].

¹³By his spirit he hath garnished the heavens; his hand hath formed the crooked serpent.

¹⁴Lo, these are parts of his ways: but how little a portion is heard of him? but the thunder of his power who can understand? (KJV)

In another classic reference to the God-dragon combat, in chapter 26 Job once again relates a great deal of information regarding the Creation. After rebuking his friend Bildad, Job again begins to praise God's great power as evidenced by His defeat of the "crooked serpent", identified in verse 12 as Rahab, and the creation of the heavens and Earth from her body. And as we shall see, once again there is a great deal of enciphered information here regarding the specifics of the Creation that can only be understood in the context of the divine conflict creation motif.

First off, the word for death in verse 6 (translated as "hell" in the KJV) is in fact Hebrew שְׁאוֹל *sheol*. This is interesting because, as we have seen, there is a reference to a dragon in the Ba'al myths named "Shalyat of the seven heads," also called "Lotan," whom Ba'al fought and defeated:

> If thou smite Lotan, the serpent slant,
> Destroy the serpent tortuous,
> Shalyat of the seven heads...[80]

Shalyat is used here in parallel with Lotan, and is considered to be another name for the same creature. Thus Leviathan apparently was also known by the variant names of "Lotan" and "Shalyat", and like Shalyat, was identified as having seven heads (cf. also Ps. 74:13-14). It is also possible that the Ugaritic (Canaanite) name *Shalyat* is cognate to the Hebrew word *sheol* in the same way that the Babylonian word *Tiamat* is related to the Hebrew word *tehom*.

As we saw with *tehom* (deep water), *yam* (the sea), and Lotan/Leviathan, the Hebrews tended to adopt the names of foreign gods, reducing them from divine beings to impersonal and/or symbolic concepts. This occurred with several other Canaanite gods, including Ba'al, the king of the gods of Canaan, whom the Israelites reduced to בַּעַל *ba'al*, "owner, lord" (Ex. 21:28); Ashtoreth, the Canaanite goddess of fertility, whom the Israelites reduced to עַשְׁתֶּרֶת *ashtoreth*, "increase" (Deut. 7:13); Dagan, the Canaanite god of grain (and fish), was reduced to דָּגָן *dagan*, "grain" (Deut. 7:13); Tirsu, god of wine, was reduced to תִּירוֹשׁ *tirosh*, "wine," (Deut. 7:13); and Resheph, god of plagues, was reduced to רֶשֶׁף *resheph*, "pestilence" (Hab. 3:5). Similarly, it is likely that Shalyat/sheol reflects the same kind of cognate "borrowing". In other words, as we saw with the Babylonian name *Tiamat* (*Tiam*, "deep water" + *-at*, "lady" = *Tiamat*, "lady sea"), we may also see in the term *sheol* yet another Israelite appropriation and depersonalization of the name of a foreign divinity, this time Ugaritic: *Sheol*, "hell," + *-at*, "lady," = Sheolat, or *Shalyat* — "lady hell" or "lady abyss." This is appropriate as *sheol*, or "the abyss," is often linked with the deep sea, more specifically as being located under it. Also, in Job, the abyss is mentioned repeatedly in the context of God's description of Leviathan, and in my retranslation of the creation accounts in Job in chapter VI, the two can even be seen as one and the same. Thus, verse 6, by mentioning that Sheol, or "Shalyat" was uncovered as a result of God's creative action, proves both that

---

[80]H.L. Ginsberg, trans.,"Poems about Baal and Anat," in *Ancient Near Eastern Texts Relating to the Old Testament*, 3d ed., ed James B. Pritchard (Princeton: Princeton University Press, 1974), 138.

this chapter fits well into the divine conflict creation paradigm, and also provides us with yet another name for the dragon.

Verse 7 also shows several excellent examples of the Hebrew tendency to adopt and depersonalize foreign deities into demythologized "loan words". These words include צָפוֹן *tsaphon*, "north" תֹהוּ *tohu*, "empty place" and אֶרֶץ *eretz*, "earth".

Zeus' battle with the serpent-monster Typhon should be considered yet another example of the great creation conflict in the Bible as interpreted within the context of pagan theology. Originally derived from Canaanite-Ugaritic creation mythology, Mt Zaphon became the serpent-monster "Typhon" of Greek myth, but simply became known as "north" in the rigidly monotheistic Hebrew Bible.

Tsaphon, typically translated as "north", was likely originally derived from the name of a mountain in the north of Israel called Mt. Zaphon (modern Mt. Aqraa in northwest Syria)[81] where, in one of the Canaanite creation myths, Ba'al defeated some sort of a serpentine monster. Similarly, it is believed that the later Greek myth of Zeus's battle with a monster named "Typhon" was derived from this Ba'al myth.[82] As a result, the word "Zaphon", literally, "mountain of the north," or "monster of the north", was adopted and denigrated to the level of a simple direction — in this case *tsaphon*, "north", which was then put into general use in the Bible to designate a place of dark foreboding that is to be avoided. Thus Typhon should be considered to be some sort of "mountain monster" — i.e., a monster made of rock, like the demon Asag who lives in the divine mountain, the "Kur", in the Sumerian creation myth, "The Feats and Exploits of Ninurta" discussed previously. This creature, who was also believed to be serpentine in character, is likely not the equivalent of Tiamat or Behemoth, but a lesser creature that

---

[81] Mt. Zaphon was an important divine mountain in Canaanite/Ugaritic myth, where their high god Ba'al was believed to live in a palace of silver and lapis lazuli. http://en.wikipedia.org/wiki/Mount_Aqraa

[82] Day, *God's Conflict with the Dragon and the Sea*, 32-33. Cf. also http://www.eliyah.com/cgi-bin/strongs.cgi?file=hebrewlexicon&isindex=6828 and http://langkjer.dk/origin/1-12.htm.

fought by their side, just as Kingu fought by the side of Tiamat in *Enuma Elish*.[83]

Tohu, usually translated as "void" or "waste", may also have its origins as yet another name for the dragon. As we have seen in our analysis of Genesis 1, the name for the deep sea, *tehom*, appears to have been an Israelite appropriation and demythologization of the name of the dragon *Tiamat* from the Babylonian myths. If so, then it may be that the very similar word *tohu*, that appears both here and in Genesis 1:1, is also a demythologized version of *Tiamat*, except shortened a bit in order to rhyme with *bohu*, with which it appears in parallel in Genesis 1:1, translated together as meaning "without form and void" in the KJV. If so, then, *Bohu* may also be the shortened version of the name of some sort of primordial monster, most likely the earth-monster Behemoth, which is described just before the dragon Leviathan in Job 40. Thus the *tohu wa bohu*, "without form and void" of Genesis 1:1 may actually be better

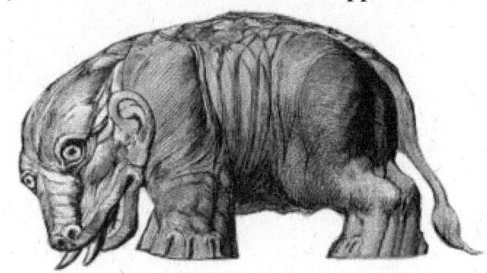

"Behemoth" by William Blake. From "Behemoth and Leviathan", Illustrations to "The Book of Job" (1825) Eretz, like Behemoth and Typhon, appears to have its roots as the name of an ancient mythological creature who fought alongside Leviathan against God at the Creation.

translated as "Tiamat and Behemoth", hearkening back to the water-monster/earth monster pairing of Tiamat and Kingu of *Enuma Elish*, and of Leviathan and Behemoth in Job 40-41, except Tiamat is paired with Behemoth instead of Kingu in Genesis 1:1. Moses may have done this intentionally in order to create a link between the two traditions, without overtly recognizing the legitimacy of *Enuma Elish* or the existence of the false gods of the Babylonians.

Eretz, "earth", may also have its origins as a mythological monster that God fought against at the Creation. Day explains, "Just as Leviathan ultimately derives from the Ugaritic dragon *ltn* [Lotan], so Behemoth has its origin in an ox-like creature of the water called Arṣ

---

[83] Wikipedia, "Asag": http://en.wikipedia.org/wiki/Asag. Cf also http://en.wikipedia.org/wiki/Kur, where the "Kur" was shown to be one of the monstrous serpents that accompanied Tiamat in her battle against Marduk in *Enuma Elish*.

or *'gl 'il 'tk* 'El's calf Atik', who is twice mentioned alongside the dragon in the Ugaritic texts."[84] Day and others believe that the fundamental concept that lies behind the Hebrew word commonly translated as "earth", *'eretz*, is that of an "earth monster" named Eretz that fought against God at the Creation in Canananite-Ugaritic creation mythology. *Eretz* was thus also, like *tsaphon*, a Canaanite/Ugaritic loan word that was appropriated by the Israelites, and denigrated to simply mean "earth" or "ground", with all personal and divine aspects removed. Therefore, though most of the time that *'eretz* appears in the Bible it should be translated as simply "earth", "land" and/or "ground", in the context of the creation battle motif as it is here in Job, it should be symbolically understood to be a beast that came up out of the Earth to fight against God at the Creation. This fits well with *Enuma Elish* and the other Creation passages we have studied in the Bible thus far.[85]

As such, verse 7 has a very different translation, based upon the supposition that this verse speaks specifically about the "earth monster" *Eretz* that accompanied the dragon (named *Shalyat* in verse 6) in her fight against God at the Creation. Both *tsaphon*, "north" and *'eretz*, "earth" appear to originally have been two different names for the same earth monster that the dragon "gave birth to" in order to help her in her fight against God, appearing in parallel to communicate to the reader that these two creatures from two different traditions are in fact one and the same. This monster came forth from the Earth through some heretofore unknown process, explaining why in verse 6, Sheol and Abaddon are said to have no covering – part of Earth itself was removed, leaving the underworld literally exposed to the open air. Then in verse 7, the text describes in detail what happened to the earth monster, named in parallel as both *Tsaphon* and as *Eretz*. First, the earth monster was "turned away" (Heb. נָטָה "stretched out, turned away") over *tohu* (Tiamat) and then it was set there, hanging in space over the defeated dragon (Heb. תָּלָה *talah*, "to hang up, suspend in a balance").[86] Thus, verse 7 should probably be translated something like "He turned aside the earth monster and suspended it in space over

---

[84] Day, *God's Conflict with the Dragon and the Sea,* 86.

[85] This "Beast from the Earth" concept was likely the inspiration for the second beast that comes out of the earth in Revelation 13:11-18. This concept will be covered in depth in Chapter VII.

[86] Interestingly, *talah* is also used to describe a type of punishment, specifically, crucifixion.

the dragon". Or, more scientifically, "He turned the mass of rock that He had removed from Earth and set it in orbit around Earth". As such, since "the dragon" is actually a metaphor for the Earth, then the earth monster *Tsaphon/Eretz* may actually refer not to the creation of Earth, but specifically to the creation of the Moon, which does indeed hang in space over Earth and, astronomers now believe, was ejected from Earth's mantle as the result of a collision with an object roughly the size of Mars.[87] This idea, that the creation of the Moon is actually being described in verse 7, is backed up by the fact that the Moon is again specifically referenced in verse 9 (כִּסֵּה *cisaih*, "Moon").

Verses 8-12 then review how God divided the waters above from the waters below, and set boundaries that they could not pass, just as we have seen in other biblical and ancient Near Eastern creation accounts. Verse 8 is particularly interesting as it contains the word צָרַר *tsorair*, "he created, he fashioned", typically used to describe the creation of an earthen vessel. In the Ninurta myth, Ninurta's weapon, a great mace named *Sharur*, was used by Ninurta to smash Asag and release the waters from the divine mountain. It may well be that the specific use of this form of the word יָצַר *yatsar, tsorair*, may have been used by the author of Job intentionally to refer to the *Sharur* mace that Ninurta used to defeat Asag the earth monster, using *Sharur* to smash the mountain monster like a potter's vessel and releasing the waters therein, without, once again, specifically mentioning the deity by name and thereby giving glory to a foreign deity.[88] The rest of verse 8 also syncs up nicely with both the Ninurta myth and *Enuma Elish*, where both Ninurta and Marduk were both described as releasing and channeling the waters of the dragon, and creating rigid barriers between the "waters above" from the "waters below".

Verses 9-10 then focus once again on the creation of the Moon. The first part of verse 9, מְאַחֵז פְּנֵי־כִסֵּה *me'ahaiz penay-kisaih*, literally means, "He took hold of the face of the Moon". *Kisaih,* which essentially means something that is covered with light, can mean either "throne" or "Moon", but in the context of the Creation, and of the surrounding verses, "Moon" is clearly the preferred translation. The

---

[87] We will discuss this topic in depth in chapters III and V.

[88] See http://www.gatewaystobabylon.com/myths/texts/ninurta/exploitninurta.htm for a detailed explanation of the myth of Ninurta. Notice also Jesus' description in Revelation 2:27 of shattering the nations with a rod of iron like potter's vessels, in the context of a mysterious "star".

second part of verse 9, פֵּרְשֵׁז עָלָיו עֲנָנוֹ *pereshaiz 'alayv 'ananow*, "He spread upon it his cloud" or "He spread darkness upon it", ably describes how the Moon to this day has a "dark side" which is never seen from Earth.[89]

Verse 10 then describes the behavior of the newly created Moon, specifically the Earth-facing side, and how it would now be used to set the appointed times of festivals (חֹק־חָג *ḥoq-ḥag*, "appointed festival times") and, by extension, the reli-

God created the Moon from the Earth and set it in orbit "over the face of the waters" as a memorial of his victory over the dragon — specifically, its helper, Behemoth. Ever since, this "heavenly bull" has marked the times and the seasons with the alternating light and dark patterns that the ancient thought of as its "horns".
Image from VisualParadox.com.

gious calendar year. Thus the Moon would not only be used to determine the religious calendar, but also would, by its very presence, continuously commemorate God's victory over Behemoth, hanging in space over Earth for all to see just as a hunter would hang the head of his quarry above his mantelpiece to impress others of his superior martial prowess (cf. also Psalm 89:37, Job 16:19). The motion of this newly created Moon would be highly accurate, to the point of being perfect, or at least so reliable that it could be used as a reliable marker of time until the end of time — thus the author of Job uses the term עַד־תַּכְלִית *ad-takeliyt*, "until the perfection" or "until the end", to describe its duration. Finally, regarding its behavior, the author of Job says that the Moon would move עַל־פְּנֵי־מָיִם *'al-penay-mayim*, "over the face of the waters", i.e., over Earth's ocean-dominated face, and have alternating periods of light and dark אוֹר עִם־חֹשֶׁךְ (*'owr im-ḥoshek*, literally, "light with darkness").

Thus, all together, verses 9-10 should be retranslated, "He grabbed hold of the Moon and set it so one side would always face away from

---

[89] The so-called "dark side" of the Moon actually receives around the same amount of Sunlight as the side facing the Earth, but it is still called "the dark side" as it is completely invisible from Earth. http://en.wikipedia.org/wiki/The_Moon#Two_sides_of_the_Moon

Earth. Thereafter, until the end of time, the side of the Moon that faced Earth would define the yearly religious calendar via alternating patterns of light and darkness." This new translation correlates perfectly with previous verses in this chapter (Job 26:6), other Creation passages in the Bible, *Enuma Elish*, and of course with established scientific facts about how we now know the Moon actually moves around the Earth.

Verses 11-13 hold fewer surprises when looking into the Hebrew, except of course verse 12, which contains yet another reference to the dragon Rahab, incorrectly translated in the KJV as "the proud", but correctly translated in the NIV as "Rahab". Verse 13 then once again recounts God's destruction of the dragon Rahab and the creation of the heavens from its body, paralleling the previous verses and affirming the dominance of the creation conflict motif in this chapter.

In all Job 26 appears to be essentially a collection of many of the most common creation myths throughout the ancient Near East, specifically *Enuma Elish*, *The Feats and Exploits of Ninurta*, and one or more Canaanite myths, combined into one pithy chapter with God given the glory instead of the gods of the nations from which these stories came. The author of Job very cleverly combined the various names of the dragon and its chief helper from these various mythologies into one brilliant passage that neatly summarizes the process of Creation, without actually overtly naming any foreign deities whatsoever. Job 26 is thus a masterpiece of ancient Creation literature that until now had been largely misunderstood.

✛ Job 38:1, 8-11
[1] Then the LORD answered Job out of the whirlwind, and said,
[8] Who shut up the sea with doors, when it brake forth, as if it had issued out of the womb?
[9] When I made the cloud the garment thereof, and thick darkness a swaddlingband for it,
[10] And brake up for it my decreed place, and set bars and doors,
[11] And said, Hitherto shalt thou come, but no further: and here shall thy proud waves be stayed? (KJV)

The divine conflict creation theme once again surfaces in Job 38, when God finally appears and begins to chastise Job for questioning His sovereignty. God then begins to openly take credit for the creation of Earth and, like Job, also describes that creative activity using the same divine conflict imagery that we have seen throughout the Bible to this point. Job 38, however, focuses on the "waters" of the dragon, specifically on keeping them from escaping their bounds and causing destruction. This theme, predictably, also has a very close cognate with *Enuma Elish*:

> *Then the lord paused to view her dead body,*
> *That he might divide the form and do artful works.*
> *He split her like a shellfish into two parts:*
> *Half of her he set up as a covering for heaven,*
> *Pulled down the bar and posted guards.*
> *He bade them to allow not her waters to escape.*
> *(Enuma Elish IV:35-40)*

Note that much of the same imagery is used in both Job and *Enuma Elish*, including the waters bursting forth from the dragon, even the use of "bars" to keep her waters from escaping again and causing flooding and destruction. This idea of channeling and controlling waters issuing forth from the defeated foe, as we have seen, also has a clear cognate with the Sumerian poem, *The Feats and Exploits of Ninurta*.

In Tablet V of *Enuma Elish*, Marduk is then described as channeling the waters of Tiamat that burst forth from her into lakes, oceans, rivers, clouds and the entire weather cycle on Earth. This earthly "river" is matched by a heavenly river, the "Durmah", a "great band" that circles somewhere out in space:

> *Taking the spittle of Tiamat*
> *Marduk created . . .*
> *He formed the clouds and filled them with water.*
> *The raising of winds, the bringing of rain and cold,*
> *Making the mist smoke, piling up . . .*
> *These he planned himself, took into his own hand.*
> *Putting her head into position he formed thereon the mountains,*
> *Opening the deep which was in flood,*
> *He caused to flow from her eyes the Euphrates and Tigris,*
> *Stopping her nostrils he left . . . ,*
> *He formed from her breasts the lofty mountains,*
> *Therein he drilled springs for the wells to carry off the water.*

> *Twisting her tail he bound it to Durmah,*
> *. . . Apsu at his foot,*
> *. . . her crotch, she was fastened to the heavens,*
> *Thus he covered the heavens and established the earth.*
> *. . . in the midst of Tiamat he made flow,*
> *. . . his net he completely let out,*
> *So he created heaven and earth . . . ,*
> *. . . their bounds . . . established.*
> *(Enuma Elish V:48-76)*

So when God created the Earth, not only did He create the Moon from the Earth, moved Earth to a new orbit, and gave it an axial tilt, at the same time He created the seas and the atmosphere. Moreover, somewhere in space well separated from Earth, there is an additional source of heavenly waters that he set in a specific place in heaven, described at the end of verse 11 as בִּגְאוֹן גַּלֶּיךָ *big'own galeiyk*, "a collection of glittering stones" — most likely a description of the asteroid belt, which is indeed a collection of rocks and frozen ice that circles the Sun like a string of precious stones and glittering pearls. And there is much more to this chapter, and indeed the entire Book of Job, as we shall see in Chapter VI.

✞ Job 40:6, 9-19, 41:1-2 7-8:
⁶Then the LORD answered Job out of the whirlwind, and said:
⁹Have you an arm like God?
Or can you thunder with a voice like His?
¹⁰Then adorn yourself with majesty and splendor,
And array yourself with glory and beauty.
¹¹Disperse the rage of your wrath;
Look on everyone who is proud, and humble him.
¹²Look on everyone who is proud, and bring him low;
Tread down the wicked in their place.
¹³Hide them in the dust together,
Bind their faces in hidden darkness.
¹⁴Then I will also confess to you
That your own right hand can save you.
¹⁵ "Look now at the behemoth, which I made along with you;
He eats grass like an ox.
¹⁶See now, his strength is in his hips,
And his power is in his stomach muscles.

¹⁷ He moves his tail like a cedar;
The sinews of his thighs are tightly knit.
¹⁸ His bones are like beams of bronze, his ribs like bars of iron.
¹⁹ He is the first of the ways of God;
Only He who made him can bring near His sword.
¹ Can you pull in the leviathan with a fishhook or tie down his tongue with a rope?
² Can you put a cord through his nose or pierce his jaw with a hook?
⁷ Can you fill his hide with harpoons or his head with fishing spears?
⁸ If you lay a hand on him, you will remember the struggle and never do it again!

Job 40-41 is the last of the overtly creation-oriented passages in the Book of Job, and one of the most famous. Typically these two chapters — which appear to actually be part of one longer passage — are translated rather benignly as the description of two of God's more prominent animal creations: Behemoth, a mysterious land creature, and Leviathan, a mysterious sea creature. Both of these mysterious creatures appear, on the face of it, to be merely large creatures that God had created, with no apparent mythological connections whatsoever. However, as we have seen in our analysis of the divine conflict creation motif to this point, Leviathan and Behemoth are clearly central figures in the original Creation battle as the enemies of God — both in the beginning and, as we shall see, in the end times.

In the first part of Job 40, God describes Himself arraying himself with great majesty and splendor, as if preparing for war. The description is highly reminiscent of Marduk's preparation for battle against Tiamat:

> *In front of him he set the lightning,*
> *With a blazing flame he filled his body....*
> *For a cloak he was wrapped in an armor of terror;*
> *With his fearsome halo his head was turbaned.*
> *The lord went forth and followed his course,*
> *Towards the raging Tiamat he set his face.*
> *(Enuma Elish IV:39-40, 57-60)*

God then talks about shattering and binding "everyone who is proud", which undoubtedly refers to the proud helpers of Tiamat, whom Marduk is also described as having shattered and bound:

> Her band was shattered, her troupe broken up;
> And the gods, her helpers who marched at her side,
> Trembling with terror, turned their backs about,
> In order to save and preserve their lives.
> Tightly encircled, they could not escape.
> He made them captives and he smashed their weapons.
> Thrown into the net, they found themselves ensnared;
> Placed in cells, they were filled with wailing;
> Bearing his wrath, they were held imprisoned.
> And the eleven creatures which she had charged with awe,
> The whole band of demons that marched on her right,
> He cast into fetters, their hands he bound.
> For all their resistance, he trampled them underfoot.
> And Kingu, who had been made chief among them,
> He bound and accounted him to Uggae.
> *(Enuma Elish IV:106-120)*

God had shattered and defeated the dragon's helpers and buried them in dust. This included Kingu, their chief whom, as we have seen, symbolized the Moon, which we now know is literally covered in a very fine dust.[90] By accounting Kingu to Uggae, the Sumerian god of death, the authors of *Enuma Elish* were likely engaging in clever wordplay, as Uggae is very similar to the Sumerian word *duggae*, "pot of clay". All together, Kingu is described as having been reduced to a lifeless mass of clay, covered in dust, which as we now know is an excellent description of our Moon. God not only "killed" Kingu and "hid him in dust", he also did this to the eleven other monsters that the dragon had created to help defend herself — burying them in dust and setting them as monuments to His victory over the dragon until the end of time (*Enuma Elish* V:71-76).[91]

---

[90] http://en.wikipedia.org/wiki/Moon_dust
[91] The entire text of *Enuma Elish* is available online at http://www.cresourcei.org/enumaelish.html. We will discuss the identity and fate of the eleven other helpers of the dragon in Chapter IV.

One possible solution for the identity of Behemoth is the Aurochs, an extinct species of cattle that was commonly bred throughout the ancient world as early as 8000 years ago. Standing 6 feet at the shoulder and weighing over a ton, the Aurochs fits many of the characteristics of the biblical Behemoth, though not all. In either case, this is probably the beast described as the "Reem" in Job 39:9. Image from http://en.wikipedia.org/wiki/Aurochs.

Behemoth, as we have seen, is the biblical equivalent of Kingu, the chief helper of the dragon in her fight against God at the Creation. Thus it makes perfect sense that God then mentions Behemoth next in verse 15 as one of his creations. Comparing Behemoth to a bull, the passage tends to imply that Behemoth is a normal Earth creature, leading most scholars to believe that God is describing some sort of huge, oxlike creature like the *Reem*, an ancient, oxlike creature mentioned in the previous chapter of Job (39:9). Scholars have variously interpreted this beast to be anything from a hippopotamus to some sort of extinct, wild bull such as the Aurochs, but no satisfactory solutions to the question have been found in the animal kingdom, either living or in the archaeological record.[92]

It is interesting to note, however, that word Reem, רְאֵם *re'aim*, is derived from the root word רָאַם *ra'am*, "to be high, lofty". This may mean that what is meant here is that the Moon, which is "on high", is considered to be a sort of "heavenly bull", whose "horns", in the form of a crescent, mark the times, and the seasons, and the years. The Moon is clearly described as having "horns" that define the times and the seasons of the year in *Enuma Elish* (V:12-20), so this conclusion is not only logical, but once again in perfect accord with ancient Near Eastern thought. It also fits neatly with the fact that the word *behemoth*, as we have seen, is very similar to the Hebrew בָּמוֹת *bamoth*, "high places". Perhaps intrinsic to the meaning of *bamoth* is that the Moon was being worshiped in these "high places"? And since

---

[92] Gesenius, W., & Tregelles, S. P. (2003). *Gesenius' Hebrew and Chaldee Lexicon to the Old Testament Scriptures* (751). Bellingham, WA: Logos Research Systems, Inc. It is likely that the extinct Aurochs, a type of cattle that stood six feet at the shoulder, is in view here, but not even the Aurochs perfectly matches the decription given of Behemoth. http://en.wikipedia.org/wiki/Aurochs.

cattle were typically sacrificed on the altars of these high places, the conclusion that Behemoth symbolically represents the Moon in this passage seems to be irresistible.

And though there is much to discuss in the short but pithy passage, it is necessary to analyze one more important fact about the original Hebrew in this chapter before we move on to the description of Leviathan. In verse 19, Behemoth is described as "the first of the ways of God". This makes little sense in the context of Genesis 1 and 2, however, as the oxen and similar creatures were not created first. Plant life was created first, followed by creatures of the water, creature of the air, and then creatures of the land (Genesis 1:11-12, 20-25). Moreover, it cannot mean that Behemoth is the largest creature that God created, as the elephant and other ancient land creatures well outsized even the Aurochs, and of course the great whales are many times larger than even an elephant. So, it is impossible for this passage to literally mean that Behemoth was the first creature, or even the largest creature, that God created.

However, if we look at the original Hebrew, we see that the word translated as "first" רֵאשִׁית *rai'shiyth*, in this verse is actually the exact same word as the first word that appears in the Bible, except for the beginning preposition: בְּרֵאשִׁית *be-rai'shiyth*, typically translated as "in the beginning". The specific use of this word probably means that the author of Job wished to indicate that Behemoth was indeed created "in the beginning", i.e., when the Earth and its Moon were formed, as we discovered previously in this chapter. Modern scientists believe now that the Moon was created as the "offspring" of an impact between Earth and another large body early in Earth's formative period, so the use of the word *berai'shiyth* here may have been used on purpose to make that connection. In short, "Behemoth", our Moon, was created as a result of the conflict between God and the early Earth, "in the beginning".

Finally, the reference to Leviathan in this Creation passage just after the discussion of the origins and nature of Behemoth makes the association clear that Job 40-41 is yet another example of the divine conflict creation motif to be found in the Old Testament. Whether she was named Leviathan, Tiamat, Rahab, Tannin, Shalyat, or simply "the dragon", it is clear that the primordial Earth was symbolized in ancient Near Eastern creation cosmography as a monstrous, dragonlike creature that was a threat to life, light and civil order in the cosmos. By defeating the dragon and its helpers led by Behemoth, God imposed peace and divine order upon the primordial Earth so that the creatures that He intended to plant on its face could be fruitful and multiply in an environment that was amenable to such life. However, it is prophesied that near the end of human history, the dragon and its allies would arise once more to threaten the divine order and destroy mankind and the other creatures God created to multiply and subdue the defeated Earth. This new arising is prophesied in the apocalyptic books of the Bible, specifically, the Book of Revelation, wherein the dragon and its chief helper make a prominent reappearance.

THE ANCIENT CREATION TRADITION IN THE NEW TESTAMENT

Though throughout the history of the world the sea dragon and its ally, the earth beast, lay dormant, nursing their wounds from the defeat they suffered at the hands of God at the great Creation battle, in the end times the dragon and the beast will awaken and rise again in another attempt to usurp the power of God and take dominion over Earth for themselves. And despite the fact that the imagery regarding the dragon and the beast of the end times appears to describe people and governments more than planetary objects such as the Earth, Moon, and possibly one or more other members of our solar system, the same wicked spirits lay behind both the rebellion of the Earth against God's cosmic order in the beginning times, and the rebellion of mankind against God's cosmic order in the end times.

In the end times, the dragon and its ally, the earth beast, will awaken from their long slumber and rise again to fight against the Second Coming of Christ. Image "Dragon Eye" by Morka, http://www.graffiti.org/morka/morka_3.html

However, that is not to say that the end times will not involve events that will take place on a planetary scale. On the contrary, Jesus' description of the end times in Matthew 24:29, where He says that "the powers of the heavens" will be shaken, is believed to actually be a reference to the planets, the Moon, and possibly even the Earth being shaken from their places. This plus the fact that, in the following verse, Jesus refers to a mysterious "Sign of the Son of Man" that will appear in the heavens and cause great dread to all the peoples of the Earth, tends to imply that the divine conflict will once again take place on a planetary scale. As such, we can expect references in apocalyptic literature, both in the Old and New Testaments, to also contain references to the divine conflict creation theme that, as we have discovered, lies at the heart of all of the Creation material in the Old Testament.

Revelation: The Divine Conflict in the End Times

The dragon from the sea and the beast from the earth, despite numerous appearances in the books of Genesis, the Psalms, Isaiah and Job, disappear completely from the biblical narrative until the Book of Revelation, when they return in a most powerful way:

- Revelation 12:

    [1] And there appeared a great wonder in heaven; a woman clothed with the Sun, and the Moon under her feet, and upon her head a crown of twelve stars:

    [2] And she being with child cried, travailing in birth, and pained to be delivered.

    [3] And there appeared another wonder in heaven; and behold a great red dragon, having seven heads and ten horns, and seven crowns upon his heads.

    [4] And his tail drew the third part of the stars of heaven, and did cast them to the earth: and the dragon stood before the woman which was ready to be delivered, for to devour her child as soon as it was born.

    [5] And she brought forth a man child, who was to rule all nations with a rod of iron: and her child was caught up unto God, and to his throne.

    [6] And the woman fled into the wilderness, where she hath a place prepared of God, that they should feed her there a thousand two hundred and threescore days.

    [7] And there was war in heaven: Michael and his angels fought against the dragon; and the dragon fought and his angels,

    [8] And prevailed not; neither was their place found any more in heaven.

God's Conflict with the Dragon in the Sea

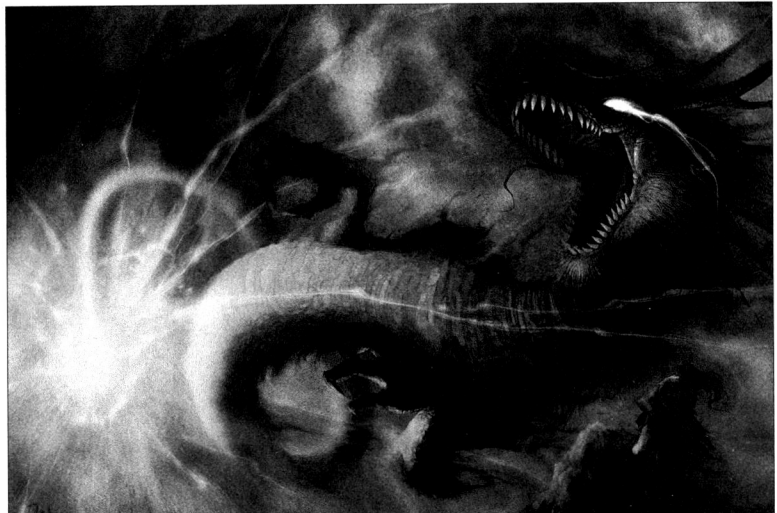

Satan, the great dragon, will be cast down from heaven to Earth in the end times, dragging down 1/3 of the angels with him. At that time he will persecute and destroy Christendom as an organized political force. "Dragon" by ~Tahra: <http://tahra.deviantart.com/art/dragon-59537759>.

[9] And the great dragon was cast out, that old serpent, called the Devil, and Satan, which deceiveth the whole world: he was cast out into the earth, and his angels were cast out with him.

[13] And when the dragon saw that he was cast unto the earth, he persecuted the woman which brought forth the man child.

[14] And to the woman were given two wings of a great eagle, that she might fly into the wilderness, into her place, where she is nourished for a time, and times, and half a time, from the face of the serpent.

[15] And the serpent cast out of his mouth water as a flood after the woman, that he might cause her to be carried away of the flood.

[16] And the earth helped the woman, and the earth opened her mouth, and swallowed up the flood which the dragon cast out of his mouth.

[17] And the dragon was wroth with the woman, and went to make war with the remnant of her seed, which keep the commandments of God, and have the testimony of Jesus Christ. (KJV)

Here in Revelation 12, both the dragon and, as we shall see, the beast from the earth, make a prominent reappearance. The first reference back to the great Creation battle occurs in verse 4, where the dragon's tail is said to have swept a third of the stars to the Earth. As we saw in *Enuma Elish,* Tiamat's tail was twisted to form the heavens, which is also clearly alluded to in Psalm 89 and Isaiah 51. The mention of the "rod of iron" in Rev. 12:5 is likely an indirect reference to the Sharur-weapon that Ninurta used to smash Asag like a clay pot and release the waters, and is also specifically mentioned by Jesus in Revelation 2:27 (apparently quoting Psalm 2:9) and again in Revelation 19:15. It is interesting to note that in all three references, this mysterious "rod of iron" is always used as a weapon to smash the nations, who are easily shattered like clay pots — much in the same way that Ninurta used Sharur to smash Asag and release the waters.

Almost as if to emphasize this point of smashing the enemy and releasing the waters trapped therein, after being defeated by God and cast down to Earth, in verses 7-15 the dragon opens up its mouth, and instead of fire, as one might expect from a typical dragon from Western mythology, water comes forth, with the intent of drowning and destroying God's chosen. However, in verse 16, the Earth is described as "opening its mouth" and drinking the water that was released by the dragon. This is particularly interesting because in Job 40:23, in the original Hebrew, Behemoth is described as being so huge, that he is confident that he can drink up the entire Jordan River. The Hebrew says יִבְטַח כִּי־יָגִיחַ יַרְדֵּן אֶל־פִּיהוּ *yivtaḥ ki-yagiaḥ yardain el-piyhoow,* literally, "he is confident that that the headwaters of the Jordan will fit into his mouth." Further, the word יָגִיחַ *yagiyaḥ,* which means "burst forth", referring to the "bursting forth" of the headwaters of the Jordan, is also used in Job 38:8 to describe the "bursting forth" of the waters of the dragon when she was defeated by God. So, clearly, this passage was influenced by the creation imagery of Job, and thus should be considered a prime example of the ancient creation tradition that is revived in the New Testament.

The "beast from the earth", only alluded to in Rev. 12, clearly rises again in Rev. 13, where he is shown once again as the greatest ally of the newly revived dragon in its ongoing war with God:

⚛ Revelation 13:1-2, 11-14:
¹ And I stood upon the sand of the sea, and saw a beast rise up out of the sea, having seven heads and ten horns, and upon his horns ten crowns, and upon his heads the name of blasphemy.
² And the beast which I saw was like unto a leopard, and his feet were as the feet of a bear, and his mouth as the mouth of a lion: and the dragon gave him his power, and his seat, and great authority.
¹¹ And I beheld another beast coming up out of the earth; and he had two horns like a lamb, and he spake as a dragon.
¹² And he exerciseth all the power of the first beast before him, and causeth the earth and them which dwell therein to worship the first beast, whose deadly wound was healed.
¹³ And he doeth great wonders, so that he maketh fire come down from heaven on the earth in the sight of men,
¹⁴ And deceiveth them that dwell on the earth by the means of those miracles which he had power to do in the sight of the beast; saying to them that dwell on the earth, that they should make an image to the beast, which had the wound by a sword, and did live.
(KJV)

In Revelation 13, the dragon reappears, delegating her power to a great seven-headed "beast from the sea", the dragon once again clearly associated with the deep sea, as she has been since Genesis 1. Then, in verse 11, the dragon's puppet, the "beast from the sea", which is apparently some sort of multifaceted political entity[93], is joined by her partner and apparent prophet, the "beast from the earth". Climbing out of the Abyss, this end-time Behemoth will be given birth to by the dragon as its defender against God in the end times, just as Tiamat "gave birth" to Kingu in order to take the lead in her defense against God at the Creation.

Interestingly, in Rev. 9:11, another beastlike entity, perhaps the same "beast from the earth" mentioned in chapter 13, is also shown as rising up out of the earth — specifically out of the Abyss (NIV, "angel of the Abyss"). This terrible fallen angel, who apparently had been chained in the Abyss possibly since before the Flood (or possibly longer), rises again from the Abyss in the End Times to enslave and destroy mankind. And whereas the link with the "beast from the earth"

---

[93] We will discuss the likely identities of the two beasts in Chapter VII.

initially appears tentative, an analysis of Job once again gives us the necessary clues that give us the true identity of the dragon's chief ally in the end times.

As we saw previously in our analysis of Job 26:6, one of the results of the divine creation conflict between God and "the dragon" was that a huge chunk of Earth was carved out by God and then used to form the Moon. As a result, as described in Job 26:6, the Abyss was literally open to the air, and "destruction" was no longer covered over. And as we saw in our analysis of the verse, שְׁאוֹל *sheol*, "the Abyss" is most likely a loan word from the Ugaritic word *Shalyat*, the name of a seven-headed dragon in Canaanite mythology that fought against the high god of their pantheon in one of their creation myths. So, the seven-headed dragon-beast of Revelation 13 (and elsewhere) was most likely derived from this ancient, symbolic concept of the primordial Earth a seven-headed dragon.

However, though the dragon, or "beast from the sea" is clearly referenced in Job 26:6 as *sheol*, or "Shalyat", where is the beast from the earth? If we look at the Hebrew, we

Isis and the newborn Horus-King. The pharaoh of Egypt was considered to be an extension of the throne, with the matriarchy and the priesthood as the true political power behind the scenes, as one can clearly see from this imagery. In ancient Egypt, Isis was conceived of as not only the mother of the newborn pharaoh, but also as his throne. So it was, and will be, with the dragon and the antichrist, the Beast from the Sea, and the Beast from the Earth.

again have the answer. The word translated "destruction" in Job 26:6 (KJV) is actually the Hebrew word אֲבַדּוֹן *abaddon*, "Abaddon", which, as we have seen, is also used as the name of the "angel of the Abyss" that rises out of the Abyss in Revelation 9:11. So in Job 26:6, the dragon and the earth beast are once again paired together and cryptically named "Sheol" and "Abaddon" so as to once again avoid directly citing the names of foreign deities in Scripture.

In Rev. 9:11, however, Abaddon is openly named as the angel of the Abyss, and is described as rising up out of the Abyss, or *sheol* which, as we have seen, is actually a cryptic reference to the seven-headed dragon *Shalyat* from Canaanite myth. In this sense, Shalyat is meant to be seen as "giving birth" to Abaddon in order to defend herself in the end-times, just as Tiamat "gave birth" to Kingu in order to defend herself against God in the beginning. Abaddon, literally, "father-lord" or perhaps "overlord", will literally rise again in the end times to be the king of the earth, backed up and supported by the dragon, who will give him all of her power and authority in order to fight against the Second Coming of Christ. Thus, just as Leviathan and Behemoth fought against God in the beginning, the sea dragon and the earth beast, Shalyat and Abaddon, will rise again in the end-times to fight against God once more.

✝ Revelation 20:1-15:
> [1] And I saw an angel come down from heaven, having the key of the bottomless pit and a great chain in his hand.
> [2] And he laid hold on the dragon, that old serpent, which is the Devil, and Satan, and bound him a thousand years,
> [3] And cast him into the bottomless pit, and shut him up, and set a seal upon him, that he should deceive the nations no more, till the thousand years should be fulfilled: and after that he must be loosed a little season.

However, the dragon and the earth beast will be defeated once again, the beast destroyed and the dragon, finally definitively identified as Satan, will be thrown back into the pit for a thousand years. And though the dragon will rise again once more after the millennium is over, only to be once again defeated and finally destroyed forever, the earth beast is never again mentioned in the narrative of the Bible.

CHAPTER I: PRELIMINARY CONCLUSIONS

After a thorough analysis of the Creation passages in both the Bible and parallel ancient Near Eastern mythology, we have discovered that the dominant creation motif throughout both the Bible and the entire ancient Near East describes the Creation symbolically as a combat between God and a "dragon". In this "divine conflict" creation motif, which is found in some form in every major reference to the Creation in the Bible, God is described as defeating this heavenly dragon, and creating heaven and Earth from its body. In the process of analyzing these Creation passages, we also discovered that the Moon was also created, or "born" from the body of this dragon, a determination that we now know corresponds with modern scientific discoveries that have independently determined that the Moon was indeed created from the Earth's mantle as the result of some sort of cosmic cataclysmic event.

This ancient creation tradition, we theorized, was handed down from Adam all the way down to Noah, and thence to the rest of the post-diluvian world. The knowledge of the ancient creation tradition spread throughout the world, along with the peoples who emigrated forth from the ark. Over time, however, errors and the names of foreign deities crept into the narrative, degrading and corrupting the understanding not only from a scientific point of view, but also giving the glory not to the one true God, but to the false gods of the nations. These other traditions, most notably the *Enuma Elish* of the Sumerians and later Babylonians, retained much of the knowledge of the creation encoded in the form of mythology. These traditions retained echoes of the ancient creation tradition, but only one tradition remained perfectly intact: that kept by Abraham, which he passed on to his descendants, the Israelites, and through them eventually becoming codified into the Bible we have today.

But is the idea that a cataclysm occurred in the early, formative stages of Earth, resulting in the Earth being moved to a new location closer to the Sun to be taken seriously? Is it easier to take the current translations of the Genesis account as is and simply ignore the numerous references to a "divine conflict" at the Creation throughout the Old Testament? I believe it is not. I believe that an understanding of the full implications of the divine conflict model of the Creation will have fundamental ramifications upon how we perceive many of God's key actions in history, particularly concerning the Creation, the Star of Bethlehem phenomenon at the Nativity and the "Sign of the Son of Man" phenomenon that Jesus prophesied would herald His Second Coming (Matt. 24:30). And as we shall see throughout the course of this book, these three events are inextricably linked.

Understanding the Bible in its ancient Near Eastern context is one of the keys to accurate biblical interpretation. Therefore, in order to more fully comprehend the "divine conflict" model of the Creation in its ancient Near Eastern context, we must study ancient Near Eastern religion in depth. And as we shall see in the following chapter, the religions of the ancient world were essentially a diverse collection of religious worldviews unified by one common element: the worship of the planets.

II

THE ASTRONOMICAL RELIGIONS OF THE ANCIENT NEAR EAST

And when you look up to the sky and see the Sun, the Moon and the stars — all the heavenly array — do not be enticed into bowing down to them and worshiping things the LORD your God has apportioned to all the nations under heaven.. (Deuteronomy 4:19)

Long ago, in a land far, far away, men raised a tower that reached "to the heavens." This tower was in the land of Mesopotamia, in the city of Babylon, and the people who raised it are an ancient, mysterious people known as the Sumerians. This event is recorded both in Genesis 11 and in *Enuma Elish*. In Genesis 11, the tower is presented as primarily a symbol of man's rebellion against God's rule, the first major rebellion since before the Flood. God's reaction to this new rebellion was to confuse their languages. This had the effect of scattering mankind over the face of the Earth, ending mankind's attempt to found a Godless, one-world government in Babylon. Thus, by confusing their languages and scattering them, God had effectively crushed the rebellion in one swift stroke.

"The Confusion of Tongues" by Gustave Doré (1865) depicting the Tower of Babel event. Instead of spreading abroad and living simply, as they were intended to do, mankind instead centralized their power and began to rebuild the wicked pre-Flood civilization that God had destroyed. Unwilling to destroy mankind again, God instead confused their languages so that they could not rebel against Him again in any sort of coordinated way. It is unclear as to whether the tower was intended to be a communications tower, an observatory, or perhaps something more sinister.

THE TOWER OF BABEL IN THE BIBLE

☧ Genesis 11:1-9:
¹And the whole earth was of one language, and of one speech. ²And it came to pass, as they journeyed from the east, that they found a plain in the land of Shinar; and they dwelt there. ³And they said one to another, Go to, let us make brick, and burn them throughly. And they had brick for stone, and slime had they for morter. ⁴And they said, Go to, let us build us a city and a tower, whose top *may reach* unto heaven; and let us make us a name, lest we be scattered abroad upon the face of the whole earth. ⁵And the LORD came down to see the city and the tower, which the children of men builded. ⁶ And the LORD said, Behold, the people *is* one, and they have all one language; and this they begin to do: and now nothing will be restrained from them, which they have imagined to do. ⁷ Go to, let us go down, and there confound their language, that they may not understand one another's speech. ⁸ So the LORD scattered them abroad from thence upon the face of all the earth: and they left off to build the city. ⁹ Therefore is the name of it called Babel; because the LORD did there confound the language of all the earth: and from thence did the LORD scatter them abroad upon the face of all the earth. (KJV)[1]

Man was never intended to be unified under a centralized, one-world government as was attempted at Babylon. In fact, the first commandment God had given mankind was to spread out over the face of the Earth, not concentrate in one area: "Be fruitful, and multiply, and replenish the earth, and subdue it: and have dominion over the fish of the sea, and over the fowl of the air, and over every living thing that moveth upon the earth." (Gen. 1:28, KJV). After God had defeated "the dragon" Earth, He then created mankind to finish the job

---

[1] The Hebrew word for "confused" is *balal,* which Moses used as a play on the name Babel (lit., "gateway of the gods"), turning Babylon from "the gateway of the gods" to "the place of confusion."

of subduing and controlling it. Thus, mankind was never meant to be independent of God, but instead exists solely for the purpose of subduing the dragon, of keeping it from ever rising again so that God should not have to defeat it again. The ongoing subdual of the dragon is thus mankind's "prime directive", and any deviation from this prime directive would surely result in swift correction, lest the dragon rise again.

At Babylon, however, mankind broke the divine prime directive and attempted to be independent of God, showing the same rebellious spirit, the same "mystery of iniquity", that the dragon had displayed in the beginning that led to God's decision to conquer and subdue the Earth. As a result, God then decided to chastise mankind for taking the side of the dragon, His subdued but still-living enemy. But since God had promised to never again destroy man with a Flood, He then chose to simply break their unity by destroying their ability to communicate. Communication is of course the most important single factor to any organization, just as the brain is the most important organ in the human body, so the destruction of man's ability to communicate was the next best alternative to destroying man physically.

The question remains, however, how did God accomplish this confusion of languages? Did He simply make a *fiat* command, and it was done, or did he accomplish the confusion using other means? The breakdown of communication on such a massive scale can really only be caused by physical destruction of the centers of communication. Men simply don't "forget" how to communicate with each other, particularly not on such a massive scale. Apparently some sort of natural disaster had happened at Babylon, some huge catastrophe that had caused so much destruction that the men who had built the tower were unable to recover. But are there any records of such a natural disaster?

As we saw in Chapter I, around 2000 B.C. the Sumerian Empire had been utterly devastated by the sudden appearance of some sort of heavenly "wind" that had destroyed the major city centers of Sumer. Thus the "confusion of languages" at Babel, as described by Moses, may actually be an account of the physical destruction of the Sumerian Empire and the inevitable breakdown in communications that would follow between the different parts of their empire.

Interestingly, the "Tower of Babel" account in the Bible actually lies between the genealogy of the sons of Noah and their descendants

(Gen. 10), and the first appearance of Abraham in the biblical narrative (Gen. 12). Furthermore, the remainder of chapter 11, after the description of the tower is completed, is taken up by the specific genealogy of Abraham, starting again with Shem.[2] If Moses had not intended the life of Abraham and the tower of Babel to be closely linked, he would not have placed them so closely together, let alone in the same chapter; he would instead have completed the genealogy of Abraham earlier, in chapter 10, along with the rest of the descendants of Shem. Instead, he actually combines the destruction of the tower *along with* the genealogy with Abraham. As such, the strategic placement of the tower account in the midst of the genealogical data presented in Genesis 10, and continued in Genesis 11:10-32, leads me to the conclusion that the confusion of languages at Babylon had actually occurred around the same time Abraham had fled Sumer. Thus, "Shinar" should be equated with the Sumerian Empire, the "confusion of languages" should be equated with its destruction, and the Lord's command for Abraham to leave Ur of the Chaldees was to save him from the destruction that was sure to come, much like Lot was later to be taken out of Sodom just before fire fell from heaven and destroyed that city as well.

The Divine Wind

The confusion at Babel, according to the biblical account, was similar in scale to that of the chaos and destruction that this mysterious "divine wind" had left in its wake, according to the Sumerian chronicles of the downfall of Sumer and Ur.[3] The downfall of the Sumerian Empire appears to have been triggered by some sort of enormous natural disaster that originated in heaven, much like that of the tower, causing a similar degree of confusion and destruction. Moreover, both events must have happened around the same time, as the Sumerian Empire ceased to exist around 2000 B.C., the same time

---

[2] Interestingly, the name of Shem (שֵׁם), the son of Noah, mentioned again in Gen. 11:10 as the ancestor of Abraham, is identical to the word used in Gen. 11:4 as the "name" (שֵׁם) that mankind wanted to build for themselves so as to not scatter over the face of the earth. The reuse of the identical word in this passage for both the ancestor of Abraham and the "name" that the Gentiles wished to make for themselves cannot have been a coincidence, and may indicate a very important hidden theme that is part of a cryptic, epic substratum that runs throughout the entire Bible.

[3] Kramer, trans., "Lamentation over the Destruction of Ur," and "Lamentation over the Destruction of Sumer and Ur," in *ANET*, 455–63, 611–19.

period that Abraham was born. And since the destinies of both Abraham and the Tower of Babel appear to have been linked in the biblical record, it would be reasonable to conclude that the Tower of Babel event and the destruction of Sumer were both caused by the same disaster of heavenly origin.

A Mesopotamian "Dark Age"

Just as the downfall of the Roman Empire had led to the "Dark Ages" of European history, the downfall of the Sumerian Empire no doubt also resulted in a similar "dark age", where the loss of the common language and culture that had bound the empire together caused the unity of the empire, and all who depended upon it, to crumble. Thus, when central authority collapsed in the wake of the heavenly storm, followed by wave after wave of barbarian invaders, the influence of the Sumerian language and culture probably fell off dramatically. In effect, the "one language and common speech" was lost, and over time, the languages gradually became confused. This theory is supported by the fact that Akkadian cuneiform, the Sumerian equivalent of Latin, has been found scattered, in various forms, throughout Mesopotamia and the surrounding lands, as far west as Asia Minor, indicating that that form of communication had been in general usage in some form or another throughout the entire ancient Near East.

As a result of the collapse of the Sumerian Empire, Sumerian culture, like Roman culture, was gradually forgotten over time, except for bits and pieces which remained in both the Babylonian and Hebrew cultures, among others. Abraham was probably forced to emigrate to Canaan either due to the collapse of the Sumerian Empire and the subsequent chaos, or because he was called out just before the divine wind from heaven came, just as Lot was called out of Sodom before it too was destroyed by a mysterious "fire from heaven".

In either case, the situation after the collapse of the Sumerian Empire would have been very chaotic, as bands of raiders would have taken advantage of the situation in order to pillage and plunder. This would explain why Abraham maintained a force of trained warriors that he would later use in the battle against the Mesopotamian confederation that later invaded Canaan (Gen. 14). It is possible that The Book of Job was also set in this situation, as Job's house and all his children, flocks, and all of his property were also destroyed by a mysterious "fire from heaven" and a "wind from the wilderness" (Job

1:13-19). Around the same time, wandering bands of Sabeans and Chaldeans also plundered his flocks. Job lived in the land of Uz, a "suburb" of Sumer that is believed to lie in the northern part of the Arabian Desert between ancient Sumer and ancient Canaan, so he was not too far from Sumer.[4]

THE TOWER OF BABEL IN BABYLONIAN MYTH

A reconstruction of the "Great Ziggurat of Ur" in what is now Nasiriyah, Iraq. Since this temple was built only in the 6th century B.C., the ziggurat that inspired the "Tower of Babel" was most likely the much older Ziggurat of Marduk in Babylon, the E-Temen-Anki (lit., "Temple that Connects Heaven and Earth", that was built prior to the reign of Hammurabi, ca. 1900 B.C.

In *Enuma Elish,* the Tower of Babel is seen more as a temple where the Sumerians could worship their gods, Marduk in particular. From this tall tower, they could more easily observe and worship their gods, whom they believed were immanent in the Sun, Moon and stars, and particularly in the planets. This temple, or "stage-tower," was probably something like the ziggurats whose ruins can still be found in Iraq today, that were aligned with the rising and setting of the Sun, Moon, stars and planets in order to more easily track their rising and setting and pay them homage at the times they deemed appropriate.

In their creation epic, *Enuma Elish,* the Babylonians actually credited the creation of the city of Babylon and its stage-tower to a group of deities known as the "Anunnaki" who, along with a similar group known as the "Igigi", were believed to be visible from Earth as the brightest stars in the sky. In *Enuma Elish,* Marduk is enthroned over this heavenly assembly of deities, an assembly which includes these mysterious Anunnaki.

---

[4] Gesenius, W., & Tregelles, S. P. (2003). *Gesenius' Hebrew and Chaldee Lexicon to the Old Testament Scriptures* (614). Bellingham, WA: Logos Research Systems, Inc.

Samuel Noah Kramer explains in *The Sumerians: Their History, Culture and Character*, "The Sumerian pantheon was...conceived as functioning in an assembly with a king at its head."[5] Strangely, the assembly of the gods over which the Babylonian god Marduk reigned actually consisted of Sumerian deities. This was due to the fact that the Babylonians had conquered the Sumerians, and when the Babylonians rewrote the ancient Sumerian creation epic *Enuma Elish* to fit their own political agenda, they carried on the ancient tradition of replacing the chief deity of the conquered people with their own chief deity, in this case replacing the Sumerian deity Enlil with their own patron deity, Marduk.[6] However, instead of replacing all of the rest of the gods of the Sumerians with Babylonian deities, they actually retained most of the Sumerian gods. The reason for this is actually very simple. Although the Babylonians had defeated the Sumerians and symbolically "dethroned" their gods, in order to maintain social order, it was important for the Babylonians to allow the Sumerians to continue to worship their own gods. It is easier to govern people to whom you show respect than it is to govern people whom you daily dishonor by casting dispersion upon those things they hold most dear. Thus the enthronement of the Babylonian deity Marduk over the preexisting Sumerian pantheon of deities was, in effect, a very wise way of impressing Babylonian rule upon the conquered Sumerians.

A Sumerian votive figurine depicting one of the Annunaki, who were believed to have built, or have directed the building of, the Etemenanki, the "Tower of Babel" of the Bible. The Annunaki were most likely the same Nephilim, or "fallen angels" mentioned in Genesis 6 and afterwards.

---

[5] Samuel Noah Kramer, *The Sumerians: Their History, Culture and Character* (Chicago: The University of Chicago Press, 1963), 114–15.

[6] Indeed, Enlil had superseded the older Sumerian deity Anu as the state god of Sumer and the central figure of the ancient creation epic, possibly as a result of the Akkadian conquest of the Sumerians under King Sargon around 2300 B.C. This sort of idolatrous "replacement theology" was common practice in the ancient Near East.

Though the Sumerians still had some political representation in the new order, symbolized by the "congress" of Sumerian deities present in the heavenly court, the Babylonian kings still had the final word in governmental affairs, just as Marduk had final word over the Sumerian gods in his heavenly court.[7]

The Sumerian Pantheon

The Sumerian pantheon over which Marduk was enthroned was made up of three main groups: a group of seven chief gods, a group of fifty greater gods, and a group of 600 lesser gods that were apparently divided into two groups: 300 "Annunaki" and 300 "Igigi." According to Samuel Noah Kramer, "The most important [group] in this assembly consisted of seven chief gods who 'decree the fates.' "[8] These seven chief gods, all of which were associated with either the Sun, Moon or one of the planets, are as follows:

- *Anu:* There is good reason to believe that An, the heaven-god, was at one time conceived by the Sumerians to be the supreme ruler of the pantheon, although in our available sources reaching to about 2500 B.C. it is the air-god, Enlil, who seems to have taken his place as the leader of the pantheon.... An[u] continued to be worshiped in Sumer throughout the millennia, but he gradually lost much of his prominence. He became a rather shadowy figure in the pantheon, and he is rarely mentioned in the hymns and myths of later days; by that time most of his powers had been conferred upon the god Enlil. The planet Anu was associated is currently unknown, though it may come and go in the heavens, just as Anu himself came and went in the Sumerian pantheon. The name "Anu" literally means "heaven" or "star", and Anu's symbol is the Sumerian "An" starlike symbol shown above. This symbol, also known as the DINGIR, is the generic Sumerian symbol for all stars and planets, and indeed for all deities, but specifically symbolizes

---

[7]For a more in-depth study of the interrelationship of religion, society, economics, and politics in the ancient world, see my thesis, *YHWH Against the Ba'als of Canaan: Contextualizing the Old Testament* (Wheaton, IL: Wheaton College [Buswell Library], 1992).

[8]Kramer, *The Sumerians*, 115.

the star of Anu, one specific planet that rules over all — even when it is not clearly visible....

✦ *Enlil:* By far the most important deity in the Sumerian pantheon, one who played a dominant role throughout Sumer in rite, myth, and prayer, was the air-god, Enlil. The events leading up to his general acceptance as a leading deity of the Sumerian pantheon are unknown; but from the earliest intelligible records, Enlil is known as "the father of the gods," "the king of heaven and earth," "the king of all the lands."... From later myths and hymns we learn that Enlil  was conceived to be a most beneficent deity who was responsible for the planning and creation of most productive features of the cosmos. He was the god who made the day come forth, who took pity on humans, who laid the plans which brought forth all seeds, plants, and trees from the earth...[however,] among the earliest Sumerian compositions published, there was an unusually large proportion of lamentation types in which, of necessity, Enlil had the unhappy duty of carrying out the destruction and misfortunes decreed by the gods for one reason or another. Overall, however, we find Enlil glorified as a most friendly, fatherly deity who watches over the safety and well-being of all humans and particularly, of course, over the inhabitants of Sumer. Enlil may have been associated with Jupiter, or perhaps the same mysterious planet as Anu, representing the same planet as would the later Babylonian deity Marduk.

✦ *Enki:* The third of the leading Sumerian deities was Enki, the god in charge of the abyss, or, in Sumerian, the *abzu*. Enki, also known as Ea, was the god of wisdom, and it was primarily he who organized the earth in accordance with the decisions of Enlil, who only made the general plans. The actual

details and executions were left to Enki, the resourceful, skillful, handy, and wise. Enki appears to be closely associated with Earth, particularly Earth's oceans, as indicated by the water and fish that are typically shown issuing from his shoulders.

✡ *Ninḫursag.* Fourth among the creating deities was the mother-goddess Ninḫursag, also known as Ninmah, "the exalted lady." In an earlier day this goddess was probably of even higher rank, and her name often preceded that of Enki when the four gods were listed together for one reason or another. Her name may  have originally been Ki, "(mother) Earth," and she was probably taken to be the consort of An [Anu], "Heaven," — An and Ki thus may have been conceived as the parents of the gods. She was also known as Nintu, "the lady who gave birth."... She was regarded as the mother of all living things, the mother goddess pre-eminent. Ninḫursag was, like Enki, associated with the planet Earth, indicating the ancient Sumerians understood that Earth was indeed a celestial body in its own right.

In addition to these four leading deities, there were also three important astral deities to round out the seven chief gods:

 ✡ *Nanna.* The Moon-god Nanna, who is also known by the name of Sin, which is probably of Semitic origin. Nanna, who was the son of Enlil, was typically represented simply as a lunar crescent.

✡ *Utu.* Nanna's son, the Sun-god. Utu was believed to rise and set every day between the twin peaks of a great mountain called "the Mountains of the East" in the morning and "the Mountains of the

West" in the evening. He is cognate to the Akkadian Sun-deity Shamash, who shows up in the Hebrew Bible as simply שֶׁמֶשׁ *shemesh*, "the Sun".

- *Inanna.* Nanna's daughter, the goddess Inanna, known to the Semites as Ishtar. Ishtar was typically associated with the planet Venus.[9]

These seven Sumerian gods make a prominent appearance in *Enuma Elish* as the "seven gods of destiny" (VI:81) who preside over the enthronement of Marduk as king of the gods.[10] In the Epic, it is these seven deities who, along with the Annunaki, built Babylon and its stage-tower as a reward to Marduk for his defeat of the dragon Tiamat. This stage-tower was actually built to be Marduk's throne, and ever afterwards, it was intended that this tower would provide a connection between heaven and Earth, a gateway or portal that the gods could use to easily travel between both realms.

The Tower of Babel — A Gateway to Heaven?

The Babylonian Creation Epic, which describes how the heavens and Earth were created in their present form, also describes the creation of the *Etemenanki*, the temple-throne that was built to honor Marduk, the chief god of the Babylonians, for his victory over the evil dragon-goddess Tiamat. *Etemenanki*, which literally means "The Temple that Connects Heaven and Earth", is most likely the same "Tower of Babel" described in Genesis 11, not only because both structures appear to have been built, or rebuilt, around the same time, but also because both structures were intended to somehow connect heaven and Earth. What is not overtly discussed in the Tower of Babel account, however, is that the word *Babel*, that forms the root of the word "Babylon", literally means "gateway of the gods". This makes sense because in *Enuma Elish*, the Etemenanki ziggurat built to honor Marduk is described as being built not by men, but by the Annunaki and the Igigi.

---

[9]Bulleted paragraphs adapted from Kramer, *The Sumerians,* 118–22. Inanna/Ishtar was identified with the planet Venus.

[10]Kramer, *The Sumerians,* 122–23.

(47) *Marduk, the king of the gods divided*
All the Annunaki above and below.
He assigned (them) to Anu to guard his instructions.
(50) Three hundred in the heavens he stationed as a guard.
In like manner the ways of the Earth he defined
In heaven and on earth six hundred (thus) he settled.
After he had ordered all the instructions,
To the Anunnaki of heaven and earth had allotted their portions,
The Anunnaki opened their mouths
And said to Marduk, their lord:
"Now, O lord, thou who hast caused our deliverance,
What shall be our homage to thee?
Let us build a shrine whose name shall be called
(60) 'Lo, a chamber for our nightly rest'; let us repose in it!
Let us build a throne, a recess for his abode!
On the day that we arrive we shall repose in it."
When Marduk heard this,
Brightly glowed his features, like the day:
"Construct Babylon, whose building you have requested,
Let its brickwork be fashioned. You shall name it 'The Sanctuary.' "
The Annunaki applied the implement;
For one whole year they molded bricks.
When the second year arrived,
(70) They raised high the head of Esagila equaling Apsu.
Having built a stage-tower as high as Apsu,
They set up in it an abode for Marduk, Enlil (and) Ea
In their presence he was seated in grandeur.
To the base of Esharra its horns look down.
(*Enuma Elish* Tablet VI:47–90)

The Watchers

So, according to The Babylonian Creation Epic, this mysterious tower was built either by or with the help of these mysterious Annunaki. But who were these beings, and how do they figure into human history? The most likely answer, based upon the fact that the Sumerian term *an-una-ki* translates as "those who came down from heaven to earth", are the same beings described in the Bible as the *Nephilim*, (lit., "those who came down") and as the "Watchers" in the *Book of Enoch*, who "left their first estate" and came down from heaven to earth to intermarry with human women. (Jude 1:6) It is said in the Book of Enoch, chapter 7, that when the fallen angels took human wives to themselves, they taught first their wives, then others various "enchantments" — what we today would call the arts and sciences:

"Eye Idols" from Tell Brak, Syria. These mysterious idols date back to the earliest times in mankind's history, to the early Uruk period, around the time of the foundation of Sumer and beginning of civilization in ancient Mesopotamia (ca. 4000 B.C.). They most likely represent votive offerings to the Watchers, divine beings whose primary function was to watch over mankind like divine shepherds. The fact that civilization started soon after supports the biblical and apocryphal emphasis on how the watchers "left their first estate" and began to start getting actively involved with mankind, giving them gifts of knowledge and technology that would ultimately lead to their destruction.

1 And Azazel [the chief of the fallen angels] taught men to make swords, and knives, and shields, and breastplates, and made known to them the metals of the earth and the art of working them, and bracelets, and ornaments, and the use of antimony, and the beautifying of the eyelids, and all kinds of costly stones, and all
2 colouring tinctures. And there arose much godlessness, and they committed fornication, and they
3 were led astray, and became corrupt in all their ways. Semjaza taught enchantments, and root-cuttings, 'Armaros the resolving of enchantments, Baraqijal (taught) astrology, Kokabel the constellations, Ezeqeel the knowledge of the

clouds, Araqiel the signs of the earth, Shamsiel the signs of the Sun, and Sariel the course of the Moon. And as men perished, they cried, and their cry went up to heaven ... (1 Enoch 1-3)[11]

In the Sumerian myths, these "fallen angels" taught the Sumerians both how, where and when to build their great towers, as if both the location and the timing of the building were critical. The purpose of this was to make sure that the temple towers did indeed align with the rising and setting of the Sun, Moon and planets, so that "the gods" might be worshiped appropriately. As it is explained in *Enuma Elish*,

> *Marduk opened his mouth to speak,*
> *To say a word to the gods, his fathers:*
> *Above the Apsu where you have resided,*
> *The counterpart of Esharra which I have built over you,*
> *Below I have hardened the ground for a building site,*
> *I will build a house therein its temple,*
> *I will appoint cellas, I will establish my sovereignty.*
> *When you come up from the Apsu for assembly,*
> *You will spend the night there[in], (it is there) to receive all of you.*
> *When you descend from heaven for assembly,*
> *You will spend the night therein; it is there to receive you.*
> *I will call its name 'Babylon,' which means*
> *'The houses of the great gods.'*
> (*Enuma Elish* Tablet V:117–129)

The great tower of Babylon was designed in such a way that it appeared that the "star gods", as they rose and set in the sky, appeared to actually climb the sides of the temple and temporarily take their seats on "thrones" that the Babylonian masons had created for them on the top of the temple-tower. Probably this practice had its roots from a time when the Anunnaki star gods — the "Nephilim" of Genesis 6 and the "Watchers" of The Book of Enoch — did indeed descend from heaven to earth and give gifts of technology to mankind. Thus, by creating thrones for them on the top of a magnificent tower, the

---

[11] *The Book of Enoch,* http://reluctant-messenger.com/book_of_enoch.htm. For more information on the giants, visit Mysterious World: Giants in the Earth: http://www.mysteriousworld.com/Journal/2003/Spring/Giants/

Babylonians were likely attempting to attract these star gods to descend from heaven and bestow these gifts once more. Perhaps in some way this temple-tower was literally a "gateway of the gods", a bridge between the spirit world and the physical, through which these ancient deities would one day return again.

In sum, the main reason that the Babylonians built a stage tower from which to worship their gods was because their gods were the stars in the sky — particularly, the planets. Whether or not the Annunaki actually came down and built the tower, or whether imaginative men built the tower in order to tempt them into coming down, it is clear that the Babylonian towers were not just temples — they were temple-observatories, high places from which the pagan priests could more easily study their gods, the planets.

PLANETARY DEITIES IN ANCIENT NEAR EASTERN RELIGION

As we have seen, the pagans believed that their gods were immanent in the stars — in particular, in the planets. They failed to understand that the stars and planets were in fact millions and billions of miles away and had little effect on human affairs. Even so, in their ignorance, they deified the planets, going so far as to study their movements in order to, as they believed, discern the will of their "gods." As W.M. O'Neil explains in his *Early Astronomy from Babylonia to Copernicus*, "Most, perhaps all, early peoples have taken an interest in events in the sky. They have identified and named the brighter celestial bodies and sets (constellations) of them. They have noted their apparent motions, usually distinguishing between the fixed stars and the wanderers."[12] The stars held central roles in the religions of the ancient Near East because they were considered to be gods, and chief among the gods were the planets, the "wanderers," which were considered to be the highest of all gods. This was believed primarily because they moved about independently, while the background stars always rose and set in a

---

[12]W.M. O'Neil, *Early Astronomy from Babylonia to Copernicus* (Sydney: Sydney University Press, 1986), 1.

predictable fashion. It was also believed that their motions in the heavens relative to the background stars was their method of communicating with man, of foretelling his fate. As B.L. van der Waerden explains in his *Science Awakening II: The Birth of Astronomy*, "The stars were supposed to influence our fate, because they were regarded as mighty gods."[13] Since the pagans believed that the planets ruled over an intricately interrelated natural order, they reasoned that systematic observation of their movements could be used to determine future events. This systematic observation led to the glorification and eventual deification of the stars and planets, which led to astral worship and, eventually, to astrology.

The earliest forms of astrology had nothing to do with determining the fates of specific individuals, as is the case with the type of modern astrology we are familiar with. The earliest forms of astrology were only concerned with predicting trends and events on the national and international level—those events dealing with kings and queens, famine and plenty, war, and peace. Colin Ronan describes this mindset in *The Astronomers,*

> Their motives for observing the heavens were partly due to their curiosity about them, and partly to the belief that all the celestial bodies had their individual effects on the nation and the multifarious affairs of state. This kind of astrology, unconcerned as it was with the details of individual lives and dealing only with the larger canvas depicting the fortunes of kings and their armies, followed on the more primitive beliefs that the Sun, Moon, and stars were gods.[14]

The pagans then extended the idea that the stars and planets were gods to creating complex mythologies based on the movements of their gods through the heavens. As E.C. Krupp explains in his *Echoes of the Ancient Skies: The Astronomy of Ancient Civilizations,*

> A perusal of nearly any ancient pantheon reveals the obvious: At least some of the gods, often the most important ones, are objects in the sky. The metaphoric reasons are not difficult to understand. The regular motions of celestial objects made them agents of

---

[13]Bartel L. van der Waerden, *Science Awakening II: The Birth of Astronomy* (New York: Oxford University Press, 1974), 128.

[14]Colin Ronan, *The Astronomers* (New York: Hill and Wang, 1964), 23.

order that helped give meaning to the world below; endless repetition of their appearances and disappearances suggested immortality; their light commanded attention and connoted power. And being in the sky, with such a perspective on Earth below, it was only natural to assume that the gods must know all because they could see all.[15]

The Universal Planetary Deities

The 8-rayed star symbol of Inanna. The "star" is actually the planet Venus, with which she was closely associated.

It would appear from the religious texts of the ancient pagan religions that practically every important deity had his or her own special planet in the heavens. Even the ancient Sumerians, who were the first to have achieved significant advancements in scientific astronomy, continued on in their belief that the planets were gods. "The Sumerians had already by observation acquired a little astronomical knowledge, and [believed] the Sun and Moon and the planets were identified with gods."[16] For example, the goddess Ishtar, known to the Sumerians as "Inanna," was hailed by them as the goddess of the evening star, the planet Venus:

> The great queen Inanna, I will hail!
> The only one, come forth on high, I will hail!
> The Great Queen of Heaven, I will hail!
> The pure torch that flares in the sky,
> the heavenly light shining bright as the day,
> the great Queen of Heaven, I will hail![17]

---

[15] E.C. Krupp, *Echoes of the Ancient Skies: The Astronomy of Ancient Civilizations* (New York: Harper and Row, 1983), 62.
[16] Wooley, *The Sumerians*, 128.
[17] Jacobsen, "The Graven Image," 17–18.

Typically, Ishtar/Inanna is identified with the planet Venus which, as is alluded to in the verse, is actually the third brightest object in the heavens next to the Sun and Moon. Similarly, the ancient Persians sometimes referred to Ahuramazda, their chief god, as " 'prince,' 'the leading star of stars,' and 'the furrow of heaven.' "[18] Krupp mentions that "Any, or An, was the greatest of the Sumerian gods. His name was the word for 'sky' and 'high,' and the written symbol for his name was shared with the word *Dingir:* 'Shining'. ... The name Jupiter derives, in turn, from Dyauspitar, or Zeus-pater, 'Father Zeus.' In terms of its original Indo-European root, the name Zeus means 'resplendent' or 'shining.' And the collective Indo-European name for the celestial gods was *daevos*, 'the Bright Ones.' "[19]

During the Greek and Roman period the planet Jupiter, named after the Roman god Jupiter, was worshiped as the king of the gods. It is unclear, however, whether or not the ancient Sumerians and Babylonians also associated the chief gods of their pantheons with Jupiter, as Jupiter clearly had nothing to do with the creation of Earth, though Marduk clearly did in the Babylonian creation myths. Moreover, as we shall see in Chapter IV, it does not fit the characteristics of Marduk as a "star" given in some ancient Sumerian texts.

Each national religion had different names for the deities they believed to be immanent in the planets. However, interestingly, all of the planets held the same general roles in the major pantheons of the ancient world. For example, the planet Jupiter was uniformly considered to be the "king of the gods" by the Greeks, and continued to be the predominant planet even to the time of the Roman Empire. As Krupp explains, "In Greece, Zeus was chief of the Olympians, with dominion over the planet Jupiter.... By contrast, the Egyptians portrayed Jupiter... with the falcon head of the sky-god Horus."[20]

---

[18] James M. Fennelly, "The Persepolis Ritual," *Biblical Archaeologist* (Summer 1980), 150.

[19] E.C. Krupp, *Echoes of the Ancient Skies*, 64.

[20] E.C. Krupp, *Echoes of the Ancient Skies*, 67–68.

The Greeks and Romans actually adopted the worship of the planets primarily as a result of Alexander the Great's defeat of the Persians and subsequent adoption of Persian and Mesopotamian culture. Though he had defeated the Persians, Alexander loved Persian and Mesopotamian religion and culture so much that he actively encouraged its spread throughout the Hellenistic world.

> Following the conquests of Alexander the Great, an atmosphere of religious syncretism settles throughout the Hellenistic world, particularly in Asia Minor; and an influx of Oriental religious ideas sweeps into the Occident.... The modulating element, transforming Greek philosophy, permeating Oriental religions, and serving as a prime factor in the fusion of the East and the West, is the Babylonian psuedo-science astrology.[21]

The fusion of the Greek (and later, Roman) gods with the planets was based upon the Mesopotamian belief that the gods and the planets were one. Thus, it was not Mediterranean imaginativeness but the influx of Mesopotamian religious thought that gradually resulted in the gods of the Greeks and Romans becoming associated with the planets.[22]

Clear planetary connections can be seen between the major deities of many of the pantheons of the ancient world. The Babylonians even used a separate scientific name for each of the planets to help avoid confusing the god-names that they and other nations had given to them. As Waerden explains,

> In Babylonia, just as in Greece, two sets of names were in use, one scientific and one divine. In astronomical cuneiform texts we find the scientific names, mostly in abbreviated form. The divine names were the names of gods whose characters were similar to those of the Greek and Roman planetary gods. Thus the highest god Marduk corresponds to Zeus or Jupiter. Ishtar, the goddess of

---

[21]J.B. McMinn, "Fusion of the Gods: A Religio-Astrological Study of the Interpenetration of the East and the West in Asia Minor," *Journal of Near Eastern Studies* 15 n.4 (October 1956): 202–203.

[22]McMinn, "Fusion of the Gods," 202.

love, was identified with Aphrodite or Venus. Nergal was a warrior god, like Ares or Mars, etc.[23]

There was a fair amount of interaction between the various national religions which eventually resulted in a general uniformity of belief. Over time, with religious interaction going on between the developing nations, similar deities took on similar roles. Eventually, the gods of the nations came to be represented by the same planets, as religious myths and traditions were adopted and passed down over the centuries. Some of these similarities are outlined in the following table:[24]

Table 2.1: Summary of Parallel Gods/Planets in Babylon, Persia, Greece, and Rome

Babylonian god:	Babylonian Scientific Name:	Old Persian god:	Time of Platon (430 B.C.)	Hellenistic (330 B.C.)	Latin Name (100 B.C.)	Modern Planet Name
Nabu	Gu-utu	Tira	Star of Hermes	Stilbon	Mercurius	Mercury
Ishtar	Dili-pat	Anahita	Star of Aphrodite	Phosphoros	Venus	Venus
Nergal	Sal-bat-a-ni	Verethragna	Star of Ares	Pyroeis	Mars	Mars
Marduk	Mulu-babbar	Ahura Mazda	Star of Zeus	Phaeton	Jupiter	Jupiter
Ninib	Kaimanu	--	Star of Kronos	Phainon	Saturnus	Saturn

---

[23]Waerden, "Science Awakening II," 187. Ahuramazda and Marduk are generally considered to be associated with Jupiter, but evidence from *Enuma Elish* makes this conclusion problematical (see chapter IV).

[24]This table was brought together from a series of three tables put together by Waerden, "Science Awakening II," on pp. 186–188.

Scientific Observation and Religious Ritual

Astronomy mixed with astrology was the inevitable result when the pagan priesthoods began to systematically observe the movements of their planetary gods. B.L. van der Waerden points out that it was this combination of scientific astronomy and a pantheistic religious worldview that eventually produced the psuedo-science known as astrology. "Stellar religion…leads not only to astronomy, but also to astrology. Because the stars were considered to be mighty gods, it was supposed that they had a decisive influence on our fate."[25] The pagan priests attempted to divine the will of their gods by various means, often using a combination of astronomy and divination (casting lots, examination of animal entrails, analysis of unusual or miraculous events) to do so. For example, Otto Neugebauer in *The Exact Sciences in Antiquity* points out that "important events in the life of the state were correlated with important celestial phenomena, exactly as specific appearances on the livers of sacrificial sheep were carefully recorded in omen literature."[26] Clearly, pantheism and scientific astronomy were thoroughly mixed into the earlier stages of Babylonian astronomy, resulting in a thorough mixture of science and superstition. Ronan explains,

> Although modern scientific work has made belief in astrology of any sort as outmoded as ideas of the unicorn or the phoenix, in Babylonia and Egypt it was a logical application of astronomy, and the fact that both nations used astronomers as court astrologers should cause us no surprise. To the Babylonians, astrology acted as a stimulus to astronomical observation and brought in its train scientific knowledge, just as their use of the entrails of animals, in particular the liver, for divining the future, led them to amass a considerable quantity of anatomical facts.[27]

---

[25]Waerden, "Science Awakening II," 3.

[26]Otto Neugebauer, *The Exact Sciences in Antiquity* (Princeton, Princeton University Press, 1952), 95.

[27]Ronan, *The Astronomers*, 23–24.

THE RISE AND DEVELOPMENT OF SCIENTIFIC ASTRONOMY

As we have seen, astronomical science had its first beginnings as an attempt on the part of pagan priests to understand the will of their "gods" in heaven. As a result, "admiration of the stars and the belief in their divinity had the direct effect of interesting mankind in the movements of the celestial bodies.... This same belief led to astrology, which in turn required astronomy as an auxiliary science, and therefore promoted it."[28] O'Neil agrees, saying, "Prescientific astronomical activity, involving observation, classification and the noting of broad regularities, ultimately gave rise to primitive or proto-scientific astronomy, which later developed into scientific astronomy."[29] The need to understand and predict the positions of their gods in the heavens then, over time, gradually resulted in the rise and development of scientific astronomy among the emerging nations of the ancient world.

A depiction of a temple observatory in Alexandria, Egypt showing the legendary astronomer-priest Hipparchus (190-120 B.C.) measuring the heavens with a cross staff, a mariner's astrolabe and an armillary sphere sitting nearby on the floor. The cross staff and armillary sphere were actually invented during the Hellenic Period of Egyptian history and thus fit into this scene, but this type of astrolabe would not be invented until around the 13th Century a.d. (Source: Camille Flammarion, Astronomie Populaire: Description générale du ciel, Paris: 1880).

This development of scientific astronomy, however, did not progress at equal rates in every country in the ancient world. Some nations forged quickly ahead, while others never fully emerged from a state of primitive, proto-scientific astronomy. A. Aaboe distinguishes between these two levels of prescientific astronomy in his article, "Scientific Astronomy in Antiquity":

> To the less advanced level I assign astronomical achievements such as the naming of prominent stars and constellations; drawing the distinction between fixed stars and planets; the

---

[28]Waerden, "Science Awakening II," 3.
[29]O'Neil, *Early Astronomy*, 13.

awareness of the morning star and the evening star being just different appearances of one and the same celestial body, namely, Venus; the realization that a fixed star which is not circumpolar always rises and sets on the same two places on the horizon, while the Sun, Moon, and planets do not; the discovery that the first appearance of a fixed star after its interval of invisibility happens at the same time of year and may be used as a seasonal indicator.[30]

Aaboe goes on to point out that the Egyptians used the first appearance of "Sothis" (our *Sirius*) as a herald for the flooding of the Nile, and uses it as an example of his "less advanced level." This is not to say that the Egyptians were ignorant, simply more superstitious and less mathematically inclined than were their Mesopotamian peers.[31] Aaboe assigns the more advanced level to the Mesopotamians, who tended to be more logical, more mathematical in their approach.[32] The Babylonians drew up long lists of observations and tables of ephemerides (predictions of where planets will be in the sky at any given time), and were also able to predict solar and lunar eclipses with a high degree of accuracy, skills which the Egyptians never mastered. Even so, Aaboe continues, "However different such early astronomies may be in their aim and approach, they have as a common characteristic that they employ various cycles concerning the motion of the Sun, Moon, and the five classical planets...Mercury, Venus, Mars, Jupiter and Saturn."[33] These cycles include the "Metonic" cycle which was used as the basis of the Athenian calendar, the "Venus cycle" of eight years, during which Venus becomes a morning star five times and an evening star five times, and eclipse cycles, all of which had varying degrees of accuracy depending on the level of development of each country. And even though all of the major nations of the ancient world had achieved astronomical skill of some degree, evidence

---

[30]Aaboe, A, "Scientific Astronomy in Antiquity" in *The Place of Astronomy in the Ancient World,* eds. D.G. Kendall, et al (London: Oxford University Press, 1974), 21.

[31]A good general overview of Egyptian astronomy J. Norman Lockyer, *The Dawn of Astronomy* (London: Cassell and Company Limited, 1894).

[32]A good resource for ancient mathematical astronomy is Otto Neugebauer, *A History of Ancient Mathematical Astronomy,* Part One of Studies in the History of Mathematics and Physical Sciences, ed. M.J. Klein and G.J. Toomer (New York: Springer-Verlag, 1975).

[33]Aaboe, "Scientific Astronomy in Antiquity", 22.

suggests that all ancient Near Eastern astronomy had actually originated from one particularly ancient land: Sumer

Sumer: The Cradle of Astronomy

Archaeological research in this century has made many new discoveries that have dramatically changed many assumptions about ancient Near Eastern history and religion. These discoveries have in turn shaped the course of biblical studies, and greatly legitimized the Bible's status as a book firmly entrenched in the context of the ancient world. As we saw in chapter I, near the beginning of this century, in southern Mesopotamia (modern Iraq), a vast and ancient civilization known as "Sumer" was discovered. And what was unusual about Sumer was that, even though it had been in existence over 3,000 years before Christ, it appeared that the Sumerians had actually attained a level of scientific achievement that had remained unmatched until the time of the Roman Empire. Moreover, their advances in the field of astronomy were so great that they remained unsurpassed until even the time of the Enlightenment (ca. A.D. 1700). The Sumerians were not only astonishingly advanced in the fields of astronomy and mathematics, they were also superb in many other fields such as medicine and architecture.

The Sumerians, in fact, had been observing and recording the stars and planetary movements since the fourth millennium B.C.[34], and had amassed a significant amount of information on the subject,[35] though much of it appears to have been lost or misplaced during the Akkadian conquest and subjugation of Sumer[36] or perhaps due to the disaster that befell Sumer around 2000 B.C. However, bits of it have surfaced over the past century, and much of what has been uncovered reveals a degree of scientific and astronomical sophistication previously thought impossible for such an early civilization.

Perhaps the most well-known and important discovery was a circular astrolabe (Figure 2.1), a sort of "star map," which showed a schematic diagram for dividing the visible heavens into three bands of 60 degrees each. The Sumerians referred to these divisions as the "way of Anu" (the central band), the "Way of Enlil" (the northern band),

---

[34]O'Neil, *Early Astronomy*, 10.

[35]Edwyn Bevan, *Ancient Mesopotamia: The Land of the Two Rivers* (Chicago: Argonaut Pub., 1968), 25.

[36]Wooley, *The Sumerians*, 84.

and the "Way of Ea" (the southern band), which are shown radiating concentrically from the center of the astrolabe. The Way of Anu corresponds with the celestial equator, and stretches 30 degrees above and 30 degrees below it. The Way of Enlil comprises all the visible heavens north of the Way of Anu (30 to 90 degrees north latitude), and the Way of Ea comprises all the visible heavens south of the Way of Anu (30 to 90 degrees south latitude).[37]

This astrolabe is further subdivided into twelve sections which radiate longitudinally from the center of the astrolabe, crossing perpendicularly over the three concentric sections to create a total of thirty-six subsections. These twelve sections define the months by means of the major zodiacal constellations, one for every month, each month assigned its own constellation. The existence of this astrolabe indicates that the Sumerians were aware that the heavens were arrayed on a 360-degree sphere relative to Earth. They were also the first to chart the movement of Earth relative to the Sun based on a twelve-month cycle, a cycle which even today still forms the basis of our calendar. As Colin Ronan explains, "The brighter stars were mapped and the band of constellations over which the Sun, Moon, and wandering stars moved was studied particularly carefully. It was divided into twelve sections, a method we still employ, and these twelve sections were themselves broken down into smaller ones, so it is clear that their astronomical knowledge had reached a significant level of sophistication."[38]

The constellations are also considered to be Sumerian in origin, or possibly even older, based on a tradition that the Sumerians had inherited from their predecessors in the Near East. Hartner explains, "It is possible to establish a continuity of tradition that can be traced even farther than to Sumer: It had its origin about or even some time before 4000 B.C. with the prehistoric settlers of Persia, Elam, and Mesopotamia, and it was taken over by the Sumerians and Akkadians, from where it eventually passed over to the Greeks."[39] These prehistoric settlers could only have been, as we saw in chapter I, the

---

[37]"Ea" is also known as "Enki," the third of the three most important Sumerian gods.

[38]Ronan, *The Astronomers,* 24.

[39]Willy Hartner, "The Earliest History of the Constellations in the Ancient Near East and the Motif of the Lion-Bull Combat," *Journal of Near Eastern Studies* 24 ns.1–2 (January–April 1965): 2–3.

descendants of Shem, the son of Noah, who had settled in that region after the Flood.[40]

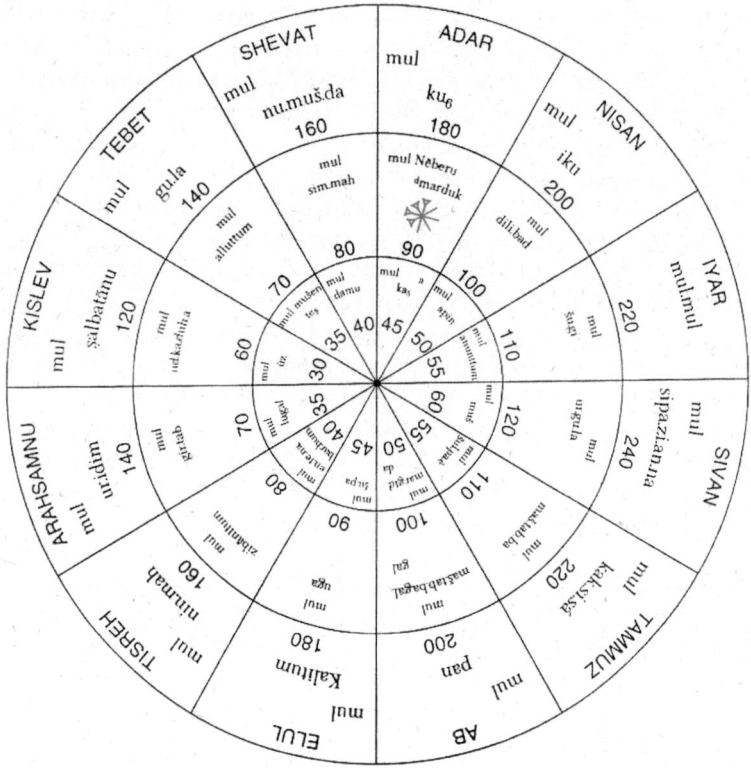

Figure 2.1. A reconstruction of a Sumerian astrolabe. Though the ancient Sumerians did not have astrolabes as sophisticated as those later developed in Europe, those astronomical tools they had at their disposal worked adequately to record the major stars, planets and constellations and their relative positions in the heavens. Marked with a red DINGIR is the record of the "star" of Marduk, the true identity of which remains a mystery. According to this astrolabe, the planet "Marduk" or "Neberu" is in its ascendancy, or perhaps first appearance, around the beginning of March.

---

[40]For a solid biblical perspective on the constellations, consult the following books: Joseph A. Seiss, *The Gospel in the Stars* (Grand Rapids: Kregel, 1972 [reprint of Philadelphia: E. Claxton and Company, 1882]); E.W. Bullinger, *The Witness of the Stars* (Grand Rapids: Kregel, 1967 [reprint of 1897 edition]); Donald B. DeYoung, *Astronomy and the Bible: Questions and Answers* (Grand Rapids: Baker Book House, 1988); G. Shiaparelli, *Astronomy in the Old Testament* (Oxford: The Clarendon Press, 1905), 10.

The Decline and Fall of Ancient Scientific Astronomy

Much of Sumer's advanced astronomical knowledge was lost, however, when Sumer was destroyed around 2000 B.C. by a mysterious force of heavenly origin, followed by wave after wave of barbarian invaders seeking to take advantage of Sumer's weakened state. Despite the fact that some of Sumer's advanced scientific knowledge was retained and recovered by its conquerors, the Babylonians, the vast majority remained buried under the rubble of Sumer's shattered cities until archaeologists rediscovered much of it in the early part of this century, nearly 4,000 years later. Further, though the Babylonians had indeed retained much of Sumer's interest in astronomy, over time the Babylonians introduced more and more pantheistic, astrological beliefs. As a result, scientific astronomy became greatly degraded and was nearly lost for many centuries, not to return in any sort of "pure" form until around 500 B.C. As A.T. Olmstead summarizes in his article, "Babylonian Astronomy—Historical Sketch,"

> Toward the end of the third pre-Christian millennium [ca. 2000 B.C.], there came an extraordinary development of mathematics which reached a level little surpassed in later centuries either by Babylonians or by Greeks. Thus were furnished the tools by which later scholars were to build up astronomy as a science, but the question why this must wait some fifteen centuries cannot be answered. Is it possible that astrology exerted here its malign influence?[41]

Most modern historians automatically assume, based upon social evolutionary theories, that human society gradually rose from savagery to civilization over thousands of years. However, the facts prove that the Sumerians were a high peak in the history of advanced civilization and scientific achievement, to be succeeded by a long dark age with relatively few and brief periods of scientific advancement. Around 1900 B.C. the shattered remnants of the Sumerian Empire were conquered by the Babylonians, and centuries after that conquest much of their advanced technical knowledge was gradually lost or forgotten, leading to a period of scientific ignorance which lasted for nearly 1,500 years.

---

[41] A.T. Olmstead, "Babylonian Astronomy—Historical Sketch," *The American Journal of Semitic Languages and Literatures* LV No.2 (April, 1938), 116.

The Renaissance of Ancient Scientific Astronomy

After that extended period of scientific ignorance, however, the Babylonians began to regain the knowledge that had been lost as a result of the conquest of Sumer. "Genuine science may be said to begin [again] in the late Assyrian period. The first advance is attributed to the Babylonian king Nabu-nasir, whose era, beginning 747 B.C. and remembered to late classical times, introduced a nineteen-year cycle of intercalation which was later modified but never abandoned in principle."[42] Later, "Around 700 B.C., under the Assyrian empire, we meet with systematic observational reports of astronomers to the court."[43] The Assyrian astrologer-priests began to take detailed records of the movements of their "gods" relative to the stellar background, and used these movements to make predictions of future events. These predictions were primarily on the national scale, and were believed to determine the will of their gods concerning what actions to take concerning war, trade, and politics.

King Shamshi-Adad of Assyria, ca. 811 B.C. Ancient astronomy reached a relatively high peak under the Assyrians and Babylonians. Here the king is shown pointing to the "gods" in heaven, the planets, represented by the symbols in the upper-left-hand corner of this stela.

This systematic report of eclipses, of course, could not have come about without some significant mathematical and scientific ability. The Assyrians and Babylonians had recovered and refined their astronomical skills to the point where, by around 400 B.C., they could predict eclipses, conjunctions, and unusual astral portents, and this ability was to "form the very backbone of Babylonian mathematical astronomy."[44] This renaissance of scientific astronomy continued through the period of the Persian Empire (c.a. 550-330 B.C.), and seems to have reached its highest level of sophistication during the time of the Seleucids and Parthians, the descendants of the Persians.

---

[42] Olmstead, "Babylonian Astronomy—Historical Sketch," 117.

[43] Neugebauer, *The Exact Sciences in Antiquity*, 96.

[44] Neugebauer, *The Exact Sciences in Antiquity*, 97.

"Mathematical astronomy is fully developed at about 300 B.C."[45] The high degree of astronomical knowledge attained during the Parthian period forms the most probable link between the Magi of the Achaemenid Persian period and the Magi who came upon the scene at the Nativity.

THE MAGI: THE INHERITORS OF THE ANCIENT CREATION TRADITION

Though much has been written on the Magi by many different sources in antiquity, only some of these sources, such as Herodotus, are reliable enough to use in any in-depth discussion of the Magi. Questions of who they were, and what role they played in ancient Near Eastern history arise in our quest to understand why their appearance at the Nativity was accorded such a place of prominence in the Gospels. Understanding who the Magi were will then serve as a prelude to a more in-depth study of the "Star of Bethlehem" phenomenon, as we come to understand how the Magi form the link between the Creation and the Nativity.

The Classical Image of the Magi

Representations of the Magi and the Star of the Nativity are among the most popular Christian symbols come Christmas time. Yet, understandings of whom the Magi were and what they truly represented are often confusing, oversimplified, or factually inaccurate. For example, John MacArthur points out that "...most of the popular notions about the Magi are misleading. It is doubtful that they were anything like the camel-riding travelers we usually see portrayed in pictures and Christmas pageants. Even the old standard Christmas song 'We Three Kings of Orient Are' may be wrong on several counts. There's no evidence that there were three of them — only that they brought three kinds of gifts (Matt. 2:11). Furthermore, Scripture does not say that they were kings; in

---

[45]Neugebauer, 97. See also Olmstead, 114.

fact, they almost certainly were not."[46] David Haag also debunks some of the mythology that has arisen around the story of the Magi over the centuries, pointing out that much of it appears to have been embellished. "Folklore has even given names to the 'three wise men,' calling them Melchior, Balthasar, and Caspar — making them kings from Egypt, India, and Greece. Some even say that they were later baptized by Thomas and that Helena, the mother of Constantine, discovered their bones and had them placed in the church of Saint Sophia at Constantinople."[47]

Interestingly, the Magi represent the only significant Gentile authority in the Gospels to affirm that Jesus was, in fact, the Messiah. It could be that Matthew intended to convince the Jews of the divinity of Christ by including with the genealogy of Christ in his Gospel an account of Gentile authority that corroborated his witness. Certainly King Herod held the Magi in high esteem (Matt. 2:1-7), enough so to slaughter all the young babies in Bethlehem upon their affirmation that the Messiah had just been born there (Matt. 2:16, 18; cf. also Micah 5:2 and Jeremiah 40:1). An understanding of who the Magi truly were, then, as seen from the perspective of their historical and cultural context, could shed more light on their importance as a witness to the Nativity.

The True Image of the Magi

The Magi did not represent Shem, Ham, and Japheth, or the peoples of the Near East, Africa, and Asia, respectively. Though there are many things we do not know about the Magi, we *can* be sure of one thing: "What we do know of the mysterious Magi is this: They...came from Persia or Parthia."[48] But Persia was a very large and complex place, having once been a very large empire that had been conquered by Alexander the Great several centuries before the Nativity took place. Therefore, we must be more specific: where in Persia did the Magi live, and what was their cultural background? Further, what sort of role did they play in Persian religion and society?

---

[46]John F. MacArthur, *God With Us: The Miracle of Christmas* (Grand Rapids: Zondervan, 1989), 100.

[47]David Haag, "The Star in God's Window," *Fundamentalist Journal* (December 1984), 40–41.

[48]Kent R. Hughes, "The Magi's Worship" *Christianity Today* 29 (13 Dec. 1985): 27; M.A. Screech, "The Magi and the Star" in *Histoire de l'exegese au XVI siecle* (Geneva: Librairie Droz S.A., 1978), 408.

Persian Magi offering a bull to one of the gods of Persia, most likely Ahura Mazda. The magi were the priestly class of ancient Persia, just a step below the royalty. They were primarily responsible for maintaining good communications between the gods and men, keeping careful track of the stars and planets and how their interactions determined the destiny of the state.

Edwin Yamauchi, in his seminal work *Persia and the Bible*, explains, "According to Herodotus [1.101], the Magi (Greek *magos*, plural *magoi*) were originally one of the tribes of the Medes."[49] James A. Moulton in his *Early Zoroastrianism: The Origin, the Prophets, the Magi* agrees with this, pointing out that "There were six tribes … in Media … we are only concerned with two, the Αριζαυτοί and the Μάγοι. The former word is obvious Persian, *Ariyazantava*, 'having Aryan family' — or perhaps *Arizantava* 'having noble family'.... The Magi are accordingly outside the ruling caste."[50] Moulton has the idea that the Magi were part of a race subject to the Aryan nobility, who gave the Magi their name, an Aryan name which denotes their status in the Aryan-dominated society:

There appears to be reason to believe that it was a name which the Magi themselves did not use; they kept it out of the Avesta, except in one passage. If the other tribal names of Media are Aryan, as is probable, there is a presumption that this will be. And there happens to be a phonetically exact Indo-European equation available, which, as I read it, will give the meaning "slave." It was then a contemptuous title given by Persian conquerors to a subjugated populace, and especially to the caste which had been foremost in resistance, as the revolt of Guamata would lead us to expect. We remember how Cambyses, when he heard of the Magian revolt, adjured those present, and

---

[49] Edwin M. Yamauchi, *Persia and the Bible* (Grand Rapids: Baker, 1990), 467. This is a primary reference for anything to do with ancient Persia.

[50] James H. Moulton, *Early Zoroastrianism: The Origins, the Prophets, the Magi* (Amsterdam: Philo Press, 1972), 183-84.

especially the Achaemenians, not to let the kingdom go to the Medes, of whom the Magi are simply a leading tribe.[51]

The Magi, according to Moulton, were part of a subjugated people — the Medians — who were more of a weaker partner in a forced alliance with the Persians than they were actual slaves. The more-or-less equal footing between the Medes and Persians can be seen in the free intermixing between Median and Persian warriors in the elite guard of the Persian army, the "Ten Thousand Immortals," as displayed on the eastern stairway of the Apadana at Persepolis.[52] Though this would imply political unity, there were most likely still tensions between the Medians and the Persians, as is witnessed by the fact that when a man named Guamata the Magos usurped the throne of Persia, he was supported by the populace, which was predominantly Median.[53] Another witness to the Median origin of the Magi is Gnoli, who in *The Encyclopedia of Religion* explains that one of the meanings of "the Old Persian word *magu*, rendered in Greek by *magos* ... may originally have meant 'member of the tribe'.... The term is probably of Median origin, given that Herodotus mentions the 'Magoi' as one of the six tribes of the Medes."[54]

Thus the Magi were not three wise men who represented the three branches of mankind from the three major geographic regions of the ancient world — the Near East, Africa, and Asia — but were from Persia, most likely coming from the Median peoples, possibly even from a caste persecuted by the ruling classes. But what was their role in Medo-Persian society? Yamauchi explains that "the Magi ... functioned as priests and diviners under the Achaemenian Persians (600 to 400 B.C.). Herodotus (1.132) wrote that 'no sacrifice can be offered without a Magian.' The Magi also interpreted dreams (Herodotus 1.107, 120, 128).... The Persians continued to use derivations from the word *magus* as a word for 'priest' down to the end of the Sasanian era around 650"[55] Gnoli confirms this observation, explaining,

---

[51] Ibid, 185–86.

[52] Yamauchi, *Persia and the Bible,* 351.

[53] Moulton, *Early Zoroastrianism,* 186.

[54] G. Gnoli, "The Magi" in *The Encyclopedia of Religion,* ed. Mercia Eliade (New York: Macmillan, 1986), 79.

[55] Yamauchi, *Persia and the Bible,* 467–68.

The Magi were technicians of and experts on worship: it was impossible to offer sacrifices without the presence of a Magus. During the performance of a ritual sacrifice, the Magus sang of the theogony (the Magi were possibly the custodians of a tradition of sacred poetry, but we know nothing about the relationship of this tradition to the various parts of the Avesta) and was called upon to interpret dreams and to divine the future.[56]

The Magi were the ubiquitous priestly class of Media-Persian society, a tribe of holy men like the Israelite Levites in social function, who were the only ones whom, it was believed, could effectively commune with the state gods of Persia. Scholars are divided on exactly what sort of relationship the Magi had with Zoroastrianism, the state religion of Persia inaugurated by Cyrus the Great,[57] but what is certain is that they were the inheritors of a tradition of sacred poetry: a "theogony," or a song about the creation of the gods. This song was probably heavily influenced by *Enuma Elish*, which was, besides being a creation story, also a story about the creation of the gods of the Babylonians. Moreover, the fact that the ancient Persians had conquered and subjugated the ancient Babylonians makes it certain that they

Two of the Persian "Ten-Thousand Immortals" are immortalized in this brick frieze in the Louvre, taken from the Apadana, Darius the Great's famous palace at Persepolis (modern Iran). The Immortals were unique partly because they were an integrated force, made up of both Persians and Medians, the latter of which was considered to be a lesser people by the lordly Persians.

did indeed inherit the ancient Creation tradition, and had made it a crucial part of their understanding of how the Earth had been created as the result of the combat between the most high God and a "dragon".

---

[56]Gnoli, The Magi", 80.

[57]Cf. Moulton, *Early Zoroastrianism*, 183; Yamauchi, 436–7, 468–9; Gnoli, 80; Jack Finegan, *The Archaeology of World Religions* (Princeton: Princeton University Press, 1952), 77–78, 89; R.C. Zaehner, *The Teachings of the Magi: A Compendium of Zoroastrian Beliefs* (London: Sheldon Press, 1956), 12; Mircea Eliade, *A History of Religious Ideas, Volume I* (Chicago: The University of Chicago Press, 1978), 309–10.

The Magi and the Stars

Unfortunately, after the collapse of the Persian Empire, not much direct evidence concerning the Magi can be found. However, secondary accounts of their involvement with astronomy and astrology are not uncommon. For example, Aus explains, "Herodotus notes that the Magi not only interpreted dreams. They also interpreted celestial phenomena for King Xerxes. The Greek historian states that while the Sun is the prophet of the Greeks, for the Magi it is the Moon. That is, they deal primarily with the nocturnal heavens. When the Magi from the East in Matt. 2:2 state that they have seen (at night) the Star of him born king of the Jews and then follow it (at night) to Bethlehem in verses 8-9, it thus belonged to a normal realm of their concern."[58] It sounds here that the Magi were considered the astrologers of the court of Xerxes. But the question remains as to whether their knowledge of the stars was merely astrological and psuedo-scientific, or approaching a true science.

The Magi appear to have astrological knowledge as one of their major attributes. "All independent references to the Magi make much of their astrology."[59] It is unusual, however, that much of Zoroastrianism seems to ignore the stars and astrology. "Apart from the special cult of Tishtrya[60] and his fellow regents, we find very little star-lore in the Avesta: there is, however, just enough to make this connection."[61] Actually, Anahita, the most prominent Persian goddess, appears in some writings in connection with the stars (the Anahita Yasht),[62] Anahita being equated with the planet Venus. However, even this connection is surprisingly limited.

However, despite the relative unimportance of astrology within Zoroastrianism, the Magi were still strongly identified with both astrology and Zoroastrianism. This may imply that the Magi were not

---

[58] Roger David Aus, "The Magi at the Birth of Cyrus, and the Magi at Jesus' Birth in Matthew 2:1-12," in *New Perspectives in Ancient Judaism, Vol. II: Religion, Literature, and Society in Ancient Israel, Formative Christianity and Judaism,* eds. Neusner, Borgen, Frerichs, Horsley (New York: University Press of America, 1977), 111–12.

[59] Moulton, *Early Zoroastrianism*, 201.

[60] The star Sirius, also prominent in Egypt as *Sothis*, the star used as an indicator of agricultural seasons.

[61] Moulton, 201.

[62] Moulton, 212. The Persian fertility goddess Anahita was associated with the planet Venus, and paralleled other fertility goddesses such as Venus, Aphrodite, Ishtar, Astarte, and Asthoreth who were also associated with the planet Venus.

pure Zoroastrians, or it may be that they were not Zoroastrian at all, their association with Zoroastrianism being a mistaken assumption on the part of outside observers. In any case, the evidence makes it clear that the Magi were essentially astrologers. As Yamauchi explains,

> From the fourth century B.C. on the Magi were increasingly associated with the Chaldeans as astrologers.... A factor that has contributed to the identification of the Magi with the Chaldeans and astrologers is their association with Zoroaster. The Greek spelling of Zoroaster's name, *Zoroastres*, was first recorded by Xanthos of Lydia. The Greeks saw in this name the word *aster* ("star"). Hermodorus, a pupil of Plato, explained Zoroaster's name as *astrothutes* ("star worshiper"). Because of these associations, a mass of astrological matter circulated under the name of Zoroaster.[63]

Yamauchi points out that the term "Chaldean" was once used to denote a people-group in lower Mesopotamia, but later came to mean one who practiced divination and astrology — Babylonian, Greek, or otherwise. These "Chaldeans" became the astrologer/astronomers who began to learn scientific astronomy for religious reasons. The Magi, as astrologers, probably fit into this generic term of "Chaldean," explaining their close association with astronomy and astrology.

At this point, we can only say one thing conclusively: the Magi were definitely astrologers. However, exactly when in the evolution of Magian beliefs this happened is open to conjecture. Moulton believes that it occurred when "The Persians and Magi reached Babylon before the end of the sixth century B.C. and there they became acquainted with Babylonian astrology and astronomy."[64] Over time, during the later Seleucid and Sasanian periods of Persian history, through practice and gradual improvement of technique, their astronomy no doubt became more and more scientific. This would correspond to the scientific trend in Mesopotamia at the time where, as Yamauchi points out, "The development of 'Chaldeans' in a professional as well as an ethnic sense derived from the interest in astronomy/astrology developed by priestly scholars among the Chaldeans of Mesopotamia."[65]

---

[63]Yamauchi, *Persia and the Bible,* 472, 74.
[64]Moulton, *Early Zoroastrianism,* 137.
[65]Yamauchi, 473.

At that time the Magi no doubt also picked up the knowledge of *Enuma Elish*, the creation epic/theogony of the Babylonians, which they may have used to form the basis of their own theogony. As we have seen, the Persians also worshiped the planets. And since their gods were the planets, then any story about the creation of the gods must also be a description of the creation of the planets. This would make sense in the context of their predominantly astral theology, and would explain their great interest in the appearance of the "new Star" that appeared at the Nativity.

III

THE STAR OF BETHLEHEM: A TENTH PLANET?

Now when Jesus was born in Bethlehem of Judaea in the days of Herod the king, behold, there came wise men from the east to Jerusalem, saying, "Where is he that is born King of the Jews? for we have seen his star in the east, and are come to worship him".
(Matthew 2:1-2)

Although to this point we have examined what role the stars played in ancient religion, we have yet to study the phenomenon of the "Star of Bethlehem" in depth. Other passages in the Bible use astral imagery, but by far the most prominent appearance of a star is in Matthew 2, where a Star announces the birth of Christ. This Star was followed by a group of wise men called "Magi" who came from the east, men whom we now know to be Persian astrologers — philosophers and scientists renowned throughout the ancient world for their expertise in understanding the night sky.

"The Wise Men Guided by the Star" by Gustave Doré (1865).

These men had inherited ancient astronomical traditions that had been handed down for millennia, traditions that may have dated from the earliest days of Sumer, possibly even from the days before the Flood. Thus, by mentioning their presence at the Nativity, Matthew was basically saying that no less than the world's most esteemed authorities on the subject of heavenly signs and portents had recognized the Star of Bethlehem as the Sign that the Son of God had been born.

THE MAGI AND THE STAR OF BETHLEHEM

The teachings of the prophet Daniel may have strongly influenced the magi of both ancient Babylon and Persia.

Not many researchers into the Star of Bethlehem phenomenon take into account the possibility that the Magi's knowledge of the true nature of this mysterious star may have actually come from the prophet Daniel. Daniel, in his exalted position as head of the wise men in the court of Babylon (Daniel 2:46-49; 5) — and later, after the Persian conquest, as a powerful man in the court of Persia (Daniel 5:30-6:3; 6:28)[1] — undoubtedly influenced the beliefs of the Magi of both the Babylonian and Persian courts.

As a result of God's work through Daniel, both Nebuchadnezzar, king of Babylon (Dan. 2:47; 3:29; 4:34, 37), Darius, king of Persia (Dan. 6:26), and Cyrus, king of Persia (2 Chronicles 36:22-23; Ezra 1:1-2; Isa. 44:28; 45:1-4) not only recognized and worshiped the LORD, but actually commanded His worship throughout their empires. This no doubt gave the Hebrew Scriptures great weight in the eyes of the Magi, the leading religious experts in Persia at that time. Moreover, the existence of Jewish colonies in eastern Persia — left over from the Babylonian dispersion — also made the Hebrew Scriptures easily available to the Magi. As Hughes explains, "The Magi of our story were probably influenced by expatriate Jews who shared their sacred writings, thus instilling in them the expectation of a coming kingly Jewish figure."[2] Numbers 24:17 was probably particularly influential in the minds of the Magi:

> *I shall see him, but not now:*
> *I shall behold him, but not nigh:*
> *there shall come a Star out of Jacob,*
> *and a Sceptre shall rise out of Israel,*

---

[1] For an excellent analysis of how the various kings and events described in the Bible are corroborated by archaeologically established history see "King Belshazzar and Darius the Mede" BibleHistory.net, http://www.biblehistory.net/Belshazzar_Darius_Mede.pdf.

[2] Kent R. Hughes, "The Magi's Worship," *Christianity Today* 29, 13 Dec. 1985, 27.

> *and shall smite the corners of Moab,*
> *and destroy all the children of Sheth.*

Numbers 24:17, which is actually a prophesy of Balaam — a magus of similar pagan beliefs as the Magi — most likely helped convince the Magi that the Messiah would be preceded by a Star. It would also help clarify in their minds in what country, and to what people, the Messiah would be born, as Balaam, per God's direct orders, specifically blessed the nation of Israel.[3]

Balaam, despite being a pagan prophet specifically hired to curse Israel, instead blessed them, as that is what God showed him in his visions. (Cf. Numbers 22-24.)

Messianic Expectations Preceding the Birth of Christ

During the previous few centuries before the birth of Christ, the expectation of the coming of a messianic figure had been widespread throughout the ancient world. For example the Zoroastrians, a Persian religious order to which the Magi appear to have been related, had been expecting the birth of a great savior of mankind for some time. The Zoroastrians had a belief in a messianic figure, which they called the *Saoshyant,* the "Savior of the Future."[4] The founder of Zoroastrianism, the prophet Zoroaster had, just a few centuries before the time of Christ, predicted that this "Savior of the Future" was soon to come to Earth. Thus the Magi were probably already expecting a messianic figure to appear.

In fact, in the period immediately before the birth of Christ, it was commonly believed throughout the ancient world that the arrival of a messianic figure was imminent:

---

[3] It is also interesting to note that both the birth of Israel, and the birth of Christ, the King of Israel, were both prophesied by "wise men from the east".

[4] Edwin M. Yamauchi, *Persia and the Bible* (Grand Rapids: Baker, 1990), 481. Zoroaster was the founder of Zoroastrianism, one of the primary religions of ancient Persia. There is some question as to whether or not the Magi were Zoroastrians. Even if they were not, they most certainly would have been aware of its basic tenets.

Suetonius (*Vespasian* iv) and Tacitus (*Histories* v.13), two Roman historians who lived in the first century, said there had long been a belief throughout the East (Palestine, Syria, Babylon) that near the first century a king would be born of the Jews who was destined to rule the world. Virgil also told of the dawning of the golden age in that period (*Eclogue* iv).[5]

This general belief that a messianic figure was soon to appear was probably supported by the fact that many different astronomical signs occurred immediately before and during the time of the birth of Christ. "Astronomical indications show that seven major conjunctions took place in 3/2 B.C."[6] The reason conjunctions and like phenomena had such an effect on the people of the ancient world is that astral apparitions at that time were generally believed to herald people and/or events of great significance. "Ancient people tended to think that a strange astral apparition was a herald of the birth of someone who would be prominent."[7] The question is, however, how do these "astral apparitions" relate to the Star of Bethlehem account in Matthew 2? The exact nature of what the Star of Bethlehem was has been the subject of great debate for centuries, a debate that has accelerated in the past century with the advent of new technologies and a greatly improved understanding of the intricacies of our solar system

Popular Theories on the Star of Bethlehem

The true nature of the Star of Bethlehem has long been a point of controversy. Explanations have ranged from something as mundane as a meteor shower to a theophany of God who appeared as a star. In fact, according to Edwin Yamauchi, "There are over five hundred books, articles, and reviews on the subject of the 'Star,' offering a variety of explanations."[8] Out of all the theories, three have received the most support: (1) a nova, (2) a comet, or (3) a conjunction of planets. Yet despite their overwhelming support, even these three theories still have problems which, in my opinion, are insurmountable:

---

[5]Ernest L. Martin, "The Celestial Pageantry Dating Christ's Birth," *Christianity Today* (December 3, 1976), 18.

[6]Martin, "The Celestial Pageantry," 18.

[7]William E. Phipps, "The Magi and Halley's Comet," *Theology Today* 43 No.1 (April, 1986): 9.

[8]Yamauchi, *Persia and the Bible*, 482.

- *The Star of Bethlehem as Nova:* Carl Richards explains, "At unpredictable intervals a new star may appear in the sky, flaring up in a few days to a brilliancy that makes it quite prominent (novae)."[9] Yamauchi points out that according to Chinese records, there was a nova near the star Alpha Aquilae for seventy days in 5 B.C.[10] However, novae have occurred before and since the birth of Christ, but nothing of any significance had happened at those times. So if the Star of Bethlehem were a nova, it would be something less than unique. Also, novae are fixed, and do not "move" as the Star of Bethlehem was said to have done (Matt. 2:9).

- *The Star of Bethlehem as Comet:* Richards feels that the planet Venus and Halley's Comet appearing together may have formed what appeared to be a "new star."[11] However, Venus was already worshiped universally as the heavenly symbol of the fertility goddess Ishtar (a.k.a. Inanna, Ashtoreth, etc.), being "one of the chief objects of worship among the ancients."[12] Venus was one of a  triad of important astral deities among the ancient pagans, and was therefore an inappropriate candidate to be the Star of Bethlehem, as this Star was apparently unique. "The Magi, being familiar with the apparent movements of the heavenly bodies, would not regard so well known and so regular a visitor as Venus to be the Sign they sought."[13] Hughes also denies the comet theory any validity: "Halley's comet appeared around 12–11 B.C., a considerable time before

---

[9]Carl P. Richards, "The Star of Bethlehem," *Sky and Telescope* (December 1956), 67.

[10]Yamauchi, *Persia and the Bible,* 482.

[11]Richards, "The Star of Bethlehem," 66.

[12]David Hughes, *The Star of Bethlehem: An Astronomer's Confirmation* (New York: Walker and Company, 1980), 134.

[13]Richards, "The Star of Bethlehem," 66.

Jesus' birth — and a comet is not a star.... Moreover, comets were thought to herald catastrophes, not births."[14] Wolters agrees, explaining, "As a rule, comets were taken to portend some catastrophe."[15] Comets are also relatively common. Halley's Comet, for example, passes near Earth every 76 years or so, making its appearance hardly unique enough to herald the birth of the King of the Universe. And even if a comet passed near enough to Venus to form what would appear to be a "new star," this apparition would not last for more than a few hours, as comets are relatively fast-moving, and Venus' position in the sky relative to Earth is constantly in motion.

⚴ *The Star of Bethlehem as a Conjunction of Planets:* The most popular and scientifically sustainable theory, the "Planetary Conjunction" theory, deals with the fact that Jupiter and Saturn came very close together in the sky around 7 B.C. appearing, as some speculate, as one unusually bright star. "The great astronomer Johannes Kepler speculated in the early seventeenth century that the 'star' was in fact a thrice-repeated conjunction of Jupiter and Saturn in the 'sign' of Pisces that occurred in 7 B.C."[16] Martin, however, argues that it was Jupiter and Venus, and not Jupiter and Saturn, that may have formed the "Star of Bethlehem" phenomenon.[17] Though interesting, the problem with Kepler's theory is that Jupiter and Saturn never actually came together, just very close to each other, and even then only briefly. Furthermore, the types of conjunctions described by Kepler and Martin are rare, but not unique, as they reoccur every few centuries. Thus, though they were in fact unusual, they were certainly not unique enough to herald the birth of the King of the Universe.[18]

---

[14] Richards, 66.

[15] Al Wolters, "Halley's Comet at a Turning Point in Jewish History," *The Catholic Biblical Quarterly* 55 (1993): 687.

[16] Roy A Rosenberg, "The 'Star of the Messiah' Reconsidered," *Biblica* 53 (1972): 8.

[17] Ernest L. Martin, *The Star That Astonished the World* (Portland, Oregon: Ask Publications, 1991).

[18] Hughes, "The Magi's Worship," condensed from p.27.

On top of the fact that these various theories don't hold water, there is still something vaguely dissatisfying about the idea that a God who in the Old Testament was described as totally transcendent, even "wholly other," should be preceded by a typical astronomical phenomenon — even if that phenomenon were relatively rare. The way that the Magi episode was presented in the Bible made it sound as if the appearance of this Star itself was of absolutely Earth-shattering importance. This was no ordinary comet or conjunction of planets; the Star that heralded the birth of Christ was, like the one whom it heralded, "wholly other."

A NEW THEORY ON THE STAR OF BETHLEHEM: A TENTH PLANET
During the school year 1988–89, while I was working on my undergraduate degree at Southern Illinois University, I became powerfully overcome by the feeling that something great was to happen in my lifetime, that Christ was going to return soon and that I should set aside my own personal agenda and priorities and instead put a priority on looking for signs of His return. As I studied the Scriptures concerning what sort of signs would precede His return, I came across Matthew chapter 24, the "Olivet Discourse," in which Jesus' disciples asked Him this very same question: "'Tell us,' they said, 'when will this happen, and what will be the Sign of your coming

and of the end of the age?'" (Matt. 24:3). He answered their question saying that, at the climax of many awesome and terrible events, many of which involved "signs and wonders" in the heavens, His "Sign" would appear in heaven, a Sign that would bring great terror to His enemies. For some reason, in my mind I automatically equated the Sign that would precede Christ's second advent with the Sign that preceded His first advent: the Star of Bethlehem. It just seemed logical that the same Christ would not be heralded by two different, unrelated, heavenly signs.

I then started to keep a regular watch on the night sky, hoping to see something that might be this Sign. As I kept my nightly vigil, I often wondered at how the Sign could appear more than once, even though each of its two known appearances would be separated by at least 2,000 years. No star or known planet fit this description, and comets were too common to be equated with this unique Star. One night I noticed one unusually bright star, a planet, and decided to track its movements to see whether it was one of the known planets or perhaps some other phenomenon which would prove to be the Sign I sought. I tracked and recorded its movements over a period of months, checked its apparent motion with that of known planets, and was disappointed to find that it was actually the planet Jupiter. However, as a result of having studied Jupiter's apparent motion against the fixed background stars, I learned a fair amount about basic planetary motion. I later took a class in astronomy, and spent much of my free time in astronomical research trying to find the answer to the Star of Bethlehem/Sign of the Son of Man enigma. Near the end of my search I accidentally stumbled upon some material that later proved to be the nucleus for a revolutionary new understanding of the Star of Bethlehem event.[19]

The Star of Bethlehem account in Matthew 2 has always intrigued me. It intrigues me that Jesus could be represented by some sort of heavenly Sign. Surely this Sign, in order to represent the very Son of God, must be, like He whom it proclaims, truly exceptional. This must be a Sign *par excellence,* a Sign without equal. No mere comet or predictable conjunction of planets could proclaim the birth of the King of the Universe. Furthermore, it seems proper that the Sign that heralded Jesus' first advent should naturally be the same object that

---

[19]Though I disagree with many of his conclusions, there can be no doubt that Zechariah Sitchin's revolutionary book, *The 12th Planet,* laid the foundations upon which the core premise of this book is based.

will herald His second advent. It just doesn't seem fitting that the same LORD would signify each of His two advents with two different Signs. These assumptions, confirmed by my research into ancient Near Eastern religion, modern astronomy, and the Bible that can be found throughout this volume, allow me to state with confidence that the Star of Bethlehem should be considered the same heavenly body as the "Sign of the Son of Man," mentioned in Matthew 24:29-31:

> Immediately after the tribulation of those days shall the Sun be darkened, and the Moon shall not give her light, and the stars shall fall from heaven, and the powers of the heavens shall be shaken: *then shall appear the sign of the Son of man in heaven*: and then shall all the tribes of the earth mourn, and they shall see the Son of man coming in the clouds of heaven with power and great glory. And he shall send his angels with a great sound of a trumpet, and they shall gather together his elect from the four winds, from one end of heaven to the other. (Matt. 24:29-31, KJV, emphasis mine.)

The Sign of His return, as it is described here, seems to be associated with highly destructive forces, forces powerful enough to rock the planets — particularly Earth. However, it is not clear whether it is responsible for these forces, or simply accompanies them. Let us presume, however, for the sake of argument, that this Sign might actually be the *cause* of these terrible disasters. If we are willing to assume this, along with the proposition that the Star of Bethlehem and the Sign of the Son of Man are indeed one and the same object, then this Sign must have the following basic characteristics, based upon the data to be found in the Bible:

- It is unusually bright upon its appearance, brighter than all the heavenly bodies, save the Sun and the Moon;
- It apparently moves independently of the background stars (Matt. 2:9), indicating it must be a planet or similar body;
- It remains visible for at least the amount of time it took the Magi to travel from Persia to Palestine, which was probably at least three months. It is therefore not a brief phenomenon like a nova, a comet, or a conjunction of planets;
- It comes and goes in a cyclical manner like a planet, explaining why it can appear more than once;

- ✞ It is capable of shaking the "powers of the heavens," i.e., alter the orbital paths of the planets;
- ✞ It is capable of causing the Sun and Moon to turn dark;
- ✞ It is capable of inflicting lightning, earthquakes, and intense meteoric activity ("stars" falling from heaven) upon Earth.

It is clear that only a planet-sized object could account for all of these anomalies — perhaps a tenth planet that lurks on the fringes of our solar system, intruding into our system occasionally to wreak havoc on the outer planets, and possibly even Earth itself. Could an unknown tenth planet, a "Planet X", be the answer to this mystery of mysteries?

Though I am intrigued by Matthew's account of the mysterious "Star" that heralded Christ's birth, I am even more intrigued by the possibility that this "Star" will return sometime in the future to herald the *Second Coming* of Christ, bringing with it great disaster for those who are not prepared. My search to understand what this Star/Sign is, however, has been far from easy. In order to fully understand what exactly this mysterious "Planet X" is and how it came into being, I found my research diversifying into many different subcategories of astronomy — in particular, theories on how our solar system was created.

In the Beginning: The Creation of Our Solar System

Astronomers have, in their investigation of star-formation processes, come up with a working theory on how stars like our Sun form. It is currently believed that stars like our Sun form from a large cloud of gas and dust called a "nebula."[20] This nebula, at first huge and shapeless, begins to shrink, collapsing in on itself because the molecules of gas and grains of dust in the nebula are attracted to each other by a sort of cumulative gravity. As it collapses, however, the infalling material is met with resistance from the material at the center of the cloud. As a result, the energy of the infalling material is vectored away from the center of the cloud, causing the whole of the cloud to rotate. The centrifugal force from this rotation then causes some of the material to flow outward from the central mass of the cloud, causing the nebula to take on the appearance of a flattened disk with a central bulge. It is in this flattened disk that the planets form. While the disk forms, the central mass of the nebula continues to collapse until the heat and pressure from the inrushing elements becomes so great that fusion reactions begin at its center. When this occurs, the rest of the central mass then quickly ignites and a star, like our Sun, is born. The remnants of the disk are then blown away by the blast, halting the formation of the planets.

There is solid evidence to confirm this theory of stellar formation. With the advent of the latest generation of optical and radio telescopes, astronomers have been able to deduce how our solar system formed by studying the formation of other solar systems. As William Kaufmann explains in his classic astronomy textbook, *Universe*, "By observing the process of star formation elsewhere in our galaxy, astronomers can deduce the conditions that led to the formation of our own solar system."[21] This new data has come in from such sources such as the Hubble Space Telescope and the Very Large Array (VLA), both of which are able to overcome the limitations of standard optical telescopes:

---

[20]For more on the early formation of planetesimals from dust, see Bennett Daviss, "Dust Demon: Physicist David Peak has Big Plans for Small Dust Balls," *Discover*, March 1992, 114–15. Peak's experiments show that the early collections of dust formed in basically the same way dust balls do under one's bed. After a while these dust balls grew larger and larger, until they began to compress into denser, rockier materials due to the great weight of their combined mass, forming protoplanets. "In theory, at least, it's a short step from a miles-wide dust bunny to an embryonic planet" (p.116).

[21]William J. Kaufmann III., *Universe*, 2d ed. (New York: W.H. Freeman and Company, 1968), 136. For a nice overview of the current understanding of how our solar system was formed, see Douglas N.C. Lin, "The Chaotic Genesis of Planets," *Scientific American*, https://www.scientificamerican.com/slideshow.cfm?id=the-genesis-of-planets

Turning the Hubble Space Telescope toward the Orion Nebula, astronomers have discovered and photographed fifteen infant stars surrounded by dense, flattened disks of dust. These images provide the strongest evidence to date, they say, that many young stars develop the dust rings required for planet formation. The presence of such a large number of protoplanetary disks in the Orion Nebula — a typical gaseous, star-forming region in the constellation Orion — suggests that many suns besides our own possess the ability to evolve planets, according to C. Robert O'Dell of Rice University in Houston, who led the imaging project.[22]

Though not all stars develop these planet-forming disks of dust and gas, enough of them do that astronomers are confident they may begin finding planets revolving around other stars in our galaxy. The most definitive evidence for this theory has come from a group of astronomers who have found what they believe to be planets revolving around a dead star, a pulsar. "In April [1994], radio astronomers said new observations confirmed the existence of two and possibly three large planets around a pulsar, the spinning remnant of an exploded star. This was generally regarded as the first definitive evidence of planets around stars other than the Sun."[23]

Thus, according to the nebular hypothesis, our solar system was basically formed out of a mass of gas and dust. Kaufmann explains the process in detail: "Initially, the solar nebula was quite cold. Temperatures throughout the cloud were probably less than 50 K [50 degrees on the Kelvin scale, 0 being absolute zero]. Snowflakes and ice-coated dust grains must have been scattered abundantly across the solar nebula."[24] These icy particles then began to gain heat and momentum as they came closer and closer together through gravitational attraction.

> The gravitational pull of the particles in the solar nebula on one another caused them to begin a general drift toward the center of the solar nebula. Density and pressure at the center of the solar

---

[22]D. Pendick, "Hubble Scopes Possible Planet-Forming Disks," *Science News* 142 (Dec. 19 & 26, 1992): 421.

[23]John Noble Wilford, "Stellar Nursery May Spawn Planets," *The New York Times*, no date, 1994, C1.

[24]Kaufmann, *Universe*, 137–38.

nebula began to increase, producing a concentration of matter called the *protosun*. Because of gravitational attraction, temperatures deep inside the solar nebula began to climb.... Temperatures around the newly created protosun soon climbed to 2,000 K.[25]

The majority of the materials coalesced in the center of the nebula, causing our Sun to ignite when the pressure from the inrushing materials was great enough to start fusion reactions. Meanwhile, the heavier, rocky materials had begun to coalesce in the part of the solar disk nearest the Sun. As Nigel Henbest explains in his article, "The Birth of the Planets," "The smaller solid worlds were built up from microscopic, solid grains...fragments of rock, carbon, and ices, generally less than a micrometer across."[26] These primarily rocky worlds would become the inner, terrestrial planets Mercury, Venus, Earth, and Mars.

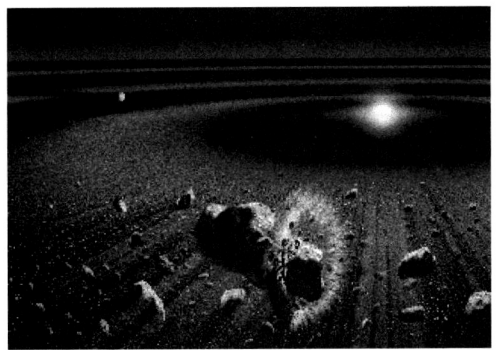

Early in the formation of our solar system, the dust from the nebular cloud gathered into small "dust bunnies" which over time accreted into small rocks. These small rocks over time combined into large rocks, which crashed into and combined with each other to eventually form the rocky inner planets we know today. The outer, "gas giants" were formed via a similar, though less destructive, process.
Illustration courtesy Kouji KANBA.

The formation of the four inner planets was dominated by the fusing together of solid, rocky particles. Initially neighboring dust grains and pebbles in the solar nebula collided and stuck together by electrostatic or gravitational forces.... These accumulations of dust and pebbles continued to coalesce into objects called *planetesimals*.... During the next stage, the gravitational attraction

---

[25]Kaufmann, 136.
[26]Nigel Henbest, "The Birth of the Planets," *New Scientist* 24 (August 1991): 30.

between the planetesimals caused them to collide and coalesce into still larger objects called *protoplanets*.[27]

As Kaufmann explains, these small fragments continued to crash and clump together violently, becoming larger and larger bodies called "planetesimals" until, like a snowball rolling down a hill, a single, massive body was formed. The lighter, gaseous materials further out on the solar disk then quickly coalesced to form the gas giants Jupiter, Saturn, Uranus, and Neptune. The reason the inner planets are primarily rock is due to their proximity to the Sun. The heat of the Sun and the force of the solar wind drove most of the lighter, more volatile gases into the outer solar system, leaving the heavier, rockier materials behind. "In the inner region of the disk around the young Sun — out to the present orbit of Jupiter — the gas became hot enough to boil away ice. As a result,
the planets that formed closest to the Sun are mainly rock, while the bodies in the outer part of the solar system are largely ice or water (along with hydrogen and helium captured from the gaseous disk)."[28]

Though astronomers are now generally in agreement about the processes involved in the formation of the planets, why the planets formed at their present distances from the Sun has been a matter of controversy for some time.

Bode's Law

The controversy concerning why the planets formed at certain distances from the Sun began in 1766, when the Prussian astronomer Johann Daniel Titius discovered a mathematical formula that he believed could be used to predict the positions of yet-to-be-discovered planets in our solar system.[29] During his time, no one knew of the existence of any planets beyond Saturn. Neptune was first officially discovered by accident in 1781 by William Herschel, but telescopes able to view Neptune and Pluto would not be available for nearly a century. And even if the astronomers of the eighteenth century *did* have access to telescopes powerful enough to see Neptune and Pluto, they would not have known where to look for them without some sort

---

[27]Kaufmann, *Universe*, 136.

[28]Henbest, "The Birth of the Planets," 33.

[29]Robert Matthews, "The Ghostly Hand That Spaced the Planets," *New Scientist* (9 April 1994): 13.

The Star of Bethlehem: A Tenth Planet?

Johannes Bode, 1747-1826. Bode was the German astronomer and Director of the Observatory of Berlin who published the famous equation now known as Bode's Law, that was created in order to predict the positions of planets further out than Saturn, the furthest known planet at that time.

of reference point. Thus, Titius' mathematical formula provided the first step in the search that culminated in the discovery of Neptune and, eventually, Pluto.

Titius' formula was also promoted by one of his contemporaries, a scientist by the name of Johannes Bode, and later erroneously came to be known as "Bode's Law." Titius' formula, more commonly known now as "Titius-Bode's Law," goes something like this:

✣ Write down the sequence of numbers 0, 3, 6, 12, 24, 48, 96 (Note that each number after the second one is simply twice the preceding number.)

✣ Add 4 to each number in the sequence.

✣ Divide each of the resulting numbers by 10.

The final result is a series of numbers that corresponds remarkably well with the distances of most of the planets from the Sun. (Note: The term "A.U." stands for "astronomical unit," a basic unit of measure used by astronomers equal to the mean distance between Earth and the Sun.)

Table 3.1: Bode's Progression Compared to Actual Distances of the Planets from the Sun[30]

Planet:	Bode's Progression:	Actual Distance: (A.U.)
Mercury	(0+4)/10 = 0.4	0.39
Venus	(3+4)/10 = 0.7	0.72
Earth	(6+4)/10 = 1.0	1.00

---

[30] Text and table from Kaufmann, *Universe*, 321.

Mars	(12+4)/10 = 1.6	1.52
(Asteroid Belt)	(24+4)/10 = 2.8	(2.75)
Jupiter	(48+4)/10 = 5.2	5.20
Saturn	(96+4)/10 = 10	9.54
Uranus	(192+4)/10 = 19.6	19.18
Neptune	(384+4)/10 = 38.8	30.06
Pluto	(768 + 4)/10 = 77.2	39.44

As you can see, the numbers correspond remarkably well, with three major exceptions. One of the major problems with Titius-Bode's Law at its inception was the fact that there was no known planet between Mars and Jupiter, though the theory predicted that there should be one there, at 2.8 A.U. In order to confirm the validity of his theory, Bode convinced a group of astronomers to help him search for the missing planet between Mars and Jupiter. And after only a few years of searching, they found something. "Five years later it turned up: the 'minor planet' Ceres, 1,000 kilometers across and orbiting at 2.8 astronomical units from the Sun — just where the Titius-Bode Law had predicted."[31] Yet, though Ceres fit into Bode's calculations perfectly, it did not qualify as a planet, because it was too small.

However, in 1802, a year after Ceres was discovered, another object was found. This object, named "Pallas" by its discoverer, had a mean distance from the Sun which was close to that of Ceres — 2.77 A.U. Because both of these objects were far too small to be planets, astronomers began to speculate that they were perhaps the remnants of a shattered planet that had once orbited at around 2.8 A.U. "The discovery of two small objects with similar orbits at the distance expected for the missing planet led astronomers to suspect that Bode's missing planet might have somehow broken apart or exploded."[32] Over the course of the nineteenth century, as telescopes and techniques improved, astronomers following up on these initial discoveries found

---

[31] Matthews, "The Ghostly Hand," 13.
[32] Kaufmann, *Universe*, 322.

more and more minor objects orbiting at around 2.8 A.U. These discoveries accumulated in number until today more than 20,000 objects have been discovered orbiting at around 2.8 A.U., over 3,000 of which are officially confirmed.[33] These objects, or "asteroids," make up what is today known as the "asteroid belt."

Though these discoveries seemed to confirm Titius-Bode's Law, more problems arose upon the discovery of the planets Neptune and Pluto. Though all of the other planets from Mercury to Uranus appeared to have been accounted for by Titius and Bode's calculations, the orbits of both Neptune (discovered in 1842) and Pluto (1930) did not. As a result, "Bode's Law" is now considered to be an interesting, but flawed, formula. Currently, the most popular explanation for the apparent deviations in the orbits of Neptune and Pluto is that a planet-sized object had, at some time in the primeval past, invaded our solar system and disturbed their orbits. Passing near Neptune, according to this theory, that rogue planet ripped one of Neptune's satellites out of its orbit and set it in an independent orbit around the Sun, a satellite that we now know as the planet Pluto.[34] If such a planet exists, it is also possible that it may have been responsible for the destruction of the planet that is missing from the sequence at 2.8 A.U., the only known remnant of which is the asteroid belt.

The intrusion of a planet-sized object into our solar system would explain many of its otherwise unexplainable eccentricities. Our solar system should, theoretically, be well-balanced and orderly, without any significant anomalies. However, our solar system actually displays numerous eccentricities for which astronomers have yet to find an explanation. I believe that these numerous eccentricities in our solar system can best be explained by the existence of a planet-sized object, the orbit of which regularly brings it into conflict with many of the planets. If such a planet exists, it could be the answer to some of the more enigmatic passages in the Bible concerning heavenly signs and wonders, particularly those dealing with the Creation, Nativity, and Second Coming. If such a planet exists, it would be the perfect candidate to fit the role of both the "mighty wind" God used to create

---

[33] "3,000 Asteroids and Still Counting." *Sky and Telescope* 68, November 1984, 412; Kaufmann, *Universe,* 323. As of 2010, hundreds of thousands of asteroids have been catalogued, and millions more are believed to exist. For more information, see http://en.wikipedia.org/wiki/Asteroid_belt.

[34] This near collision with Neptune may have also caused Neptune's orbit to shift, explaining its deviation from Bode's Law, but there is not enough evidence to confirm this.

the Earth, the "Star of Bethlehem" that He used to herald the first coming of His Son Jesus, and the "Sign of the Son of Man" which will herald His Second Coming. This theoretical "tenth planet," has actually been the subject of an intensive search by leading astronomers for over a century which, for lack of a better name, they have named "Planet X."

Planet X

Ever since the discovery of Neptune in 1846, astronomers have hunted for yet more planets beyond. The hunt for "trans-Neptunian" planets, planets with orbits beyond Neptune, became particularly intense after evidence was uncovered that pointed to the possible existence of yet another planet beyond Neptune. This evidence was stumbled upon indirectly when astronomers, studying the orbits of the planets Uranus and Neptune, noted that these planets appeared to be moving erratically. When astronomers attempted to observe them, they found that Uranus and Neptune actually appeared to be several arc seconds[35] away from where the astronomers' calculations said they were supposed to be in the sky. Astronomers need to calculate the positions of the planets they want to observe very carefully, because

In 2008, a group of Japanese scientists re-raised the possibility of the existence of a "Planet X" beyond Pluto, theorizing that it has a 1,000-year, elliptical orbit. Image courtesy Cosmos magazine/Kobe University, cosmosmagazine.com/node/1874

their powerful telescopes focus on a very small part of the sky. So, if their calculations are even slightly off, they may have difficulty finding the planet they want to view. Therefore, since Uranus and Neptune were not showing up at the exact points in the sky the astronomers'

---

[35]The heavens are mapped according to longitudinal and latitudinal lines, just as Earth's surface is. There are 360 latitudinal and longitudinal divisions, measured in "degrees," which can be further divided into 60 arc "minutes." These minutes can also be further divided into 60 arc "seconds," which are 1/3,600 of a degree each. An arc second seems to be a relatively small amount of area, but when dealing with such a vast area as space, an entire galaxy could easily fit into an arc second, depending on its distance. This is true even with relatively small, nearby objects, such as planets in our solar system.

calculations said they would, they could conclude only one of two things: either their calculations were flawed, or there was yet another planet even farther out in the solar system whose gravitational pull was affecting the orbits of Uranus and Neptune. After verifying the accuracy of their calculations, they were forced to conclude that there must be another planet in our solar system that orbits beyond Neptune. Thus the race to find this mystery planet, this "Planet X," was on.

The most famous researcher in the quest for Planet X is an astronomer by the name of Clyde Tombaugh. Tombaugh, who grew up on farms in Kansas and Illinois, had developed an interest in astronomy, ancient history, the Bible, and other, related disciplines from an early age. He had a brilliant mind which was constantly in motion. Levy explains, "Clyde's mind was always so active that he had no trouble keeping it occupied.... For instance, one day after farm work he calculated the number of cubic inches in Betelguese, the bright star on Orion's east flank: his solution was 1 duodecillion (39 zeroes)."[36]

> Early in high school Tombaugh took a course in general science that included both physical and biological studies. As a freshman he also developed an interest in ancient history. He read voraciously, continuing his daytime reading into the night with an old kerosene lamp. At first he concentrated on two books, the Bible and an encyclopedia. He read the entire Bible, a considerable feat for a young person who read it more out of sheer interest than from deep religious feelings. Eventually he studied his father's books on trigonometry and physics and even learned a little Latin and Greek. Not all Tombaugh's leisure hours were spent reading, just most of them. He carried this enthusiasm throughout his life, devouring books, underlining passages, and writing marginal notes.[37]

Tombaugh, growing tired of the farm routine, wrote a letter in 1929 to the Lowell Observatory in Flagstaff, Arizona asking for information about how he could go about becoming an astronomer. To his surprise, they gave him an offer for a job helping in what turned out to be a search for planets beyond Neptune — more specifically, for a mysterious planet they called "Planet X" whose gravitational influence, they

---

[36]David H. Levy, *Clyde Tombaugh: Discoverer of Planet Pluto* (Tucson: The University of Arizona Press, 1991), 21.

[37]Levy, *Clyde Tombaugh,* 17–18.

believed, was responsible for the perceived deviations in the orbits of Uranus and Neptune. His job was to make a systematic, comprehensive search of the heavens for Planet X with a device called a "blink comparator." Tombaugh was to use a telescope-mounted camera to take two separate pictures of the same area of the sky at different times, which he would then overlay and compare using this blink comparator. Since the background stars were too far away to change position due to parallax, any relatively close objects, such as unknown planets in our solar system, would appear to shift position from one plate to the other relative to the background stars. As Tombaugh explains,

Famed astronomer Clyde Tombaugh using a "blink comparator" at the Lowell Observatory in Flagstaff, Arizona to search for the elusive Planet X. By comparing numerous photographs taken of the night sky at different times he finally discovered in 1930 what he hoped would be the elusive Planet X. Unfortunately, it turned out to be a minor planet that we now know as "Pluto", so the hunt for Planet X continues. http://en.wikipedia.org/wiki/Clyde_Tombaugh

> I started hunting for a planet beyond Neptune in 1929 at Lowell Observatory in Flagstaff, Arizona. The task required taking pairs of photographic plates with the thirteen-inch Lawrence Lowell Telescope (now called the Pluto Telescope) and examining them with a blink-microscope comparator. It was in this way that I found Pluto the next year, in 1930.[38]

To everyone's surprise, Tombaugh found a planet — Pluto — after only a year of searching. It was at first assumed to be the mysterious "Planet X," but later observations proved Pluto to be far too small and its gravitational field far too weak to have any significant effect on the orbits of Uranus and Neptune. So, the search for Planet X continued. Tombaugh searched for Planet X for another thirteen years, but never found it. "By July of 1943 he had photographed the entire sky visible from Flagstaff, from Canopus to Polaris.... His final tally of individual stars photographed and blinked numbered 45 million — 90 million

---

[38]Clyde W. Tombaugh, "Plates, Pluto, and Planets X," *Sky and Telescope,* April 1991, 360.

paired images. He had spent 7,000 hours at the blink microscope...."[39] Tombaugh's search for other planets then ended in 1943 as he was drafted into the Navy.

The search continued on, however, headed up by a number of established astronomers who were convinced that Planet X indeed exists. These included, among others, Thomas C. Van Flandern and Robert S. Harrington of the U.S. Naval Observatory, Daniel P. Whitmire and John J. Matese of the University of Southern Louisiana, John D. Anderson at NASA's Jet Propulsion Laboratory, and Conley Powell of Teledyne-Brown Engineering. Ken Croswell, an astronomer and prolific writer on the subject of Planet X, neatly summarized our understanding of the outer edge of our solar system around the end of the 1980s:

> All is not well with these remote planets. "I think there is something affecting our observations of the outer solar system," says Kenneth Seidelmann of the U.S. Naval Observatory in Washington D.C. Seidelmann used to be able to blame the deviations in the motions of Uranus and Neptune on another distant object — Pluto. Ten years ago, however, scientists discovered the startling truth: Pluto is actually five hundred times less massive than Earth, much too tiny to perturb either Uranus or Neptune. Yet discrepancies in the motions of Uranus and Neptune persist, which causes some astronomers to search for an unseen "Planet X" that lies far beyond Pluto.[40]

However, there were other astronomers, such as Myles Standish of NASA's Jet Propulsion Laboratory, who disbelieved the "Planet X" theory. They felt that the inconsistencies in the orbits of Uranus and Neptune were not due to the gravitational pull of a "Planet X" beyond Pluto, but rather to errors in previous observations of Uranus and Neptune, which may have caused astronomers to miscalculate their orbits. "They believe that any remaining inconsistencies come from the measuring process itself."[41] Since the calculations for the orbits of these planets are based partly on data that was gathered around the turn of the century, the possibility exists that the less accurate

---

[39]Mark Littman, *Planets Beyond: Discovering the Outer Solar System* (New York: John Wiley and Sons, 1990), 196.

[40]Ken Croswell, "The Pull of Planet X," *Astronomy*, August 1988, 30.

[41]Gail S. Cleere, "Planet X," *Natural History*, June 1993, 62.

equipment in use at that time may have resulted in readings flawed compared to modern standards. In order to check this possibility, Standish checked the original records of the observations of these planets, and found what he believes to be errors in the measurements of their orbits. "Hidden in ninety-year-old records of the U.S. Naval Observatory, Standish found errors in the observation of Uranus' orbit. From his research he concludes that the planetary wobbles were more likely the artifact of human fallibility than heavenly cause."[42] Standish has also analyzed data on Neptune collected by the *Voyager* space probe which recorded the mass of Neptune as being slightly higher than previous estimates. "It turns out, Standish says, that 'previous estimates were too high by about one-half-of-one-percent.' Neptune's mystery mass is an important clue in the search for Planet X, because once its updated mass is accounted for, the anomaly in the orbit of Uranus largely disappears."[43]

Another possible problem with the Planet X hypothesis is that not one of the *Pioneer* probes have ever detected any gravitational changes that would point to the existence of a tenth planet. *Pioneer 10*, for example, has reached 50 A.U. from the Sun, and still has not detected any gravitational tugs which could indicate the existence of Planet X. "According to [John] Anderson, minute Doppler shifts in *Pioneer*'s feeble signal should betray any tugs of gravity. 'If there are any unmodeled forces extraneous to known gravitational sources,' says Anderson, 'they would show up as small perturbations in the trajectories.' "[44]

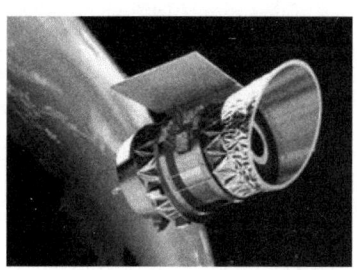

The IRAS (InfraRed Astronomical Satellite) was designed to map the entire heavens in infrared light in order to determine if there are any objects, including unknown planets in our solar system that may only be visible via infrared light. Image courtesy NASA/JPL.

Another attempt to locate Planet X, the Infrared Astronomical Satellite (IRAS), has met with mixed results:

> On January 25, 1983, NASA launched the Infrared Astronomical Satellite (IRAS), a joint endeavor by the United States, the

---

[42]John Kross, "Planet X: Will X Ever Mark the Spot?" *Ad Astra*, Sept./Oct. 1993, 47.
[43]Kross, 47.
[44]Kross, 48.

Netherlands, and Great Britain. Scientists realized that this 22-inch (57-centimeter) telescope with infrared sensors would have a reasonable chance of detecting a tenth planet if it exists. A distant planet would receive and reflect very little sunlight and therefore be hard to find with optical telescopes and photography. But the meager energy it absorbed from the Sun and converted to heat could make this planet stand out clearly in infrared wavelengths.[45]

One of the reasons that IRAS was launched was because it was believed that Planet X either has a "low reflectivity or [is] located deep in the southern sky,"[46] which would explain why Tombaugh's visual search had missed it. Unfortunately, the IRAS project has, as yet, not found Planet X. "The Infrared Astronomical Satellite (IRAS) launched in 1983 was expected to be an excellent search instrument for such cool, distant bodies. However, careful examination of the IRAS data so far has turned up nothing."[47] This is not to say that Planet X does not exist, however, simply that the IRAS data so far had not revealed its position. IRAS would have detected Planet X. The problem probably

---

[45]Littman, *Planets Beyond,* 207.

[46]Littman, *Planets Beyond,* 203.

[47]Paul R. Weissman, "Are Periodic Bombardments Real?" *Sky & Telescope,* March 1990, 266. Some researchers feel that Planet X *was* detected by IRAS, but that its discovery was quickly covered up for reasons of national security. This belief is based on a *Washington Post* story ("Mystery Heavenly Body Discovered," Dec. 31, 1983, p.1) that explained that IRAS had, in fact, found something, and that something, some speculate, may pose a very real threat to Earth: "A heavenly body possibly as large as the giant planet Jupiter and possibly so close to Earth that it would be part of this solar system has been found in the direction of the constellation Orion by an orbiting telescope aboard the U.S. infrared astronomical satellite [IRAS]. So mysterious is the object that astronomers do not know if it is a planet, a giant comet, a nearby 'protostar' that never got hot enough to be a star, a distant galaxy so young that it is still in the process of forming its first stars, or a galaxy so shrouded in dust that none of the light cast by its stars ever gets through.... The most fascinating explanation of this mystery body, which is so cold it casts no light and has never been seen by optical telescopes on Earth or in space, is that it is a giant gaseous planet, as large as Jupiter and as close to Earth as 50 billion miles [over 500 A.U.]." This story was never followed up, however, and the information was quietly buried. This of course only fueled speculation as to whether this object was in fact the mysterious Planet X, and whether or not it presents a threat to Earth, particularly since soon after its discovery NASA scientists had speculated that it might in fact be headed toward Earth. NASA's vagueness as to the planet's size and distance leave plenty of room for speculation concerning this object's size, orbital characteristics, and distance from Earth, which will be discussed in depth in this and the following chapters.

lies in the fact that not all the IRAS data has been analyzed. For example, the scientists who analyzed the data, Thomas J. Chester and Michael Melnyk of the Jet Propulsion Laboratory, significantly narrowed their search parameters in order to expedite the search. Because they had to sift through over 600,000 objects, they concentrated on those parts of the heavens with the fewest stars. As of 1990, however, they had covered only one-tenth of the sky, and hadn't even begun to search in the plane of the Milky Way Galaxy, where the stars are most concentrated. Furthermore, it appears that much of the sky may never be searched. "The unsearched sky remaining [includes] the Milky Way, where the stars are so numerous that a complete search of the IRAS data performed by human beings would be so lengthy and tedious it would be impractical."[48] Thus the IRAS data as yet cannot be relied upon to either support or deny the existence of a tenth planet.

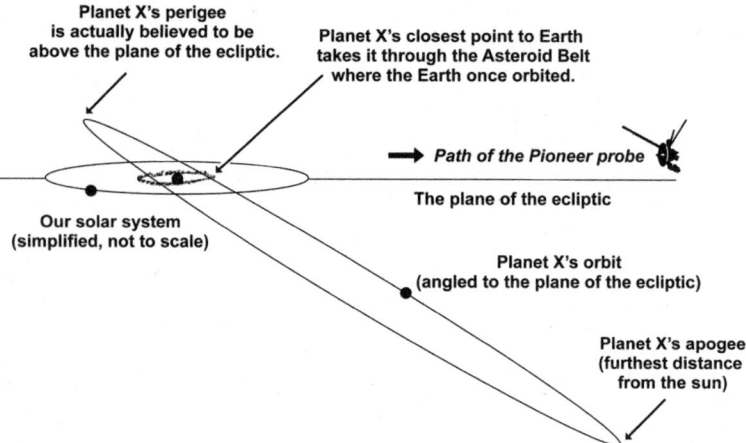

Figure 3.1. The Pioneer's failure to detect Planet X does not negate the possibility of its existence, as some astronomers, such as Robert Harrington, have theorized that Planet X's orbit is actually highly inclined to the ecliptic, and thus undetectable by the Pioneer probes, that remained in the planet of the ecliptic.

Robert S. Harrington of the U.S. Naval Observatory, however, remains undaunted by attempts to debunk the Planet X theory. Harrington's calculations for the size and orbit of Planet X place it far from the

---

[48]Littman, *Planets Beyond,* 213.

Pioneer probes, so they cannot detect its gravitational pull. As Croswell explains, "Although Harrington acknowledges that the deviations in Uranus and Neptune could be spurious, he is not worried about the negative results from the *Pioneer* spacecraft. Neither *Pioneer 10* nor *Pioneer 11* traveled near Harrington's Planet X, so neither should feel its gravitational pull. In fact, Harrington predicted negative results from the *Pioneer* data even before it was analyzed."[49] (See Figure 3.1.)

Another leader in the search for Planet X, John Anderson of the Jet Propulsion Laboratory, has also dismissed the naysayers, particularly Myles Standish and his negative assessment of the orbital perturbations of Uranus and Neptune.

> Anderson had confidence in almost all the observational data — new and old. He therefore concluded that an unseen outer planet had been disturbing Uranus and Neptune before and during the nineteenth century but that the planet was now too far away for its gravitational effects to be noticeable on the planets or even on the two tiny and distant *Pioneer* craft. Thus Planet 10, he surmised, must have a highly elliptical orbit that carries it far enough away to be undetectable now but periodically brings it close enough to leave its disturbing signature on the paths of the outer planets. He put the orbital period at 700 to 1,000 years. The suspect planet also had to have a highly inclined orbit so as to have produced no detectable deflection of either of the *Pioneers*. Finally, to create the planet perturbations reported in the Naval Observatory data, he concluded that the planet must have a mass of about five Earths.[50]

Harrington and Van Flandern's Planet X also has a highly elliptical orbit which takes it well outside of the known solar system and thus well away from the *Pioneer* probes. "A circular orbit beyond Neptune would have been detected by *Pioneer*...advancing the theory that the unknown planet has a highly eccentric orbit. This is consistent with other irregular orbits at the extreme edge of the solar system, such as that of Pluto and Triton's orbit around Neptune."[51]

---

[49]Ken Croswell, "The Hunt for Planet X," *New Scientist* 22 (29 Dec. 1990): 37.
[50]Littman, *Planets Beyond,* 204.
[51]"Pioneer Data Support Theory of Tenth Planet," *Aviation Week,* 6 July 1987.

The majority opinion on Planet X is that it is significantly different than most of the other planets because its orbit is highly elliptical and, some believe, at an angle to the ecliptic. Furthermore, most believe that it is a fairly massive body, and that its orbit is so large and elongated that the planet actually leaves our solar system for many centuries at a time. "'We keep coming up with masses on the order of two to five earths,' says Harrington. Planet X is therefore intermediate in mass between the largest inner planet — Earth — and the smallest outer planets — Uranus and Neptune. Most estimates place the planet at a distance between 50 and 100 A.U. from the Sun, which gives Planet X an orbital period between 350 and 1000 years."[52]

Table 3.1: Comparison of Leading Planet X Theories

Theorist	Evidence for Planet X	Mass (Compared to Earth's)	Shape of Orbit	Orbital Period	Max. Distance from Sun
Thomas C. Van Flandern (U.S. Naval Observatory)	Perturbations in orbits of Uranus and Neptune; problems with Neptunian system indicate near-collision with large object; Pluto once satellite of Neptune.	2 to 5 times greater	Highly elliptical, inclined to ecliptic	Around 800 years	50 to 100 A.U.
Robert S. Harrington (U.S. Naval Observatory)	As above.	2 to 5 times greater	Highly elliptical, inclined to ecliptic	Around 800 years	50 to 100 A.U.
John D. Anderson (Jet Propulsion Laboratory)	Perturbations in orbits of Uranus and Neptune point to a tenth planet; *Pioneer* data irrelevant	5 times greater	Highly elliptical, inclined to ecliptic	700 to 1,000 years	Unknown

---

[52]Croswell, "The Pull of Planet X," 38. Cf. also 2 Peter 3:8: "But, beloved, be not ignorant of this one thing, that one day is with the Lord as a thousand years, and a thousand years as one day."

Daniel P. Whitmire & John J. Matese (University of Southwest Louisiana)	Comets are taken from a cloud of icy materials just outside our solar system (the "Oort Cloud") and thrown into our solar system occasionally by Planet X.	Up to 5 times greater	Highly elliptical, inclined about 45 degrees; precesses over time, changing angle to ecliptic	700 years	80 A.U.
Conley Powell (Teledyne-Brown Engineering)	Analysis focusing on more recent (and more accurate) data on perturbations in orbit of Uranus	2.9 times greater	Somewhat elliptical, inclined by 8.3 degrees	494 years	60.8 A.U.

Planet X has so intrigued astronomers that some have jokingly put out a "wanted" notice for this mysterious planet:

WANTED on cosmic charges:
- Disturbing the motion of Uranus and Neptune
- Smuggling short-period comets (like Halley's) into the inner solar system[53]
- Suspected of trespassing at Neptune, driving Triton and Nereid berserk, and kidnapping Pluto.
- Repeated assaults on Earth with deadly comets, causing periodic mass extinctions of life.

DESCRIPTION of fugitive: One to five Earth masses; eccentric, with odd inclination; likes to leave subtle clues to tantalize astronomers; lives in trans-Plutonia, constantly on move, no known address, might repeat movements every 700 years; knows how to hide.[54]

---

[53]This particular point reflects a currently held view that there is a cloud of comets surrounding our solar system called the "Oort Cloud," from which this theoretical planet occasionally brings comets into our solar system through gravitational attraction.

[54]Littman, *Planets Beyond,* 203.

PLANET X: THE EVIDENCE

My initial search into evidence for the existence of a tenth planet was based solely on the apparent delays in the orbits of Uranus and Neptune. However, as my research went deeper and deeper, it quickly became clear that the mountain of suspicious clues in our solar system could only be explained by the existence of a tenth planet of the kind hypothesized by leading astronomers.

There are, specifically, ten clues that point to the existence of a tenth planet in our solar system. The first two of these ten clues have already been suggested by mainstream astronomers. However, clues three through ten are my own invention, based on the theory that Planet X's elliptical orbit actually takes it far into our solar system, possibly as far as what is now the asteroid belt. Evidence suggests that on one of its journeys into the inner solar system, Planet X passed near the primordial Earth, which originally orbited where the asteroid belt now lies, between the orbits of Jupiter and Mars. As it passed near Earth, one of Planet X's Moons struck Earth and shattered it into pieces. Much of the ejecta from the impact remained in Earth's original orbit to form the asteroid belt, while the majority of the shattered Earth was moved closer to the Sun, to its present position between the orbits of Venus and Mars.[55] If this theory is correct, then all of the planets from the asteroid belt on out should also show some sign of having been affected by this planet to some degree. In fact, as we shall see, various eccentricities present in *all* of the outer planets could only have been caused by a large, planetlike object intruding into our solar system.

---

[55] This theory is actually not original, but a modification of the same basic theory proposed by Zechariah Sitchin in his book, *The Twelfth Planet* (New York: Avon, 1976).

Clue #1: Pluto: Enigma on the Edge of the Solar System

The planet Pluto is the first of many eccentricities in our solar system which could be best explained by the existence of a tenth planet. First, it is much too small to be a planet, having only one fifth the mass of Earth's Moon.[56] Secondly, its orbit is highly irregular, being both highly elliptical and at a 17 degree angle to the ecliptic.[57] Thirdly, it bears little resemblance to the other outer planets. "Pluto has little in common with its neighbors in space, Uranus and Neptune."[58]

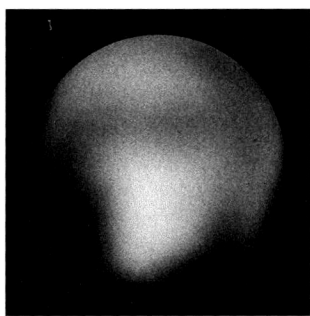

"Planet" Pluto, as seen from the Hubble Telescope. Pluto is most likely not one of the original planets that formed during the initial formation of the solar system, but a satellite of Neptune that was ripped from its orbit by our theoretical "Planet X".
http://en.wikipedia.org/wiki/Pluto

This conclusion is nearly universal among astronomers, who see in Pluto a key to understanding the origins of our solar system. Richard Wagner explains in his article "Nein on Nine? The End of the Line May Open up a New Road to the Rest of the Solar System" that Pluto may not in fact be the last planet in our solar system. Instead, according to Wagner (and a growing number of astronomers), a study of Pluto's unusual orbital dynamics may in fact be the key to finding the enigmatic Planet X:

> Lurking on the outskirts of the solar system, Pluto remains an enigma, a bit of an oddball, or so it seems, in the land of the gas giants. Recently, though, theorists have come to have a new appreciation for the ninth planet as a key to understanding our solar system, its early days, and the possibility that nine is not a magic number.[59]

---

[56]"Pluto and Charon Weigh In," *Sky & Telescope,* January 1993, 9.

[57]George Lovi, "Rambling through the Skies: A 'Far Out' Planet," *Sky & Telescope,* March 1990, 295.

[58]Ken Croswell, "Pluto: Enigma on the Edge of the Solar System," *Astronomy,* July 1986, 9.

[59]Richard Wagner, "Nein on Nine? The End of the Line May Open Up a New Road to the Rest of the Solar System," *Ad Astra,* September/October 1993, 39.

Figures 3.2 and 3.3: Pluto's orbit is highly unusual, being angled to the ecliptic, and even crossing the orbit of Neptune, leading astronomers to believe that Pluto is actually an escaped satellite of Neptune. Neither planet should have an orbit that deviates from the plane of the ecliptic, and certainly should not have an orbit that elliptical, indicating that a planet-sized object must have entered into our solar system at an oblique angle, imparted some of its characteristics to these two objects, and hurled Pluto into a new orbit altogether.

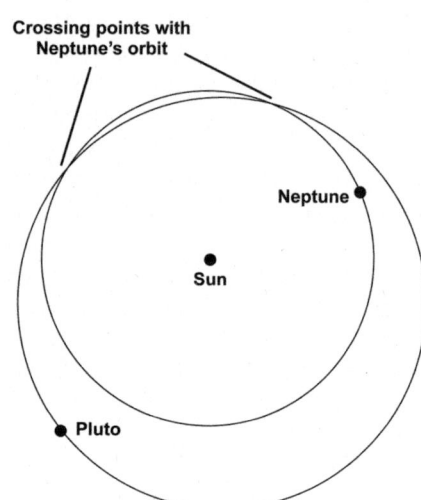

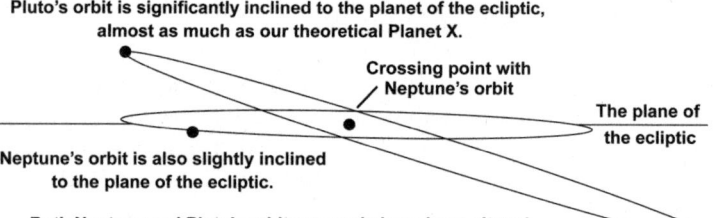

Pluto is so unlike the other planets in size, composition, and orbit, in fact, that some scientists are tending more toward the idea that Pluto and its Moon, Charon, are actually escaped satellites of one of the other outer planets: Neptune. They believe that a near flyby of Planet X had ripped Pluto out of Neptunian orbit and flung it into its own, independent orbit around the Sun. (See Figures 3.2 and 3.3.) They also believe that the orbits of the two other major satellites of Neptune, Triton and Nereid, were similarly affected by a near flyby of Planet X. (See Figures 3.4 and 3.5.) Kaufmann explains,

> In their size, mass, and density, Pluto and Charon resemble the icy satellites of the Jovian planets. Especially in view of Pluto's unusual orbit around the Sun, it is reasonable to wonder whether Pluto might be an escaped satellite that once orbited Neptune.

Some sort of cataclysmic event might have occurred in the ancient past to reverse the direction of Triton's orbit, fling Nereid into its highly elliptical orbit, and catapult Pluto away from Neptune altogether.[60]

The primary reason astronomers believe Pluto was originally a satellite of Neptune is the fact that the orbits of Neptune and Pluto actually cross. Wagner explains, "For a long while, researchers [have] believed Pluto to be an escaped Moon of Neptune, somehow belted out of Neptune's orbit, perhaps by a passing star or a near-collision with Neptune's Moon Triton. The fact that the two planets' orbits cross, and that researchers thought the planets could therefore pass nearby one another, laid the foundation for this belief."[61] Another reason astronomers came to the conclusion that Pluto is an escaped satellite of Neptune is the fact that Pluto closely resembles Triton, a Moon of Neptune. "Although Pluto is usually classified as a planet, its closest relative in the solar system appears to be Triton, Neptune's largest satellite."[62] This similarity is based on the fact that Triton and Pluto are very similar in both size and composition. In fact, the mass of Pluto, when combined with that of its Moon Charon, is very close to the mass of Triton.[63] It is believed that Charon may have been formed as a result of a collision between Pluto and another large body, which would explain Charon's unusually large size and close orbit to Pluto. "A large body struck the original Pluto — possibly then a satellite of Neptune — knocking off a lot of ice that formed in surface layers, and leaving a denser, mainly rocky body. Some of these ejected materials may have formed Charon."[64] Thus, Pluto's original mass, including that of Charon, was probably approximately the same as that of Triton, yet more evidence that Pluto was once a satellite of Neptune.

---

[60]Kaufmann, *Universe*, 316.

[61]Wagner, "Nein on Nine," 41.

[62]Tobias C. Owen, et al., "Surface Ices and the Atmospheric Composition of Pluto," *Science* 261 (6 August 1993): 745.

[63]Jonathan I. Lunine, "Triton, Pluto, and the Origin of the Solar System," *Science* 261 (6 August 1993): 697; Ken Croswell, "Tantalizing Triton," *Space World*, November 1986, 28.

[64]"The Planet That Came in from the Cold," *New Scientist* (29 September 1988): 43.

Clue #2: Neptune and Its Disturbed Moons

Planet X may have also, as we have seen, severely disturbed the orbits of Triton and Nereid, the two largest Moons of Neptune, at the same time it liberated Pluto. Explains Kaufmann, "Perhaps Triton, Nereid, and Pluto all once orbited Neptune along well-behaved, regular orbits in the ancient past. Then, in a near collision, the hypothetical planet severely perturbed the orbits of all three satellites. Triton and Nereid were swung into their present unusual orbits. At the same time, tidal forces from the unknown planet tore Pluto into two pieces, while catapulting it into a heliocentric orbit."[65] Van Flandern and Harrington could only find one plausible explanation for the problems with Triton, Nereid, and Pluto. "Could the gravitational energy to force Triton into a retrograde revolution have come from an outside source—the same source that they felt was disturbing the outer planets? Could that intruder have been a planet?"[66]

Triton's orbit around Neptune is highly inclined; that is, its orbit is at an angle to the plane of the ecliptic, like that of Pluto. Apparently Planet X's influence upon these bodies included transferring to them some of its own characteristics. These characteristics were born from the harsh angle with which it approached the outer edge of our solar system, which dramatically affected Planet Neptune, particularly its satellite system. (See Figures 3.4 and 3.5)

The tremendous difference in the angles of momentum between the Neptunian system and the incoming Planet X caused a dramatic effect in the characteristics of both systems, the net effect of the interaction being that Planet X, previously a rogue body passing through the outer edge of our solar system, was now a part of our solar system, with its own, highly elliptical solar orbit. In the process of becoming a member of our solar system, Planet X left an unmistakable path of destruction in its wake, which clearly could only have been caused by the intrusion of a planet-sized object.

---

[65] Kaufmann, *Universe*, 316.
[66] Littman, *Planets Beyond,* 198.

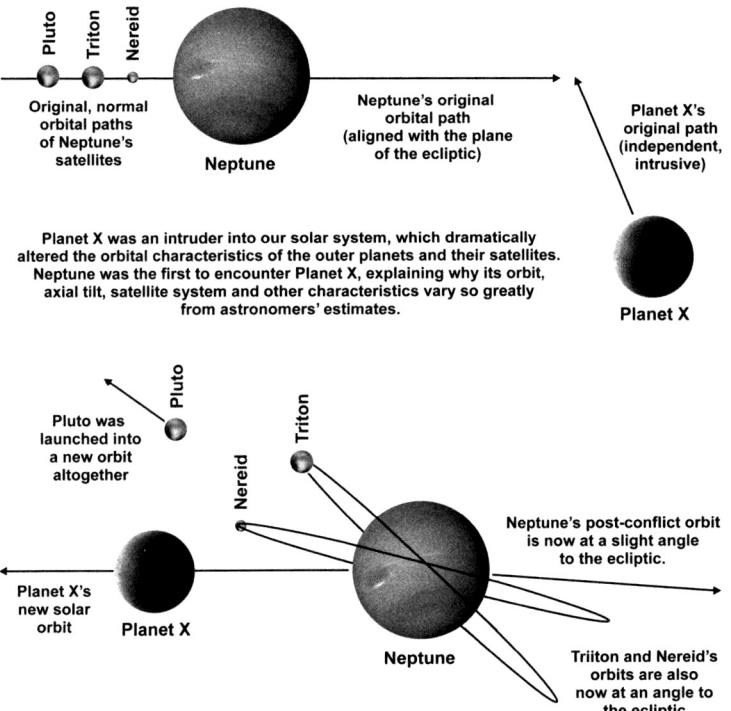

Figures 3.4 and 3.5: Planet X was an intrusive body not native to our solar system. It first came into conflict with the outer planet now known as Neptune, the interaction with which brought Planet X into our solar system as a new planet with a new, solar orbit. Neptune's orbital and other characteristics were dramatically affected by this conflict, its orbital path now slightly eccentric and at a slight angle to the ecliptic, with an axial tilt of over 28 degrees. Its satellites were most dramatically affected. Triton's orbit was now retrograde and highly inclined to the ecliptic, Nereid's orbit is highly eccentric, seven times long as it is wide. Pluto was affected most of all, being ripped out of the system altogether into a new orbit of its own. (Note: figures not to scale.)

Despite its detractors, the Planet X theory remains the most plausible explanation for the strange orbits of Pluto, Triton, and Nereid. Thomas Van Flandern, one of the leading proponents of this theory, explains how he believes it may have happened:

> I begin with the conjecture that the solar system formed with a few additional major planets beyond Neptune. Occasionally, a passing star will approach the Sun close enough to disrupt the orbital motion of one such planet, causing it to cross the orbit of

another further in. Sooner or later these worlds will have a close approach. This remains true even if initially the orbits are inclined, because such orbits must precess until they eventually intersect. If the two worlds are comparable in mass, the most probable result of a close encounter is that one gets ejected from the solar system, while the other assumes an elongated orbit that crosses the orbit of the next planet inward. This process continues in domino fashion until the remaining outermost planet with an eccentric orbit is not sufficiently massive to disrupt the motion of planets nearer the Sun. But it may still be massive enough to affect the *satellites* of the outermost "regular" planet, Neptune.[67]

In 1978, Van Flandern and his colleague, Robert Harrington, ran computer simulations in an attempt to see if an object like Planet X could have thrown the Neptunian system into such disarray. After several trials, they found that a planet around three times the mass of Earth passing near Neptune would result in a situation strikingly like that of the Neptunian system. "Some encounters left one of Neptune's regular Moons moving retrograde (as does Triton), another near the threshold of escape (as is Nereid), and a third pushed from the Neptune system completely and into a solar orbit that crossed the orbit of Neptune. This one, I submit, is Pluto."[68]

> They made computer simulations of planets of different sizes intruding into the Neptunian system at different distances, speeds, and angles. From their computations emerged a nominee — a planet with two to five times the mass of Earth in a highly inclined and elliptical orbit 50 to 100 astronomical units from the Sun with an orbital period of about 800 years. In one brief visit long ago, the intruder had reversed the motion of Triton, warped the orbit of Nereid, and cast the Moon Pluto out of the Neptune family into a planetary orbit of its own.[69] (See Figure 3.5.)

Planet X's legacy to the outer planets, then, was a multitude of eccentricities, for both the outer planets and their satellites. For example, Triton's orbit is not only angled to the ecliptic, it is *retrograde*; that is, it moves in the opposite direction of the planets and

---

[67] McKinnon and Flandern, "Worlds Apart," 341.
[68] *Ibid.*
[69] Littman, *Planets Beyond*, 198.

most other satellites in our solar system.[70] Nereid's orbit, like that of Pluto, is highly elliptical. "Nereid's orbit is the most eccentric of any satellite in our solar system. The distance between Nereid and Neptune varies from 1.4 million to 9.7 million miles km as this tiny Moon moves along its highly elliptical path. Triton completes its backward orbit in only 6 days, but Nereid takes nearly 360 days to go once around Neptune."[71]

The 1989 *Voyager* flyby confirmed the irregular orbits of Triton and Nereid, and found many more problems with Neptune, all of which seem to indicate some sort of catastrophic encounter with one or more planet-sized bodies in the past. One of these problems was the existence of six more tiny moons, some orbiting so close to Neptune that they lay within what is called Neptune's "Roche limit."

> *Voyager 2*'s discovery of six satellites close to Neptune — four of which are at least 150 kilometers across — has left celestial mechanicians in a quandary. The physics of planetary formation argues that Moons cannot form inside what is termed the Roche limit, where gravity's ability to hold a fluid body together is overwhelmed by tidal effects and centrifugal acceleration. For Moons consisting mostly of ice, the Roche limit is about 65,000 kilometers from Neptune's center, and at least three of *Voyager*'s six new finds lie within the "forbidden zone."[72]

In other words, according to planetary physics, the three satellites within the Roche limit should not exist. They must, therefore, have originally been formed further out from Neptune, and then thrown into a closer orbit by some sort of outside force. This outside force could only have been the gravitational force of another planet, as only another planet could have had the force necessary to alter the orbits of these satellites. Thus, the existence of these Moons within the Roche limit is yet more evidence for the existence of Planet X.

Another important new find was a ring system around Neptune. The rings are complete, but some of the sections of the rings are thicker and thus more easily visible. As a result, from a distance Neptune appears to have ring arcs rather than complete rings. These rings

---

[70]William B. McKinnon and Thomas Van Flandern, "Worlds Apart," *Sky & Telescope*, October 1991, 340.

[71]Kaufmann, *Universe*, 311.

[72]"Neptune's 'Forbidden' Moons," *Sky & Telescope*, July 1992, 7.

around Neptune were actually detected as early as 1984.[73] The *Voyager* flyby confirmed the existence of these rings, and scientists concluded that they must be the remains of one or more small Moons shattered by some object that must have intruded into the Neptunian system. "The observation that Neptune's arcs are so few in number and clustered so closely in orbital longitude suggests that they may well have had their origin in the collisional disruption of a small Moon."[74] The six small Moons orbiting close to Neptune are probably also fragments of this shattered Moon.[75]

---

[73] J. Eberhart, "Signs of a Puzzling Ring around Neptune," *Science News* 127 (January 19, 1985): 37.

[74] Carolyn C. Porco, "An Explanation for Neptune's Ring Arcs," *Science* 253 (30 August 1991): 1000.

[75] Despite the weight of evidence in favor of Planet X, some scientists still feel the need to disprove its existence. Instead, they argue, the object that had intruded into the Neptunian system was not a mysterious "Planet X," but the satellite, Triton, which they believe had originally had an independent orbit before its capture by Neptune. They argue that Triton's destructive conflict with a former Moon of Neptune had slowed Triton's motion sufficiently to allow it to be grabbed by Neptune's gravity. The shattered remains of the former Moon then remained as partial ring arcs circling Neptune. Triton's intrusion, according to their theory, also caused Nereid to be thrown into its elliptical orbit (P. Goldreich, et al., "Neptune's Story," *Science* 245 (4 August 1989): 501). However, besides confirming the existence of rings around Neptune, *Voyager* also found a third Moon which has a very normal-looking orbit in contrast to that of Triton and Nereid. "The new Moon, 1989 N1, orbits Neptune every 1 day 3 hours in a nearly circular orbit at the planet's equator.... The orderly nature of its orbit contrasts sharply with the other two known Neptunian Moons, Triton and Nereid, which follow very unusual paths around the planet." (John Mason, "Neptune's New Moon Baffles the Astronomers," *New Scientist* (22 July 1989): 31). Mason believes that the existence of this new Moon defeats the theory that Triton had been "captured" by Neptune, which some astronomers hold to as an explanation for the odd orbits of Triton and Nereid. " 'If Triton were a relative newcomer to the Neptune system...it would have passed near enough to the low orbit of any pre-existing Moon, such as 1989 N1, either to collide with it or sweep it up, through gravitational attraction.' " (*Ibid.*)

The captured-Triton hypothesis also has other problems. For one, it fails to take into account the fact that both Triton and Pluto are nearly identical in size and composition, indicating that they may have originally been part of the same planetary system. The captured-Triton hypothesis posits that both Pluto and Triton were two examples of a large collection of small, icy bodies that, theoretically, orbit just outside the known solar system. However, the odds of two unrelated bodies being so similar in size and composition are rather small, and this theory also fails to explain why Pluto's orbit is so elliptical and angled to the ecliptic, why an object as small as Pluto has a Moon, and why its Moon is so large and orbits so closely. Also, assuming that Pluto *was* once a satellite of Neptune, Triton's mass is insufficient to have hurled Pluto out of Neptunian orbit. The captured-Triton hypothesis also fails to address the problems with Neptune's rotational and magnetic axes, perhaps Neptune's most unexplainable mystery.

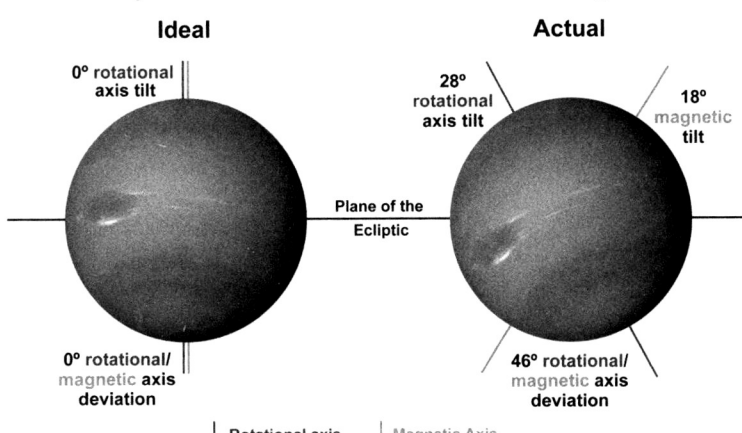

Figure 3.6: According to the standard solar system formation model, all of the planets should have rotational and magnetic axes that are 90° perpendicular to the plane of the ecliptic. Neptune, however, has rotational and magnetic axes that are radically misaligned, both with the plane of the ecliptic, but also to each other, to the point where astronomers have concluded that only a conflict with another planet-sized object could have caused such radical anomalies.

The planet Neptune itself also displays anomalies that can only be explained by a near-collision with Planet X. Neptune, formerly assumed to have its rotational and magnetic axes perpendicular to the Sun, actually turns out to have axes that are radically tilted. (See Figure 3.6.) "Neptune's rotation axis is tipped nearly 29 degrees toward the Sun."[76] A tilt in a planet's rotational axis is not unusual in our solar system, but the magnetic axis of a planet is usually closely aligned with its rotation axis. Not so with Neptune, where "the magnetic axis is tipped almost 47 degrees with respect to Neptune's spin axis."[77] To add to the puzzle, the orbit of Triton is tilted 21 degrees to the equatorial plane of Neptune, which is already tilted at 29 degrees to the ecliptic plane, so that Triton's orbital plane is inclined to the plane of the ecliptic by up to 50 degrees. Only the

---

[76] Thorpe, "Enigmatic Triton and Nereid," 485; J. Kelly Beatty, "Welcome to Neptune," *Sky & Telescope*, October 1989, 358; " 'Ring' Discovered around Neptune," *Astronomy* 13, April 1985, 60.

[77] J. Kelly Beatty, "Getting to Know Neptune," *Sky & Telescope*, February 1990, 146.

intrusion of a massive, planetlike object such as Planet X could account for such a gross deviation.

In order to cause these anomalies, the theoretical Planet X would have to have entered our solar system from below, at an extreme angle to the ecliptic, as Harrington and Van Flandern have proposed. This angle may have been 45 degrees or more, as Whitmire and Matese have suggested. Its interaction with Neptune would have caused Neptune's Moons to be severely disturbed, and Neptune itself would have taken on a tilt to accommodate Planet X as the direction of movement and the angles to the ecliptic of the two conflicting planets attempted to equalize each other. Neptune, the larger of the two bodies, was less affected than was Planet X. Planet X had its angle to the ecliptic significantly altered, to the point that after its interaction with Neptune it was pretty much aligned to the plane of the ecliptic. The gravitational influence of the Sun and the other Jovian planets then caused Planet X's orbit to further precess over time, gradually pulling it more closely in line with the plane of the ecliptic.

Despite the fact that Planet X was the definite loser in this gravitic tug of war, Neptune did not escape unscathed. As a result of the gravitational interaction with Planet X, Neptune's rotational axis was now tilted to the ecliptic plane by 29 degrees. Its magnetic axis was also dramatically affected, probably because of an electrical discharge between the two planets. Neptune's Moons were, of course, thrown around like billiard balls by this encounter. Triton's orbit was reversed and set at an angle to the ecliptic that approximated Planet X's original angle to the ecliptic, and Nereid's orbit was altered so that it reflected the elliptical shape of Planet X's new orbit around our Sun. A third Moon may have been shattered by Planet X, its remnants being the ring arcs, the six Moonlets, and the re-formed Moon 1989 N1.[78]

Pluto, of course, was thrown out of the system entirely, and perhaps dragged for some distance, its new orbit imitating Planet X's orbit with its elliptical shape and angle to the ecliptic. Or, perhaps Neptune itself had had been dragged for some distance from its original orbit at around 38–40 A.U., leaving Pluto behind. This would help justify the problems with Bode's progression. According to Bode's Law, the next planet out from Uranus should be orbiting at 38.8 A.U., but Neptune actually orbits at 30.06 A.U. The 38.8 A.U. figure, however, fits closely with the 39.44 A.U. figure for Pluto's current (mean) orbit,

---

[78]Beatty, "Getting to Know Neptune," 150.

suggesting that Pluto may have been left behind while the rest of the Neptunian system was pushed or dragged some 8 A.U. toward the Sun by its encounter with Planet X. This is a good explanation for three important reasons. First, it justifies Bode's Law, which before Neptune had been (with one important exception) fairly accurate. Second, it clears up any doubt concerning the relationship between Neptune and Pluto. Third, it helps support the existence of Planet X, as only a fast-moving, planet-sized body could have had such an effect on Neptune.

Clue #3: Uranus' Odd Inclination

The planet Uranus also appears to have been involved in a collision with some sort of large planetary body. For example, its axis of rotation is tilted even more than that of its twin, Neptune. Its axis is so radically tilted, in fact, that it is nearly in line with the plane of the ecliptic. Furthermore, its magnetic axis is out of alignment with its rotation axis by 59 degrees, and its north and south poles have been flipped over almost completely. (See Figure 3.7.) These anomalies initially baffled astronomers. "Neither Earth nor other planets in the solar system have magnetic fields aligned exactly with their geographic poles, but this *much* of a tilt had only been seen previously in certain exotic astrophysical objects, such as pulsars."[79] Reichhardt explains,

> Uranus is once again unique, because all the other planets have their rotational and magnetic axes nearly aligned. For instance, both Earth and Jupiter have their magnetic axes inclined by less than 11 degrees from their rotational axes. What could have caused such a misalignment on Uranus? One explanation might be that Uranus's magnetic field might be undergoing a reversal, a phenomenon known from geological data to have occurred on Earth, but never actually observed in progress anywhere. Another possibility is that the misalignment of Uranus's magnetic field came from one or more catastrophic collisions with planet-sized bodies that also tilted the planet's rotational axis. The Uranian Moons seem to show evidence of such collisions.[80]

---

[79] Tony Reichhardt, "Uranus is a Magician (Part 2)," *Space World,* April 1986, 31.
[80] Kaufmann, *Universe,* 307.

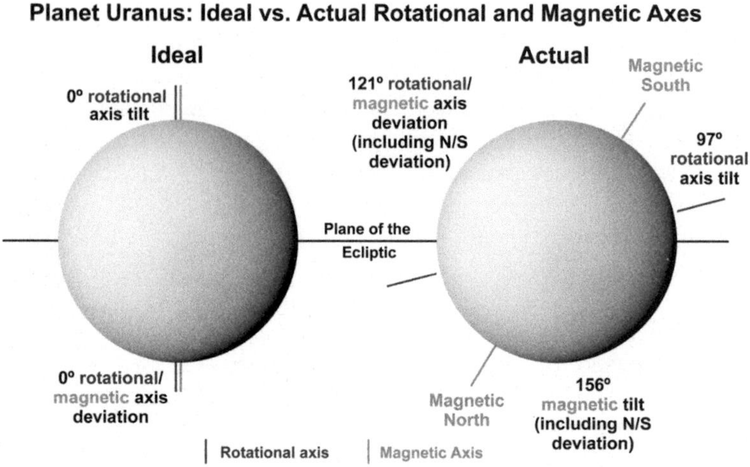

Planet Uranus: Ideal vs. Actual Rotational and Magnetic Axes

Ideal
- 0° rotational axis tilt
- 121° rotational/magnetic axis deviation (including N/S deviation)
- Plane of the Ecliptic
- 0° rotational/magnetic axis deviation

Actual
- Magnetic South
- 97° rotational axis tilt
- 156° magnetic tilt (including N/S deviation)
- Magnetic North
- Rotational axis | Magnetic Axis

Figure 3.7: Planet Uranus' rotational and axial tilts are even more radically variant from the expected norm than that of Neptune, the rotational axis being an amazing 97° from the standard vertical orientation relative to the ecliptic plane, with the effect that Uranus is actually spinning on its side. The magnetic axis is an incredible 156° variant from the norm, being almost completely reversed. Once again, only a near-collision with a planet-sized object could have caused such radical anomalies.

Baffled, astronomers were forced to conclude that Uranus had been knocked over by a collision with another large object, which some believed to be one of the large planetesimals which had combined to form Uranus. However, it would require a massive planetesimal traveling at a tremendous speed to literally knock the planet on its side, and the accretion models run to simulate the creation of our solar system from planetesimals don't seem to be able to explain how a planetesimal could be accelerated rapidly enough to do that much damage to Uranus. Moreover, an impact with a large planetesimal would not have knocked Uranus back away from the Sun, with its rotational poles pointing almost directly at the Sun as they are now, but on its side, where the poles would never point at the Sun. In order to knock over Uranus as it is now, the conflicting object would have to have come either from the direction of the Sun, or from outside of the solar system. Also, except for its twin, Neptune, none of the other planets display such radical tilts, even though they too were formed from planetesimals. Thus, a more likely explanation for the problems with Uranus' rotation and magnetic axes is a catastrophic encounter with Planet X, the same explanation given for the problems with the Neptunian system. Uranus appears to have basically been bowled over by some massive body that had smashed into its southern hemisphere, tilting the planet on its side so that its rotation axis now points almost directly toward the Sun. And not only is the rotation axis skewed, but Uranus' magnetic axis is nearly upside down, relative to its rotational axis. (See Figure 3.7.)

A view of the south pole of Planet Uranus. Uranus is actually tilted on its side, explaining why its ring system, unlike Saturn's, is perpendicular to the ecliptic. The Voyage probes discovered that Uranus was basically a train wreck, its rotational and magnetic tilts even more radically off kilter than Neptune. Such radical differences between the expected and actual characteristics of Neptune led astronomers to conclude that Uranus had also come into conflict with some sort of planet-sized object.

At first, this apparent anomaly was passed off by scientists as a natural event. Earth's poles have shifted position many times in the past, leading some to believe that this feature may be typical of all the planets. However, there is no hard evidence that this reversal happens naturally. In fact, the evidence seems to suggest that the reversals happen suddenly, leading some to the conclusion that the changes were caused by the near flyby of other planets, or collisions with large asteroids. Some have even suggested periodic shifts in Earth's crust over the Mohorovičić Discontinuity, a highly lubricious, or "slippery" area that lies between Earth's crust and mantle. However, the fact that Neptune's rotation and magnetic axes are in a condition similar to that of Uranus made the hypothesis that Uranus' magnetic field was undergoing a natural reversal extremely unlikely. The odds of both planets undergoing changes in the positions of their magnetic poles at the same time were so small as to be not worth considering. As Berry explains, "When they had data from Uranus, scientists were inclined to dismiss the planet as a freak, or explain the magnetic field by assuming that Uranus was observed at an odd moment. They reasoned that Uranus must occasionally reverse its magnetic polarity, just as Earth does. Neptune changed that. If the probability of catching Uranus during a magnetic reversal was small, the likelihood of catching two planets in the act would be infinitesimal."[81] Furthermore, the differential between the rotation and magnetic axes of the two planets were similar, 47 degrees for Neptune and 59 degrees for Uranus.[82] Thus another explanation needs to be found, and a collision or near-collision with Planet X fits the bill perfectly.

Uranus' Moons also present an interesting dilemma. Uranus has five Moons: Oberon, Titania, Umbriel, Ariel, and Miranda. They all travel in circular, prograde orbits around Neptune's equator, and in general seem to be perfect examples of how satellites should behave, with one important exception.

> The known Uranian satellites travel in virtually circular orbits, and except for Miranda their orbital planes coincide with the planet's equatorial plane to within a few tenths of a degree. Although the satellite orbits are quite regular, the orientation of the entire system is unusual: it is tilted on its side, so that the rotation axes of the planet and its Moons lie nearly in the planet's orbital plane. Some workers attribute Uranus' odd orientation — as well as the less extreme inclinations of other planetary axes — to the impact of a planetesimal early in the planet's history. It has [also] been suggested that such a catastrophe would have affected the evolution of the Uranian satellites....[83]

Because the Moons of Uranus have very regular orbits, they could only have formed *after* the collision that had knocked over Uranus. It is probable that the collision that had knocked Uranus on its side had also left ejecta floating in orbit around the planet, ejecta which later migrated to Uranus' equator and accreted into satellites and its ring system. If the satellites had existed before the impact, their orbits would be extremely chaotic, probably similar to that of Neptune. However, they are in fact extremely orderly, proving that they were created as a result of the same collision that had knocked Uranus on its side. But no minor planetesimal could have packed the kind of punch needed to knock such a massive planet on its side. Only a fast-moving, planet-sized body — Planet X — could have done it.

---

[81]Richard Berry, "Neptune Revealed," *Astronomy,* December 1989, 26.

[82]J. Kelly Beatty, "Getting to Know Neptune," *Sky & Telescope,* February 1990, 146. Note that this number for Uranus does not take the north/south differential into account.

[83]Robert Hamilton Brown and Dale P. Cruikshank, "The Moons of Uranus, Neptune, and Pluto," *Scientific American* 253, July 1985, 38-48.

A great deal of material would have been thrown up when Uranus was struck by Planet X, and this material would have gradually moved to Uranus' equator due to the centrifugal force generated by the planet's rotation, forming a ring of material probably very similar to that of Saturn. Over time this material accreted into a series of five Moons and a ring system of material that remained unassimilated.[84] Since the rings also circle Uranus' equator, it stands to reason that they too were formed as a result of the collision. Unlike the Moons, however, the material in the rings, perhaps as a result of gravitational forces from Uranus and its new satellites, never formed into a Moon. Or, perhaps the ring system is the result of a more recent collision, and has not had enough time to re-form. Either way, a collision with Planet X is also the best explanation for the eccentricities in the Uranian system.

Clue #4: Saturn's Rings

Saturn, with its trademark rings, may also have been affected by Planet X, which may have created Saturn's rings as well as its 29° axial tilt as it passed by on its way to the inner solar system.

Perhaps the most beautiful sight our solar system has to offer, the rings of Saturn have long been a source of controversy. Originally thought to be a single, flat sheet of material by some renaissance astronomers, we now know the rings to be a collection of dust and ice particles ranging in size from tiny grains to massive Moonlets. The combined gravitational attraction of Saturn and its Moons upon the rings causes the rings to be spread out and divided into as many as 100,000 different divisions. Small Moons or "shepherd Moonlets" within the rings themselves also contribute to the variety of divisions. "With modern radar and spacecraft, the ring particles resolve into red-tinged snowballs that range in size from sand grains to enormous boulders. Large satellites that lie beyond the ring system carve features within it, such as the

---

[84]See J. Eberhart, "Sustaining the Uranian Rings," *Science News* 134 (December 24 & 31, 1988): 407.

scimitar-sharp edges and scalloped hems. Tiny Moonlets embedded within the rings may knot them, braid them, clump them, and cut slices out of them."[85]

The origin of the rings of Saturn is believed to have been similar to that of the rings of Uranus and Neptune, that is, the result of one or more satellites shattered by an external influence, perhaps that of another planet. This assumption is made because most scientists now believe that Saturn's rings, like the rings of Uranus, had formed some time after the planet's initial formation.

> During the past ten years...many scientists have been forced to abandon the long-established notion that the rings of Saturn are as ancient and enduring as the solar system itself. It now appears that the rings could not have formed along with the planet.... Rather, they are a recent addition.... Once considered unique, Saturn's rings now represent merely the most spectacular specimens of a cosmic species known to circle every giant world—from Jupiter's diffuse, dusty halo to the narrow, dark hoops of Uranus to the demi-rings that appear to trace a line of dashes around Neptune.[86]

But how could these ring systems have formed *after* the planet's formation? The only explanation is an outside source — Planet X once again. Planet X apparently passed near enough to Saturn to destroy one of its Moons, as it had apparently done with Uranus and Neptune. Sobel explains,

> Rings, most researchers agree, are Moons gone to pieces — or captured comets, caught on the fly and then torn to shreds by competing gravitational forces. If you scooped up all the scattered particles of ice and dust in the glittering ring system of Saturn and packed them together, you could mold a Moon about the size of Saturn's Moon Mimas — a little under 250 miles in diameter. Such a satellite probably existed quite close to the planet 100 million years ago. Then along came a comet or another big body on a collision course and blasted the Moon to bits.... This ill-fated Moon lay within Saturn's Roche limit...defined as the region close to a planet where competing gravitational forces are strong

---

[85]Dava Sobel, "Secrets of the Rings," *Discover,* April 1994, 89.
[86]Sobel, "Secrets of the Rings," 89.

enough to shatter unstable satellites or prevent them from forming in the first place.... The Moon that became Saturn's rings was too close to the massive planet to pull itself back together. Once it was smashed to bits, the pieces — large and small — all went into orbit in a cloud of debris. These particles eventually fell into a disk around the planet's equator.... Today the great circle spreads out into a disk more than 180,000 miles wide but scarcely 60 feet high.[87]

Though it is suggested that perhaps the rings are made up of captured comets, this is unlikely since even the largest comets are only 10 kilometers (6.21 miles) across and thus not nearly large enough account for the large amount of material in the rings. Furthermore, no other planets show such extensive ring systems as Saturn, though they come into contact with comets just as frequently if not more so. The idea that a Moon of Saturn could have been pulverized by a comet is similarly unlikely, as comets are much too small to significantly affect, let alone pulverize a Moon of the size suggested by Sobel. However, Planet X is quite capable of destroying a satellite of that size, as the evidence from the other outer planets suggests. Planet X may have even come close enough to strike Saturn itself, causing the 29 degree tilt of its rotation axis.

Clue #5: Jupiter's Rings and Retrograde Moons

The existence of a ring around Jupiter makes this feature typical of the Jovian planets, the gas giants Jupiter, Saturn, Uranus, and Neptune. Jupiter's ring system has divisions in it, like those of Saturn.[88] Also, like Neptune, Jupiter has a number of small inner Moons. All together, "This ring, the small inner Moons, and the Galilean satellites together form a system of orbiting material that apparently is a common feature of Jovian planets."[89] Another feature Jupiter shares with Neptune is its odd combination of satellites with "normal" orbits and satellites with eccentric orbits.

---

[87]Sobel, "Secrets of the Rings," 89. Cf. also Jeffrey N. Cuzzi, "Ringed Planets: Still Mysterious—II," *Sky & Telescope,* January 1985, 22–23.

[88]J. Eberhart, "The Ring of Jupiter: Evidence for Ringlets," *Science News* 122 (November 6, 1982): 294.

[89]Kaufmann, *Universe,* 267.

A total of sixteen satellites are now known to orbit Jupiter, three of which were discovered during the *Voyager* flybys. These newly identified Moons, along with Amalthea and the Galilean satellites, all orbit Jupiter in the plane of that planet's equator. In contrast, the remaining eight Moons are all extremely tiny, with estimated diameters typically of less than 50 km, and circle Jupiter along large orbits that are inclined at steep angles to the planet's equatorial plane. Furthermore, the four outermost satellites all have retrograde orbits.[90]

Jupiter, like Neptune, has satellite(s) with orbits that are retrograde and/or angled to the ecliptic. This may be evidence that Planet X had at one time passed near enough Jupiter to disrupt its satellites, as it had done with Neptune. This condition could not have come about as the result of natural evolutionary processes — the Jovian system, like the Neptunian system, requires an external force to explain its eccentricities.

Jupiter also has a small ring system along with numerous satellites with eccentric, even retrograde orbits, all of which were most likely caused by interactions with Planet X.

Jupiter's ring and collection of small inner Moons may also be evidence that Planet X had at one time smashed into one or more of Jupiter's satellites, their remains migrating to Jupiter's equator due to the centrifugal force of the planet's spin. There they formed a ring and new satellites that have near-perfect orbits — a situation similar to that of the Uranian and Neptunian systems. Some of these remnants may have never re-formed due to gravitational tides from the planet and its nearby Moons, resulting in the formation of Jupiter's small ring system — a feature shared with both Neptune, Uranus, and Saturn.

Unlike the other Jovian planets, there is no evidence that either Jupiter or its satellites have ever been influenced by the impact of a planetesimal, which mitigates against the idea that it was the impacts of planetesimals that caused these planets to be tilted. Jupiter's

---

[90]Kaufmann, *Universe*, 267.

rotation axis is tilted to the plane of the ecliptic by only 3 degrees, compared to 28.8 degrees for Neptune, 97.9 degrees for Uranus, and 29 degrees for Saturn. If we are to believe that the axial tilts of the outer planets were caused by the impact of massive planetesimals during the end of their initial formative periods, then Jupiter should have been affected similarly. However, Jupiter's axial tilt is almost nonexistent.

Furthermore, the fact that Jupiter's satellites are made up of both regular *and* irregular satellites — a situation analogous to that of Neptune — proves that a planetesimal could not have created Jupiter's satellites. The ejecta thrown up by the impact from a planetesimal would not have created Moons with retrograde or elliptical orbits; all of Jupiter's Moons in that case would have circular, prograde orbits around its equator, as is the case with Uranus. Therefore the only plausible answer is that the Jovian system, like the other outer planets, must have experienced a near flyby from Planet X. Apparently Planet X narrowly missed Jupiter, hitting instead one or more of its satellites. These satellites were destroyed, their scattered remains eventually forming a ring like that of Saturn, only smaller. Over time most of their remains re-accreted into new Moons that have near-perfect orbits around Jupiter's equator. The satellites that were not destroyed by Planet X's near flyby were affected in other ways; they were thrown into orbits that were either elliptical, retrograde, and/or angled to the ecliptic, or both. Jupiter's small axial tilt might have been caused by the gravitational pull between the two planets as they passed by one another, or perhaps by a glancing impact with Planet X itself.

If Planet X did indeed come close enough to Jupiter to disrupt its satellites, then this leaves us with an interesting question. How far into our solar system does Planet X's orbit reach? Robert S. Harrington suggests that Planet X's perihelion (closest approach to the Sun) lies somewhere between the orbits of Uranus and Neptune, but none of the other Planet X theorists, to my knowledge, have attempted to guess where its perihelion lies. Yet the evidence suggests that Planet X's orbit reaches deeper into our solar system than any mainstream scientist has previously dared theorize. Should we place the perihelion of Planet X near the orbit of Uranus, or Saturn, or Jupiter, or should we look even deeper into our solar system for yet more clues? Do any of the planets in the inner solar system show signs of having been struck by a large, planetlike object at some time in the primordial past? In fact, one does: Earth. Along with the clues from the outer solar system, more clues pointing to the existence of Planet X can be uncovered through a thorough examination of the inner solar system, particularly Earth and its Moon. Still more clues can be obtained by analyzing the asteroid belt and the comets, as we shall see.

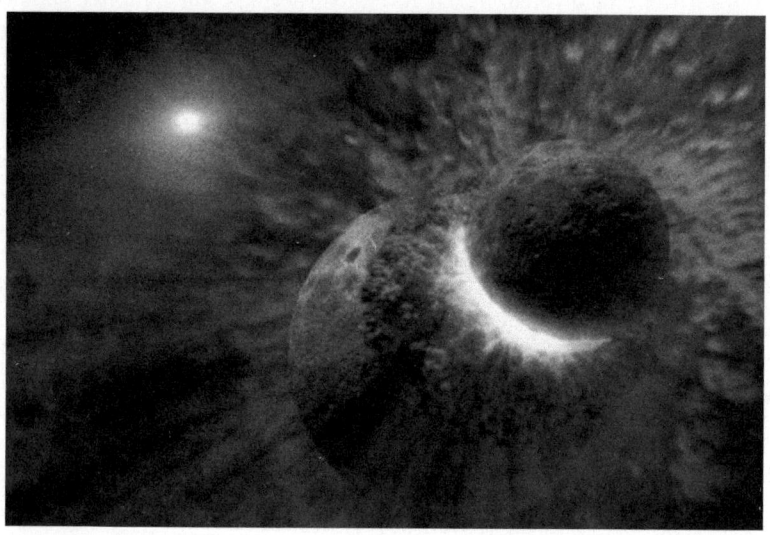

The "Giant Impact Theory" posits that the Moon was formed as the result of a "giant impact" between Earth and another large body approximately the size of Mars. This impact is also largely responsible for the many unique features Earth exhibits today.

Clue #6: The Moon

There is conclusive evidence indicating that the Moon was created as the result of a relatively large body colliding with Earth. This collision, it is believed, gouged out a large section of Earth's crust and mantle, throwing it into space. The material ejected from Earth's mantle then remained in orbit around Earth, over time gradually accreting into the Moon.[91] This theory is known as the "Giant Impact Theory," a theory that is also used to explain several other questions about Earth's formation, including its axial tilt, its relatively fast rotation rate, and the prodigious amounts of water on its surface.

The Giant Impact Theory was first formulated in 1976 by two scientists working independently: Al Cameron and William Ward. These men had both deduced, based on the fact that the rotation rate of

---

[91] Kaufmann, *Universe*, 216–17.

Earth was too fast to be explained by conventional accretion models, that some sort of outside force must have somehow accelerated Earth's rotation rate during its formative period. This outside force, according to their calculations, was an object roughly the size of Mars. Hartmann explains, "Al Cameron and William Ward independently published the same basic idea arrived at from studies of the angular momentum of the Earth-Moon system. Their work also led them to estimate that the secondary impactor was roughly the size of Mars."[92] Traveling at around 40,000 kilometers per hour, according to their calculations, this object had struck Earth at a moderate angle, accelerating Earth's rotation in the process. This giant impact also carved out a substantial portion of Earth's mantle, forming the Moon.

In order to rigorously test this hypothesis, Al Cameron then teamed up with Arizona physicist Jay Melosh and several other researchers and used the CRAY supercomputer at Los Alamos National Laboratory in Los Alamos, New Mexico in to run simulations of what would happen during a catastrophic encounter between Earth and a Mars-sized body. (See Figure 3.8.) Hartmann explains the results of this experiment in his article, "Piecing Together Earth's Early History":

> The results of the scientists' years of work include a simulation that details the collision process as it unfolds over a period of several hours. The calculations show that the impactor probably struck a glancing blow, shearing off much of the mantles of primordial Earth and the impactor itself in a stupendous cloud of luminous vapor. Initially, most of the iron core impactor traveled on, though slowed by the impact. But unable to escape Earth's gravity, it looped back to crash into the disrupted Earth, eventually merging into our planet's core. Much of the mantle debris from both bodies also crashed back into Earth. But a small fraction of the mixture of both objects' mantles stayed in orbit where it eventually coalesced to form the Moon. The Cameron-Melosh simulation greatly interested geophysicists because it predicted that Earth's mantle would have been melted. The shock of the impact would have dumped so much energy into Earth that

---

[92]William K. Hartmann, "Piecing Together Earth's Early History," *Astronomy,* June 1989, 30. It is important to note here that impactor was *not* Mars, as the impactor was destroyed as a result of the impact.

most of the mantle had its temperatures raised perhaps to more than 2,000 kelvins, far above the melting point of its rocks.[93]

The supercomputer models confirmed Cameron and Ward's theory that the Moon could have been formed as the result of a Giant Impact. They also observed that the iron core of the impactor would have fallen back into the now molten Earth, sinking in and combining with Earth's original iron core. This could explain the 12.5 degree tilt in Earth's core, recently discovered by seismologists at Harvard University.[94]

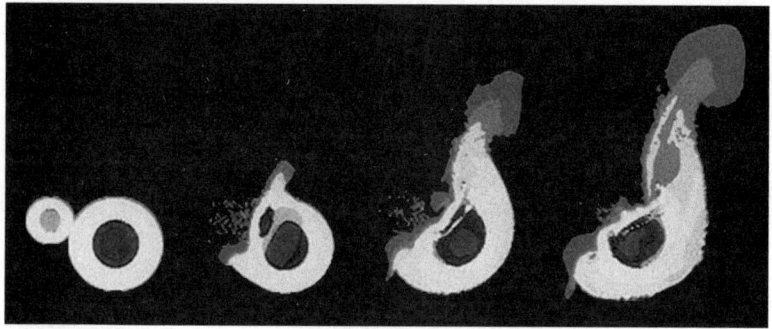

Figure 3.8: During the 1980s, astronomers Al Cameron and Jay Melosh used a Cray supercomputer at the Los Alamos National Laboratories to simulate what would happen if an impactor slightly larger than the size of Mars struck Earth. What resulted was a revolutionary new understanding of how our Moon was created, as the impactor, it was found, created a body from the mantle of earth of the same size, composition and orbital characteristics of our Moon. This "giant impact" theory of lunar formation has been the accepted theory ever since. In the above image can be seen, left to right, the impactor impacting, and the materials that would later form the Moon being launched into orbit around Earth. In this model, the impactor remains embedded in Earth, throwing much of the mantle into space to form the Moon.

Before the Giant Impact Theory was generally accepted as valid by the scientific community in 1984, there had been three other hypotheses about how the Moon had been created. "Ideas about how the Moon came to orbit around Earth fell roughly into three categories: (1) fission — a piece of Earth spun off in a chunk, (2) capture — Earth attracted nearby material into its orbit, and (3) double-planet — Earth

---

[93]Hartmann, "Piecing Together Earth's Early History," 30, 32; Thomas J. Ahrens, "The Origin of the Earth," *Physics Today,* August 1994, 40.

[94]"Earth's Core out of Kilter," *Science News* 145, 250.

and the Moon formed at the same time from the same material."[95] However, these theories were about to be replaced in a rapid turnaround unprecedented in the scientific community.

In 1984, G. Jeffrey Taylor of the University of Hawaii, along with William K. Hartmann of the Planetary Sciences Institute in Tucson and Roger J. Phillips of Washington University, organized a conference in Kona, Hawaii in which they would attempt to achieve a consensus theory among the scientific community on how the Moon was created. This conference included geologists, astronomers, astrophysicists, and anybody else who could offer evidence to help solve the riddle of how the Moon was born. They expected one of the three traditional theories to be adopted, but were surprised when the Giant Impact Theory, a relative newcomer to the scientific arena, was adopted almost unanimously.

But its adoption was no accident. The Giant Impact Theory was adopted almost unanimously partly because the three previous theories had failed so miserably in the face of new evidence produced by geologists and astrophysicists at the Kona conference. These three theories had their merits, but they also had critical flaws which proved to be their downfall:

⚚ *The Capture Theory:* In its original form the capture theory held that Earth seized a fully formed Moon that came whizzing in from elsewhere in the solar system. In principle, such capture is possible but unlikely. A body passing near Earth would probably collide with it or get a gravitational boost that would alter its orbit so much that it could never meet up with Earth again. The chances of the orbits of the Moon and Earth being exquisitely right for a capture is so miniscule that all but a few scientists had rejected the idea. The Apollo mission [also] helped to put [this] theory to rest. Lunar samples showed that the Moon and Earth have similar quantities of oxygen isotopes, suggesting a close kinship. If the Moon had formed elsewhere in the solar system, it would probably have had a different isotopic oxygen composition from that of Earth.

---

[95]Ray Spangenberg and Diane Moser, "Birth of the Moon," *Space World,* August 1988, 20.

⊕ *The Fission Theory:* This theory has a long and honorable history. George Darwin, the second son of Charles' ten children, first proposed it. He postulated that Earth, during a period after it formed a core, was at one time spinning extremely fast. It bulged so much at the equator that eventually a small blob spun off, becoming the Moon. The scenario would account nicely for a crucial feature of the Moon deduced by astronomers more than 100 years ago. Based on the satellite's orbital characteristics and size, the investigators calculated that the Moon must be less dense than Earth. The low density implies that the Moon must have only a small metallic core, if it harbors one at all. The fission idea would explain this fact: a fissioned Moon is composed mostly of the Earth's mantle (the layers between the crust and the core). Subsequent calculations showed that Earth would have to have been rotating once every 2.5 hours in order to have spun off the material that became the Moon.... [However,] the Earth-Moon system of today does not have nearly the amount of momentum needed to initiate separation of the two bodies from one another.

⊕ *The Double Planet Theory:* The third classic idea is the double planet theory, by which the Moon and Earth formed concurrently from a cloud of gas and dust. Thus, the raw materials for the Moon came from a ring of material in orbit around Earth. As Earth grew, so did the ring and the embryonic Moon within. This theory always had trouble explaining why the Moon has such a small metallic core compared with that of Earth.... Although the binary planet hypothesis explains the similarity of the composition of Earth and the Moon with respect to oxygen isotopes, it does not account for the differences in volatiles and refractories. Most important, it runs into the angular momentum problem. That is, it does not explain how Earth's rotation came to be twenty-four hours, which is faster than predicted by simple accretion models, and how the ring could have acquired enough circular motion to stay in orbit.[96]

---

[96]Taylor, "The Scientific Legacy of Apollo," 41–42.

For these reasons, these theories were rejected, and the Giant Impact Theory was adopted almost unanimously.

- *The Giant Impact Theory:* "The new theory, proposed by Cameron and William Ward, proposes that a planetary body struck Earth, causing material from the mantles of both objects to be thrown into space. Within a few hours, the new material moved far enough from Earth to accrete by its own gravity and form the Moon. Because the lunar material came solely from the outer regions of both objects, it would contain little iron from the cores. The high temperatures produced by the collision would have vaporized the more volatile elements....The most recent calculations assume the colliding body to be one-seventh as massive as the proto-Earth, a value approximately equal to the mass of Mars. Each body consists of an iron core, which makes up one-third of its total mass....The collision occurs at a relative speed of 11 kilometers per second. The colliding body is partially destroyed by the impact and its iron core completely separates from the mantle. Four hours after the initial collision, the core strikes Earth again and is swallowed. Some of the mantle material thrown into space by the collision clumps together by self-gravity to produce a granite object orbiting Earth that is almost exactly the Moon's mass."[97] This encounter occurred about 4.4 billion years ago, and "the impact could have raised the temperature of Earth and the Moon by between 3,000 and 4,000 kelvin, more than enough to melt rock."[98] As a result of these extreme temperatures, "'Some of Earth's mantle is vaporized along with the projectile. Slower-moving vapor stays around Earth for about 1,000 years, causing the planet to glow like a dim star.' "[99] Furthermore, "The Giant Impact model also accounts for the lack of volatiles and water on the Moon. 'The jetted vapor gets rid of the volatiles,' Melosh said.... Assuming that 50 to 100 percent of the lunar material

---

[97]"Was the Moon Formed by a Giant Collision?" *Astronomy*, July 1986, 69.

[98]"The Day an Object Struck Earth and the Spin-off Formed the Moon," *New Scientist* (1 April 1989): 27.

[99]Betty Nolley, "Lunar Origins: The Giant Impact Theory," *Space World*, June 1986, 31.

is derived from the projectile, S.R. Taylor said, solves the problem of discrepancies in composition between the Moon and Earth's mantle. And, Taylor added, the Mars-sized projectile model accounts for the large angular momentum of the Earth-Moon system."[100]

The Three Major Stages of Earth's Early History

The Primordial Earth
A lifeless, barren rock like the other inner planets.

Transitional Earth
Struck by a Mars-sized impactor, Earth was transformed...

Modern Earth
...into a water-covered planet with its own large moon

Figure 3.9: Earth has gone through three major stages: the "primordial" stage, the state Earth was in after it had finished its gradual process of accretion from the solar disc, the "transitional" stage that it went through as a result of being impacted by a body roughly the size of Mars, and its "modern" stage, where it remains today.

Most astronomers now support the Giant Impact Theory. However, they believe that the Mars-sized object that struck Earth was a planetesimal, the last and largest remaining planetesimal out of the thousands that had, over time, combined to form Earth. However, though I do believe the Moon was created by a Giant Impact, I do not believe that the impactor was a planetesimal.

The scientists who developed the Giant Impact Theory needed to find a suitable candidate large enough and fast enough to create the kind of powerful impact necessary to thrust enough of Earth's mantle into space to create the Moon. In doing so, however, they may have jumped to the conclusion that the body that disrupted Earth was a planetesimal. Though I admit that the planetesimal theory seems the most plausible on the surface, there is one significant assumption lying behind it that I find troublesome.

The planetesimal is believed to have collided with Earth at about 40,000 kilometers per hour, or 24,840 miles per hour. This was the

---

[100]Nolley, "Lunar Origins: The Giant Impact Theory," 31.

speed a Mars-sized planetesimal would have needed to be moving in order to generate enough energy to throw a large portion of Earth's mantle into space, according to the CRAY simulation. However, Earth currently orbits the Sun at approximately 66,621 miles per hour, so this theoretical planetesimal must have been going over 90,000 miles per hour. The scientists who came up with this figure never explained how this planetesimal could have accumulated so much extra momentum.[101] Thus I believe this is a critical error in the planetesimal theory, as it seems unlikely that a planetesimal could have been moving quickly enough to strike Earth with sufficient force to create the Moon. It is difficult to account for such a dramatic difference in speed between the two bodies using the accretion model, since that process was very slow and gradual, and would not have produced such a high difference in relative velocity between the two bodies.

So is the Giant Impact Theory in error? I don't think the problem lies in the theory itself, but rather in the conclusion that the body that struck Earth was a planetesimal. Since evidence from the outer planets seems to suggest that all of them had come into conflict with Planet X at least once in their history, it may be that at one time Earth had also come into conflict with this same planet. One of Planet X's satellites may have struck early Earth, the Moon forming from the ejecta. The same impact may have also knocked Earth into a new orbit closer to the Sun, simultaneously tilting its rotational axis 23.5 degrees to the ecliptic and giving it a much faster rate of rotation. Some of the ejecta from this impact stayed at Earth's original orbit, 2.8 A.U., forming the asteroid belt. The comets may also have originated from water and rock that had been thrown from Earth's mantle, as we shall see.

Though this theory seems, on the surface, to be largely speculative, it actually has a surprising amount of support from scientific data gathered since the late 1980s. Based upon this data, I have formulated a new theory which explains the creation of Earth, the Moon, Earth's seas and atmosphere, the asteroids, and the comets.[102] This theory is essentially a combination of the Planet X Theory and the Giant Impact Theory, which I will henceforth refer to as the "Planet X/Giant Impact Theory" or "PX/GI Theory". This theory, as we shall see, explains

---

[101]See Richard A. Kerr, "Theoreticians Are Putting a New Spin on the Planets," *Science* 258 (23 October 1992): 548.

[102]This theory is actually not original, but a modification of the same basic theory proposed by Zechariah Sitchin in his book, *The Twelfth Planet* (New York: Avon, 1976).

many of the eccentricities of the inner solar system which otherwise have no explanation.

Clue #7: Earth's Spin Rate, Axial Tilt, and Orbit

The Giant Impact did more than melt Earth and create the Moon. It also significantly accelerated the rotation rate of Earth, tilted Earth's axis (as it had done to Neptune, Uranus and possibly Saturn), and may have even moved Earth to a new orbital station (as it had done with Pluto and possibly Neptune).

1) Earth's Rapid Rotation Rate: Until recently, scientists studying computer simulations of planets forming from planetesimals believed that Earth's rotation was caused by the accumulated impacts of these planetesimals. Over time, they believed, the massive amounts of planetesimals impacting Earth's surface during its formative period gradually caused Earth to spin on its axis, explaining why it rotates.

> Over the past twenty-five years, calculations of how planetesimals would collide with a protoplanet showed a slight excess of the off-center hits that would impart prograde spin over hits that would twist the planet in the opposite direction.... It was thought to stem from a subtle interplay between the slightly different speeds of planetesimals orbiting on either side of a growing planet and the elliptical shape of the planetesimals' orbits.[103]

Recently, however, scientists have come to the conclusion that Earth's rotation rate is too fast to have been derived solely from a series of small impacts with minor planetesimals. Instead, they now believe that Earth's relatively fast rotation rate was the result of one giant impact —the same Giant Impact that had created the Moon. (See Figure 3.8.)

Luke Dones and Scott Tremaine, two scientists at the University of Toronto, have found that the amount of rotational momentum derived from the early accretion of the protoplanet was not nearly enough to account for Earth's current rotation rate. "The simulated bombardment leaves a growing planet spinning once a week at most, not once a day."[104] But one impact by a large object late in Earth's formative period, the same kind of object proposed by the Giant Impact Theory,

---

[103]Kerr, "Theoreticians Are Putting a New Spin on the Planets," 548.
[104]Kerr, "Theoreticians Are Putting a New Spin on the Planets," 548.

could account for Earth's excess rotational speed. "If that theory is right, say Tremaine and Dones, the impact that formed the Moon almost surely gave Earth its spin. They argue that the effect of a single impact would overwhelm any net spin accumulated from the innumerable and largely self-canceling impacts of smaller bodies."[105] Melosh's model of the Giant Impact confirms this. "According to Melosh's model, very soon after Earth formed 4.5 billion years ago, a planet about 1.5 times more massive than Mars (or 15% as massive as Earth) struck the newborn Earth at an oblique angle. The impact vaporized a large part of crust and upper mantle, spewing it up into space like a jet. The blast also accelerated Earth's rotation, spinning the planet like a child's top."[106]

However, the question remains, was the giant impactor a planetesimal, or one of the satellites of Planet X? In fact, an analysis of the inner planets Mercury and Venus provides evidence that helps refute the conclusion that the object that struck Earth was a planetesimal. For example, both Mercury and Venus have extremely slow rotation periods compared to that of Earth, though their rotation periods should be significantly faster if they too had experienced a Giant Impact with a large planetesimal during their formative periods. Mercury rotates only once every 58.65 Earth days, while its orbital period is only

The two inner rocky planets, Mercury (top) and Venus (bottom), display none of the characteristics of the outer planets from Earth outward, including no significant axial tilt, satellites, or ring systems. Both also rotate very slowly compared to the fairly rapid rotation of the rest of the planets, indicating that these two planets were never influenced by the hypothetical Planet X that would explain the existence of these anomalous behaviors in the rest of the planets.

---

[105]Kerr, 548.

[106]Damond Benningfield, "Mysteries of the Moon," *Astronomy* 19 n.12, December 1991, 52.

slightly longer — 87.97 Earth days.[107] Venus rotates so slowly that it actually orbits the Sun more frequently than it rotates around its own axis. Its orbital period is 224.7 Earth days, but its rotation period is only 243.01 Earth days. Furthermore, Venus' sluggish rotation is retrograde, or "backwards," so that on Venus the Sun actually rises in what we would perceive to be the western horizon.[108] Apparently neither Mercury nor Venus, with their slow rotation rates and lack of satellites, had been significantly affected by the theoretical large, last planetesimals to strike them — though this is believed to be true of the rest of the planets. Their ponderous rotations have apparently remained unchanged since they first accreted. But since the planetesimal accretion model demands that each of the planets was struck by one huge planetesimal in the final stage of their formation, an impact which is supposed to have, among other things, dramatically accelerated their rotation rates, why are the rotation rates of Mercury and Venus so ponderously slow? Furthermore, why do Mercury and Venus lack satellites, or orbiting material of any kind?

It is important to note that Mercury and Venus are the only two planets in the entire solar system that rotate so ponderously slowly. They are also the only two planets without satellites of any kind, in contrast with all the other planets in our solar system. This contrast is particularly apparent when comparing Mercury and Venus to the outer planets, as all the outer planets have particularly complicated satellite and ring systems, as well as surprisingly rapid rotation rates, considering their size (Neptune makes one full rotation at an amazingly fast rate of 16 hours, 6 minutes, 36 seconds relative Earth time).

This is predictable, of course, according to the Planet X/Giant Impact Theory. Planet X's orbit never took it far enough into the inner solar system to allow it to affect Mercury and Venus directly. These two planets should therefore be considered pristine examples of what the other planets would have been like if Planet X had never existed: slow and/or retrograde rotation rates, little or no axial tilts, no ring systems, and no satellites. In short, it is arguable that Planet X is responsible for most of the anomalies in our solar system. It is also possible that axial tilts, satellites, and ring systems should also be considered anomalous to a well ordered system. The evidence seems to point to the idea that most, if not all these anomalous conditions in our

---

[107]Kaufmann, *Universe*, 146.

[108]Kaufmann, *Universe*, 164–65.

solar system were all created by catastrophic encounters with Planet X, and not by normal accretion mechanisms as has been assumed to this point. Most astronomers agree that the Moons of Uranus, the rings of Saturn, and Earth's Moon at the very least were created by catastrophic encounters between these bodies and one or more other planet-sized bodies. I would like to suggest that all of these types of anomalies present in our solar system were created by Planet X, which travels regularly through our solar system "seeding," in effect, the various planets and producing "offspring" in the form of satellite and ring systems. The fact that Mercury and Venus are so very different from the rest of the planets in this manner, combined with their relative distance from the Sun, is therefore yet more evidence supporting the Planet X/Giant Impact Theory.

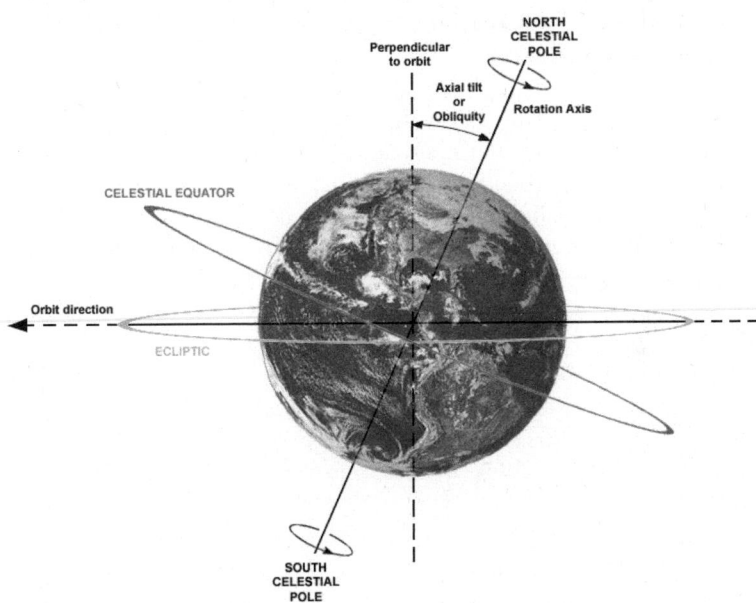

Figure 3.10: Earth's axial tilt of 23.5° is higher than average for our solar system, and much higher than Mercury and Venus, indicating the need for some sort of significant interaction with another planetary body to explain the anomaly. As with the outer planets, Planet X fits the bill perfectly. Image courtesy Wikipedia.

2) Earth's Axial Tilt. The Giant Impact is also responsible for Earth's 23.5 degree axial tilt. Not only did the mysterious impactor significantly accelerate Earth's rate of spin, it also altered the angle of Earth's rotational axis relative to the plane of the ecliptic. Richard Kerr explains in "Making the Moon, Remaking the Earth" how the Giant Impact not only created the Moon but also dramatically changed, among other things, Earth's axial tilt:

> Researchers considering how the solar system formed from a ball of dust and gas have been driven to the conclusion that one of the last acts of creation was the collision of the partially formed proto-Earth with a body about the size of Mars. That catastrophe could have splashed enough debris into Earth orbit to form the Moon and guarantee terrestrial lovers their Moonlit nights. It could also have knocked Earth into its 23-degree tilt, ensuring the procession of the seasons.[109]

If it were not for this tilt, Earth would not have seasons. "The seasons occur primarily because Earth's rotation axis isn't perpendicular to the plane of its orbit around the Sun. Instead, the inclination of the rotation axis, or obliquity, is about 23.5 degrees. The axis always points the same direction in space — the north pole points toward the star Polaris — as Earth orbits the Sun."[110] Because of the tilt in Earth's axis, as Earth orbits around the Sun its surface is exposed to sunlight of varying degrees of intensity. Sunlight can strike Earth directly at latitudes between 23.5 and -23.5 degrees, but above or below those latitudes on Earth the sunlight is indirect. This has the effect of making Earth's surface temperature more uniform overall. Without the seasons, Earth would be a place of extremes, and uninhabitable by mankind.

3) A New Orbit for Earth. Could it be possible that the Giant Impact also propelled Earth into a new orbit? This possibility has yet to be proposed in mainstream science, mainly because until recently there has not been enough evidence to form a coherent hypothesis. Now, however, there is mounting evidence that Earth had originally orbited not at 1 A.U., its current position, but at around 2.8 A.U., where the

---

[109]Richard A. Kerr, "Making the Moon, Remaking Earth," *Science* 243 (17 March 1989): 1433.

[110]Neil F. Comins, "A New Slant on Earth," *Astronomy*, July 1992, 45.

asteroid belt now lies. The impact with a satellite of Planet X may not only have shattered early Earth, it also may have thrown its shattered remains into a new orbit closer to the Sun. A small part of the shattered remains of Earth may have been thrown clear, however, remaining at Earth's original orbit to form the asteroid belt.

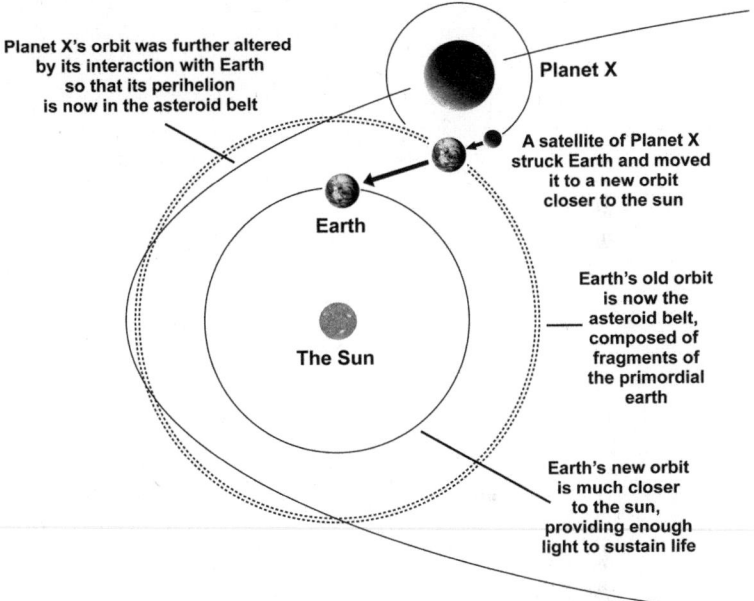

Figure 3.11: Planet X conflicted with the primordial Earth in its original orbit where the asteroid belt now lies, moving it to a new orbit closer to the Sun where there is adequate Sunlight to support life. The other results of the collision were the creation of Earth's Moon, Earth's rapid spin rate, its axial tilt and of course the countless asteroids in the asteroid belt, the forever-circling debris that remains as an eternal witness in heaven of the conflict between Earth and Planet X.

The idea of a planet orbiting at 2.8 A.U. is not an original one. In fact, the search for a planet at 2.8 A.U. first started nearly two centuries ago, as we have seen, in 1801. A group of astronomers, led by Johannes Bode, was searching for a planet that, according to Bode's Law, should orbit at around 2.8 A.U. from the Sun. During their search, they failed to find a planet, but they did discover the asteroids Ceres and Pallas. When they found these asteroids, they came to the conclusion that they must be the remnants of a planet that had once orbited at around 2.8 A.U. but had been somehow destroyed.

Since then hundreds of thousands of asteroids have been sighted and cataloged, and millions more, ranging all the way down to the size of a dust particle, remain to be discovered. All together, they make up a "belt" of asteroids that circle the Sun. But the question first raised by Bode and his colleagues remains unanswered: are these asteroids the shattered remains of a planet that once orbited at 2.8 A.U.? The presence of a belt of shattered rocks circling at 2.8 A.U. seems to indicate that there was indeed once a planet orbiting there, a planet which at one time had met with a sudden, disastrous fate.

Asteroid Gaspra, as imaged by the Galileo spacecraft in 1991. Gaspra is a typical S-Type, or "stony" asteroid, primarily composed of olivine and pyroxene that circles on the inner edge of the asteroid belt. Olivine and pyroxene are also the predominant minerals in Earth's mantle, leading some to believe that the asteroids originated from Earth due to the Giant Impact.

Bode and his colleagues assumed that this belt of asteroids accounted for all of the material that made up this shattered planet, that no parts of that primordial planet were moved away from that planet's original orbital position at 2.8 A.U. However, there are a number of problems that make this assumption untenable. First of all, there is not enough material in the asteroid belt to account for an entire planet. As Kaufmann explains, "The combined matter for all the asteroids, (including an estimate for those not officially known) would produce an object barely 1,500 km in diameter, considerably smaller than our Moon. Therefore, if the asteroids are fragments of Bode's missing planet, it cannot have been large enough to rank with the terrestrial planets."[111] Second, until recently it was not known how this planet could have been shattered. "Geologists and physicists have never been able to produce a good theory to explain how a planet could fragment or explode."[112] One popular explanation for the existence of

---

[111] Kaufmann, *Universe*, 324.

[112] Kaufmann, *Universe*, 324.

the asteroids is that they are planetesimals left over from a planet whose formation was stopped by the immense gravitational influence of nearby Jupiter. "Constant gravitational perturbations caused by the enormous mass of Jupiter probably kept planetesimals from ever accreting into a larger object in the region between Mars and Jupiter. As a result, the missing planet never had a chance to form."[113] The problem with this explanation, however, is that it fails to take into account the fact that there is not nearly enough material in the asteroid belt to create an object even the size of our Moon, let alone a planet. It also assumes that the forming Jupiter had accumulated enough mass quickly enough so that its gravitational pull was sufficient to disturb the missing planet's formation. It would be much easier to simply rely on the same theory that explains the problems with the outer planets to explain the existence of the asteroid belt: the asteroid belt is the partial remnants of a catastrophic encounter between a planet at 2.8 A.U. and Planet X.

But since there are not enough asteroids to account for a planet-sized object, most of that planet must have been moved elsewhere. Could this explain the origin of Earth? If Earth had originally orbited at around 2.8 A.U., it would explain both the existence of the asteroid belt *and* Earth's Moon, axial tilt, and rapid rotation rate. A Giant Impact with one or more satellites of Planet X might have been powerful enough to thrust Earth into an orbit closer to the Sun, with a small amount of residual material in the form of a ring of rocky debris circling the Sun as evidence of the impact. Since Planet X is at least three times as massive as Earth, any sort of conflict between the two planets would most certainly have resulted in a significant shift in Earth's orbit.

Despite the fact that Bode's Law may have helped us discover the original orbit of Earth, ironically, it cannot be used to support the Planet X/Giant Impact Theory. This is because Bode's Law states that planets must have formed at *both* 1 A.U. *and* 2.8 A.U., whereas the Planet X/Giant Impact Theory holds that no planet ever formed at 1 A.U —only at 2.8 A.U. However, even though Bode's Law has proven fairly accurate in predicting the distances of most of the planets from the Sun, it is important to remember that it is based upon *current* conditions in our solar system; it is based upon the assumption that Earth always orbited at 1 A.U., which is not necessarily the case, as we

---

[113]Kaufmann, *Universe,* 324.

have seen. Actually, a much simpler equation can be derived if we remove Earth (or any planet) from the 1 A.U. position altogether, and recalculate the progression based upon the idea that Earth did in fact originally form at around 2.8 A.U.

For example, if we remove Earth from the sequence at 1 A.U., making the original, pre-Impact sequence of planets Mercury (.39 A.U.), Venus (.72 A.U.), Mars (1.52 A.U.), Earth (2.75 A.U.), Jupiter (5.2 A.U.), Saturn (9.54 A.U.), Uranus (19.18 A.U.), and Neptune (proposed original orbit of 39.44 A.U., Pluto's mean orbit), we see an even simpler equation. Assuming that Neptune originally orbited around where Pluto orbits, around 39 A.U., each planet is seen to be roughly twice the distance away from the Sun as the previous planet (approximately 1.91 times as distant, on average). Using this system, there is no need to count out numbers, add, and then divide by ten. In this system, each of the planets is simply twice (1.91 times) the distance from the Sun as the previous planet.

Table 3.1: Elwell's Law
Compared to Actual Distances of the Planets from the Sun[114]

Planet:	Elwell's Progression:	Actual Distance: (A.U.)	% Deviation
Mercury	(1 x .39 = .39)	0.39	(0%)
Venus	.39 x 1.91 = **.74**	0.72	2.8%
Mars	.74 x 1.91 = **1.42**	1.52	6.6%
Earth	1.42 x 1.91 = **2.72**	(2.75)	1.1%
Jupiter	2.72 x 1.91 = **5.19**	5.20	0.2%
Saturn	5.19 x 1.91 = **9.91**	9.54	3.7%
Uranus	9.91 x 1.91 = **18.94**	19.18	1.3%
Neptune/Pluto	18.94 x 1.91 = **36.17**	39.44	8.3%

---

[114]Text and table partially borrowed from Kaufmann, *Universe,* 321.

As you can see, Elwell's Progression, or "Elwell's Law" is as close or even closer to reality than Bode's Law, and it is much simpler. The fact that each of the planets is approximately 1.91 times as far away as the previous planet instead of two times might be explained by the fact that, over the hundreds of millions of years that the planets have orbited the Sun, they have slowly but inevitably surrendered some of their territory to the Sun's relentless gravitational pull. It is important to note that the planets are not traveling in perfect circles around the Sun, but are actually traveling in huge spirals that will inevitably lead them to crash back into the Sun that bore them. They maintain their orbits for such long periods of time because there is almost no friction in space. As such, they do not decelerate over time as do objects on Earth, which quickly succumb to the friction caused by the resistance of air and solid objects to motion, as well to the overpowering gravity of Earth. However, over aeons of time, even the planets gradually slow down, resulting in a gradual diminishing of their orbital distances from the Sun, as Elwell's Law reveals.

Not only does the existence of a ring of shattered rocks at around 2.8 A.U. indicate that a planet once orbited there, but also the fact that removing the point of Earth's origin from 1 A.U. to 2.8 A.U. creates a much simpler mathematical progression all but proves the validity of the Planet X/Giant Impact Theory. And there is much more evidence to come.

Clue #8: Earth's Seas and Atmosphere

Until recently, the scientific community has taken the existence of Earth's oceans for granted. They assumed that the oceans had formed along with Earth gradually, over time. They also believed that the oceans have been in their present state since the beginning, one of the unique features of Earth that distinguished it from its relatively arid neighbors in space.

However, this view has gradually changed, a change which has dramatically accelerated since the middle of this century as our scientific understanding of Earth's seas and atmosphere has rapidly progressed. Most scientists now believe that Earth's seas were created suddenly, when water was, for some reason, forcefully ejected from Earth's interior. "Researchers had hypothesized since the 1950s that the terrestrial atmosphere was created by gases emerging from the interior of the planet...about 4.4 billion years ago."[115] Scientists have recently confirmed this conclusion, having found that the chemical makeup of Earth's mantle includes a significant quantity of water. We now know that the majority of water on Earth is not in the oceans and atmosphere, but in Earth's mantle, chemically bonded with the rocks themselves. Raymond Jeanloz explains in his article, "The Hidden Shore,"

> Where is most of the water on Earth? The answer seems obvious, spelled out by the areas of vivid blue in a Rand McNally atlas: surely the oceans that cover two-thirds of the planet's surface constitute the bulk of terrestrial H_2O. Indeed, that eminently reasonable assumption was endorsed for many years by the geological community. But nature is not so conveniently self-evident. In the past decade more than a few doubts have been raised about the magnitude, distribution, and location of Earth's water supply.... A growing number of geologists...are becoming convinced that most of the water on Earth may lie unseen, deep below the surface, dissolved into the rocks of the mantle and the core.[116]

These geologists arrived at this conclusion after experimenting with minerals known to exist in abundance in Earth's mantle. In order to test how these minerals reacted to the extreme pressures found in Earth's mantle, they applied simulated amounts of pressure by compressing small samples of these minerals in a specially designed press. Though olivines and pyroxenes—the most common types of minerals found in Earth's mantle—simply deformed under the pressure, hydrous, or "water carrying" minerals such as serpentine and talc (which are produced when olivine and pyroxene react with water), made loud crackling noises as they were put under pressure. This crackling noise, they deduced, came from a chemical reaction caused by the extreme pressure of the press that had actually caused the molecules in the samples to rearrange themselves into new substances. As Jeanloz explains, "When we compressed the hydrous materials between the diamond anvils, we obtained startling results: frequent bursts of sound over a wide range of pressures and temperatures.

---

[115]Claude J. Allegre and Stephen H. Schneider, "The Evolution of the Earth," *Scientific American*, October 1994, 69.

[116]Raymond Jeanloz, "The Hidden Shore," *The Sciences*, January/February 1993, 26.

Crystal structures became unstable in the serpentine even at pressures exceeding 250,000 atmospheres."[117]

The crackling sound, as these scientists discovered, was the sound of water being released from the serpentine and talc. The extreme pressures had actually initiated a chemical reaction that had caused the water to separate from the serpentine and talc, forming the elements olivine, pyroxene and water. Therefore, they surmised, this sort of reaction must also occur in the mantle, where serpentine and talc are fairly common.

Water is routinely outgassed from earth's mantle via geysers and volcanoes, but only on a small scale, as seen here with the "Rainbow and Castle Geyser" in Yellowstone National Park. In order to release enough water from the hydrous minerals in Earth's mantle to form Earth's oceans and atmosphere, a massive impact from a very large object would have been required.

Based upon these facts, they came to the conclusion that the majority of Earth's water supply resides not in the oceans, but in Earth's mantle: chemically bonded to the rocks, waiting for a sudden, massive increase in pressure to release it. Furthermore, they deduced that Earth's seas and atmosphere must have been formed early in Earth's history as a result of a sudden, massive outgassing of this water from Earth's mantle. This hypothesis, surprisingly, was largely unchanged from the scenario first hypothesized in the 1950s by William W. Rubey:

Rubey argued that the composition of Earth's hydrosphere corresponds roughly to gases and fluids that emanate from volcanic eruptions, hot springs, and geysers. All the water now lying at Earth's surface, he maintained, was purged from the interior via pathways to the surface. Thus according to conventional wisdom, the mantle was hot enough early in geologic time to cook out all of the water inside it. The entire planet was degassed in one giant, and fairly rapid, burst. That start set in motion the hydrological cycle, through which the

---

[117]Jeanloz, "The Hidden Shore," 29.

hydrospheric balance is exquisitely maintained: water is taken up into the atmosphere by evaporation and returned to the surface through precipitation.[118]

This rapid outgassing created both the atmosphere and the seas as we know them today. "The rapid outgassing of the planet liberated voluminous quantities of water from the mantle, creating the oceans and the hydrologic cycle."[119] But what could have caused this sudden massive outgassing from the mantle? These massive fountains of water emanating from the deepest parts of Earth could not have simply "happened" without some sort of massive influx of energy into the Earth's mantle. But is there a catastrophe on record that would fit into the 4.4 billion B.C. time frame? According to the Giant Impact Theory, Earth was struck by a Mars-sized object approximately 4.4 billion years ago. This correlates perfectly with the need for a catastrophic "cause" for the rapid outgassing of water from Earth's mantle. In fact, the Giant Impact theorists, aware of the 4.4 billion B.C. date, probably chose this date for the impact because an object the size of Mars impacting Earth would be an excellent trigger for the kind of explosive outgassing geologists are describing. When the Giant Impact occurred, according to their theory, the mantle was superheated and jetted into space, at which time all the water and other volatile (easily evaporated) elements were "cooked" out of it. This left a cloud of volatile materials, primarily water, hanging in space, where astronomers believe it formed a ring system. Most of the materials in this cloud then eventually settled back down to Earth's surface to form Earth's seas and atmosphere, and the rest of the ejected mantle remained in space to form the Moon.

As we have seen, two of the primary reasons scientists concluded that the Moon was formed from Earth's mantle were (1) the Moon and Earth's mantle are very similar in composition, both being primarily made of olivines and pyroxenes, and that (2) the Moon's interior is completely devoid of water and other volatile materials, the only explanation being that the materials it is made up of had had all the volatiles "cooked" out of them by extreme temperatures. These temperatures were so high that they could *only* have been caused by an impact between Earth and a large, fast-moving body. Therefore, the

---

[118]Jeanloz, "The Hidden Shore," 30.

[119]Allegre and Schneider, "The Evolution of the Earth," 70.

Moon *must* have been formed by a Giant Impact—no other explanation fits. Comins explains,

> First, the Moon has essentially the same chemical composition as Earth's mantle. Specifically it has few refractory, or high melting-point, materials such as iron and nickel. This makes sense if the Moon came from our mantle, since most of the refractory elements in Earth sank to the core long before the alleged collision occurred.... Second, the Moon lacks volatile, or low melting-point, materials like water and carbon dioxide in its rocks. These should not have all outgassed from the Moon rocks by now. By comparison, we still observe outgassing on Mercury today. The new theory neatly explains this. The energy generated by the intruder's impact would have created temperatures on Earth far greater than any it had ever experienced before. The Moon-forming collision would have created enough extra energy to heat the rocks in Earth's mantle sufficiently to bake out much of the carbon dioxide and water trapped in them.... Consequently, the mantle rocks splashed into orbit around Earth by the impact would have had few volatiles, and so the Moon started with an extreme deficit of frozen gases and water.[120]

Astronomers now believe that Earth had a ring system formed from materials that had been thrown into orbit around Earth by the Giant Impact. These smaller and more volatile materials eventually precipitated back down to Earth to form the oceans, continents and Earth's atmosphere, whereas the larger chunks of Earth's mantle remained in orbit and combined together to form the Moon.

---

[120] Neil Comins, "The Earth without the Moon," *Astronomy*, February 1991, 53.

The water that had been outgassed from the melted mantle then froze in space or fell back to Earth to form the seas and atmosphere. That which stayed in space combined with the dust and rocks that were blown into close orbit around Earth. Since computer simulations show that a single asteroid only 10 kilometers across could throw so much dust and rocks into space that the entire Earth would be covered by a blanket of deep darkness, the Giant Impact must have made a thick blanket indeed. "According to computer simulations, the real problem would have been the plume of vaporized rock and other debris from the impact, which would have exploded outward into space. Quickly spreading around the world, the plume would have enveloped the planet in a blanket of rock vapor having a temperature of 2,000K, and a pressure about 100 times that of our modern atmosphere."[121] The material that would later form the Moon, however, was thrown well clear of Earth, and thus did not mix with the water (in the form of ice) now orbiting around Earth with the rest of the lighter materials that had been thrown up by the Giant Impact. Eventually this lighter material settled back down to Earth, forming the atmosphere, seas, and the upper part of Earth's crust.

So, Earth's seas and atmosphere were also created as a result of a cataclysmic encounter between Earth and Planet X. But did all of the materials ejected from Earth's mantle by the Giant Impact stay within Earth's gravitational field, or was some of it thrown clear? Perhaps some of this ejected material was thrown clear of Earth's gravity and/or carried away by Planet X, if Planet X is indeed the culprit behind the Giant Impact. If so, can we locate any of this free-floating material anywhere in our solar system? Any remnant of the Giant Impact would have to be of the same composition of Earth's mantle: i.e., primarily olivines, pyroxenes, and some iron, among other things. Furthermore, it would have to have at least some trace amounts of water, as a large amount of water was also ejected into space by the Giant Impact. In fact, the asteroid belt has all of these things, and more.

---

[121]M. Mitchell Waldrop, "Goodbye to the Warm Little Pond?" *Science* 250 (23 November 1990): 1078.

Clue #9: The Asteroid Belt

The links between Earth and the asteroid belt are numerous and growing. For example, scientists studying the IRAS[122] data have found that Earth's orbit is actually embedded in a ring of dust which they believe came from the asteroid belt. "Astronomers have found indirect evidence that Earth is embedded in a ring of asteroidal dust particles that orbits the Sun."[123] Moreover, Earth has many minor asteroids orbiting nearby, which are also the same composition as the asteroids in the asteroid belt. These asteroids, called "Near Earth Asteroids," or NEAs, are distinguished from the asteroids in the asteroid belt, which are referred to as "belt asteroids." (See Figure 3.12.)

> Earth shares the inner solar system with a swarm of objects—some of which pass closer to us than the Moon. Astronomers know relatively little about these roughly 200 odd-shaped bodies, called near-Earth asteroids (NEAs), which range from 40 kilometers to 10 meters in length. A few thousand more of these NEAs—some with the potential to crash into our planet—may await discovery.... NEAs represent only a tiny fraction of the million or so asteroids 1 km or larger in diameter thought to orbit the inner solar system. Most asteroids reside in a belt-shaped region that lies between the orbits of Mars and Jupiter.[124]

There are also other groups or "families" of asteroids with elliptical orbits that periodically take them in and out of the inner solar system, all of which intersect with Earth's orbit:

> The NEAs so far detected may represent just the tip of the iceberg. Astronomers estimate that there exist 5,000 to 10,000 near-Earth objects with diameters of 0.5 kilometers or larger. These objects come in three classes: Amors, Apollos, and Atens. Amors cross the orbit of Mars and approach that of Earth, and 10 percent of them cross Earth's path over the course of a few hundred to a few thousand years. Apollos cross Earth's orbit, and a few even come closer than the Moon. Atens, for most of their

---

[122] The InfraRed Astronomical Satellite, mentioned earlier in this chapter.

[123] Ron Cowen, "New Link between Earth and Asteroids," *Science News* 144 (November 6, 1993): 300.

[124] Ron Cowen, "Rocky Relics: Getting the Lowdown on Near-Earth Asteroids," *Science News* 145 (February 4, 1994): 88.

orbit, lie closer to the Sun than Earth does, but may intersect Earth's path at their farthest point from the Sun.[125]

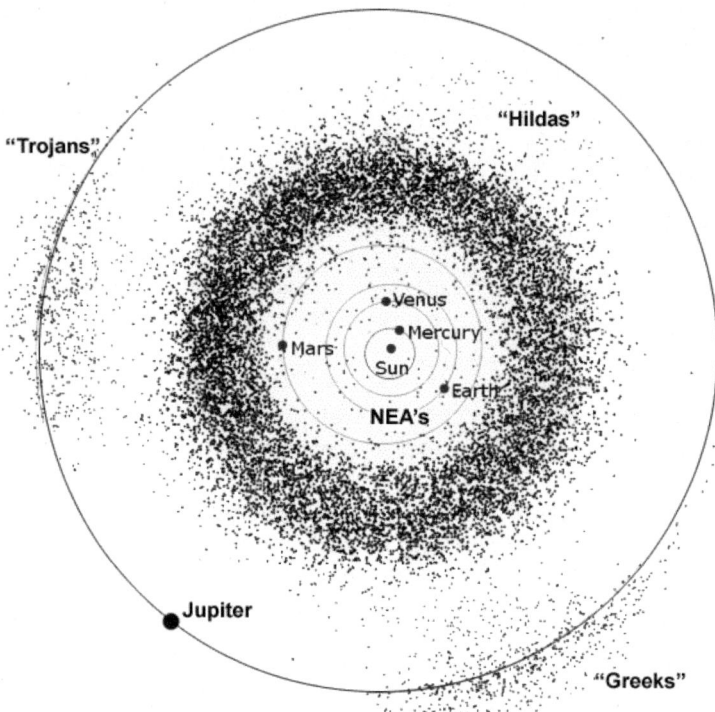

Figure 3.12: The "Asteroid Belt", indicated by the thick ring of dots, actually occupies a very wide swath of area between Mars and Jupiter. However, despite the fact that the above figure appears to indicate that the region is very crowded, asteroids are in fact very widely spread apart. Many asteroids can be grouped into "families" or groups of related asteroids, with some 20-30 families identified as of the date of this writing (May 2010). Some of these families, such as the "Greeks" and "Trojans", actually share their orbits with the planet Jupiter. There are also other groups closer to the Sun such as the group known as "Near Earth Asteroids" (NEAs), which are divided into the Amor, Apollo and Aten families, but the asteroid belt has by far the most known asteroids.

There is so much asteroidal material orbiting in sync with Earth that some astronomers have suggested that there may be another, minor asteroid belt orbiting close to Earth. This was first suggested in 1993

---

[125]Cowen, "Rocky Relics," 88.

by Tom Gehrels, David L. Rabinowitz, and James V. Scotti, astronomers at the University of Arizona at Tucson.

> "Rabinowitz and his colleagues suggest that the unexpectedly large number of NEAs argues for the existence of another asteroid belt — this one near Earth. Gehrels proposes two sources: debris gouged out of the Moon, when other, larger asteroids slam into it; or further breakup of the main-belt asteroids already fragmented by collisions within the belt."[126]

The fact that there may be another, minor asteroid belt in which the Earth orbits may help explain where much of the residual debris from the Giant Impact was thrown. Even excluding the portions of the mantle which later became the Moon and that which settled back down to Earth, there must have been billions of tons of debris that was thrown up by the Giant Impact. And not all of it would have remained behind when Earth was thrown into its new orbital station at 1 A.U. Apparently some of this debris accompanied Earth on its way in, which accounts for the existence of the Amor, Apollo, and Aten families of asteroids as well as the large amount of lesser asteroidal debris recently discovered sharing Earth's orbit.

Until recently, astronomers have been unsuccessful in their attempts to connect the origin of the NEAs and other asteroidal material with that of the belt asteroids. This connection has always been assumed, but never proven. They have also tried to compositionally link both NEAs and belt asteroids with meteorites, which they believe are simply bits of NEAs which survive the descent through Earth's atmosphere. Their assumption is that all of the asteroidal material in the inner solar system, including that which falls to Earth in the form of meteorites, originated in the asteroid belt. "Scientists have long sought to identify similarities between certain types of meteorites, chunks of space rock that fall on Earth, and asteroids, large blocks of rock orbiting the Sun which astronomers study largely by spectra measured through telescopes."[127]

---

[126] *Ibid.*

[127] Jonathan Eberhart, "Carbonaceous Meteorites and Asteroids," *Science News* 136 (November 18, 1989): 334.

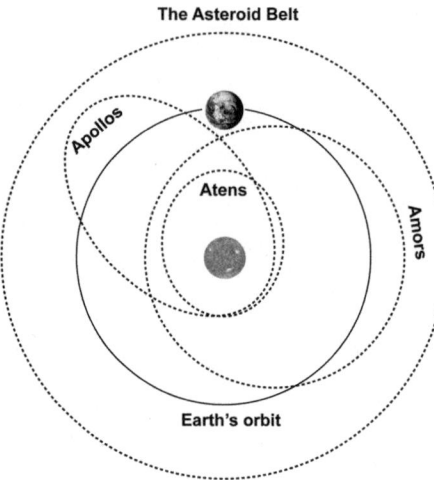

Figure 3.13: Besides the main asteroid belt there are three independent families of what are called "Near Earth Asteroids" or NEAs, that orbit within the inner solar system. Two of these families, the Amors and the Apollos, have orbits that cross over that of Earth, and may have been responsible for various mass extinctions throughout Earth's history. The existence of these belts, which also cross across the main asteroid belt, supports the thesis that Earth had been dragged in from the asteroid belt by some powerful force, leaving a trail of asteroids behind it as evidence for its point of origin within what is now the asteroid belt.

A common origin *has* been determined for both Apollo asteroids and meteorites,[128] so if all asteroids originated from the belt, therefore the meteorites almost certainly also originated from the belt. Meteorites, also known as "chondrites," *are* made of the same material that makes up the majority of Earth's mantle: olivine and pyroxene, and also usually contain significant amounts of magnetic iron. As Binzel explains, "More than 80 percent of the meteorites falling to Earth are stone-like assemblages of olivine and pyroxene that are classified as ordinary chondrites."[129]

Though past attempts to prove that meteorites and belt asteroids come from a common source have been unsuccessful, recently one belt asteroid — 3628 Boznemcova — was found to be compositionally similar to most of the meteorites that fall to Earth.

> Although ordinary chondrite material dominates meteorite falls, the identification of a main-belt asteroid source has remained elusive. [However,] from a new survey of more than 80 small main-belt asteroids comes the discovery of one having a visible and near-infrared reflectance spectrum similar to L6 and LL6 ordinary chondrite meteorites.... the discovery of a spectral match

---

[128]"Meteors from Asteroids," *Sky & Telescope,* March 1989, 246.

[129]Richard P. Binzel, et al, "Discovery of a Main-Belt Asteroid Resembling Ordinary Chondrite Meteorites," *Science* 262 (December 3, 1993): 1541.

may indicate the existence of ordinary chondrite material within the main asteroid belt.[130]

This discovery forms a clear link between meteorites and belt asteroids and thus also between Near Earth Asteroids and belt asteroids. These compositional similarities make it all the more likely that all asteroids in the inner solar system had a common origin.

But do NEAs come directly from the asteroid belt, or are they simply secondary remnants of the Giant Impact? If they are simply secondary remnants of the Giant Impact, how can they be so similar to the belt asteroids? Most astronomers currently believe that the NEAs and meteorites are simply belt asteroids that were thrown toward Earth as a result of impacts with other asteroids, combined perhaps with the gravitational influence of Jupiter. However, their theories are unconvincing. The answer, as I see it, is actually very simple. All of the asteroids, whether NEA or belt asteroids, were thrown from Earth's mantle as a result of the Giant Impact. But why are the majority of the asteroids still orbiting at an average distance of 2.8 A.U. from the Sun? Because that is where Earth originally orbited before the Giant Impact threw it into its new orbit at 1 A.U. NEAs are probably those remnants of Earth's mantle that followed Earth in as it was moved into its new orbit closer to the Sun, explaining why many of them have orbits that stretch between Earth and the asteroid belt. (See Figure 3.13.)

The compositional similarities between meteorites, Near-Earth Asteroids, belt asteroids, and Earth's mantle don't stop there. Other tests of the spectra of belt asteroids have revealed many other compositional similarities with Earth. For one, tests have shown that many meteorites and belt asteroids have been in contact with liquid water — impossible unless they had originally been part of a larger, warmer planetary body.

> A particularly intriguing possible parallel exists between a class of meteorites known as carbonaceous chondrites (primarily types C1 and C2) and the so-called C-type asteroids. Studies of their compositions suggest that water was involved in the formation of both.... Two overlapping lines of evidence are involved. Larry A. Lebovsky of the University of Arizona in Tucson and Thomas D.

---

[130]Binzel et al, "Discovery of a Main-Belt Asteroid Resembling Ordinary Chondrite Meteorites," 1541.

Jones, now with the Central Intelligence Agency in McLean, VA, report that the infrared spectra of some C-type asteroids include absorption bands with a 3.0-micron wavelength characteristic of water of hydration — a sign that water was present when the asteroids formed — and indicating the presence of clay minerals called phyllosilicates.... Faith Vilas of NASA's Johnson Space Center in Houston, and Michael J. Gaffey of Rensselaer Polytechnic Institute in Troy, N.Y., report high-resolution, visible light spectral absorption features that they say are due to iron oxide in such clays. Spectral measurements of the asteroids indicate the oxidation state of the iron, which researchers can compare to the iron oxide in carbonaceous chondrites.[131]

The fact that some belt asteroids and meteorites show evidence of once having been in contact with liquid water is powerful evidence to link them with the Giant Impact. "Liquid water has modified minerals on the surfaces of certain asteroids, according to recent spectroscopic observations. Additionally, direct evidence for so-called aqueous alteration of asteroid material has been found in meteorites collected from the stratosphere by aircraft."[132] As we have seen, all of the water was cooked out of that part of the mantle which later became the Moon. As a result of this rapid evaporation of millions of tons of water out of the hydrous minerals in Earth's mantle, a massive amount of water was left floating in space along with other secondary ejecta from the Giant Impact. Some of this water eventually settled back to Earth to form Earth's seas and atmosphere, but apparently the rest of it then combined with the secondary ejecta from the Giant Impact, forming the icy, rocky asteroids of the asteroid belt. It could be that before the water had completely frozen, it had reacted chemically with the hot surfaces of the newly formed asteroids. Or, perhaps the liquid water now known to exist inside the mantle reacted with the other minerals there, and then later those minerals were ejected by the Giant Impact. Either way, it is highly unlikely that water could have ever been warmed sufficiently to become liquid on the near-absolute zero surface

---

[131]Eberhart, "Carbonaceous Meteorites and Asteroids," 334.
[132]"Wet Asteroids," *Sky & Telescope,* December 1990, 590.

temperature of an asteroid, and there is no explanation as to how the water had gotten there in the first place.[133]

Therefore, an alternative explanation needs to be found, and the Planet X/Giant Impact Theory fits perfectly: After the Giant Impact, the majority of the material that was thrown clear of Earth's gravitational field remained in Earth's original orbit, forming the icy, rocky asteroids of the asteroid belt. Meanwhile, as Earth was hurtling toward its new orbital station at 1 A.U., some of the ejecta from the impact followed it in, taking on elliptical orbits of varying sizes depending upon where they became detached from Earth's gravitational pull. In this way, the Amor, Apollo, and Aten classes of asteroids were formed. The remainder of the ejecta that followed Earth all the way in to its current orbital station then continued to circulate along Earth's new orbit as a ring of dust and small asteroids. These ejecta, along with the occasional NEA, occasionally fall back to Earth in the form of meteorites.

Despite the plausibility of this evidence, it is still not absolute proof that the asteroid belt originated from Earth's mantle. But there is other evidence that proves irrefutably that the asteroids *must* have come from the interior of a planet that once orbited at 2.8 A.U. This startling evidence came to light in October, 1991 when the *Galileo* space probe flew near the asteroid "Gaspra" on its way to Jupiter.[134]

Before the flyby, astronomers had assumed that Gaspra, and all the belt asteroids, were simply remnants of planetesimals that had failed to accrete into a planet, largely due to the interference of Jupiter's gravity. Thus by studying Gaspra, they felt they could gain an insight into the conditions accompanying the formation of rocky planets like Earth. Richard Talcott, writing before the *Galileo* data was fully analyzed, explains what he and other astronomers were expecting the data to reveal: "Gaspra, like many asteroids, is probably the fragment of an older and larger asteroid. Thus *Galileo*'s flyby of Gaspra should provide a new perspective on the conditions prevailing in the early solar system. It should tell us about collisions among the planet-forming bodies."[135]

---

[133] More recent analysis has confirmed substantial amounts of water on at least two asteroids: "Scientists Find Second Asteroid with Water on It", MailOnline.com: http://www.dailymail.co.uk/sciencetech/article-1319278/Scientists-discover-second-asteroid-water-answer-life-Earth.html

[134] Richard Talcott, "Galileo Views Gaspra," *Astronomy*, February 1992, 53.

[135] Talcott, "Galileo Views Gaspra," 53.

However, as the data on Gaspra slowly trickled in, the astronomers were shocked to find that Gaspra has a magnetic field ... a seeming impossibility which immediately disproved their theory that the asteroid belt is merely the remnants of a planet that simply failed to accrete. In fact, it not only disproved their theories, it totally blew them out of the water. The editors of *Astronomy* magazine explain the dilemma that astronomers now face:

> *Galileo*'s images of Gaspra taken in 1991 quickly became the classic textbook examples of what an asteroid looks like. But this "typical" asteroid has taken on a unique character. This past December [1992] *Galileo* mission scientists announced that this 16-kilometer-long chunk of rock appears to have a magnetic field. It was a surprising discovery. Small asteroids aren't supposed to have magnetic fields—such fields are generated by the churning of molten iron cores, *and only large worlds such as planets are candidates for molten cores*.... The origin of Gaspra's field is a mystery. Gaspra is certainly too small to have a molten core itself. But it does imply that Gaspra has a great deal of iron in its composition. Gaspra's irregular shape—it measures 16 by 14 by 12 kilometers—suggests that it is the fragment of something bigger. *Perhaps Gaspra was once part of the iron-rich core or mantle of a larger object.* Despite whatever catastrophic event shattered its parent world, Gaspra managed to retain traces of its magnetic field [emphasis mine].[136]

Only a planet-sized object could have been the point of origin for Gaspra, a planet which had been shattered so completely that part of its core had been ejected into space. The large amount of iron in Gaspra could only have been formed in the core of a planet — there is no other possible explanation for this phenomenon. Rich iron deposits, particularly magnetized iron, can only originate from the core of a large body. This is because only planet-sized bodies have interiors that are sufficiently molten so that the relatively heavy iron can float down to the molten center of the planet, where over time it becomes concentrated and magnetized.

However, even if you put together all the known (and estimated) asteroidal material in our solar system into one large body, there

---

[136]"Asteroid Gaspra Surprises Astronomers," *Astronomy,* April 1993, 20–21.

would still not be nearly enough to create a body even the size of our Moon, let alone a planet. Therefore, the only explanation is that a planet-sized object once orbited at 2.8 A.U. — a planet that had been partly destroyed, the majority of its remains moved elsewhere. And as we have seen, the only planet that fits the profile is Earth. The most likely candidate to be a remnant of a planet that once orbited at 2.8 A.U. is Earth because Earth clearly suffered from a Giant Impact early in its history. This scenario also explains why many meteorites are magnetic — they, like their cousins in the belt, originated from the lower mantle and core of Earth.[137] Another reason the planet-of-origin for the asteroids has to be Earth is that it is one of only three large, rocky bodies in our solar system known for sure to have magnetic fields: Mercury, Earth, and Ganymede, a satellite of Jupiter.[138] Since it is obviously neither Mercury nor Ganymede, Earth is the only possible point of origin for the asteroids.

The last bit of evidence for linking the asteroids with Earth is the fact that organic materials have been found on some meteorites and, recently, on at least one asteroid. This asteroid, "130 Elektra," contains significant amounts of water as well as many organic materials previously thought only to exist on Earth. "The carbonaceous chondritic meteorites are known to contain organic matter.... Asteroid 130 Elektra [also] contains a vast array of complex organics, including alkanes, alkenes, purines, amino acids, and so forth."[139] The existence of these organic materials is strange enough, but the existence of amino acids —the complex building blocks for proteins — on an asteroid is nothing short of incredible. Yet the facts speak for themselves. How could such complex organic materials spontaneously form on a freezing, lifeless asteroid? There is probably barely enough heat to initiate chemical reactions, and conditions aren't exactly ideal for the formation of relatively complex chemicals such as amino acids. Only Earth could have had an environment in which amino acids and similar organic materials could have formed in abundance.

The existence of amino acids and other organic materials on an asteroid should be enough to question whether or not it might have

---

[137]Richard A. Kerr, "Magnetic Ripple Hints Gaspra is Metallic," *Science* 259 (January 8, 1993): 176.

[138]"Jupiter Moon In Select "Magnetic Club," *Daily Herald* (Illinois), 12 December 1996, sec. 1, p.2. (Associated Press release.)

[139]D.P. Cruikshank and R.H. Brown, "Organic Matter on Asteroid 130 Elektra," *Science* 238 (October 9, 1987): 183–84.

originated from Earth, but the combined witness of liquid water, concentrated, magnetized iron, and organic materials cries out for an Earth origin. What other conclusion could one draw from these facts? Thus as it turns out, the men who first discovered the asteroids Ceres and Pallas were correct. The asteroids *were* the remnants of a shattered planet — Earth. But only now do we have the ability to prove it.

Clue #10: The Comets

Comet Hale-Bopp, which passed near Earth in 1997. Hale-Bopp clearly showed a comet's two distinct tails, the white-colored dust tail on top, and the blue-colored ion tail on the bottom. The "dust tail" is actually caused by the sublimation of water ice on the surface of the comet, where the water ice rapidly converts directly from ice to vapor, which is highly reflective. Without this water ice present on the surface, the comet would be just like any other asteroid. Comets also tend to have long, highly elliptical orbits, indicating that an object with a highly elliptical orbit must have imparted some of its orbital characteristic upon them sometime in our solar system's ancient past.

Of the many interesting things that have been recently discovered about the comets, perhaps the most interesting thing is the fact that they are more similar to the asteroids and their cousins, NEAs and meteorites, than had been previously thought. In fact, some had theorized as early as a century ago that comets and asteroids are so closely related that they only differ in appearance. "As far back as 1861 the American astronomer Daniel Kirkwood declared, 'Meteors and meteoric rings are the debris of ancient but disintegrated comets, whose matter has become distributed around their orbits.' Hard evidence for this came with Giovanni Schiaparelli's proof that the Perseid meteors of mid-August belong to an orbit very similar to that of Comet Swift-Tuttle (1862 111). Many other relationships between comet and meteor orbits are now known."[140] Another link between comets and asteroids is the fast-moving object named 3200 Phaethon, which was recently discovered, "traveling in virtually the same orbit as

---

[140]"Meteors from Asteroids," 245.

the Geminid meteors."[141] These meteors travel in elliptical orbits that bring them across Earth's orbit. The elliptically shaped orbits of some NEAs and comets forms further links between them. (See Figure 3.14.)

"And new evidence provides further hints that asteroids — NEAs in particular — may be closely related to two other relics from the solar system's infancy — comets and meteorites. 'These bodies [NEAs] may provide the missing links between meteorites, comets, and main-belt asteroids'"[142] This new evidence is the newly discovered fact that the comets, like many asteroids, also contain large amounts of water ice *and* organic matter. Cowen explains,

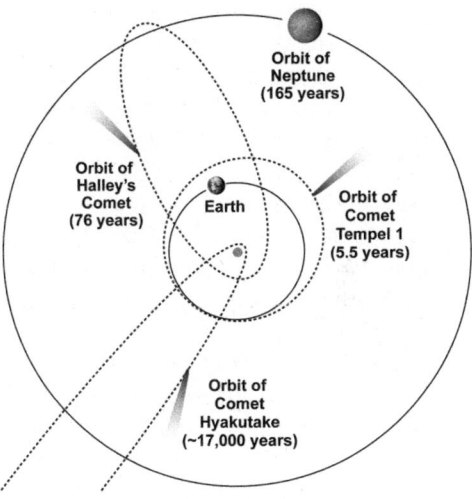

Figure 3.14: *This diagram shows three different comets with very different orbital periods to demonstrate the wide variety of orbital characteristics displayed by comets. Comets are generally categorized into two classes based upon their orbital periods: short-period comets with orbital periods of less than 200 years such as Halley's and Tempel 1, and long-period comets with orbital periods in excess of 200 years such as Comet Hyakutake. More recent analysis, however, shows that the comets are no different than asteroids, except for the relative abundance of water ice on their surfaces. Moreover, many of their orbits are the same. For example, the orbit of Comet Tempel 1 is very similar to that of some near-earth asteroids.*

Another source of NEAs may be the mixtures of ice, dust, and frozen organic goo known as comets. Typically, the Sun's warming radiation evaporates some of the volatile compounds in comets whenever they visit the inner solar system. The expelled gas drags dust out with it, forming the fuzzy coma around the nucleus of the comet as well as its familiar tail. Such an object would seem to bear little resemblance to the rocky

---

[141]*Ibid.*
[142]Cowen, "Rocky Relics," 88.

body of an asteroid. But near the end of its lifetime — after passing through the inner solar system hundreds or thousands of times — a comet may have little gas to expel and thus lack the raw materials to form a coma or tail. Evidence also suggests that over time, a crust of inert dust forms over a comet's frozen nucleus. Its volatile compounds trapped beneath this crust, the comet would appear dormant. And since scientists classify as NEAs all near-Earth objects that lack a coma and a tail, a "dead" comet would indeed fit the description.[143]

And there are asteroids that fit this description. One example is an Apollo asteroid called 1979 VA. Modern observations of the asteroid classified it as a simple asteroid. However, after a search through old astronomical records, it was discovered that 1979 VA had already been spotted and cataloged — as a comet. "On a plate exposed Nov. 19, 1949, he found an object at the same place that calculations indicated 1979 VA should lie. However, the object had a faint, but definite, tail. Indeed, in 1949, astronomers identified the object as a comet and dubbed it Wilson-Harrington. Researchers now say that the comet and the asteroid are one and the same."[144] Another enigmatic object is the asteroid 2060 Chiron. Though it was originally officially classified as an asteroid, recent changes in its behavior have made this classification problematic. "In the past few years ... as Chiron's orbit has brought it closer to the Sun, it has begun to shine. Chiron is emitting gas, and it is surrounded by a faint halo: it is a comet, not an asteroid. And as comets go, it is a whopper: Halley's Comet is only 15 km across, while Chiron, according to Dr. Mark Sykes of the University of Arizona, could be up to 370 km across, if it is as dark as other comets."[145]

> The unusual object 2060 Chiron has developed a gas coma of cyanogen.... Chiron, which orbits between Saturn and Uranus, was classed as an asteroid when it was discovered in 1977 and assigned minor planet number 2060. But in mid-1989, astronomers discovered that it had developed a faint coma of dust and so more properly ought to be classed as a comet. The new finding emphasizes Chiron's cometary nature. Cyanogen (CN) is

---

[143]Cowen, "Rocky Relics," 89.
[144]*Ibid.*
[145]"Flickerings in Outer Darkness," *The Economist,* 9 March 1991, 85.

commonly found in the spectra of the nuclei and ionized gas tails of comets, but it has never before been detected at such a great distance from the Sun. Cyanogen results from the breakup of a parent molecule such as hydrogen cyanide (HCN) or from more complex polymer grains.[146]

With its cyanogen coma, Chiron forms the missing link between asteroids and comets, proving that they have a common origin.

Despite the reality that the facts show that there are only cosmetic differences between comets and asteroids, and that the evidence clearly points to an origin point of the comets in the inner solar system — specifically, from the mantle of Earth — many astronomers continue to maintain that the comets actually originated in the "Kuiper Belt", a band of small, icy objects that surrounds our solar system. This theory took yet another blow in 2006, however, when the *Stardust* unmanned probe was launched. The *Stardust* probe was designed to visit a recently discovered comet named "Wild 2" in order to collect dust from its tail in order to verify its point of origin from within or outside of our solar system. They assumed that Wild 2, like all comets, was from the Kuiper Belt, but when the dust samples from Wild 2 were brought back to Earth and studied, they discovered that not only was Comet Wild basically an asteroid in composition, its origin is from our inner solar system!

The Stardust Probe was launched in 2006 to take samples of the tail of Comet Wild 2, which it did successfully. However, when scientists analyzed the data, instead of finding proof of their assumption that Comet Wild 2 — like all comets — originated in the outer solar system, they found that Comet Wild 2 actually originated in the inner solar system — a dramatic affirmation of the Planet X/Giant Impact theory.

Studies of samples the craft brought back from the comet Wild 2 are causing some of those same astronomers to reconsider what comets actually are. For instance, although Wild 2 orbits like a

---

[146]"Chiron: Cyanogen Gas Emission Detected," Astronomy, May 1991, 22.

comet, it's built like an asteroid.... A chemical analysis of the Stardust samples resembled objects from the inner solar system's asteroid belt instead of the pristine and ancient materials expected to be deep-frozen in the much more distant Kuiper Belt, beyond Neptune, said Hope Ishii, the California-based Lawrence Livermore National Laboratory physicist who led the research. "The first surprise was that we found inner solar system materials, and the second surprise was that we didn't find outer solar system materials," Ishii said. For some astronomers, the results come as a relief that a handful of prevailing computer models aren't seriously flawed. The models had been indicating a major shake-up in the formation of the solar system that would have scattered materials far and wide — causing, for instance, inner solar system materials to reach the outer solar system.[147]

All of the evidence clearly points to the fact that the comets, like the asteroids, originated within the inner solar system. Moreover, this evidence corroborates the majority opinion that our solar system experienced some sort of "major shake-up" that caused a great deal of chaos in what would otherwise have been a highly ordered system. This "space invader" that disrupted the formation of our solar system, as we have seen, is fully answered by the Planet X-Giant Impact theory that we have been proposing, where a planet roughly 3-5 times the size of Earth invaded our solar system and, over time, came into conflict with all of the outer planets and some of the inner planets, from Neptune to Earth. When it struck Earth, it shattered it and moved the greater part to an orbit closer to the Sun, leaving remnants behind in the form of the asteroids and comets, which continue to circle the Sun to this day as an eternal witness in heaven of the greatness of God and His defeat of the dragon.

CONCLUSION

If these ten clues indeed point to an existence of a tenth planet, a Planet X in our solar system, then it is the obvious choice for our mysterious "Star of Bethlehem." This planet may have entered our solar system in the primeval past, disrupted the orbits of several

---

[147] Anne Minard, "Comet Built Like an Asteroid, Scientists Find", *National Geographic News*, January 24, 2008, http://news.nationalgeographic.com/news/2008/01/080123-comet.html. Cf. also David F. Coppedge, "The Message in Surprise Effects", *Acts & Facts*, August 2008, 15.

planets and their satellites, and even created Earth from the remains of a planet that once orbited where the asteroid belt now lies. Its highly elliptical orbit around the Sun makes it so that this theoretical Planet X can only be seen by the naked eye once every thousand years or so, if even then. If this planet does exist, and if it is visible from Earth at its closest approach, it is very likely that it was an object of worship among the ancients. Could it be Planet X that the ancient Sumerians worshiped as Enlil, the chief god of their pantheon? Could it be this same planet that the Babylonians worshiped as Marduk, the Assyrians worshiped as Assur, and the Persians worshiped as Ahuramazda? Could it be that an awareness of the existence of Planet X was part of the Sumerian astronomical legacy that the Magi inherited from the Babylonians? Further, could it be that this planet and the "Star" of Bethlehem were one and the same? If so, then the discovery of Planet X may usher in a new era of religious understanding, the understanding that Planet X was for millennia worshiped as the symbol of the most high God, the same symbol which signaled the advent of the Son of God.

IV

"WHEN ON HIGH": THE ASTRONOMICAL INTERPRETATION OF THE ENUMA ELISH

O LORD my God, thou art very great; thou art clothed with honour and majesty. Who coverest thyself with light as with a garment: who stretchest out the heavens like a curtain: Who layeth the beams of his chambers in the waters: who maketh the clouds his chariot: who walketh upon the wings of the wind: Who maketh his angels spirits; his ministers a flaming fire: Who laid the foundations of the earth, that it should not be moved. (Ps. 104:1-6, KJV)

Now that I had come to the conclusion that the Star of Bethlehem was probably a tenth planet in our solar system, the question still remained as to how this planet fit into the biblical and historical records. Surely a planet of this size and importance would have been known among the astronomer-priests and Magi of ancient Sumer, Babylon, Assyria, and Persia, whose entire lives were spent searching the heavens in search of such unusual phenomena. The ancient Mesopotamians, who worshiped the planets as gods, would certainly have exalted Planet X as the greatest of all their gods. I further reasoned that the existence of Planet X might also explain many of the more

Two of the tablets upon which was found written Enuma Elish, more generally known as "The Babylonian Creation Epic". On these famous tablets, recovered by the legendary British archaeologist Henry Layard in 1849 in the ruined library of Ashurbanipal at Nineveh, is a story of the creation of Earth that has many parallels with that given in the Bible — particularly the idea that Earth was created by God from the body of a "dragon".

enigmatic passages in the Bible, particularly those dealing with the Creation, Nativity, and Second Coming.

The Planet X theory, unlike all of the other theories attempting to explain the Star of Bethlehem phenomenon, fits all of the necessary requirements for the unusual Star described in the text of Matthew 2. Furthermore, since Planet X may become visible to Earth every 1,000 years or so, its existence could explain some of the more enigmatic references to a certain unusual star in the ancient astronomical texts and records of the Sumerians and Babylonians. This is important because, as we have seen, the Magi had been the inheritors of an ancient astronomical tradition passed on to them by the Babylonians. By studying astral references in Babylonian religious texts, then, we may be able to find references to Planet X and use this information to help us understand how the Magi knew that the Star of Bethlehem was a sign that the Son of God had been born. As always, understanding the Bible in its cultural context is crucial to proper interpretation.

> Many of the earliest attempts at a scientific explanation of the celestial phenomena alluded to in Matt. 2:1-12 fell short because almost nothing was known about Babylonian astronomy.... Hence, many different explanations have been proposed by astronomers, professionals as well as amateurs. Some of these authors have not only completely ignored Babylonian astronomy and its astrological implications, but sometimes have not even considered the original Greek text of the gospel.[1]

D'Occhieppo believes that the Star was a conjunction of Jupiter and Saturn, based on the fact that the Babylonians during the Seleucid era (around 300 B.C.) had accurately predicted this conjunction based on past observations of these two planets.[2] However, as we have seen, this interpretation is unlikely. Furthermore, after one compares the Matthew account with Babylonian references to an unusual "star" that they believed had created Earth, it appears even more likely that the Star of Bethlehem phenomenon and Planet X are one and the same.

---

[1] Konradin Ferrari-D'Occieppo, "The Star of the Magi and Babylonian Astronomy," in *Chronos, Kairos, Christos: Nativity and Chronological Studies Presented to Jack Finegan*, eds. Jerry Vardaman and Edwin M. Yamauchi (Winona Lake, IN: Eisenbrauns, 1989), 41.

[2] Occieppo, "The Star of the Magi," 44ff.

"When On High": The Astronomical Interpretation of Enuma Elish

ENUMA ELISH REINTERPRETED

As we saw in chapter I, the most important religious text to the ancient Babylonians was their creation myth, *Enuma Elish*. This ancient text, the name of which means, literally, "When on High," describes the creation of their gods, of heaven, and of Earth. The hero of the story, the god Marduk, in order to save the other gods from destruction at the hands of the evil dragon-goddess Tiamat, kills Tiamat and creates heaven and Earth from her dead body. As we have seen so far in this book, we have found this story to be instructive in helping us better understand the Creation references in the Bible that make mention of a combat between God and a dragon that results in the creation of Earth. However, what makes it particularly interesting to our present study is the fact that in it the Babylonians referred to their god Marduk as a "star." In *Enuma Elish,* Marduk is described as a star that continually crosses "in the midst" of the gods, and even "shepherds" their movements (VII:27-32). Marduk is also described as continually moving through the heavens, regularly returning to the place where he defeated Tiamat and created heaven and Earth, which

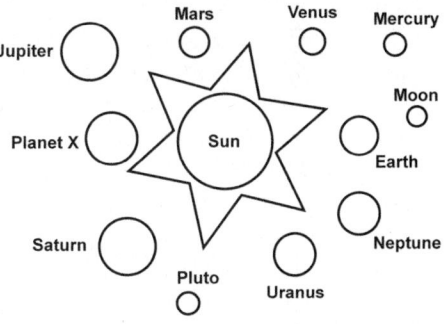

A Sumerian cylinder seal depicting the gods in assembly (top). In between the heads of the two deities on the left is what some believe is actually a depiction of our solar system, which we have reproduced here (bottom). Zechariah Sitchin in his book, The Twelfth Planet believes that the central disk with the extended rays is the Sun, and the rest of the circles surrounding it are actually depictions of all of the planets in our solar system, including the mysterious "Planet X". He believes the Sumerians were aware of Planet X, calling it NI.BI.RU c literally, "the Star of the Crossing" — so called because this planet's cometlike orbit "crosses" over that of the outer planets, taking it into our inner solar system.

213

is of course an excellent description of how a planet moves through space.

Thus, though Marduk is described as a "star" in *Enuma Elish* and other texts, the description of this star's characteristics could only describe a planet. First of all, how can a "star" create Earth? And how can a "star" cross between the "gods," the planets, and even affect their orbits? No *star* could do this, but a planet could. Clearly this is a reference to Planet X. Since the gods of the Sumerians and Babylonians were the planets, and since the orbit of our theoretical Planet X also regularly crosses between the inner and outer planets, it is only logical to assume that the star "Marduk" and Planet X are one and the same.

Of course, the Sumerians and Babylonians had never developed the kind of sophisticated technology necessary to understand how Planet X's orbit could actually cross "in between" the planets. However, as we have seen, one of the premises of this book is that God had given Adam a scientifically accurate description of how He had created Earth — a "Creation story." Adam then told this Creation story to his children, and they to theirs, forming a creation tradition that lasted thousands of years. This tradition was then carried on by Noah and his sons into the post-Flood world. As the sons of Noah divided and multiplied over the face of the Earth, the old Creation story likewise became divided into numerous variant forms over time, many of which strayed significantly from the original story. Abraham, when he fled Ur, took with him the only truly accurate version of the ancient Creation tradition, the version that would later be used by Moses and the Prophets for all the Creation material to be found in the Old Testament.

The Babylonians, of course, had their own variant version of the ancient creation tradition: *Enuma Elish*. However, unlike Abraham, the Babylonians had derived their knowledge of the Creation from the Sumerians, whose former territories they had conquered and subjugated sometime after the downfall of the Sumerian Empire around 2000 B.C. The Babylonians were in turn conquered and subjugated by the Persians around 600 B.C., who then in turn took control of the accumulated learning of the conquered Babylonians as part of the spoils of war. As a result, the priestly class of Persia, the Magi, inherited the ancient knowledge of the Sumerians, via the Babylonians, for their own use. They even adapted *Enuma Elish* for use in the state religious ceremonies of Persia. And since the information acquired from the Babylonians included their extensive knowledge of both the Creation and of astronomy, the Magi became experts in both fields. As a result, the Magi became increasingly associated with astronomy and astrology to the point where the name "Magi" became practically synonymous with "star worshiper."

Centuries later, it is quite probable that the descendants of these Magi used the information codified in *Enuma Elish,* along with other pertinent astronomical information derived from the Babylonians, and from the Hebrews in exile, to determine that the Star of Bethlehem was indeed "Marduk" — Planet X — returned. This explains their belief that the Son of God had been born — no less than the planet of the most high God had returned, and its return must, as they had deduced from the writings of the Hebrew exiles, signal the advent of the Messiah Himself.

Since we know that the Magi were in fact the inheritors of the religion and astronomy of the Babylonians, and that the Magi recognized the Star of Bethlehem as the Sign of the birth of the Son of God, then it is reasonable to assume that *Enuma Elish* may have been one of the primary sources for their understanding of the Star of Bethlehem event. If this is true, then *Enuma Elish* may be more than just a religious text; it may actually be a strikingly accurate scientific account of how Earth had been created in its present form—as the result of a collision with a satellite of Planet X.[3]

Marduk: The Star of the Crossing
Nebiru [Marduk] shall hold the crossings of heaven and Earth, so that they (the gods) cannot cross above and below, they must wait on him.
Nebiru is the star which in the skies is brilliant.
Verily he holds the central position, they shall bow down to him,
Saying, "He who in the midst of the sea restlessly crosses,
Let 'Crossing' be his name, who controls its midst.
May they uphold the course of the stars of heaven;

---

[3]To give credit where credit is due, this idea was originally proposed by Zechariah Sitchin in *The Twelfth Planet* (New York: Avon Books, 1976), 178. To be more precise, his book really should have been named *The Tenth Planet.* Though I hesitate to use Sitchin as a source because much of his book is highly speculative, the material dealing specifically with his theory concerning the existence of a tenth planet in our solar system, "Planet X" does have some validity.

May he shepherd all the gods like sheep.
May he vanquish Tiamat; may her life be straight and short!
Into the future of mankind, when days have grown old,
May she recede without cease and stay away forever.
(*Enuma Elish* VII:125-134, emphasis mine)

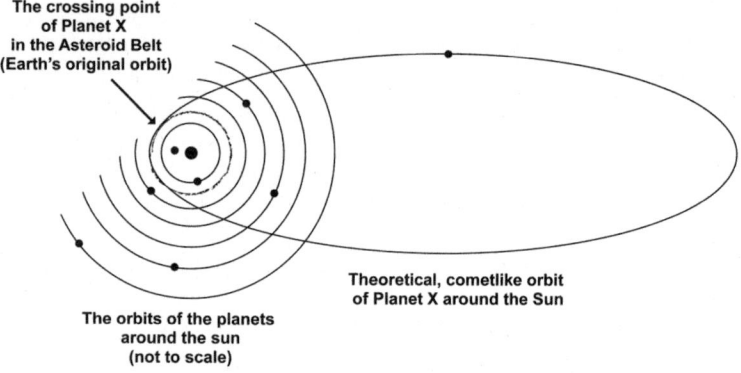

Figure 4.1: The above diagram is based upon a similar diagram in Zechariah Sitchin's seminal work, The Twelfth Planet. Here we can see Sitchin's proposed orbital path for the planet "Nibiru", the name Sitchin believes was the ancient Sumerian name for what we today call "Planet X". Based upon his astronomical interpretation of Enuma Elish, as well as theories regarding Planet X that were in circulation during the time of writing (the early 1970's), Sitchin was able to put together this probable ephemerides (orbital path) for the mysterious Nibiru. This orbital path is much like that of a comet, "crossing through" the commonly understood solar system, finding its perigee (closest approach to the Sun) in what is now know as the asteroid belt. Thus the Sumerian name for the planet: NI.BI.RU, literally, "Planet of the Crossing".

The orbit of the planet "Marduk," according to the Babylonians, is unusual. Its orbit is among the other "gods," the planets, but it is in what they call "the central position," through which it is constantly "crossing." The planets are, of course, bound to roughly circular orbits that cause them to constantly circle, with the exception of Pluto, at approximately the same distance from the Sun. However, the planet Marduk's orbit is special in that it "crosses" the orbits of the other planets. In other words, Marduk regularly crosses through our solar system, literally passing through the orbits of the outer planets, to "the central position," in between the inner and outer planets, where the asteroid belt now lies. Thus, the gods "above and below," i.e., the inner and outer planets, each restricted in their orbits to remain at a constant distance from the Sun, have to "wait," for Marduk to come to them.

According to *Enuma Elish,* then, the planet Marduk does not orbit like a "typical" planet. Its orbit is actually elliptical, just as Planet X's orbit is believed to be. Marduk's orbit is so elliptical, in fact, that it takes Marduk deep into our solar system, past the outer planets, all the way to the "central position" between the inner and outer planets. And, just like our theoretical Planet X, the Babylonians believed that the planet Marduk struck and divided a planet that once orbited in between the inner and outer planets, dividing it into the asteroid belt and what we now know as the planet Earth.

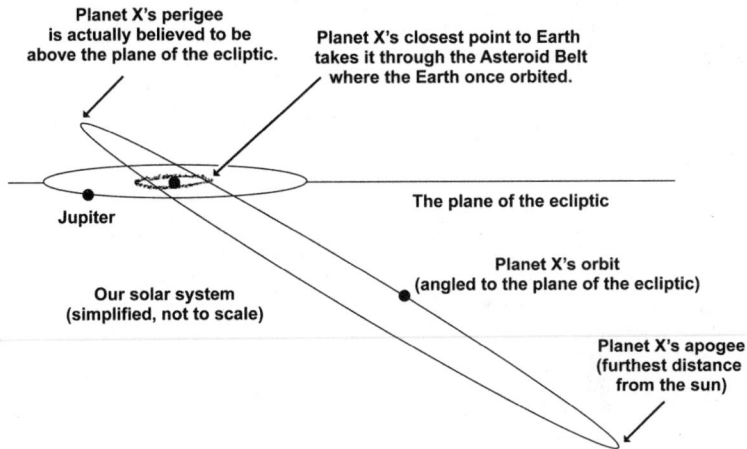

Figure 4.2: *Another view of the orbital path of Nibiru/Planet X. Astronomers believe that Planet X's orbit is actually inclined to the ecliptic plane of the solar system like that of some long-period comets, so that not only does the planet pass in and out of our solar system, but also above and below it. Furthermore, some astronomers believe that Planet X's orbital path precesses over time, so that it occasionally comes in line with the plane of the ecliptic, at which times no doubt it wreaks great havoc with the outer solar system, coming into conflict with "the gods", which would explain many of the eccentricities of the outer planets.*

It is through this "sea" of asteroids in the belt region that Marduk regularly crosses, a feature so distinctive of this planet that the Babylonians also called Marduk "Nibiru" — literally, "Crossing." The metaphor of "the sea" used to describe the asteroids is appropriate because, as we saw in Part III, one of the results of the Giant Impact was the expulsion of massive amounts of water from Earth's mantle, much of which remained in space to combine with some of the rocky ejecta to form the icy, rocky boulders typical of the asteroid belt. Apparently, the Babylonians retained in their creation tradition the knowledge of the water in the asteroid belt by referring to it as the heavenly "sea." This tradition was also clearly upheld by the Hebrews, who likewise referred to the asteroid belt as "the waters above" (Gen. 1:6-8).

Since the asteroid belt is in the midst of the other planets, and Planet X regularly crosses through the asteroid belt, Planet X was believed by the Babylonians to control "the midst" of the planets. It was also believed to be the "shepherd" of the gods, as it was believed to significantly influence the orbital paths of the planets.

A Sumerian cylinder seal depicting a warrior deity vaulting over the dragon/sea. The belief that Earth was created by a great sky god from the body of a sea dragon is one of the most ancient religious motifs in the world, spanning several civilizations over thousands of years. The great "sea" that Marduk is describing as crossing and re-crossing again and again is most likely the asteroid belt, which recent studies have shown does indeed contain a fair amount of water ice. Thus the Hebrew and Babylonian conception of the asteroid belt as a "heavenly sea" in space.

The Dragon in the Sea

Later, in Tablet VII of *Enuma Elish*, Marduk is also described as the one "Who the wide-spreading Sea vaults in his wrath, crossing (her) like a bridge at the place of single combat" (VII:74-75). Here, the "sea" mentioned earlier is clearly identified both with the place where the "star" Marduk defeated and divided Tiamat, and as a place where that "star" still crosses through. Of course no star can cross through our solar system, as its massive gravity would fling the planets out of the solar system entirely, so a planet-sized object must be in view here. And since a planet that fits this description may exist according to mainstream astronomy, it is not too much of a reach to propose that that planet is the one being discussed here. Thus, the basic meaning of this passage is that the asteroid belt is both the place where Earth was divided, and the place where the "star" Marduk — Planet X — regularly returns.

The Heavenly Shepherd

The second concept communicated in this passage is the fact that the "star" Nebiru/Marduk has a significant effect on the orbits of the outer planets. This "star" not only crosses through our solar system, but it also controls, or "shepherds" the planets like sheep. As we saw in Chapter III, a large planet like Planet X would most certainly have an effect on the orbits of any planets it passed near, as is apparently the case with Uranus and Neptune. This "shepherding" concept is corroborated in Tablet VII of *Enuma Elish*, where Marduk is described as the one "Who established for the gods the holy heavens; who keeps a hold on their ways, determines *[their courses]*" (VII:16-17). Thus, according to the Babylonians, Marduk is a "star" that affects the "courses," or orbits, of the planets.

And there are still other references to Marduk as a star. One reference, from a Babylonian astronomical record, calls Marduk a "great star" that moves like a planet (the determinative *mul* before certain words indicates that the word following is the name of a planet):

> When the stars of Enlil have finished,
> the great star shining faintly,
> that halves the sky and stays there,
> is ^{mul}*Marduk, nibiru,* ^{mul}*sag.me.gar;*
> he changes his place and wanders along the sky.

B.L. van der Waerden, an expert on ancient astronomy, believes that this text refers to Jupiter, but cannot explain why Jupiter, one of the brightest objects in the night sky, is referred to as "shining faintly." In his words, "The predicate 'shining faintly' apparently contradicts the name 'great star.' "[4] Jupiter is actually one of the brightest objects in the night sky, so the appellation "shining faintly" is probably not meant as a reference to Jupiter.

Another interesting passage describes the star Marduk in much the same way, except it describes Marduk as a "red star":[5]

> The red star, that, when stars of the night have finished,
> stays where the south wind comes from,
> halves the sky and stays there,
> is the god *nibiru, Marduk*.

Interestingly, Waerden is similarly unable to explain why Jupiter would be referred to as "the red star." "Why Jupiter was called the 'red star' is obscure; perhaps 'red' meant merely 'faint.'[5] However, the appellation "red star" would seem much better suited for Mars, so the Babylonians would surely not have used it to describe Jupiter, especially since Jupiter is not red in color. However, Mars is not a faint object in the sky either, contradicting the first reference. Also interesting is the reference to how the planet Nibiru/Marduk "stays where the south wind comes from" — in other words, it comes from the south of the ecliptic, at an angle to the ecliptic, just as modern astronomers have predicted (See Figure 4.2). I suggest that these descriptions refer to how Planet X appears as it first becomes visible: as a faint, reddish star coming up from the south that gradually grows brighter (and whiter) as it passes through the outer system toward its perihelion in the asteroid belt.

ENUMA ELISH: AN ACCOUNT OF THE CREATION OF OUR SOLAR SYSTEM

I believe that *Enuma Elish* is, in essence, an astronomical text. *Enuma Elish* was, as we have seen, the primary religious text of the Babylonian astronomical religion, a religion where all of the major deities of the pantheon were clearly identified with the Sun, Moon, and planets. Thus, since *Enuma Elish* is a description of how the Babylonian gods came into being, and since the gods of the Babylonians were the Sun, Moon, and planets, then *Enuma Elish* must

---

[4]B.L. van der Waerden, "Babylonian Astronomy. II. The Thirty-Six Stars," *Journal of Near Eastern Studies*, Vol. 8, No. 1 (Jan., 1949), 12.

[5]B.L. van der Waerden, "Babylonian Astronomy. II. The Thirty-Six Stars," 12, note.

"When On High": The Astronomical Interpretation of Enuma Elish

therefore be a description of the formation of the Sun, Moon, and planets.

Though this would seem obvious, one major problem with this theory is the fact that only one of the deities mentioned in the Babylonian version of the Epic, the chief Babylonian god "Marduk," is specifically identified on known Babylonian star charts with a planet (Jupiter). This, despite the fact that none of the descriptions (or actions) of the star Marduk sound anything like Jupiter. The rest of the deities mentioned in *Enuma Elish* are not specifically identified with the planets on any Babylonian star charts. The most likely explanation for this is the fact that the Babylonian version of *Enuma Elish* was a heavily edited version of a Sumerian original, an idea which, as we saw in chapter I, has been the general consensus among scholars in the field of ancient Near Eastern religion. As Heidel points out, "Not only do all the gods, with the exception of Tiamat, appear to have Sumerian names but some of the gods themselves, such as Apsu, Anu, and Enlil, are admittedly Sumerian."[6] Though Marduk replaced the Sumerian god Enlil in the Babylonian version of *Enuma Elish*, the rest of the gods in the Epic were Sumerian deities retained from the previous version, most likely as an attempt to add legitimacy to Babylon's sovereignty over the defeated Sumerians.[7] Since the Sumerians also worshiped the planets, it is likely, therefore, that the Sumerian gods in the Epic also represented the planets, albeit with names different than those used by the Babylonians.

However, despite the fact that an astronomical interpretation is the most plausible, there is simply not enough hard evidence to make a

An image from a Babylonian cylinder seal showing Marduk subduing the sea dragon Tiamat. This is how the ancient Babylonians conceived the creation and ongoing rulership of the Earth: as the defeat of a great dragon by an all-powerful deity, who returns on occasion to make sure the dragon remains subdued.

---

[6]Heidel, *The Babylonian Genesis*, 12.

[7]For a more in-depth discussion of the relationship between religion and politics in the ancient Near East, see my thesis, *YHWH against the Ba'als of Canaan: Contextualizing the Old Testament* (Master's Thesis: Wheaton College, Buswell Library, 1992).

dogmatic assertion that *Enuma Elish* is beyond a shadow of a doubt a scientifically accurate description of the formation of our solar system. Babylonian astronomy never reached the level of sophistication necessary for them to accurately speculate on the creation of the solar system. It is not even clear as to whether or not they were aware that our solar system is heliocentric, even though they had achieved a high degree of skill in predicting the motions and movements of the Sun, Moon, and planets. Yet, despite these facts, *Enuma Elish,* when translated in the context of modern astronomical science, conveys a description of the formation of our solar system that is strikingly similar to the Planet X/Giant Impact theory.

The Traditional Interpretation of the Babylonian Creation Epic
The Planet X/Giant Impact theory was originally inspired by the writings of Zechariah Sitchin. He was the first to come up with the idea that a tenth planet in our solar system had smashed into early Earth, thereby forming the asteroid belt and shifting Earth to a new orbit closer to the Sun. He also believed that the Sumerians worshiped Planet X as the most high god, and that their primary religious text, *Enuma Elish,* was not a fanciful account of the creation of the "gods" but a detailed, albeit mythologized, account of Planet X's conflicts with the planets, Earth in particular. Sitchin's astronomical interpretation of *Enuma Elish* is thus unique and quite ingenious.

Most mainstream scholars, however, feel that *Enuma Elish* is simply a description of the gradual formation of the Earth by slow geological processes. Each of the gods in the epic, they believe, were meant to represent natural forces such as earth, water, and air, all engaging in an unending process of erosion and sedimentation. Barbara Sproul explains her position on the meaning behind the symbolism of *Enuma Elish,* a position which serves as a good example of the mainstream interpretation:

> The Epic of Creation...begins with Apsu (the ocean) and Tiamat (the primeval waters) lying inert together and eventually producing the divine natural forces: Lahmu and Lahamu (silt and slime), Anshar and Kishar (the horizons of sky and Earth), Anu (the heaven, the principle of authority), and Nudimmud, (or Ea, the waters of the Earth, the principle of wisdom). As the offspring grew, they began to order the chaotic world and became rebellious. Apsu and Tiamat, resentful and angry, tried to reassert

themselves. They called Mummu (mist of the clouds, principle of entropy) and together conspired to slay the young gods they had begotten. The plan failed, however, as Tiamat withdrew out of motherly concern and the wise Ea (Earth water) slew Apsu (ocean) with his art and cunning...and locked Mummu away.[8]

Unfortunately, this interpretation fails to take into account the essentially astronomical nature of Mesopotamian religion. Despite this, scholars in this field tend to take this approach to the interpretation of *Enuma Elish* because, apparently, it never occurred to them that the Babylonians might actually have a creation epic that reflected the astronomical and astrological beliefs that were central to their religion. But even the Hebrew creation story in Genesis 1 has heavy astronomical elements, with its prominent references to the Sun, Moon, and stars, despite the fact that the Hebrews appear to have shunned any kind of astronomical research as pagan. Surely, then, the creation story of the Mesopotamians, astronomers *par excellence,* should reflect the astronomical beliefs that were central to their religion.

Thorkild Jacobsen's interpretation is basically the same as Sproul's in that it too is based on the assumption that the Babylonians viewed the creation of Earth as the result of gradual evolutionary processes, primarily erosion and sedimentation:

> The description presents the beginning of the world as a watery chaos in which the powers of the fresh waters underground, Apsu, and the powers of the salt waters in the sea, Tiamat, mingled.... Then in the midst of these waters two gods, Lahmu and Lahamu, came into being ... their names suggest that they represent silt which had formed in the primeval ocean. In their turn they engendered Anshar and Kishar, the horizon, the circular rim of heaven and the corresponding circular rim of Earth. Anshar and Kishar gave birth to Anu...and Anu engendered Nudimmud, who is more familiar to us under his other names, Enki and Ea. He is, as we have seen, the god of running waters, rivers, and marshes.... The speculations by which the ancient Mesopotamian sought to penetrate the mystery of origins were based, apparently, on observations of how new land

---

[8]Sproul, *Primal Myths,* 91.

came into being. Mesopotamia is alluvial, formed by silt brought down by the rivers. It is the situation at the mouth of the rivers where the sweet waters, Apsu, flow into the salt waters of the sea, Tiamat, and deposit their load of silt, Lahmu and Lahamu, to form new land that has been projected backward to the beginnings. This original silt was deposited along the edge of the primeval ocean to form first the horizon Anshar and Kishar, then as it grew more and more toward the center, two large discs An and Ki, heaven and Earth, which were eventually forced apart by their son, the storm god Enlil.[9]

This interpretation is somewhat forced, but not unreasonable. However, like Sproul's interpretation (from which it differs somewhat) it has the fatal flaw of failing to take into account the essentially astronomical character of Mesopotamian religion, and of ancient religion in general. *The importance of astronomy to ancient religion cannot be understressed.*

One example of ancient religion which has been similarly miscategorized is Mithraism, a Greco-Roman religion in vogue around the time of Christ. In the September/October, 1994 issue of *Biblical Archaeology Review,* author David Ulansey wrote an excellent article in which he unlocked the riddle behind the religion of Mithraism, a mystery religion that dominated the Greco-Roman world from around 100 B.C. until it was snuffed out by the rise of Christianity. Although in the past Mithraism had been difficult to understand and categorize, generally labeled as a Persian-Greek fertility cult involving bull worship, Ulansey argues that Mithraism was not based on ferililty, but upon astronomy.

---

[9]Thorkild Jacobsen, *The Treasures of Darkness: A History of Mesopotamian Religion* (New Haven and London: Yale University Press, 1976), 168–69.

"When On High": The Astronomical Interpretation of Enuma Elish

The solution to the mystery came when Ulansey stopped trying to overlay his own presuppositions over the archaeological data and instead let the data speak for itself (not always an easy task). By studying the data within its cultural context instead of attempting to overlay it with modern assumptions, Ulansey came to the conclusion that Mithraism was actually based upon astronomical principles. More specifically, Ulansey came to the conclusion that the primary symbol of the Mithra cult, that of the god Mithra killing a bull, actually symbolizes an important astronomical concept: the precession of the equinoxes.

Earth, due to the combined gravitational pull of the Sun, Moon, and planets, actually "wobbles" slightly in its orbit. Over time, this "wobble" causes Earth's axis to slowly change position — to "precess." As a result of this precession, the poles gradually change direction, describing a full circle in the heavens once every 25,920 years. This gradual shifting of the poles causes the heavens to appear to slowly change position, moving one zodiacal house (30 degrees longitude) every 2,160 years. (See Figure 4.3.)

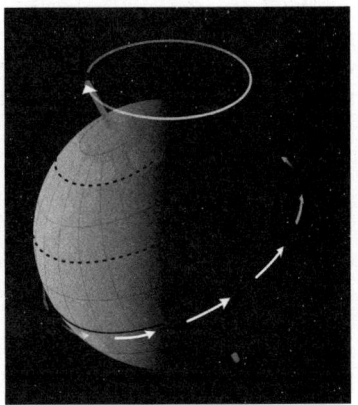

Figure 4.3: Earth's poles "precess" over time due to a slight wobble in Earth's rotation. This causes the Earth's north (and south) poles to trace a circle in the heavens every 25,920 years. Some experts believe that the (re)discovery of precession by Hipparchus led them to create the religion of Mithraism, wherein the deity Mithra was believed to be the god responsible for precession. Image courtesy <u>Wikipedia</u>.

For a long time the Greeks had been ignorant of the concept of precession, and were not even aware that Earth was a sphere. As a result, when the Greek philosopher/scientist Hipparchus (ca. 100 B.C.) discovered from some old Sumerian astronomical records that Taurus had once been the constellation to mark the vernal equinox (ca. 2000 B.C.), instead of the constellation of Aries with which he was familiar, he realized to his horror that the heavens had been slowly moving over the past 2,000 years — moved, he reasoned, by the unseen hands of a previously unknown god. Since Hipparchus was a polytheist, believing in the existence of a god for every natural phenomenon, he naturally concluded that the motion of the heavens must have caused by some mighty, unknown god working invisibly behind the scenes. He further concluded that a god with this kind of power must be mighty indeed, and that he and his fellow countrymen were in danger of falling under his wrath if they did not worship and respect this unknown god.

This fear of retribution from this unknown god caused the Greeks to quickly invent a name for him, "Mithras," and institute his worship all over the Hellenistic world. This explains why Mithraism grew so rapidly and was adopted so universally — the Greeks were afraid that if they did not pay homage to this almighty god, he would grow angry and destroy them.

Realizing that the Greeks had actually discovered the concept of the precession of the equinoxes and, further, that it was an issue of paramount religious importance to them, Ulansey came to the conclusion that the bull in the Mithras cult standard must therefore symbolize the constellation of Taurus. As Ulansey explains,

> The precession of the equinoxes...was discovered about 128 B.C. by Hipparchus. Today we know that the precession is caused by a wobble in the Earth's rotation on its axis. However, Hipparchus, who assumed that the Earth was immovable and at the center of the cosmos, could only understand the precession as a movement of the *entire cosmic sphere.* In other words, Hipparchus' discovery amounted to the revelation that *the entire universe was moving* in a way that no one had ever been aware of before. At the time Hipparchus made his discovery, Mediterranean intellectual and religious life was pervaded by astrological beliefs. It was widely believed that the stars and planets were living gods, and that their movements controlled all aspects of human existence.... In such circumstances, Hipparchus' discovery would have had profound religious implications. A new force had been detected capable of shifting the cosmic sphere: Was it not likely that this new force was the sign of the activity of a new god, a god so powerful that he was capable of moving the entire universe?[10]

---

[10]David Ulansey, "Solving the Mithraic Mysteries," *Biblical Archaeology Review* v. 20 n. 5 (September/October 1994): 50.

Hipparchus had discovered that the entire sky had shifted position from one zodiacal house to another over the past two millennia, and came to the conclusion that a god more powerful than all the other gods in heaven and on Earth was working behind the scenes, gradually moving the entire cosmos with his mighty hands. As this god had in effect "killed" the heavenly bull, the constellation of Taurus, by moving it out of its position of preeminence, "an obvious symbol for the precession would have been the *death of a bull*, symbolizing the end of the age of Taurus.... And if the precession was believed to be caused by a new god, then that god would naturally become the agent of the death of the bull — the 'bull slayer.' "[11] Thus Mithraism came into being, a religion which worshiped the new supreme god, Mithras, who was always portrayed as a man slaying a bull. And since they now believed that this god was the true power behind the universe, the god of all gods, his worship had to be enforced everywhere, over every other god. Thus Mithraism spread rapidly throughout the Roman Empire.

Mithras slaying the heavenly bull, the constellation of Taurus. This fresco of the tauroctony, (lit., "killing of the bull") from the Mithraeum in Marino, Italy shows the central concept behind Mithraism — that the constellation of Taurus was "killed" by the great god Mithras, ushering in the age of Pisces. Image courtesy <u>Wikipedia</u>.

If the gods of the ancient world had not been astral, Mithraism would not have caught on so easily. However, as we know, astral worship was the basis of ancient religion. "Given the pervasive influence in the Greco-Roman period of astrology and astral immortality, a god possessing such a literally world-shaking power would clearly have been eminently worthy of worship."[12] Further, as we saw in chapter II, the Greek emphasis on the worship of the planets was not original, but had been largely borrowed from the

---

[11]Ulansey, "Solving the Mithraic Mysteries", 50.
[12]*Ibid.*, 50–51.

Mesopotamians due to the policy of free cultural exchange embraced by Alexander the Great. "The many references to the learned traditions of Chaldeans by Greek and Roman writers indicate that the impetus for Greek developments in astrology derived from Babylonia."[13] Thus if the Greeks revered the stars so highly, how much more the Mesopotamians, from whom they had borrowed their beliefs?

Had the gods of the ancient world been merely water and silt, that is, rudimentary elements involved in gradual earthly processes of erosion as Jacobsen et al. assume, Mithraism would never have caught on so universally. But Greek religious beliefs were founded firmly upon astronomy, astronomy borrowed from Mesopotamia. And to say that Mesopotamian religion was any less astronomical in character than Greco-Roman religion would be ludicrous, particularly given the evidence analyzed in chapter II. Thus it is most likely that *Enuma Elish* was not a speculative exercise on how Earth was formed through erosion and sedimentation, as the modern interpretation holds, but rather a continuation of an ancient astronomical tradition — a scientific tradition which accurately described the creation of the Sun, Moon, and planets.

The Astronomical Interpretation of the Babylonian Creation Epic

A Babylonian cylinder seal depicting the battle between Marduk and Tiamat. Tiamat is shown standing on planet Earth, with the Moon, her servant Kingu, interceding to defend her. Marduk of course rides atop Planet X, shown here as a cherub-like creature. The ancient Babylonians clearly saw the creation combat as a battle between the two planets.

Enuma Elish is a creation epic that describes how our solar system was created, focusing particularly on the creation of Earth. Instead of using scientific terminology, however, it employs symbolic imagery, such as "gods" and "dragons," to describe the creation of our solar system and of Earth so that the average man can understand it. The genius of this method is apparent in the fact that

---

[13]F. Rochberg-Halton, "New Evidence for the History of Astrology," *Journal of Near Eastern Studies* 43 n.2 (1984): 115.

the timeless symbolism and dramatic format of the Epic allow it to be easily understood even today — if one understands what lies behind the symbolism.

At the heart of this symbolism actually lies a very cleverly composed astronomical document that describes, in amazing detail, how Earth was formed. Interpreted this way, it matches almost exactly with the Planet X/Giant Impact Theory, right down to the creation of the asteroid belt and the comets out of the shattered remains of primordial Earth. Also like the Planet X/Giant Impact Theory, *Enuma Elish* describes the creation of Earth in two stages: an initial formation, and a re-formation due to a cataclysm that divided it into two sections: heaven, and Earth. According to the Babylonian account of the creation, this "re-formation" of Earth occurred when a new planet appeared in the heavens and struck Earth with some sort of weapon, causing Earth to be divided into two parts. This planet then shattered one part, using it to form the heavens, and then hurled the other, intact part away. This intact part eventually became Earth as we know it today. This "giant impact" also formed the Moon, as well as Earth's seas and atmosphere, all of which fits perfectly with modern theories on how Earth was formed in its present state.

The Planet X/Giant Impact Theory aligns almost perfectly with *Enuma Elish,* but only if *Enuma Elish* is translated within an astronomical context. Therefore, I have decided to retranslate key sections of *Enuma Elish* using the Planet X/Giant Impact Theory as a guide. With this in mind, let us go through these sections of *Enuma Elish* line by line, so that we can see for ourselves just how scientifically accurate this ancient text really is.

TABLET I:
A GENERAL OVERVIEW OF THE CREATION OF OUR SOLAR SYSTEM

The Creation of the Sun, Mercury, and Proto-Earth

When on high the heaven had not been named,
Firm ground below had not been called by name,
Naught but primordial Apsu, their begetter,
And Mummu-Tiamat, who bore them all,
Their water commingling as a single body; (I:1–5)

Somehow, this very poetic sounding verse is the text which describes the Babylonian version of how "the gods," the Sun, Moon, and planets, were created. As we saw in chapter III, the consensus of most modern scientists concerning the creation of the solar system was that it was formed by the process of "accretion."[14] That is, a large body of minerals and gasses in outer space, a "nebula," began to rotate and condense into a large "ball" of material due to its collective gravity. As it spun, this ball flattened into a disc, growing hotter and spinning faster, while our Sun formed at its center. Meanwhile, the heavier, rocky materials gathered together nearer the center of the plane and accreted into "planetesimals," or growing planets, while the gasses gathered further out and gradually accreted into much larger but less dense gaseous planets.[15] "Terrestrial planets accrete[d] from rocky material in the warm inner regions of the solar nebula. Meanwhile, the huge gaseous, Jovian planets form[ed] in the cold outer regions."[16]

Unlike the traditional interpretation of the three "bodies" mentioned in the first five lines of *Enuma Elish* which says that "Apsu," "Mummu," and "Tiamat" symbolized salt water, clouds and mist, and fresh water, respectively, Sitchin argues, logically, that in the Babylonian astronomical religion, these three bodies must have represented the Sun, Mercury, and Earth respectively, and that the "water" which "commingled as a single body" must therefore have been the primordial mixture of minerals, frozen liquids, and gasses in the solar nebula out of which these bodies formed.

Therefore, in the beginning of our solar system's formation, according to Sitchin, "Only three bodies exist[ed]: 'primordial AP.SU' ('one who exists from the beginning'); MUM.MU ('one who was born'); and TIAMAT ('maiden of life'). The 'waters' of Apsu and Tiamat were mingled, and the text makes it clear that it does not mean the waters in which reeds grow, but rather the primordial waters, the basic life-giving elements of the universe."[17] According to the astronomical interpretation, the text that leads off the Epic of Creation does not simply describe geological processes on Earth, but the preliminary stages of our solar system, which included a developing

---

[14] I am taking this position because we can now observe other solar systems in the process of formation, and because the Bible is silent on exactly how the pre-earth universe was created.

[15] Kaufmann, *Universe*, 138–40.

[16] *Ibid.*, 138–40.

[17] Sitchin, *The Twelfth Planet*, 212.

Sun, Mercury, and a proto-Earth, the first of the bodies to accrete from the swirling elements of the solar nebula. Thus we may translate the first few verses of *Enuma Elish* in this way:

Enuma Elish I:1–5	The Astronomical Interpretation
When on high the heaven had not been named,	Before the asteroid belt had been created,
Firm ground below had not been called by name,	Before the modern Earth had been created,
Naught but primordial Apsu, their begetter,	The proto-Sun existed, from which issued the…
And Mummu-Tiamat, who bore them all,	…nebular disk in which the planets formed, the first to form being Mercury and the primordial Earth
Their water commingling as a single body;	They were the first to form out of the elements in the nebular disk.

The Creation of Mars and Venus

When no gods whatever had been brought into being,
Uncalled by name, their destinies undetermined —
Then it was that the gods were formed within them.
Lahmu and Lahamu were brought forth,
by name they were called. (I:7–10)

Although this would seem to contradict the previous passage which explains that the gods Apsu, Mummu, and Tiamat had already come into being, the reference to "the gods" in verse 7 actually refers more specifically to the creation of the "children" of Apsu and Tiamat, the first of whom were Lahmu and Lahamu. Apsu, Mummu, and Tiamat were considered to be older gods that had engendered the younger gods. And, as in the similar Greco-Roman myth of the birth of the gods, these younger gods would also overcome and destroy their parents, supplanting them as rulers over the universe.

The names "Lahmu" and "Lahamu" are subject to varying interpretations. The most straightforward interpretation of the words *lahmu* and *lahamu* is "silt" and "slime" respectively, which supports the mundane interpretations offered by Jacobsen and Sproul. Sitchin however, offers a different interpretation. "Etymologically, the names of these two planets stem from the root LHM ('to make war'). The ancients bequeathed to us the tradition that Mars was the god of war and Venus the goddess of both love and war. Lahmu and Lahamu are indeed male and female names, respectively; and the identity of the two gods of the epic and the planets Mars and Venus is thus affirmed both etymologically and mythologically."[18] This verbal root *laḥam*, לָחַם, is also the Hebrew root for "to make war,"[19] and it is interesting that both Baal and Anat, the Canaanite equivalents for these Sumerian deities, were also both considered gods of war.[20] Anat was probably associated with Venus, though Ba'al may have been associated with either Jupiter or Mars.[21] Ares and Aphrodite[22] were the Greek equivalent, and the Roman deities Mars and Venus, the deities from which we get our modern planet names are, of course also closely analogous. In fact, every major Mesopotamian and Mediterranean empire had a god and goddess of war, and in every one they were equated with the planets Mars and Venus.[23] Looked at from the context of the Babylonian astronomical religion, then, one should immediately realize that the characters "Lahmu" and "Lahamu" (lit., "god of war" and "goddess of war") were not intended to represent silt and slime (a rather degrading interpretation), but the planets Mars and Venus.

Enuma Elish I:7-10	The Astronomical Interpretation
When no gods whatever had been brought into being,	The rest of the planets formed later,

---

[18]Sitchin, 213.

[19]Gesenius, W., & Tregelles, S. P. (2003). *Gesenius' Hebrew and Chaldee Lexicon to the Old Testament Scriptures* (436). Bellingham, WA: Logos Research Systems, Inc.

[20]C.f. Arvid S. Kapelrud, *The Violent Goddess: Anat in the Ras Shamra Texts,* (Oslo: University Press, 1969).

[21]The connection between Ba'al and astral worship is not clear. I assume that he shows up in the compound name "Bel- (Ba'al) Marduk," whom we have seen was worshiped as the planet Jupiter.

[22]Homer, *The Iliad,* trans. W.H.D. Rouse (New York: Mentor/Thomas Nelson, 1938), 237ff. The warlike goddess Athena is actually a better match for Anat than is Aphrodite.

[23]For a more complete listing, see Table 2.1

"When On High": The Astronomical Interpretation of Enuma Elish

Uncalled by name, their destinies undetermined —	and their orbits took longer to determine.
Then it was that the gods were formed within them.	More inner planets formed next, taking shape between the orbits of Mercury and primordial Earth.
Lahmu and Lahamu were brought forth	These two inner planets were Mars and Venus.

The Creation of Saturn, Jupiter, Uranus, and Neptune

> Before they had grown in age and stature,
> Anshar and Kishar were formed, surpassing the others.
> They prolonged the days, added on the years.
> Anu was their heir, of his fathers, the rival;
> Yea, Anshar's first-born, Anu, was his equal.
> Anu begot in his image Nudimmud. (I:11–16)

The next planets to form were the planets Anshar, Kishar, Anu, and Nudimmud. Anshar and Kishar are described here as being much larger than any other of the planets previously formed, which is true of the planets Jupiter and Saturn. As Sitchin explains,

> With a terseness matched only by the narrative's precision, Act I of the epic of Creation has been swiftly played out before our very eyes. We are informed that Mars and Venus were to grow only to a limited size; but even before their formation was complete, another pair of planets was formed. The two were majestic planets, as evidenced by their names — Anshar ("prince, foremost of the heavens"), and Kishar ("foremost of the firm lands"). They overtook in size the first pair, "surpassing them" in stature. The descriptions, epithets, and location of this second pair easily identify them as Saturn and Jupiter.[24]

Mars and Venus had already begun their formation, but Mars and Venus accreted much more slowly than Jupiter and Saturn. Thus, though Jupiter and Saturn began their formation later than Mars and Venus, they were the first to complete their full growth. This is a

---

[24]Sitchin, *The Twelfth Planet*, 213–14.

reasonable assertion, because gas is much more malleable than rock, and thus assimilates more easily. The growing Jovian planetesimals probably attracted the free-floating gas much more easily and assimilated it much more quickly than the inner planets could attract the denser, rocky materials of the inner solar system. For example, even now, many comets and meteor swarms remain unassimilated by Earth, even though they may have passed near Earth's orbit countless times. Conversely, there is little or no significant amounts of free-floating gas in our solar system, indicating the ease with which it is assimilated.

After Jupiter and Saturn were formed, they were followed by two more planets, for a total of nine "gods." The next two planets, Anu and Nudimmud, are described as "equal." This is course corresponds perfectly with the planets Uranus and Neptune, which are almost exactly the same in appearance, size, and composition, almost to the point of being twins. Their relative distances from the Sun are also precisely described: Mars and Venus are closest, followed by the largest planets, Jupiter and Saturn, and then by the twin planets Uranus and Neptune. Clearly, the parallels are too close to ignore.

> Some time then passed ('multiplied the years'), and a third pair of planets was brought forth. First came Anu...then Anu, in turn, begot a twin planet 'his equal and in his image.' The Babylonian version names the planet Nudimmud, an epithet of Ea/Enki. Once again, the descriptions of the sizes and locations fit the next known pair of planets in our solar system, Uranus and Neptune.[25]

Uranus and Neptune are strikingly similar in size, mass, and chemical composition, so much so that at first glance they actually do appear to be twins. They bring the number of major deities/ k mentioned in the Epic to nine, a number which includes both the "elder" gods of the Sumerian pantheon (the Sun, Mercury, and Earth) and the "younger" gods of the Sumerian pantheon (Mars, Venus, Jupiter, Saturn, Uranus, and Neptune). Not coincidentally, this number matches perfectly with the total number of original bodies in our solar system. Pluto, as we have seen, was simply a satellite of Neptune that had been ripped from Neptunian orbit by Planet X, so it should not be included in the total number of planets that originally formed in our solar system. Without

---

[25]Sitchin, *The Twelfth Planet*, 213–14.

Pluto, we are left with the Sun and eight planets, for a total of nine "gods".

Enuma Elish I:11–16	The Astronomical Interpretation
Before they had grown in age and stature,	Before the inner planets had finished accreting,
Anshar and Kishar were formed, surpassing the others.	Saturn (Anshar) and Jupiter (Kishar) formed very quickly, becoming much larger than the inner planets.
They prolonged the days, added on the years. Anu was their heir, of his fathers, the rival;	After a great deal of time passed, Uranus (Anu) slowly formed, at first a very large planet;
Yea, Anshar's first-born, Anu, was his equal.	Uranus was originally as large as Saturn in its initial formative stage,
Anu begot in his image Nudimmud.	but the huge protoplanet divided into two smaller planets, forming the twin planets Uranus (Anu) and Neptune (Nudimmud).

So not only do we have a perfectly accurate scientific account of the formation of the planets in the first tablet of *Enuma Elish*, we also appear to have some information about the unique way that Uranus and Neptune may have originally formed — out of one larger protoplanet. In all we are confronted with several excellent reasons why *Enuma Elish* should be considered a scientifically accurate description of how our solar system was formed:

- ⚚ The "gods," like the planets, formed out of a chaotic mass of materials, or "waters." This conforms perfectly with modern scientific theory about how planets are formed from stellar nebulae, which are essentially "oceans" of dust, ice, and gasses that rotate around a newly formed star.

- ⚚ The planets, with the important exception of planet "Tiamat" (proto-Earth), are represented in their correct order from the Sun with accurate descriptions of their relative sizes.

⚕ The total number of major gods mentioned in the Epic equals the total number of major bodies in our solar system, correctly leaving out Planet Pluto, which was originally a satellite of Planet Neptune.

Note how exactly in the following table the number of planets matches the number of the gods mentioned in the Epic, and how their names, literally translated, match the characteristics of each of the planets so closely. So far, the Epic has described the creation of the Sun, Mercury, a planet named "Tiamat" (proto-Earth), and the planets Mars, Venus, Jupiter, Saturn, Uranus, and Neptune. However, the planet Pluto has yet to be accounted for in the Epic.

Table 4.1: Comparison of Traditional and Astronomical Interpretation of the Deities Mentioned in Enuma Elish

Major Deities Mentioned in Enuma Elish	Traditional Interpretation of Deity Names	Sitchin's Translation of Deity Names	Proposed Astronomical Equivalents
Apsu	fresh water, rivers	"One who existed from the beginning"	The Sun
Mummu	mist, clouds, entropy, "mold, matrix, archetypal watery form"[26]	"One who was born"	Mercury
Lahamu	slime	"Lady of Battles" (or "goddess of war")	Venus
Lahmu	silt	"Deity of War" (or "god of war")	Mars
Tiamat	the primeval ocean	"maiden of life" [or "lady sea"]	(proto-) Earth
Kishar	the horizon of the Earth	"prince of the firm lands"	Jupiter
Anshar	the horizon of the sky	"prince of the heavens"	Saturn

[26]Jacobsen, 170.

Anu	heaven, authority	"He of the heavens"	Uranus
Ea/Nudimmud	running water, rivers, marshes, wisdom	"Artful creator"	Neptune
Damkina, wife of Ea (minor goddess)	(No interpretation)	(No translation)	(Pluto)
Marduk	The concept of kingship personified	"Son of the Pure Mound"	Planet X

As we saw in chapter III, some astronomers believe that Pluto may be an escaped satellite of another planet, possibly Neptune:

> In its size, mass, and density, Pluto...resemble[s] the icy satellites of the Jovian planets. Especially in view of Pluto's unusual orbit around the Sun,[27] it is reasonable to wonder whether Pluto might be an escaped satellite that once orbited Neptune. Some sort of *cataclysmic event* might have occurred in the ancient past to reverse the direction of Triton's orbit, fling Nereid[28] into its highly elliptical orbit, and catapult Pluto away from Neptune altogether.... Thomas Van Flandern and Robert S. Harrington of the U.S. Naval Observatory made the intriguing proposal that *an unknown, massive, planet-like object* may have been involved in Pluto's escape from Neptune [emphasis mine].[29]

This explains why Pluto was not described as one of the original planets in the *Epic*. Pluto attained its independent orbit only after Planet X passed by Neptune and tore Pluto out of Neptunian orbit. Thus, Neptune's "wife", Damkina, who "gave birth" to Marduk, is likely the ancient Sumerian name for what we now call the "planet" Pluto.

---

[27]Pluto's orbit is highly elliptical (that is, oval-shaped), as if it was torn from its orbit by a passing planet whose orbit was also highly elliptical.

[28]Triton and Nereid are both current satellites of Neptune.

[29]Kaufmann, *Universe,* 316. Harrington is one of the leading scientists in the search for Planet X.

The Erratic Orbits of the Forming Protoplanets

> The divine brothers banded together,
> They disturbed Tiamat *as they surged back and forth*
> Yea, they troubled the (belly) of Tiamat
> By their *hilarity* (mischief? dancing?) in the Abode of Heaven.
> Apsu could not lessen their clamor
> And Tiamat was speechless at their [*ways*].
> Their doings were loathsome unto [...].
> Unsavory were their ways; they were overbearing.
> (I:21–28)

Notice here that the gods were "dancing" not on Earth, as Jacobsen and Sproul would have us believe, but in the "Abode of Heaven." The high gods of the Sumerians and Babylonians were not the rivers and the ocean, silt and slime, which are all bound to Earth; *they were the planets,* and they "danced" *in the sky.* This reference proves beyond a reasonable doubt that the gods in the *Enuma Elish* are, in fact, the planets.

This description of the planets surging back and forth correlates with the Nebular Hypothesis perfectly. The forming planets had unstable, erratic orbits due to the collision between the increasingly large planetesimals. The formative solar system was like a gigantic billiards table, and the planets ended up being knocked around a bit before they were fully formed.

The planets are also described as "troubling the belly" of Tiamat. This is based on the birth metaphor begun in I:4, where Tiamat is portrayed as the "mother" of the gods. Thus this passage is describing their troublesome "gestation" and "birth," i.e. their period of formation and differentiation from the nebular disk. This period was rife with conflict, where planetesimals collided together violently, all the way through their formation, causing the divine brothers, the planets, to "surge back and forth." And not even Apsu's great power (the Sun's gravity) was able to stop this process. "Apsu could not lessen their clamor" (I:25).

"When On High": The Astronomical Interpretation of Enuma Elish

Enuma Elish I:21-28	The Astronomical Interpretation
The divine brothers banded together,	The planets orbited the Sun
They disturbed Tiamat *as they surged back and forth*	Their combined gravitational pull had a small but significant effect on proto-Earth's orbit.
Yea, they troubled the (belly) of Tiamat	Their combined gravitational pulls disturbed the orbital path of the primordial Earth.
By their *hilarity* (mischief?) in the Abode of Heaven.	
Apsu could not lessen their clamor	Not even the Sun's powerful gravity could stop their influence,
And Tiamat was speechless at their [*ways*].	The proto-Earth was at the mercy of their emerging gravitational influence.

The Sun's Ignition and Unveiling from the Nebular Cloud

Apsu, opening his mouth,
Said unto *resplendent* Tiamat:
"Their ways are verily loathsome unto me.
By day I find no relief, nor repose by night.
I will destroy, I will wreck their ways,
That quiet may be restored. Let us have rest!"...
(Now) whatever they had plotted between them,
Was repeated unto the gods, their firstborn.
When the gods heard (this), they were astir,
(Then) lapsed into silence and remained speechless.
Surpassing in wisdom, accomplished, resourceful,
Ea, the all-wise, saw through their scheme.
A master design against it he devised and set up,
Made artful his spell against it, surpassing and holy.
He recited it and made it subsist in the deep,
As he poured sleep upon him. Sound asleep he lay.
When Apsu he had made prone, drenched with sleep,
Mummu, the adviser, was powerless to stir
He loosened his band, tore off his tiara,
Removed his halo (and) put it on himself.

> Having fettered Apsu, he slew him.
> Mummu he bound and left behind lock.
> Having thus upon Apsu established his dwelling,
> He laid hold on Mummu, holding him by the nose-rope.
> (I:35-40, 55-72)

The storyline continues. As the newly formed planets began to finalize their differentiation from the solar nebula, their combined gravitational pulls began to have a small but measurable effect on the Sun, Mercury, and proto-Earth. Mercury and Earth's orbits began to undergo small shifts over time, as they still do. The Sun was also affected by the combined gravitational pull of the planets, probably resulting in the creation of sunspots, which to a divine being would be considered "loathsome". Thus the stage was set for a conflict between the Sun and the outer planets.

In the myth, this emerging conflict between the gravitational pulls of the Sun and its planets in the latter stages of our solar system's formation is presented as a conflict between Apsu, the Sun, and Ea, the planet Neptune. This is significant, because the Sun and Neptune represent the center and outer edge of our solar system respectively, together defining the traditional boundaries of our solar system. Mary K. Wakeman's translation of this passage makes this even clearer, defining Ea's "master design" as literally a "master circle": "The progeny take the offensive position, finding a champion in Ea....By holy incantation Ea establishes a master circle (devises a master design I:61) upon the waters."[30] Thus, the passage here literally says that Ea's "master design" was actually a description of its circle, or "orbit" around the Sun! And it is this circle, the orbit of Neptune, that defines the outer edge of our solar system to this day.

---

[30]Wakeman, *God's Battle with the Monster,* 17.

"When On High": The Astronomical Interpretation of Enuma Elish

At the end of the initial formative stage of a solar system, the infalling materials in the center of the solar nebula reach a critical mass, and a star is born. This sudden ignition creates a blast of radiation known as the "T Tauri Wind", which blows away all of the remaining gas and dust in the nebular disc that has not been assimilated by the planets, so the birth of the star halts the development of the new solar system in its entirety. This nebular disc is aptly described as the "tiara" of Apsu in Enuma Elish.

Lastly, this passage describes, once again in symbolic terms, how the early formative stage of our solar system ended. In the myth, Ea is described as putting Apsu "to sleep", killing him, and then taking his tiara away from him and placing it on himself. This "tiara" is an excellent description of the disc of the solar nebula out of which the planets formed. And the description of Ea's killing of Apsu and taking the "tiara" for himself is an excellent description of how, at the end of initial solar system formation, the central mass of gas and dust finally ignites to form a star, in the process sending out a shockwave called the "T Tauri Wind" that blows away the remaining unassimilated gas and dust from the nebular disc and sends it out into space.

The protostar, at first, only has about 1% of its final mass. But the envelope of the star continues to grow as infalling material is

241

accreted. After 10,000–100,000 years, thermonuclear fusion begins in its core, then a strong stellar wind is produced which stops the infall of new mass. The protostar is now considered a young star since its mass is fixed, and its future evolution is now set.[31]

Thus the description of "killing" Apsu and taking away his "tiara" is in fact a very clever way of describing how the Sun's formative process was suddenly stopped, and how the solar nebula that surrounded it was removed and blown away into space, in the direction of Neptune. This symbolic description once again corresponds perfectly with how scientists now believe our solar system was formed. Dent summarizes the process of stellar formation, breaking it down into three main evolutionary stages:

- The initial collapse of the dense cloud to form a protostar;
- The initial ignition of nuclear reactions at the core;
- The "unveiling" of the star from the parent cloud.[32]

In short, after the newly born star ignites, the rest of the cloud around it is blown away by the T Tauri wind, and the initial, "nebular" stage of solar system formation is complete. And as we have seen, this process of how our solar system initially formed was described in *Enuma Elish* with exacting, albeit symbolic, detail, over 4,000 years ago.

Planet X

In the chamber of fates, the abode of destinies,
A god was engendered, most able and wisest of gods.
In the heart of Apsu[33] was Marduk created,
In the heart of holy Apsu was Marduk created.

---

[31] Wikipedia, "T Tauri Wind", http://en.wikipedia.org/wiki/T_Tauri_wind

[32] W.R.F. Dent, "Observing the Formation of Stars and Planets," *Endeavour* 16 n.3 (1992): 139.

[33] Pritchard translates Apsu here as "the deep." We would understand that as deep space, that is, from outside the solar system. It is unlikely that the "Apsu" mentioned here is the same "Apsu" that appeared earlier in the text, as *that* Apsu is now dead. Therefore, "Marduk" apparently came from outside of our solar system, from "the deep," or deep space.

"When On High": The Astronomical Interpretation of Enuma Elish

> He who begot him was Ea, his father;
> She who bore him was Damkina, his mother.
> The breast of goddesses he did suck.
> The nurse that nursed him filled him with awesomeness....
> When Ea saw him, the father who begot him,
> He exulted and glowed, his heart filled with gladness
> "My son, the Sun! Sun of the heavens!"
> Clothed with the halo of ten gods, he was strong to the utmost,
> As their awesome flashes were heaped upon him.
> Anu brought forth and begot the fourfold wind
> Consigning to its power the *leader of the host.*
> He fashioned..., station[ed] the whirlwind,
> He produced streams to disturb Tiamat.
> (I:79-86, 89-90, 102-107)

The text now turns swiftly to the beginning of the next phase of our solar system's formation. Whereas the end of the first phase ended with the completion of the formation of our native solar system and all of its planets, the beginning of the second phase describes how an intruder from deep space — a new "god", or planet — entered our solar system from the outside. After Ea had defeated Apsu, he retired to his former place, his "sacred chamber," which he then named "Apsu." This Apsu is to be distinguished from the Apsu who fathered the gods and whom Ea destroyed. *This* Apsu was a dwelling created by Ea for himself and his wife Damkina to live in (I:75-77). It was in *this* Apsu, translated by Pritchard as "the Deep,"[34] where Marduk was born. Therefore, Marduk apparently came from outside of our solar system, from "the deep," or deep space. This makes sense because, before Pluto was flung into its current orbit at the outer edge of our solar system, Neptune was the furthest planet from the Sun and thus anything outside of its orbit would be considered deep space. Significantly, it was Neptune, from whose orbit Pluto is now believed by modern astronomers to have been ripped by a "massive, planetlike object," that is seen in the Epic as the god/planet which "fathered" Marduk. Thus "Damkina," the wife of Ea (Neptune) and the mother of Marduk in the Epic (I:84), probably represents the planet Pluto. The gravitational attraction between Marduk (Planet X) and Ea (Neptune)

---

[34]E.A. Speiser, "The Creation Epic," in James B. Pritchard, ed., *Ancient Near Eastern Texts related to the Old Testament*, (Princeton, N.J.: Princeton University Press, 1974), 62.

apparently caused Neptune's Moons to go flying into very unusual orbits. One of these Moons was so affected by the gravity of Planet X that it flew completely out of Neptune's influence into an independent orbit around the Sun. The fact that Pluto's orbit is both elliptical and at an angle to the plane of the ecliptic can be explained by the fact that Planet X's motion was probably also elliptical and angled to the plane of the ecliptic before it interacted with Neptune.

The interaction between Planet X and the Neptunian Moons also altered Planet X's direction so that it was not only less angled to the plane of the ecliptic but was now also headed toward the inner solar system. In effect, "Ea" and "Damkina" had "given birth" to Marduk. As Sitchin explains,

> A new celestial "god" — a new planet — now joins the cast. He was formed in the Deep, far out in space, in a zone where orbital motion — a planet's "destiny" — had been imparted to him. He was attracted to the solar system by the outermost planet: "He who begot him was Ea" (Neptune).[35]

A planet-sized body had passed near enough to our solar system to be captured by the gravitational pull of the outermost planet and its Moons. As a result, its formerly aimless path was converted into a highly elliptical orbit around our Sun. This new orbital path was far from completed, however; the tenth planet, "Marduk," also came into conflict with the planet Uranus (Anu) on its journey deep into our solar system. The result of this conflict was apparently a tradeoff between the two planets. Planet X's path was now aimed even deeper into our solar system and its orbit was brought more in line with the plane of the ecliptic. This caused an equal and opposite reaction in the larger Uranus, the result being no discernible shift in orbital path but a dramatic tilt in its spin and magnetic axes. In sum, having knocked over Uranus, Marduk was now aimed directly at the inner solar system.

Enuma Elish I:79-86, 89-90, 102-107	The Astronomical Interpretation
In the chamber of fates, the abode of destinies,	Out in deep space, beyond the orbit of Neptune,

[35]Sitchin, *The Twelfth Planet*, 218.

"When On High": The Astronomical Interpretation of Enuma Elish

A god was engendered, most able and wisest of gods.	a new planet was created, possibly independently from the rest of our solar system.
In the heart of Apsu was Marduk created, In the heart of holy Apsu was Marduk created. He who begot him was Ea, his father; She who bore him was Damkina, his mother. The breast of goddesses he did suck. The nurse that nursed him filled him with awesomeness. . . . When Ea saw him, the father who begot him, He exulted and glowed, his heart filled with gladness. . . . "My son, the Sun! Sun of the heavens!"	As this planet, Planet X (Marduk), approached our solar system, its course was altered by the outermost planet, Neptune (Ea). This interaction with Neptune altered Planet X's path so that it was now pointed toward the inner solar system, more or less in line with the plane of the ecliptic. In effect, Planet X had been "born." This interaction also caused significant changes in the Neptunian system, however. Neptune was dragged from its original position at about 42 A.U. to its current position at 30 A.U. Pluto (Damkina), formerly a Moon of Neptune, was simultaneously ripped out of Neptune's orbit and flung into an independent orbit. This orbit combined elements of both Neptune and Planet X's orbits: Pluto stayed at around 42 A.U. where Neptune had originally orbited. Two other Moons of Neptune, Triton and Nereid, were also substantially altered, and are probably symbolized in the Epic as the "goddesses" whom Damkina (Pluto) used to help nurse the young Marduk. These Moons, in other words, aided in altering Planet X's path.
Clothed with the halo of ten gods, he was strong to the utmost, As their awesome flashes were heaped upon him.	As Planet X passed near the outer planets, there were intense electrical exchanges in the form of lightning that greatly strengthened its magnetic field.
Anu brought forth and begot the fourfold wind Consigning to its power the *leader of the host.* He fashioned...station[ed] the whirlwind, He produced streams to disturb Tiamat.	When Planet X struck Uranus (Anu), the result was that a great deal of material was ejected from the mantles of both planets. This material accreted into four satellites which now orbited Planet X (and several more which now orbited around Uranus). Planet X's approach toward the inner solar system was now beginning to have an effect on Earth's orbit.

The Creation of the Comets

Mother Hubur [Tiamat], she who fashions all things,
Added matchless weapons, bore monster serpents,
Sharp of tooth, unsparing of fang.
[With venom] for blood she has filled their bodies.
Roaring dragons she has clothed with terror,
Has crowned them like haloes, making them like gods,
So that he who beholds them shall perish abjectly,
(And) that, with their bodies reared up, none might turn [them back].
She set up the Viper, the Dragon, and the Sphinx,
The Great-Lion, the Mad-Dog, and the Scorpion-Man,
Mighty lion-demons, the Dragon-Fly, the Centaur —
Bearing weapons that fear not, fearless in battle.
Firm were her decrees, past withstanding were they.
Withal eleven of this kind she brought [forth] (I:132–45)

Meanwhile, while Marduk was being equipped with wondrous weapons by the other planet-gods and was clothed by them "with the halo of ten gods" (I:91-110) in order to help him defeat Tiamat, Tiamat was preparing for battle as well, to defend herself and revenge her husband, Apsu. Tiamat created eleven "helpers" to march at her side to help her fight against Marduk. These helpers were the comets,

Like the "roaring dragons" that Tiamat bore to defend herself, filling them with "venom", or water, the comets are also noted for containing water, which is the source of their glorious comas, or tails.

which had been created from the rock and water that was ejected into space by the Giant Impact. *Enuma Elish*, however, describes the creation of the comets here in Tablet I, even though the Giant Impact which resulted in the creation of the comets is not actually described in the *Epic* until Tablet IV. The Babylonians apparently shifted the order of some of the creation events to make the storyline flow smoothly. It was necessary for Tiamat to bring forth her "helpers" before the "battle" took place; bringing forth her helpers *after* the battle would make little sense in the narrative, though that is what actually happened. Therein lies the weakness of the Babylonian method of preserving the creation tradition — in order to maintain a plausible plotline, some liberties had to be taken with the facts. However, the information on how the comets were created remains essentially intact, and that is what is most important.

These "helpers" were filled with "venom," i.e., probably that which covered the body of Tiamat herself — water. These "helpers" were what we now know as the comets: "The solid part of a comet, called the nucleus, is a chunk of ice, typically measuring a few kilometers across."[36] The Giant Impact threw huge amounts of water into space along with the rocks and dust, some of which combined with the rocks and dust to form the comets. The writers of the Epic dramatized this event as the creation of "helpers" which Tiamat made to help defend her against her Marduk.

Enuma Elish I:132–45	The Astronomical Interpretation
Mother Hubur [Tiamat], she who fashions all things,	Planet Earth was the source of the Moon, comets, and asteroids brought forth by the Giant Impact.
Added matchless weapons, bore monster serpents, Sharp of tooth, unsparing of fang.	The comets were a particularly spectacular offshoot of the Impact, made of combination of rock and water from Earth's mantle.
[With venom] for blood she has filled their bodies. Roaring dragons she has clothed with terror, Has crowned them like haloes, making them like gods,	The comets, which acquired a larger share of the free-floating water left over from the impact, formed massive comas, or "tails" which created an awesome spectacle that rivaled that of the other planets,
So that he who beholds them shall perish abjectly,	a fearsome sight to behold.

---

[36]Kaufmann, *Universe*, 334.

The Creation of the Moon

> From among the gods, her firstborn,
> who formed [her Assembly],
> She elevated Kingu, made him chief among them....
> She gave him the Tablet of Destinies,
> fastened on his breast:
> "As for thee, thy command shall be unchangeable,
> [Thy word] shall endure!"
> (I:146–147, 156–57)

As with the comets, the Babylonians also understood that "Kingu", or the Moon, also had been created from the mantle of Earth, "given birth" to by Tiamat as a result of the Giant Impact. The Moon was much larger than the comets, however, so it was perceived as being their "chief" and the leader of Tiamat's heavenly army that she had created to defend herself against Marduk. The newly created Moon also had an orbit around Earth, which the *Epic* describes as a "destiny", or path that it would follow until the end of time.

Enuma Elish I:146–150, 156–61	The Astronomical Interpretation
From among the gods, her firstborn, who formed [her Assembly],	The most spectacular result of the Giant Impact was the Moon, made of molten materials jetted from Earth's mantle.
She elevated Kingu, made him chief among them....	The Moon contained the majority of the ejecta from the Impact, and was thus the largest of the objects created from Earth's mantle.
She gave him the Tablet of Destinies, fastened on his breast:	The material that had been jetted into space gradually accreted into a satellite
"As for thee, thy command shall be unchangeable, [Thy word] shall endure!"	that had a stable, permanent orbit — our Moon.

Thus the stage was set in the *Epic* for the grand confrontation between Marduk and Tiamat, a battle that would determine the fate of the solar system, of Earth, and of mankind.

TABLET IV: PLANET X AND THE GIANT IMPACT

More details regarding the characteristics of our solar system, as well as a fair amount of plot detail, are then given in Tablets II and III of *Enuma Elish*. Tiamat continues to prepare to destroy her children, the other planets in our solar system, in revenge for "killing" her husband Apsu (the Sun) and their advisor, Mummu (Mercury). Meanwhile her children, learning of her plans to kill them, begin to set their own plans in order to kill their own mother before she can do the same to them. After unsuccessful attempts by Anu (Uranus) and Ea (Neptune) to kill her, it was determined that the newly born Marduk was the only one who could defeat Tiamat and restore order to the solar system. To accomplish this, the gods, the planets set Marduk as their king, armed him with a variety of weapons and armor, and then set him on course to conquer Tiamat and restore order to the solar system.

Planet X Passes by the Outer Planets, Headed toward Earth

> They erected for him a princely throne.
> Facing his fathers, he sat down presiding.
> "Thou art the most honored of the great gods,
> Thy decree is unrivaled, thy command is Anu...."
> They conferred on him scepter, throne and *vestment*;
> They gave him matchless weapons that ward off the foes:
> "Go and cut off the life of Tiamat.
> May the winds bear her blood to places undisclosed."
> [Marduk's] destiny thus fixed, the gods, his fathers,
> Caused him to go the way of success and attainment.
> He constructed a bow, marked it as his weapon,
> Attached thereto the arrow, fixed its bow-cord.
> He raised the mace, made his right hand grasp it;
> Bow and quiver he hung at his side.
> In front of him he set the lightning,
> With a blazing flame he filled his body.
> He then made a net to enfold Tiamat therein.
> The four winds he stationed that nothing of her might escape,
> The South Wind, the North Wind, the East Wind, the West Wind.
> Close to his side he held the net, the gift of his father, Anu.
> He brought forth Imhullu "the Evil Wind,"
> the Whirlwind, the Hurricane,

The Fourfold Wind, the Sevenfold Wind, the Cyclone,
    the Matchless Wind;
Then he sent forth the winds he had brought forth, the seven of them.
    To stir up the inside of Tiamat they rose up behind him.
    Then the lord raised up the flood-storm, his mighty weapon.
    He mounted the storm chariot irresistible [and] terrifying.
        He harnessed (and) yoked it to a team-of-four,
        (Their) lips were parted, their teeth bore poison.
        They were tireless and skilled in destruction.
    On his right he posted the Smiter, fearsome in battle,
    On the left the Combat, which repels all the zealous.
    For a cloak he was wrapped in an armor of terror;
    With his fearsome halo his head was turbaned.
    The lord went forth and followed his course,
    Towards the raging Tiamat he set his face.
        (IV:1-4, 29-60)

Though the arms and armor bestowed upon Marduk by the gods, his fathers seems to more precisely describe the battle dress of an earthly warrior, they were actually intended to be symbolic, descriptive of heavenly weapons that could be used in a battle of the "gods", the planets. Sitchin explains, "These are common names for what could only have been celestial phenomena — the discharge of electrical bolts as the two planets converged, the gravitational pull, (a 'net') of one upon the other. But Marduk's chief weapons were his satellites, the four 'winds' with which Uranus had provided him with when Marduk passed by that planet."[37] Sitchin assumes that these "winds" are large bodies of swirling gasses that Planet X pulled, by means of gravitational attraction, from the planet/gods Uranus, Jupiter, and

Passing by and coming into conflict with the outer planets, Planet X, or "Marduk" acquired several new satellites, which it would then use to strike Earth, or "Tiamat" and move it to a new location closer to the Sun.

---

[37]Sitchin, *The Twelfth Planet*, 222.

Saturn when he passed by them. If Planet X had indeed collided with Uranus, the collision would have caused massive amounts of material to be ejected from the mantles of both planets, more than enough to give Planet X several large satellites. Thus, Sitchin's thesis is entirely plausible, though collision, and not gravitational attraction, is the most likely cause behind the creation of Planet X's satellites.

Enuma Elish IV:1-4, 29-60	The Astronomical Interpretation
They erected for him a princely throne. Facing his fathers, he sat down presiding. "Thou art the most honored of the great gods, Thy decree is unrivaled, thy command is Anu. . . . " They conferred on him scepter, throne and vestment;	Planet X's new orbit took it above the plane of the ecliptic, so it appeared to be the "king" of the planets.
They gave him matchless weapons that ward off the foes: "Go and cut off the life of Tiamat. May the winds bear her blood to places undisclosed." [Marduk's] destiny thus fixed, the gods, his fathers, Caused him to go the way of success and attainment. He constructed a bow, marked it as his weapon, Attached thereto the arrow, fixed its bow-cord. He raised the mace, made his right hand grasp it; Bow and quiver he hung at his side. In front of him he set the lightning, With a blazing flame he filled his body. The four winds he stationed that nothing of her might escape, The South Wind, the North Wind, the East Wind, the West Wind. Close to his side he held the net, the gift of his father, Anu.	Planet X's interaction with the outer planets left it with several satellites, which it would then use to strike Earth and move it to a new location closer to the Sun. Its orbit now set, Planet X now proceeded towards the inner solar system. The numerous satellites of Planet X, along with its powerful magnetic field, would cause great destruction to the Earth.

He brought forth Imhullu "the Evil Wind,"
the Whirlwind, the Hurricane,
The Fourfold Wind, the Sevenfold Wind,
the Cyclone, the Matchless Wind;
Then he sent forth the winds he had brought forth, the seven of them.
To stir up the inside of Tiamat they rose up behind him.

Then the lord raised up the flood-storm, his mighty weapon.
He mounted the storm chariot irresistible [and] terrifying.
He harnessed (and) yoked it to a team-of-four,
(Their) lips were parted, their teeth bore poison.
They were tireless and skilled in destruction.
On his right he posted the Smiter, fearsome in battle,
On the left the Combat, which repels all the zealous.
For a cloak he was wrapped in an armor of terror;
With his fearsome halo his head was turbaned.
The lord went forth and followed his course,
Towards the raging Tiamat he set his face.

Planet X had seven major satellites: four "Galilean" type satellites, and three additional large satellites.

Planet X also had an enormous, cometlike coma. All together, with the seven satellites, the aura of its powerful magnetic field, and its massive coma, the appearance of Planet X was truly awesome.

The Divine Conflict:
The Creation of the Modern Earth, Comets, and Moon

The lord approached to scan the inside of Tiamat,
(And) of Kingu, her consort, the scheme to perceive.
As he looks on, his course becomes upset,
His will is distracted, and his doings are confused.
And when the gods, his helpers, who marched at his side,
Saw the valiant hero, blurred became their vision....
Then joined issue Tiamat and Marduk, wisest of gods.
They strove in single combat, locked in battle.
The lord spread out his net to enfold her,
The Evil Wind, which followed behind,
he let loose in her face.
When Tiamat opened her mouth to consume him,
He drove in the Evil Wind that she close not her lips.

> As the fierce winds charged her belly,
> Her body was distended and her mouth was wide open.
> He released the arrow, it tore her belly,
> It cut through her insides, splitting the heart.
> Having thus subdued her, he extinguished her life.
> He cast down her carcass to stand upon it.
> (IV:65–70, 93–104)

Here, then, is a most original theory explaining the celestial puzzles still confronting us. Our newly forming, still unstable solar system, made up of the Sun and nine planets, was invaded at some time in the distant past by a large, planet-sized body. Planet X first encountered Neptune, whose gravity pulled Planet X into a permanent orbit around our Sun. Over time, Planet X's orbital path gradually precessed — due to the combined gravities of the Sun and planets — until it was more or less in line with the plane of the ecliptic. As a result, Planet X began to conflict with some of the other planets. It first struck Uranus, hitting it so hard that Uranus was knocked on its side. It later passed near enough to Saturn to shatter one or more of its Moons, forming its ring system. Still later, Planet X passed near enough to Jupiter to disrupt the orbits of many of its satellites.

Its orbit altered by the outer planets into a collision course with the primordial Earth, Planet X passed near enough to Earth for at least one of its satellites to collide with it and create the Moon, Earth's oceans and atmosphere, and of course the asteroid belt and the comets. According to Enuma Elish, a second satellite of Planet X called the "North Wind" then struck Earth and moved it to its present orbit between Venus and Mars, though Planet X's gravitational pull may have been enough to do the job.

As it interacted with each of these planets, its course was bent more and more towards the inner solar system. Also, in the process of interacting with the outer planets, Planet X now had four major and three additional satellites, for a total of seven, including probably numerous small satellites, a ring system, and possibly even a cometlike tail. Headed toward the inner solar system with its vanguard of seven satellites, Planet X was now set on a collision course with "Tiamat" — the primordial Earth — which at that time orbited between the present-day orbits of Jupiter and Mars. However, it is important to note here that, in the Epic, "the two planets did not collide.... It was the satellites of Marduk that smashed into Tiamat, and not Marduk himself."[38]

After Planet X had struck Tiamat/Earth with its satellite, called "the Evil Wind" in the Epic, it then imprisoned Tiamat's "helpers", what we know today as the comets, and defeated the Moon, taking away its independent orbit and placing it in a permanent orbit around Earth. Though the comets and Moon were actually created as a result of the Giant Impact, as we discussed earlier, some license was taken in order to make the narrative storyline work.

Enuma Elish IV:65-70, 93-104	The Astronomical Interpretation
The lord approached to scan the inside of Tiamat, (And) of Kingu, her consort, the scheme to perceive. As he looks on, his course becomes upset, His will is distracted, and his doings are confused. And when the gods, his helpers, who marched at his side, Saw the valiant hero, blurred became their vision. . . . Then joined issue Tiamat and Marduk, wisest of gods. They strove in single combat, locked in battle. The lord spread out his net to enfold her,	As Planet X approached the primordial Earth, Earth's gravitational field began to affect the course of Planet X and its satellites. Earth too was affected by the powerful gravity of Planet X as it approached, and the two were locked in struggle for gravitational supremacy.

---

[38]Sitchin, *The Twelfth Planet*, 224–25.

The Evil Wind, which followed behind, he let loose in her face.
When Tiamat opened her mouth to consume him,
He drove in the Evil Wind that she close not her lips.
As the fierce winds charged her belly,
Her body was distended and her mouth was wide open.
He released the arrow, it tore her belly,
It cut through her insides, splitting the heart.
Having thus subdued her, he extinguished her life.
He cast down her carcass to stand upon it.

As Planet X passed near Earth, one of its largest satellites struck deep into Earth's core, effectively destroying the primordial Earth and leaving its shattered hulk hanging in space.

The Comets Captured by Planet X

After he had slain Tiamat, the leader,
Her band was shattered, her troupe broken up;
And the gods, her helpers, who marched at her side,
trembling with terror, turned their backs about,
in order to save and preserve their lives.
Tightly encircled, they could not all escape.
He made them captives and smashed their weapons.
Thrown into cells, they found themselves ensnared;
placed in cells, they were filled with wailing;
bearing his wrath, they were held imprisoned.
And the eleven creatures which she had charged with awe,
The whole band of demons that marched on her right,
He cast into fetters, their hands he bound.
For all their resistance, he trampled (them) underfoot.
And Kingu, who had been made chief among them,
He bound and accounted him to Uggae.
(IV:105-120)

The *Epic* continues, and how Earth was created by "Marduk" is finally explained in detail. After he killed Tiamat by extinguishing her life with his "wind" and lightning, he met with Tiamat again, and took control of the "monsters" who fought by her side. First of all, who were these "rebellious gods" whom Tiamat had created to defend herself? By solving this riddle, "...we offer an explanation to yet another puzzle of our solar system — the phenomenon of the comets....The orbits of the planets around the Sun are almost circular; the orbits of the comets are elongated, and in most instances very much so — to the extent that some of them disappear from our view for hundreds or thousands of years....the comet's orbits [also] lie in many diverse planes."[39] Sitchin's theory also adroitly explains how the comets were created — as a result of the collision between a satellite of "Marduk" and the primordial Earth. This makes perfect sense, as the standard accretional model of how solar systems are formed does not allow for such radical behavior as that displayed by the comets — all material in the nebular disc originally had the same angular momentum, traveling in the same direction at approximately the same speed. It would require an invading object of significant size to create the comets, and Planet X fits the bill perfectly.

Enuma Elish IV:105-120	The Astronomical Interpretation
After he had slain Tiamat, the leader, Her band was shattered, her troupe broken up; And the gods, her helpers, who marched at her side, trembling with terror, turned their backs about, in order to save and preserve their lives. Tightly encircled, they could not all escape. He made them captives and smashed their weapons. Thrown into cells, they found themselves ensnared; placed in cells, they were filled with wailing; bearing his wrath, they were held imprisoned. And the eleven creatures which she had charged with awe, The whole band of demons that marched on her right, He cast into fetters, their hands he bound. For all their resistance, he trampled (them) underfoot. And Kingu, who had been made chief among them, He bound and accounted him to Uggae.	One of the results of the collision between one of Planet X's satellites and Earth was the creation of many asteroids, large and small. Many of these large asteroids also contained a significant amount of water, making them what today are called "comets". Planet X then "imprisoned" these comets in orbits similar to its own, long, elliptical orbits that took some of them out of the solar system entirely. The largest of the objects that were ejected from Earth's mantle as the result of the Giant Impact was then bound into an orbit around Earth, to become what we know today as the Moon.

[39] *Ibid*, 225–26.

The Earth Divided and Moved to Its Present Orbit

When he had vanquished and subdued his adversaries,
Had...the vainglorious foe,
Had wholly established Anshar's [Saturn's] triumph over the foe,
Nudimmud's [Neptune's] desire had achieved, valiant Marduk
Strengthened his hold on the vanquished gods,
And turned back to Tiamat whom he had bound.
The lord trod on the legs of Tiamat,
With his unsparing mace he crushed her skull.
When the arteries of her blood he had severed,
The North Wind bore (it) to places undisclosed.
On seeing this, his fathers were joyful and jubilant,
They brought gifts of homage, they to him.
(IV:123-134)

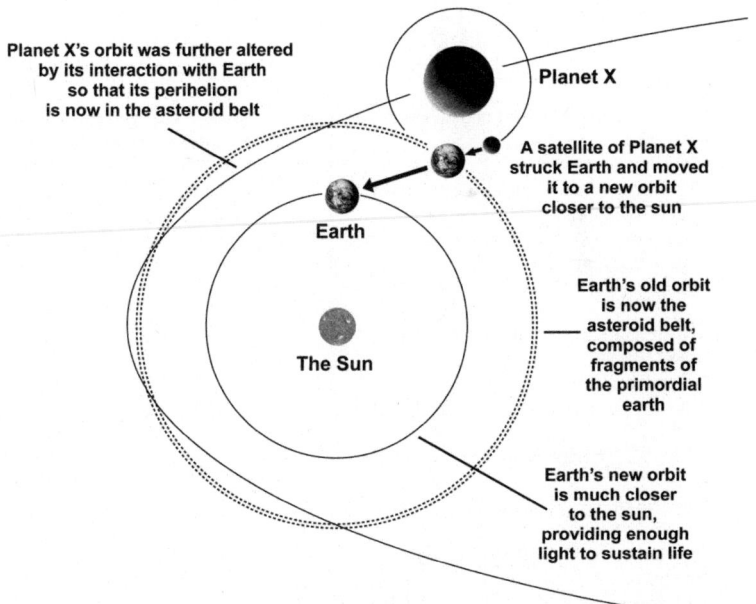

Figure 4.3: As we saw in Chapter III, Planet X conflicted with the primordial Earth in its original orbit where the asteroid belt now lies, moving it to a new orbit closer to the Sun. The other results of the collision included the creation of Earth's Moon, Earth's rapid spin rate, its axial tilt and of course the asteroid belt and the comets.

After killing Tiamat, Marduk used her body for a certain purpose: to create the heavens and Earth. Planet X had "divided" Earth with one of its satellites, smashing out a large chunk of Earth with which it created the Moon, the comets and the asteroids, then hurling the remaining, intact portion into a new orbit closer to the Sun. "Marduk... [split] Tiamat in two, severing her 'skull' or upper part. Then another of Marduk's satellites, the one called North Wind, crashed into the separated half. The heavy blow carried this part — destined to become Earth — to an orbit where no planet had been orbiting before."[40] The fact that one of the satellites of Planet X was responsible for shifting Earth's orbit is corroborated later in *Enuma Elish*, in the seventh tablet, where Marduk is described as one who had "the corpse of Tiamat carried off with his weapon" (VII:71). The Giant Impact of this satellite, this "weapon," is thus responsible not only for the creation of Earth as we know it, but its orbital position in the solar system.

Enuma Elish IV:123-134	The Astronomical Interpretation
When he had vanquished and subdued his adversaries, Had...the vainglorious foe, Had wholly established Anshar's [Saturn's] triumph over the foe, Nudimmud's [Neptune's] desire had achieved, valiant Marduk Strengthened his hold on the vanquished gods, And turned back to Tiamat whom he had bound. The lord trod on the legs of Tiamat, With his unsparing mace he crushed her skull. When the arteries of her blood he had severed, The North Wind bore (it) to places undisclosed. On seeing this, his fathers were joyful and jubilant, They brought gifts of homage, they to him.	When, after eons of having its orbit gradually altered by the outer planets, Planet X finally came into conflict into Earth. With one of its satellites it then smashed Earth into a shattered hulk of its former self, and with another it had moved Earth into an entirely new orbit, closer to the Sun.

---

[40]Sitchin, *The Twelfth Planet*, 226–27.

The Creation of the Asteroid Belt and Planet X's Orbit Determined

> Then the lord paused to view her dead body,
> That he might divide the monster and do artful works.
> He split her like a shellfish into two parts:
> Half of her he set up and ceiled it as sky,
> Pulled down the bar and posted guards.
> He bade them to allow not her waters to escape.
> He crossed the heavens and surveyed the regions.
> He squared Apsu's quarter, the abode of Nudimmud,
> As the lord measured the dimensions of Apsu.
> The Great Abode, its likeness, he fixed as Esharra,
> The Great Abode, Esharra, which he made as the firmament.
> (IV:135–45)

In this short but pithy passage, *Enuma* Elish describes how heaven was created from Tiamat's dead body. Having created Earth from Tiamat's "head" in the previous passage, Marduk is then described as taking Tiamat's body, or "tail" and using it to create the heavens. Sitchin explains, "The lower half had another fate: on the second orbit Marduk himself hit it, smashing it to pieces....The pieces of this broken half were hammered to become a 'bracelet' in the heavens, acting as a screen between the inner planets and the outer planets. They were stretched out into a 'great band'[41] The asteroid belt had been created."[42] In short, "Half of Tiamat...became the heaven, and the other half the Earth,"[43] with the upper section, or "head" of the dragon being used to create the Earth, and the lower half, or "body", being used to create the heavens. The heavens thus became the "great abode", or throne of Marduk, through which he occasionally crossed in the great thousand-year journey through the heavens.

This "great abode", or *Esharra*, is described as being fixed as the "firmament" in heaven. The Sumerian/Akkadian word *esharra*,

---

[41]*Esharra*, "great band," and *sha'ar*, "gate," are cognate both linguistically and conceptually. In Genesis 28:17, Jacob has a dream where he sees God in heaven, standing atop a "ladder" reaching from heaven to Earth, on which angels ascended and descended. Jacob refers to this "ladder" as the *sha'ar*, or "gate" of heaven, making this usage of *sha'ar* very similar to way *esharra* is used in *Enuma Elish*. In both places, these words refer to a heavenly place where the chief deity, God, dwells.

[42]Sitchin, *The Twelfth Planet*, 226–27.

[43]*Ibid.*

literally means a "great band," that circles somewhere high in the heavens, the word *Esharra* being cognate with the Hebrew word שַׁעַר, *sha'ar*, "gate." Thus this "great abode" was also thought of as a "gate" through which Marduk passed when returning on his great journey through the heavens. Another interesting point is that the word that Sitchin translates as a "bracelet" or a "great band" in heaven is the Sumerian/Akkadian word *rakkis,* which is cognate to the Hebrew word רָקִיעַ, *raqiya*. *Raqiya* is translated in Genesis 1:6 as "the firmament" which God used to separate the "waters above" from the "waters below". Both *rakkis* and *raqiya* refer to some sort of circular, ring-like object that has been hammered into shape by some powerful force — a "hammered heaven". In the context of astral religion, where the gods are the planets, this could only refer to the asteroid belt, which does indeed circle around the Sun like a great band in heaven, hammered out from the primordial Earth by a satellite of Planet X. This barrier of asteroids is also described in this passage as a "bar" which is "guarded" — traveling through the asteroid belt would be hazardous, so this metaphor is apt.

Enuma Elish IV:135-145	The Astronomical Interpretation
Then the lord paused to view her dead body, That he might divide the monster and do artful works. He split her like a shellfish into two parts: Half of her he set up and ceiled it as sky, Pulled down the bar and posted guards. He bade them to allow not her waters to escape. He crossed the heavens and surveyed the regions. He squared Apsu's quarter, the abode of Nudimmud, As the lord measured the dimensions of Apsu. The Great Abode, its likeness, he fixed as Esharra, The Great Abode, Esharra, which he made as the firmament.	The effect of Planet X's satellites striking Earth had the secondary effect of creating a "belt" of asteroids in space that circled where the primordial Earth originally orbited. The larger part of Earth was sent to a new orbit, and the shattered remnants remained in the primordial Earth's original orbit to become the asteroid belt. Planet X then settled into its new orbit, passing out of the solar system to its aphelion well beyond Neptune. Planet X then returned to its perihelion in the asteroid belt, its point of closest approach to the Sun.

"When On High": The Astronomical Interpretation of Enuma Elish

TABLET V: MORE RESULTS OF THE GIANT IMPACT

Planet X Determines Earth's Axial Tilt

Anu, Enlil, and Ea he made occupy their places.
He constructed stations for the great gods,
Fixing their astral likenesses as the Images.
He determined the year by designating the zones:
He set up three constellations for each of the twelve months.
After defining the days of the year [by means] of heavenly figures,
He founded the station of Nebiru to determine their heavenly bands,
That none might transgress or fall short.
Alongside it he set up the stations of Enlil and Ea.
Having opened up the gates on both sides,
He strengthened the locks to the left and the right.
In her belly he established the zenith.
(IV:46; V:1-11)

The beginning of Tablet V gets into the specifics of Earth's axial tilt with a fair amount of detail. As we saw in Chapter II, Figure 2.1, the Sumerians had an advanced understanding of how the heavens were arranged relative to the Earth, and organized the night sky in a way nearly identical to the way we still do today. The Sumerians and Babylonians divided the heavens into three regions: "The Way of Anu," "The Way of Enlil," and "The Way of Ea." The Way of Enlil represented the region of the sky north of what is modernly called the "Tropic of Cancer",

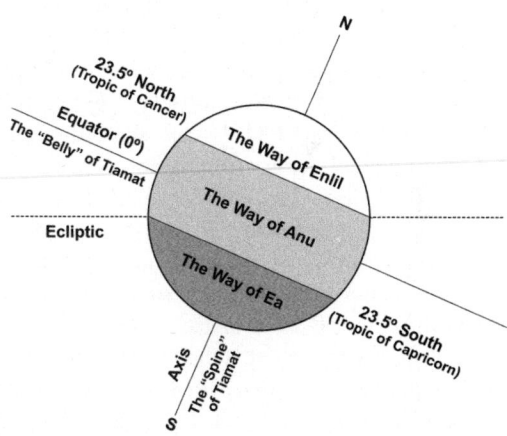

Figure 4.4: The Sumerians understood that the heavens relative to Earth are divided into three sections, defined by the movement of the Sun relative to Earth's position in its annual orbit, combined with the axial tilt also imparted by the Giant Impact with one of Planet X's satellites. Earth's equator was seen as the "belly" of Tiamat, and Earth's axis was seen as her "spine".

that part of the sky north of 23.5 degrees where the Sun is never directly overhead. The Way of Ea represented that region of the sky south of what is modernly called the "Tropic of Capricorn", that part of the sky south of 23.5 degrees where the Sun is never directly overhead. And the Way of Anu represented that region of the sky that is between the tropics, corresponding to earth's equatorial region. And since these "ways" are relative to the 23.5 tilt in Earth's axis, and the Sumerians believed that Marduk created these "stations" and "zones", *Enuma Elish* IV:46 must therefore be describing the tilting of Earth 23.5 degrees into its current axial tilt as result of the Giant Impact.

The Sumerians also divided the heavens into twelve longitudinal divisions, each of which had contained three constellations, corresponding to their twelve-month calendar, which we also still use today. These divisions can be seen in an English interpretation of the Sumerian astrolabe we saw in Chapter II, Figure 2.1:

The Sumerian calendar, divided into twelve months, is the system upon which the Western system is still based, though our modern months start approximately in the middle of the ancient months (thus the use of the term "March/April", in Figure 4.5). The Sumerians also associated one of the 12 major constellations of the zodiac with each month, which we still do today, though the constellations have shifted "houses" in the 4000+ years since the Sumerian original was created. The updated version of the Sumerian astrolabe in Figure 4.5 accounts for that shift, and shows which constellations are currently at their zenith at twelve midnight during that time period. This well-designed astrolabe was also divided radially into three sections, identifying the three major latitudinal divisions into which the Sumerians divided the night sky: the ways of Enlil, Anu and Ea, as described in Figure 4.4. These months are also the "zones" and the "stations of the great gods", the planets, mentioned in Enuma Elish IV:46, V:1-7. The "station of Nibiru" is probably the location in the sky where Planet X will first appear on its return trip which, unlike the positions of the other planets, never changes. Thus it was used as an absolute reference point by which to compare the movements of the other planets over time.

"When On High": The Astronomical Interpretation of Enuma Elish

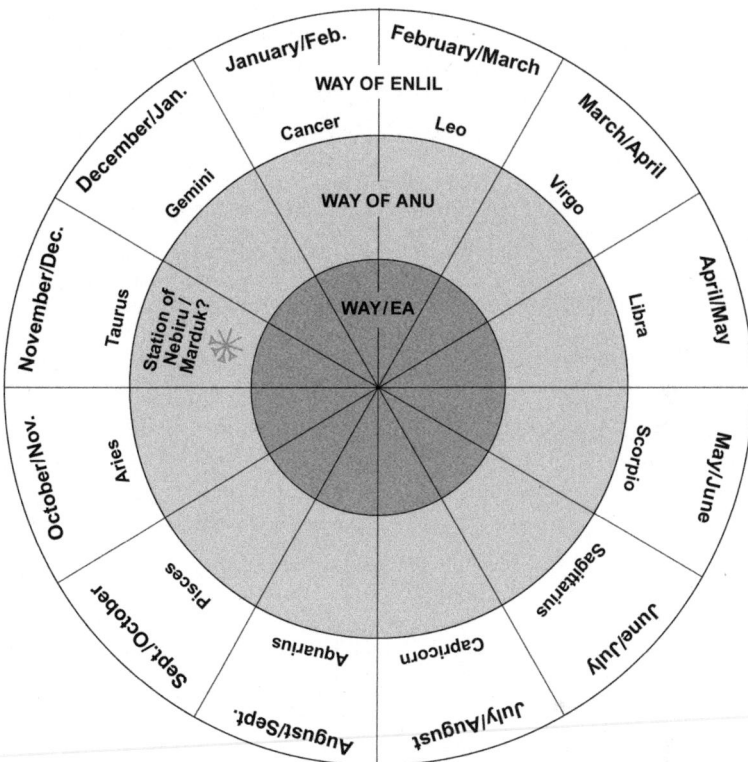

Figure 4.5: Another view of the Sumerian astrolabe we reviewed in Chapter II (Figure 2.1). This version has been translated into English, with modern months and constellation names appended.

Next, this passage describes how the ways of Enlil and Ea were like "gates" that had been opened, and then locked down again in new positions. Clearly, based upon our understanding of the Sumerian division of the heavens into three "ways", that the Sumerians understood that the positions of the stars and planets relative to the Earth had been changed as a result of the Giant Impact, and then "locked" again into new positions which would not change again until the end of time — or until Planet X returned, whichever came first. Finally, in Tiamat's belly Marduk established the "zenith", a good description of how the Sun shines most directly on Earth's equator.

Enuma Elish IV: 46, V:1-11	The Astronomical Interpretation
Anu, Enlil, and Ea he made occupy their places.	As a result of the Giant Impact, Earth's axis was now tilted approximately 23.5 degrees to the plane of the ecliptic. This caused the motions of the Sun, Moon, planets and stars in the heavens to be oriented differently relative to Earth than they had been formerly. The Sumerians divided the sky into three different zones based upon this new apparent motion, the same way we divide the night sky today.
He constructed stations for the great gods	Because Earth now had a new orbit, orbital period, rotation rate, and axial tilt as a result of the Giant Impact, the "gods," the planets, now appeared to move through the night sky differently relative to Earth. In order to more efficiently track the movements of their gods in the heavens, the Sumerians divided up the night sky longitudinally into 12 zodiacal "stations" spaced regularly along the celestial equator.[44]
Fixing their astral likenesses as the Images.	These "stations" were each assigned various constellations that told the stories of the gods associated with them.
He determined the year by designating the zones:	These 12 celestial stations formed the basis of a new calendar, with a total of twelve months per year, one per station of the zodiac, or "zone", in the sky.
He set up three constellations for each of the twelve months.	Each of the celestial stations had three constellations associated with it – one in the Way of Enlil, one in the Way of Anu, and one in the Way of Ea.[45]

[44] The Akkadian word for constellations is *manzaltu*, literally, "stations of the gods"; compare the Hebrew cognate *mazzaloth,* "constellations").

[45] The Sumerians, as we saw in Figures 2.1 and 4.5, divided the night sky into thirty-six sections: twelve longitudinal divisions (the "months") by 3 latitudinal divisions (the "Ways" of Anu, Enlil, and Ea). On the Sumerian astrolabe shown in Figure 2.1, each of the twelve months has three stars, planets, or constellations assigned to it; one in the Way of Anu, one in the Way of Enlil, and one in the Way of Ea. Thus the Sumerian astrolabe presented here conforms perfectly with the text of *Enuma Elish.*

"When On High": The Astronomical Interpretation of Enuma Elish

After defining the days of the year [by means] of heavenly figures	After having set Earth's new axial tilt and orbit,
He founded the station of Nebiru to determine their heavenly bands	the orbital path of Planet X was set as an absolute, unchanging reference point...
That none might transgress or fall short.	...against which the orbits of the other planets could be measured over long periods of time.

Planet X Establishes the Orbit of the Moon (and the Motion of the Sun)

The Moon he caused to shine, the night (to him) entrusting.
He appointed him a creature of the night to signify the days:
"Monthly, without cease, form designs with a crown.
At the month's very start, rising over the land,
Thou shalt have luminous horns to signify six days,
On the seventh day reaching a [half]-crown.
At full Moon stand in opposition in mid-month.
When the Sun [overtakes] thee at the base of heaven,
Diminish [thy crown] and retrogress in light.
At the time [of disappearance] approach thou the course of the Sun,
And [on the thir]tieth thou shalt again stand in
opposition to the Sun."[46]
(V:12-22)

The creation of the Moon is now given in pithy prose, describing in exacting detail how the Moon behaves even today. Of course the movements of the Moon are easily observable even today, so these statements are not so incredible. But what is incredible is the fact that the ancient Sumerians gave Marduk the credit for creating the Moon at the same time that Earth was moved to a new orbit, given a new axial tilt, and so forth, conclusions that modern astronomers are only just now re-discovering!

---

[46] Lines 25-44 are too broken for translation. It is clear from the traces, however, that after completing his creation of the Moon Marduk turned his attention to establishing the Sun. This means, of course, that he determined the spin rate of the Earth-cf. V:45-6.

Enuma Elish IV:123–46	The Astronomical Interpretation
The Moon he caused to shine, the night (to him) entrusting.	Planet X created the Moon as a result of the giant impact between one of its satellites and Earth.
He appointed him a creature of the night to signify the days:	The Moon was now the brightest object in the night sky, and its periods of waxing and waning were approximately thirty days long:[47]
"Monthly, without cease, form designs with a crown.	Each of these thirty-day periods formed one month. During this month, the Moon waxed and waned. At the end of its waning and the beginning of its waxing, it took the shape of a crescent, which made it look something like a crown.
At the month's very start, rising over the land,	At the beginning of the month, the "New Moon," where the Moon is at its dimmest,
Thou shalt have luminous horns to signify six days,	it will wax slowly for six days, forming a crescent that looks like a pair of horns.
On the seventh day reaching a [half]-crown.	At the end of that week, the horns will disappear and the Moon will become half full.
At full Moon stand in opposition in mid-month.	After two weeks, the Moon will be full.
When the Sun [overtakes] thee at the base of heaven,	And at the same time of the month, the Sun will begin to catch up,
Diminish [thy crown] and retrogress in light.	during which time the Moon will begin to wane again.
At the time [of disappearance] approach thou the course of the Sun,	When the Moon is waning, it will begin to approach the Sun,
And [on the thir]tieth thou shalt again stand in opposition to the Sun."	until the New Moon appears once again, completely dark.

---

[47] The Moon's actual orbital period, its "sidereal" period, is 27.3 days. The Moon's apparent orbital period, its "synodic" period (i.e., how it is perceived from Earth), is actually around 29.5 days. This period is longer as the Moon has to "catch up" with Earth, which is also moving around the Sun in its own orbit at the same time.

(Lines 25-44 are too broken for translation. It is clear from the traces, however, that after completing his creation of the Moon Marduk turned his attention to establishing the Sun. [This means, of course, that he determined the spin rate of the Earth—cf. V:45-6].)

The essence of this passage is that the Moon, created after Earth had been struck by a giant heavenly object, had been given a unique rate of rotation and revolution around Earth that gave it a very predictable cycle of waxing and waning. The Sun's apparent motion was also altered, as the Giant Impact had also significantly accelerated Earth's rotation rate. Unfortunately, most of lines V:25-44 in *Enuma Elish* describing the Sun's relative motion have been lost, but enough information remains to show that it was indeed discussed. Most importantly, it proves that the Sumerians knew that the orbital characteristics of both the Earth and the Moon were both caused by the same impact event.

Planet X and the Creation of Earth's Atmosphere, Seas, Mountains, and the Asteroid Belt

After he [had appointed] the days [to Shamash],[48]
[And had established] the precincts of night and d[ay],
    [Taking] the spittle of Tia[mat]
      Marduk created [...] ...
He formed the c[louds] and filled (them) with [water].
The raising of winds, the bringing of rain (and) cold,
    Making the mist smoke, piling up her poison:
(These) he appointed to himself, took into his own charge.
Putting her head into position he formed the[reon] the mountai[ns],
    Opening the deep which was in flood,
He caused to flow from her eyes the Euph[rates (and) T]igris,
    Stopping her nostrils he left...
He formed at her udder the lofty m[ountain]s,
(Therein) he drilled springs for the wells to carry off (the water).
    Twisting her tail he bound it to Durmah,
      [...] ... Apsu at his foot,
    [...] ... her crotch, she was fastened to the heavens,
(Thus) he covered the heavens and established the Earth.

---

[48] Shamash was the Sun god of Mesopotamian mythology. This line provides transition from the previous, lost section describing how Marduk set the motion of the Sun relative to Earth.

> [...] ... in the midst of Tiamat he made flow,
> [...] ... his net he completely let out,
> (So) he *created* heaven and earth...,
> [...] their bounds...established.
> (V:45-66)

Starting with line 45, the text becomes more legible again, and we see that the previous degraded lines were indeed discussing how Marduk/Planet X had set the relative motion of the Sun in the heavens, along with the Moon, stars and planets, using the Sun to rule the day, and the Moon to rule the night. In this passage we now see that, along with the creation of Earth in its current state and the creation of the Moon, the Giant Impact between Earth and one of Planet X's satellites also resulted in the creation of Earth's clouds, rivers and oceans — the entire atmosphere and hydrosphere — which Marduk caused to flow from the body of Tiamat. As we saw in Chapter III, modern scientists now believe that Earth's oceans and atmosphere were created as the result of a giant impactor striking Earth and releasing a massive amount of water from Earth's mantle, which was thrown into orbit and then gradually precipitated back to Earth to form Earth's oceans, lakes, rivers and atmosphere. This belief is now once again clearly corroborated in *Enuma Elish*, where the creation of Earth's oceans and atmosphere are again correctly described as having been created by waters released from the body of Earth, or "Tiamat" as a result of a Giant Impact.

At the end of this passage, the reference to heaven as a "great band" that had been stretched out into a circle in space is once again mentioned. The word *Durmah* in line 59 literally means "great band", and is also mentioned in *Enuma Elish* VII:38 as part of one of the 50 names of Marduk: "Lugal*durmah*, the king, bond of the gods, lord of the *Durmah*." This is cognate to the reference to *Esharra*, the "great band" or "great gate of heaven" that we saw in lines IV:144–145. As we discussed in that section, Tiamat was believed to have been split into two major sections, upper and lower. The lower section, or "tail" was used to create the "great band" or "hammered heaven", and the upper section, or "head", was used to create Earth. This concept is corroborated here in lines V:59-61, where Tiamat's "tail" was "twisted" and bound to this "great band" in heaven, along with some of the water that was released from Earth's mantle from the Giant Impact. These latter lines in this passage also form an excellent

"When On High": The Astronomical Interpretation of Enuma Elish

transition between this section, which describes the creation of Earth's atmosphere and hydrosphere, and the next section, which describes the creation of the comets.

Enuma Elish IV:123–46	The Astronomical Interpretation
After he [had appointed] the days [to Shamash], [And had established] the precincts of night and d[ay],	The impact from one of Planet X's satellites had determined a new, faster rotation rate for Earth, which gave the Earth 24-hour days.
[Taking] the spittle of Tia[mat] Marduk created [...] ... He formed the c[louds] and filled (them) with [water]. The raising of winds, the bringing of rain (and) cold, Making the mist smoke, piling up her poison: (These) he appointed to himself, took into his own charge.	The massive impact also released a great deal of water from Earth's mantle, which formed Earth's atmosphere.
Putting her head into position he formed the[reon] the mountai[ns], Opening the deep which was in flood, He caused to flow from her eyes the Euph[rates (and) T]igris, Stopping her nostrils he left... He formed at her udder the lofty m[ountain]s, (Therein) he drilled springs for the wells to carry off (the water).	This section may refer to a specific set of mountains known as Serabit al-Kadim in the central-western Sinai, which may be the true Mt. Sinai and the site of many other ancient mysteries. See http://www.mysteriousworld.com/Journal/2008/Spring/Artifacts/ for more information.
Twisting her tail he bound it to Durmah, [...] ... Apsu at his foot, [...] ... her crotch, she was fastened to the heavens, (Thus) he covered the heavens and established the Earth. [...] ... in the midst of Tiamat he made flow, [...] ... his net he completely let out,	Part of Earth was left behind in Earth's previous orbital position to form the asteroid belt.
(So) he created heaven and earth..., [...] their bounds...established.	Thus the asteroid belt and Earth were created.

Planet X Drags the Comets into Independent Orbits like Its Own

> When he had designed his rules (and) fashioned [his] ordinances,
> He founded [the shr]ines (and) handed them over to Ea.
> [The Tablet of] Destinies which he had taken from Kingu he carried,
> He brought (it) as the first gift of greeting, he gave (it) to Anu.
> [The go]ds who had *done battle* and had been scattered,
> He led bound into the presence of his fathers.
> Now the eleven creatures which Tiamat had made...,
> Whose weapons he had shattered, which he had tied to his foot:
> [Of these] he made statues and set (them) up
> [at the Gate of] Apsu (saying):
> "Let it be a token that this may never be forgotten!"
> (V:67–76)

After Planet X had completed its work of setting the Earth and Moon system into its current form, it then passed out of our solar system on its grand orbit past the outer planets, into the "Apsu", or deep space. On its way, however, it would have carried a great deal of material in its train, as much of the rock and water that had been ejected from Earth by the Giant Impact would have been picked up by Planet X itself and carried along with it in its own orbit, possibly imparting some of that material on some of the outer planets on its way back out of the solar system.

As we saw previously, the "gods who had done battle" mentioned in line 71, the "warriors" that Tiamat had made to defend herself against Marduk, were in fact the comets, huge bodies of rock and water ice formed as a result of the Giant Impact. Apparently the description here of Marduk "shattering their weapons" and "tying them to his foot" is a description of how Planet X had captured in its gravitational field some of the rocky, icy ejecta orbiting the post-impact Earth. These "comets," now orbiting Planet X, accompanied it to the outer solar system, "into the presence of his fathers", the planets Uranus and Neptune. As Planet X flew by Uranus and Neptune (Anu and Ea), their gravitational pulls tore the comets away from Planet X, sending them into independent orbits around the Sun. This explains why many of the comets have orbits with aphelions in the vicinity of Uranus and Neptune — so many, in fact, that some astronomers, such as Gerard Kuiper, have postulated that the comets were originally formed there (in the theoretical "Kuiper's Belt"). Thus the orbit of Ea, the Planet

Neptune, was set as the outer limit of the orbits of many of the comets that Planet X had carried away from the shattered Earth.

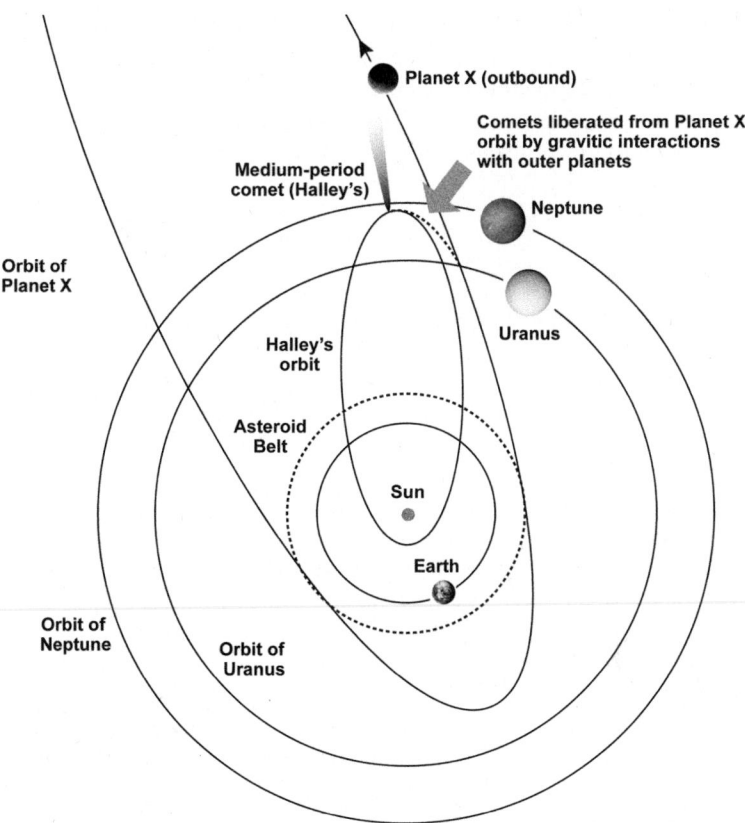

Figure 4.6: As Planet X moved out of the solar system back into deep space on the outward bound part of its orbit, it carried a fair amount of the shattered Earth with it that had been caught in its gravitational "net". Some of this material was a combination of rock and water ice, what we know today as "comets". When Planet X passed by the outer planets, many if not all of these newly created comets were stripped from orbit around Planet X, taking on independent orbits of their own and becoming the "short period" comets, of which Halley's is the most famous. These comets are the "statues" mentioned in Enuma Elish that Marduk set up at the outer edge of the solar system to commemorate the battle between himself and Tiamat. These statues were symbolically seen by the ancient Sumerians as the dead bodies of the "helpers" of Tiamat, which still circle the heavens as the comets to this day as a reminder of the divine creation battle and the defeat of the dragon and her helpers.

In conclusion, the "shrines" of the rebellious gods, described in verse 68, are the orbits of the comets. The comets themselves were the statues, or "monuments," "war trophies" which forever pass near Earth, an eternal witness in heaven continuously recalling God's glorious defeat of the dragon and the creation of Earth. The "shrines" wherein these "monuments" were placed were set "at the gate of Apsu," or deep space, the outer boundary of the solar system as defined by the orbit of Neptune — exactly where man of the comets orbit today.

Enuma Elish V:67-76	The Astronomical Interpretation
When he had designed his rules (and) fashioned [his] ordinances, He founded [the shr]ines (and) handed them over to Ea. [The Tablet of] Destinies which he had taken from Kingu he carried, He brought (it) as the first gift of greeting, he gave (it) to Anu. [The go]ds who had done battle and had been scattered, He led bound into the presence of his fathers.	When Planet X had finished recreating Earth and its new Moon, setting their orbits, rotational periods, and all of their other characteristics, it captured much of the remaining shattered material, both rock and water ice, in its gravitational field, and took it with on its journey back out of the solar system. As it passed out of the solar system, Planet X's interaction with the gravitational fields of the outer planets, particularly Uranus and Neptune, pulled many of the comets in Planet X's train out of its gravitational influence into independent orbits of their own.
Now the eleven creatures which Tiamat had made..., Whose weapons he had shattered, which he had tied to his foot: [Of these] he made statues and set (them) up [at the Gate of] Apsu (saying): "Let it be a token that this may never be forgotten!"	Of these comets and other fragments of the former Earth that had been captured in Planet X's gravitational field, 11 comets were particularly large. As Planet X passed by Uranus and Neptune on its way out of the solar system on the outbound leg of its orbital journey, these 11 comets were pulled from its gravitational field and set into independent orbits of their own. These comets regularly pass by Earth to this day as a reminder of the cosmic Creation battle, when God defeated the dragon and created the heavens and Earth from her dead body.

TABLET VI: THE CREATION OF MAN AND THE TOWER OF BABEL

The Creation of Man from the Moon

When Marduk hears the word of the gods,
His heart prompts (him) to fashion artful works.
Opening his mouth, he addresses Ea
To impart the plan conceived in his heart:
"Blood I will mass and cause bones to be.
I will establish a savage, 'man' shall be his name.
Verily, savage-man I will create.
He will be charged with the service of the gods
that they might be at ease!
Ea answered him, speaking a word to him...
"Let but one of their brothers be handed over;
He alone shall perish that mankind be fashioned....
The Igigi, the great gods, replied to him...
"It was Kingu who contrived the uprising,
And made Tiamat rebel, and joined battle."
They bound him, held him before Ea.
They imposed on him his guilt and severed his blood (vessels).
Out of his blood they fashioned mankind.
(VI:1-8, 11, 13-14, 27, 29-33)

Just after the creation of the Moon is described at the end of Tablet V, Tablet VI starts with the creation of man. In it, Marduk decides to create mankind as a sort of "slave race" that "the gods" could then use to create various structures on Earth, most notably the Tower of Babel. It was decided that in order to bring life to mankind, one of the gods would have to be killed, and the life in his blood used to bring mankind to life. After some debate, it was decided that the gods who had rebelled against Marduk should be killed, and their blood used to create mankind. And since Tiamat was already dead, and the 11 "dragons" that Tiamat had created to defend herself had been imprisoned in orbits far away in the outer solar system, only Kingu remained alive and available of the original group of deities who had rebelled against the gods. So, it was decided that mankind would be created from the blood of Kingu, the leader of Tiamat's heavenly army. The idea that mankind was created from the "blood" of Kingu is corroborated in Tablet VII, where one of the 50 names of Marduk is given as "Gishnumunab, creator of all people, who made the (world) regions, destroyer of the gods of Tiamat; who made men out of their substance" (VII:89-90).

In the astronomical context, however, the message that this passage enciphers more likely has to do with the fact that some of the material that was thrown into space by the Giant Impact separated from that part of Earth's mantle that would become the Moon and fell back down to Earth to form the original "Pangaea" continent that geologists have believed for some time was the original continent on Earth. This continent would have contained a rich mixture of minerals, as the heavier elements would have precipitated out from the lighter elements in space and fallen to Earth, leaving the lighter elements in orbit to form the Moon. And it was from this rich mixture of minerals that fell from heaven to Earth — a mixture that might otherwise not have been possible had the Giant Impact not carved out and sorted out the heavier elements from the mantle and re-deposited them back onto the surface of Earth in a concentrated form — that mankind was formed. And not only was this exceptionally rich and concentrated mixture of elements available to create mankind from, these concentrated elements would also now be more easily available for mining by the newly created mankind so they could create tall towers and fashion gold and jewel-encrusted ritual objects with which to worship the gods.

The Tower of Babel Reaching to the Apsu/Heaven

The Anunnaki opened their mouths
And said to Marduk, their lord:
"Now, O lord, thou who hast caused our deliverance,
What shall be our homage to thee?
Let us build a shrine whose name shall be called
'Lo, a chamber for our nightly rest'; let us repose in it!
Let us build a throne, a recess for his abode!
On the day that we arrive we shall repose in it."
When Marduk heard this,
Brightly glowed his features like the day:
"Construct Babylon, whose building you have requested,
Let its brickwork be fashioned. You shall name it 'The Sanctuary.'"
The Anunnaki applied the implement;
For one whole year they molded bricks.

> When the second year arrived,
> They raised high the head of Esagila equaling Apsu
> Having built a stage tower as high as Apsu,
> They set up *in it* an abode for Marduk, Enlil, (and) Ea
> To the base of Esharra its horns look down.
> (VI:47–66)

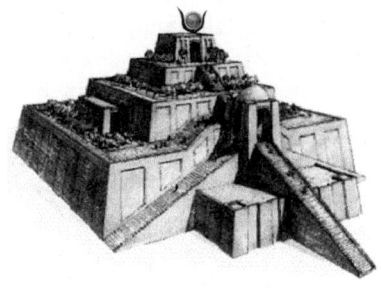

A reconstruction of what the Tower of Babel may have looked like, with the "horns" added at its peak. These mysterious horns, mentioned in Enuma Elish VI:66, may have had some important communications purpose, a purpose that may have something to do with both the beginning and end times of mankind's history on Earth.

As we saw in Chapter II, the Babylonians believed that the Tower of Babel had been built by a group of angelic divine beings known as the Annunaki, who came down from heaven and taught mankind all knowledge, including but not limited to language, writing, astronomy, mathematics, architecture, metallurgy, and possibly many other disciplines. And the reason for this was so that mankind could create a sufficiently advanced civilization so that, when these "star gods" returned, mankind would be ready to accommodate them at a level they would find acceptable, and be able to worship and serve them in an appropriate manner.

However, since Chapter III, we have learned a great deal more about the specific intentions of these divine beings who interacted with the ancient Sumerians. As we see here, in VI:47-66, the Annunaki had led a combined development effort with the ancient Sumerians to build a tower that was "as high as Apsu". As we have seen, the Apsu in Sumerian cosmology was a description of deep space beyond the orbit of Neptune. So, just as it is described in the Bible, this tower was indeed intended to reach "unto heaven". Of course, no tower could literally, physically reach to heaven, so clearly something else must be in mind here. Somehow, this tower was connected to heaven, just as Tiamat's "tail" formed a bond with the heavens in V:56, 59. In this passage, Tiamat's tail was somehow connected to the mysterious *Durmah*, which we determined was a reference to the asteroid belt, the "hammered heaven" of biblical cosmology. This may explain why, in the last line of this passage, lies the cryptic message, "to the base of Esharra its horns look down". *Esharra*, as we have seen, was a sort of "gateway of heaven" through which Planet X passed on the inner part of its long orbital journey through our solar system. The *Esharra*, based upon textual and linguistic clues, appears to be a particular part of the asteroid belt, probably where Planet X and Earth had come into conflict. As such, it would appear that these "horns", that assumedly sat atop the Tower of Babel, were somehow meant to connect to Planet X as it passed through that part of the inner solar system where it had come into conflict with Earth, "in the beginning". The origin and nature of these mysterious horns will be examined more fully in the final chapter of this book.

Enuma Elish VI:47-66	The Astronomical Interpretation
The Anunnaki opened their mouths And said to Marduk, their lord: "Now, O lord, thou who hast caused our deliverance, What shall be our homage to thee? Let us build a shrine whose name shall be called 'Lo, a chamber for our nightly rest'; let us repose in it! Let us build a throne, a recess for his abode! On the day that we arrive we shall repose in it."	A mysterious race of beings called the "Anunnaki" (those who came from heaven to Earth), and helped the Sumerians build a tower that had both religious, astronomical and related uses that was intended to be an abode for these mysterious beings whenever they visited Earth.
When Marduk heard this, Brightly glowed his features like the day: "Construct Babylon, whose building you have requested, Let its brickwork be fashioned. You shall name it 'The Sanctuary.'" The Anunnaki applied the implement; For one whole year they molded bricks. When the second year arrived, They raised high the head of Esagila equaling Apsu Having built a stage tower as high as Apsu, They set up in it an abode for Marduk, Enlil, (and) Ea To the base of Esharra its horns look down.	The Annunaki worked with the ancient Sumerians to build this temple, which was made of brick. At the top of the tower was what looked like a pair of horns that was meant to be used to communicate with the Annunaki when they returned to heaven. These horns were designed to point at the place in the asteroid belt where Planet X and Earth came into conflict.

"When On High": The Astronomical Interpretation of Enuma Elish

The "Bow-Star" in Heaven

Two examples of the classic "winged disc" used by the Sumerians, Babylonians, Assyrians and Persians to represent Planet X. The top version is the original Sumerian version, which is intended to display the "winglike" characteristics of the cometlike tail, or "flood storm" that is believed to surround Planet X as it approaches our inner solar system. Note the simplified "bow" symbol on the top of the design, identifying this as the "bow star" described in Enuma Elish VI:82-94. The bottom version shows the Assyrian equivalent of Marduk, Assur, sitting atop Planet X, holding his bow, showing that Marduk was believed to be "riding" the planet. This symbol is the ubiquitous symbol of the most high god of heaven that can be found in various forms throughout the ancient Near East.

Enlil raised the bow, his weapon, and laid (it) before them.
The gods, his fathers, saw the net he had made.
When they beheld the bow, how skillful its shape,
His fathers praised the work he had wrought.
Raising (it), Anu spoke up in the Assembly of the gods,
As he kissed the bow: "This is my daughter!"
He named the names of the bow as follows:
"Longwood is the first, the second is Accurate;
Its third name is Bow-Star, in heaven I have made it shine."
He fixed its position with the gods its brothers.
After Anu had decreed the fate of the bow,
(And) placed it in the lofty royal throne before the gods,
Anu placed it in the assembly of the gods.
(VI: 82-94, emphasis mine)

Though to this point Marduk is only assumed, based upon the context, to be a previously unknown planet in our solar system, if one is still not convinced of this fact, despite the avalanche of religious, mythological, textual and linguistic evidence presented to this point, the Sumerians and Babylonians make it absolutely crystal clear, here in VI:90, the Marduk is indeed not some abstract concept, nor a mere idol, but was indeed *a star in the sky*. And since no star could move like Marduk is said to do, this star must, in fact, be a planet. End of discussion.

Interestingly, Marduk and the "bow-star" are actually seen as two parts of the same being — Marduk being the supreme deity who controls Planet X like a weapon, in this case a bow — and the bow itself. So a further degree of detail regarding the relationship between the god of the planet and the planet itself is made here. Just as Planet X was believed to have a patron deity behind it that was spiritual in nature, so too did the other planets. So the gods of the Sumerians were perceived to be both immanent in their planets, yet transcendent — part of them, yet not limited by them. This belief was carried on by the cultural descendants of the Sumerians, the Babylonians, and from them on to the Assyrians, and from then on to the Persians. And all of them used variations on the same symbology, the classic "winged disc" symbol showed at the top left of this page which is also often associated with either a bow, or a deity carrying a bow.

Finally, this mysterious "bow-star" was placed in the heavens amongst the other gods, the other planets in our solar system — game, set and match against those interpreters who believe that Marduk and the other Sumerian deities represented lowly, earth-bound concepts such as silt and slime. Marduk, Planet X was now set amongst the other planets in our solar system, where it would remain until the end of time.

TABLET VII: PLANET X: THE STAR OF THE CROSSING

Tablet VII of Enuma Elish is preoccupied primarily with the pronouncement of the fifty names of Marduk, fifty names that describe fifty attributes of Marduk and his accomplishments in the creation of Earth, mankind, and all the animals and plants — much the same as Genesis 1-2 attributes the creation of the heavens and Earth, and all life on Earth, to God. Several of these names recall some of the specific events of the creation battle, even adding some additional details that may not have been clear in the previous tablets. And one of the most important summary names is the 49th name of Marduk, "Nebiru" which, as we saw earlier, means "the one who crosses" or, simply, "the Cross":

> (49) Nebiru shall hold the crossings of heaven and earth,
> So that they (the gods) cannot cross above and below
> They must wait on him

Nebiru is the star which in the skies is brilliant.
Verily he holds the central position, they shall bow down to him,
   Saying: "He who the midst of the Sea restlessly crosses,
   Let 'Crossing' be his name, who controls its midst.
May they uphold the course of the stars of heaven;
   May he shepherd all the gods like sheep.
May he vanquish Tiamat; may her life be strait and short!
Into the future of mankind, when days have grown old,
   May she recede without cease and stay away forever.
                    (VII:124-134)

Once again, Marduk is clearly stated to be a bright star in the sky, a planet that crosses across the orbits of the other gods, the planets. Further, it states that as a planet, he holds "the central position", the position that Tiamat, the primordial Earth, had once held before it had been shattered and moved to a position closer to the Sun. Marduk, or Planet X, is then described as the one who "restlessly crosses" through the middle of our solar system — thus the surname of *Nebiru*, "the one who crosses". In this way, Planet X has an effect on the orbits of the outer planets, which it crosses near on occasion. Finally, *Enuma Elish* sums up by cursing Tiamat and, though it curses her to recede forever, the text seems to imply that perhaps Tiamat would rise again sometime in the distant future of mankind.

SUMMARY

In summary, it is clear that *Enuma Elish* is not the work of foolish superstition, or religious zeal, but indeed the product of an ancient scientifically advanced tradition that most likely hails all the way back to the beginning of mankind. This tradition is most likely a branch of a *grundschrift*, or foundation text, upon which the creation material in the Bible is also based, a foundation text that may have been passed down all the way from the world before the Flood, through Noah and the patriarchs. As such, a study of *Enuma Elish* in the context of astronomy, as we will see, is absolutely necessary to have a complete understanding of the creation material to be found in the Bible, particularly those sections that describe the Creation as the result, as we discussed in Chapter I, of a battle between God and a dragon. And as we shall see in the next two chapters, the parallels between *Enuma Elish* and the biblical Creation material, properly interpreted within the astronomical context we have explored in this chapter, makes it clear that both the ancient Sumerians and the authors of the Bible had an understanding of the specific details of the Creation that was extremely advanced even by modern standards — so advanced, in fact, that we have yet to fully catch up to the understanding of the ancients.

V

"IN THE BEGINNING": THE BIBLICAL CREATION MATERIAL REINTERPRETED

Thou hast broken Rahab in pieces, as one that is slain; thou hast scattered thine enemies with thy strong arm. The heavens are thine, the Earth also is thine: as for the world and the fulness thereof, thou hast founded them. (Ps. 89:8-11)

Even more important than the scientific and historical evidence behind the reinterpretation of the biblical accounts of the Creation, underlying even the Planet X/Giant Impact theory and the ancient Near Eastern parallels, is the fundamental truth that God would not lie to His prophets by revealing to them a false account of the Creation. The belief that the Hebrews conceived of Earth as a flat circle over which sat a fixed dome, upon which the stars and planets moved around in an Earth-centered universe, is a result not of Hebrew ignorance but of modern arrogance. It is not the foolishness of our ancestors but our failure to properly interpret the Creation passages in the Bible which have created this error. Yet we continue to embarrass God by applying unscientific, irrational and in some cases ridiculous interpretations to these

As we saw in Chapter I, this depiction of the battle between the Babylonian deity Marduk (right) and the dragon-goddess Tiamat (left) from the Babylonian Epic of Creation ably illustrates the concept of the creation battle between the high god of the ancient Mesopotamian pantheons and a "dragon" which represented the heavenly conflict that resulted in the re-creation of Earth in its present form. As we shall see, this was not only the belief of the ancient Mesopotamians, but of the Hebrews as well.

passages, all in the name of "tradition". We must abandon this failed strategy and search for an account of the Creation that is both scientifically and exegetically sound. We must find the true path between irrational fundamentalist traditions regarding the Creation on the right, and the Godless, modernist approach on the left that presumes that God is only a myth and that His Word is merely a collection of folktales written by scientifically ignorant savages. The true path is to determine the proper exegesis of the Creation materials in the Old Testament, relying not only on interpreting the Bible in its cultural context, but also in the context of modern scientific findings regarding the creation and early history of Earth. By doing so, we will create an interpretation of the Creation material in the Old Testament that is not only scientifically accurate, but may actually be even more advanced than our modern scientific understanding is today.

The Planet X theory has been around for over a century, yet it remains the only logical explanation for the numerous anomalies in the outer solar system and, as we have seen, the inner solar system, particularly Earth. The Giant Impact theory, generally accepted and adopted by the scientific community in 1984 as the best explanation for the creation of the modern-day Earth and its Moon, only started receiving coverage by the more popularly oriented science magazines in the 1990s. Also, not until the 1990s was it determined that the water and organic materials found in the comets and on some asteroids originated from the primordial Earth. These and other scientific breakthroughs have only come to light in the last century or so, some of them coming in only the last decade or so. Only now is God allowing man to fully understand the specifics of how He created the heavens and Earth. And there is much more yet to come before we have as full an understanding of the Creation as the prophets had, those trusted few with whom God shared His secrets.

THESIS: GOD USED PLANET X TO CREATE HEAVEN AND EARTH

The thesis of this chapter, based upon our analysis thus far, is that God used Planet X to create Earth, its Moon, and the entire solar system in its present form. It is important to note that God did not use Planet X to actually *create* the solar system from nothing, but to "fine tune" a system that He had previously brought into being, particularly the fourth planet in that system, so that it would be best able to support life and allow Him to execute His plans for the creation, redemption and salvation of His chosen people. This is why only a minimal amount of

Creation information is given in the beginning of the Bible — whereas the Creation of the heavens and Earth were the critical first steps in God's plan, the vast majority of the Book of Genesis, and the rest of the Bible, is dedicated to the people of God and their eventual salvation. In this "salvation history" scenario, the creation of Earth is merely a relatively minor prolegomena to the creation, redemption and salvation of God's chosen people, which is the true and only real purpose for the Creation. And whereas the people of God will live forever, heaven and Earth will eventually pass away and be forgotten, replaced with a new heaven and a new Earth (Rev. 20:11, 22:1; 2 Peter 3:10-13). Thus, since the Creation material in Genesis and throughout the Bible describes only a temporary situation that was created specifically as a foundation for the rest of human history, a situation of planned obsolescence where the heavens and Earth in their present form would eventually be destroyed and forgotten, the Creation texts in the Bible are only important if they shed light on our understanding of God's plan of salvation. And, as we shall see throughout the rest of this book, Planet X has indeed played a crucial role in the creation, history and salvation of God's chosen people, both their past, present and future.

The Planet X Creation Paradigm

In this new paradigm, the "Planet X Creation Paradigm", we will see that Planet X was used by God as a sort of precision tool to fine-tune the heavens and Earth so they would be able to support life of a complexity sufficient for God to successfully execute His plan of salvation. In this new paradigm, Earth of course still refers to our modern planet Earth, but the word "heaven(s)" here in Genesis 1:1 actually refers not to some ethereal realm on a higher plane of existence, the entire universe, our galaxy, or even our solar system, but specifically to the asteroid belt, which was created when God shattered the primordial Earth and moved the bulk of its mass to a new orbit closer to the Sun, leaving a small, shattered remnant behind as a reminder of the cosmic Creation battle.

However, the idea of "heaven" being a lifeless zone of shattered rock between the orbits of Mars and Jupiter makes little sense from a theological perspective, particularly since the Bible specifically states that this is where Jesus ascended to heaven, sitting on the right hand of the Father (1 Peter 3:22), and where we as believers will be elevated after death (1 Peter 1:4). Thus this usage of the term "heaven" in Genesis 1 must differ from that used in other parts of the Bible.

The answer to this riddle lies in the fact that the Hebrew word שָׁמַיִם *shamayim*, "heavens" in Genesis 1:1 and elsewhere does not refer to a plural collective "heavens", i.e., the entire starry array, but to three different heavens, one of which is the eternal destiny of the saints.

Un missionnaire du moyen âge raconte qu'il avait trouvé le point où le ciel et la Terre se touchent...

The famous "Flammarion woodcut" depicting the vision of a Christian missionary who believed that he had found the connection between heaven and Earth, and had broken through the veil to peer past the first heaven (Earth's atmosphere) and the second heaven (a second sphere upon which circled the Sun, Moon and stars) to view the third heaven, in which mysterious spheres and the Merkevah, the "chariot of the Lord" flew. This woodcut ably illustrates the ancient conception of the heavens and their tripartite division, a conception that remained dominant in some circles, particularly fundamentalist ones, until well after the Enlightenment. Image from Camille Flammarion's L'Atmosphere: Meteorologie Populaire, Paris, 1888.

The Three "Heavens"

This multiplicity of heavens has caused some confusion amongst Bible scholars, who tend to fall back on the theological premise that there is only one heaven, and one hell, one place for the faithful, and another place for the damned. However, others point out that the Apostle Paul mentions not one but three heavens in 2 Corinthians 12:2, and that one believer actually traveled to the third heaven, which he described as "paradise". Let us now take a look at the information regarding the three heavens of the Bible, and analyze them in the context of our more modern, scientific understanding of how these "heavens" are actually arranged.

The first step in our understanding of what the "heavens" are and how they are arranged is to analyze the Hebrew word for heaven, שָׁמַיִם *shamayim*, and the related word רָקִיעַ *raqiya*, "firmament". *Shamayim*, as we have seen, is a plural word that literally means "heavens", meaning literally that there is more than one "heaven". *Shamayim* is based on the root שָׁמָה *shamah,* "to be high, lofty", which is closely related to the word שָׁמַם *shamam,* "empty, desolate". Thus the term *shamayim* literally means a place that high above the Earth and empty — a perfect description of outer space.

רָקִיעַ *raqiya,* "firmament" is used in the Bible almost always in conjunction with *shamayim,* appearing with *shamayim* several times in Genesis 1, and once in Psalm 19, both of which are Creation passages. *Raqiya* is based upon the root word רָקַע *raqa',* "to beat, strike or trample underfoot". *Raqa'* also contains the meaning of spreading something out by beating or hammering it flat, or shattering it into pieces, and is cognate to the Akkadian word *rakkis,* which we saw in Chapter IV was used in *Enuma Elish* to describe the "heaven" created from the "tail" of Tiamat as a sort of "hammered bracelet" that was stretched out across the heavens. Thus, from this information, we can determine that at least one of the heavens was thought of as something that had been shattered and spread out as a result of the creation of Earth.

Additional information that can help us corroborate the biblical view of the heavens with our modern scientific understanding of them can be found in the various uses of the word "heaven" throughout the Bible. In Genesis 1:20 and Jeremiah 4:25, heaven is the place where the birds fly, and in Isaiah 55:10 and Acts 14:17, heaven is the place where rain and snow are said to come from. This would correspond to our modern understanding of Earth's atmosphere, which extends some miles above Earth before it finally gives place to outer space. However, in Genesis 1:14-18, the "firmament of heaven" is also said to be the place where the Sun, Moon and stars move, which is well above the limits of Earth's atmosphere. Thus a different sphere of influence is in view here.

The most logical conclusion, then, is that the Earth's atmosphere, where birds fly and the clouds drop the rain, is the first "heaven", and that somewhere in outer space lies the second "heaven". This conclusion is further underlined by the description in Genesis 1:6-7 of the "waters above" being separated from the "waters below" by a "firmament". This "firmament", the *raqiya*, as we have seen, was seen as a "hammered bracelet" that circles in heaven, defining the outer limit of the inner solar system. The asteroid belt, modern astronomers have discovered, contains a fair amount of water ice frozen in with the asteroids, making them a sort of "supercaelian sea", a river of ice and rock that flows in the heavens. Thus the "waters below" must refer to the water present in Earth's seas and atmosphere, and the "waters above" must refer to the frozen waters of the asteroid belt, and therefore the "first heaven" is defined by the outer limit of Earth's atmosphere, and the "second heaven" is defined by the asteroid belt.

The Third Heaven: Planet X?

So if the first heaven is Earth's atmosphere, and the second heaven is the asteroid belt, what is the third heaven? In 2 Corinthians 12:2-4, the third heaven is described as a "paradise" that a Christian man had been "caught up" to. It is interesting to note that Paul was not sure as to whether or not the man had been caught up "in the body", or "out of the body", indicating that it was not necessarily a purely spiritual experience. And if it was a physical experience, perhaps this man had been "beamed up" into a "chariot of fire" as the prophet Elijah had been in 2 Kings 2 and physically taken to the third heaven?

Assuming that a man could be taken up "in the body" to the third heaven and not die, as the Bible clearly states, then could it be possible that the third heaven, like the first and second heavens, is actually a physical location in space, perhaps even in our own solar system? And if the first heaven is defined by Earth's atmosphere, and the second heaven is defined by the asteroid belt, which resides in the middle of our solar system, could it be that the mysterious "third heaven" is actually defined by the outer edge of our solar system? Could it even be defined by the orbit of Planet X, or even be Planet X itself?

Though it seems unlikely that Planet X — which is most likely an icy planet that is probably even colder than Pluto throughout much of its orbit — could be the location of the heaven promised to the saints, it is not impossible. "Heaven" tends to be thought of as a sort of "higher dimension" a "spirit realm" that is above that of the physical, though the Bible is not clear on the issue. It could well be that Planet X is the location of a great and ancient civilization, compared to which earthly civilizations are merely pale imitations — a civilization that we as Christians will inherit, ruled over by Christ Himself. It could also be that Planet X hosts a gateway between the physical realm and a higher, spiritual realm where God dwells, but we can only speculate. We will look into these interesting possibilities, along with numerous other mysterious passages in the Bible that the Planet X/Giant Impact theory may solve, in the rest of this chapter.

In sum, "heaven" or "the firmament," as it is commonly translated, may not have been conceived of originally as a hardened dome that arches over the sky — a scientifically inaccurate concept — but as circle of rocks that had been hammered fine by a destructive force — a scientifically accurate concept. Planet X smashed the primordial Earth into two pieces, smashing the lesser piece into small pieces to form the asteroid belt, and sending the larger piece into a new orbit closer to the Sun. The heavens were then divided into three divisions: 1) Earth's atmosphere, 2) the asteroid belt, and 3) Planet X. If this theory *is* true, then many verses dealing with the creation may have significantly different interpretations, beginning with Genesis 1.

GENESIS 1: GOD USES PLANET X TO (RE)CREATE HEAVEN AND EARTH

✞ Genesis 1:1-8:

> [1] In the beginning God created the heaven and the Earth.
>
> [2] And the Earth was without form, and void; and darkness was upon the face of the deep. And the Spirit of God moved upon the face of the waters.
>
> [3] And God said, Let there be light: and there was light.
>
> [4] And God saw the light, that it was good: and God divided the light from the darkness.
>
> [5] And God called the light Day, and the darkness he called Night. And the evening and the morning were the first day.
>
> [6] And God said, Let there be a firmament in the midst of the waters, and let it divide the waters from the waters.
>
> [7] And God made the firmament, and divided the waters which were under the firmament from the waters which were above the firmament: and it was so.

⁸ And God called the firmament Heaven. And the evening and the morning were the second day.
⁹ And God said, Let the waters under the heaven be gathered together unto one place, and let the dry land appear: and it was so.
¹⁰ And God called the dry land Earth; and the gathering together of the waters called he Seas: and God saw that it was good.
¹⁴ And God said, Let there be lights in the firmament of the heaven to divide the day from the night; and let them be for signs, and for seasons, and for days, and years:
¹⁵ And let them be for lights in the firmament of the heaven to give light upon the Earth: and it was so.
¹⁶ And God made two great lights; the greater light to rule the day, and the lesser light to rule the night: he made the stars also.
¹⁷ And God set them in the firmament of the heaven to give light upon the Earth,
¹⁸ And to rule over the day and over the night, and to divide the light from the darkness: and God saw that it was good.
¹⁹ And the evening and the morning were the fourth day. (KJV)

Nowhere in the Bible does it say specifically that in the beginning, God created the "universe." It simply says "the heaven(s) and the Earth." It has been *assumed* that the Genesis creation account refers to the creation of the whole universe. However, the Hebrew word for "heaven" appears to actually describe an object or region in our solar system. This distinction begins in Genesis 1, which explains first and foremost that it is the creation of Earth with which Moses is primarily concerned, and not of the universe as a whole (though clearly God created the whole universe). Grand cosmological theories were not necessary as a preface to the stories of the patriarchs. All Moses needed was a concise recapitulation of the well-known events of the creation of Earth to serve as a prolegomena to God's saving acts in history that He accomplished through the patriarchs and their descendants. Moses also wanted to avoid the polytheistic methods employed by the Babylonians in *Enuma Elish*, particularly the use of gods and goddesses to symbolize the planets.

This is why the Genesis account of the Creation is so short, comprising only the first of the 50 chapters of Genesis: Moses wanted to avoid the extended narrative technique that the Babylonians had used to describe the Creation, instead boiling it down to the bare, scientific fundamentals, focusing only on those aspects of the Creation of the heavens and Earth that were most relevant to the story. As a result, the creation of the heavens and Earth, instead of being the subject of the majority of the Book of Genesis, as it is with *Enuma Elish*, is instead merely a brief recapitulation of the creation of heavens and Earth in their present form, intended to serve as a background story that sets the context for what was truly important: the creation, redemption, and salvation of God's chosen people.

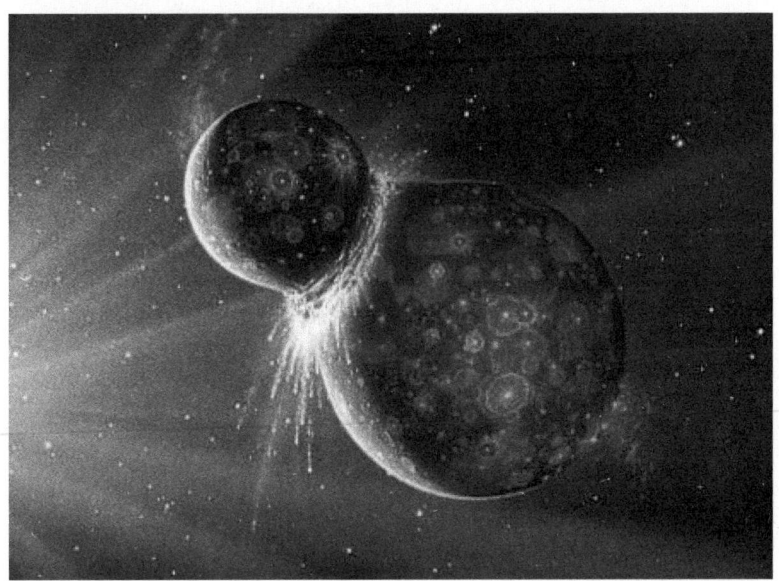

Genesis 1:1: God Uses Planet X to Divide Heaven and Earth

☥ Genesis 1:1:
¹In the beginning God created the heaven and the Earth.

The first of God's actions in history that was directly relevant to mankind was the creation of Earth, of which the creation of the heavens was a secondary result. Moses' account, as we shall see, is scientifically accurate to the extreme, corresponding perfectly with the Planet X/Giant Impact Theory. In just a few short lines, he summarizes how the primordial Earth had been shattered, made "without form and void," by a collision with one of Planet X's Moons.

Though the text does not directly state this, it is clearly implied, particularly in the context of *Enuma Elish*.

This concept can be seen as early as Genesis 1:1, where the word translated in Genesis 1:1 as "created" is actually בָּרָא *bara,* "to cut", in the sense of dividing an object into two (or more) pieces. Genesis 1:1, in the context of *Enuma Elish* and other biblical parallels to be discussed later in this chapter, would thus be most accurately translated, "In the beginning, God cut apart the heavens and Earth." Even more interestingly, the root meaning of the word רֵאשִׁית *ra'shiyth,* currently translated as "beginning", literally means "head" — i.e., something that came first, and is the most important thing of all. It can refer to a previous time or event in history, to an object that was the "first mover" in that event, or possibly a combination. It is thus translated along with the Hebrew word for stone, אֶבֶן, *'even,* as "chief cornerstone" in Zech. 4:7.[1]

Though אֶבֶן is not actually present in the text of Genesis 1:1, I propose, based upon the Planet X/Giant Impact theory, that the first word[2] in the Bible, בְּרֵאשִׁית *be-ra'shiyth,* should be translated not as "in the beginning", but as "by the chief cornerstone", "by a great stone", or perhaps most accurately, considering the astronomical context, "with the satellite of a planet". This also fits in better with the idea of God using a "divine wind", or "satellite" of Planet X to divide heaven and Earth, which we will also discuss later in this chapter. Thus, Genesis 1:1 would be best translated in the context of our new understanding of the Planet X/Giant Impact theory as "With the satellite of a planet God cut apart the heavens and Earth." This would correspond nicely with the idea of Jesus as the "chief cornerstone" that is used by God the Father to defeat His enemies (Matt. 21:42, 1 Peter 2:6), and with the idea that God routinely uses huge stones to destroy his enemies (Joshua 10:11; Judges 5:20; Daniel 2:31-35, Rev. 18:21), not to mention his command to Israel to stone to death those who

---

[1] Gesenius, W., & Tregelles, S. P. (2003). *Gesenius' Hebrew and Chaldee Lexicon to the Old Testament Scriptures* (752). Bellingham, WA: Logos Research Systems, Inc.

[2] Technically, the first word in the Bible is a preposition, בְּ *be'* – which can mean "in", "at", "with", or a few other subtle variations depending upon the context. The first true "word" is of course רֵאשִׁית *ra'shiyth,* "beginning", "former time", "head", "most important thing" and/or "first thing". Thus we can see the variety of potential interpretations based upon these two words alone.

violated the Mosaic covenant (Exodus 19:13; Lev. 20:27, Deut. 21:21, etc.)

If this is indeed the correct interpretation, then it is interesting to note that the major advents of Planet X literally form the framework in which the Bible is set. The first thing mentioned in the Bible is how God used a planet to create the heavens and Earth. Then at the beginning of the New Testament — between the Testaments — this planet is again given prominent mention as the Star of Bethlehem. Finally, at the end of the Bible, this same heavenly Sign will return to destroy God's enemies once more, and then create a new heaven and a new Earth. At the end of human history, with His enemies defeated and His people saved, God's "grand design", his "master covenant", literally comes full circle.

Moses holding the two tablets of the Ten Commandments. The tablets were most likely divided into two so as to remember the fact that God divided the primordial Earth into two parts, forming the heavens and a new Earth. These two tablets would then be a constant reminder of God's victory over the dragon, and of its ongoing subjugation.

Another interesting bit of information that can be gleaned from this single, pithy passage that is pregnant with meaning is that בָּרָא *bara* is one of the words used in the Bible to describe how the various lesser covenants between God and man were created. For example, God literally "cut" a covenant with Abraham, commanding Abraham to cut (בָּתַר *batar*)[3] some sacrificial animals in half (Genesis 15:8-18). Then, God caused what is described as "a smoking furnace and a burning lamp" to pass between the two halves of the carcasses, this ritual apparently completing the cutting (Hebrew כָּרַת *carat*)[4] of the covenant between God and Abraham that was then formally declared in Genesis 15:18.

---

[3]*Batar*, "to cut up" or "divide", is usually used in the context of slain and/or sacrificial victims Gesenius, W., & Tregelles, S. P. (2003). *Gesenius' Hebrew and Chaldee Lexicon to the Old Testament Scriptures* (149). Bellingham, WA: Logos Research Systems, Inc.

[4]Gesenius explains, "כָּרַת בְּרִית; Gr. ὅρκια τέμνειν, τέμνειν σπονδὰς, *to make a covenant*, [describes the] slaying and dividing the victims, as was customary in making a covenant (see Gen. 15:18; Jer. 34:8, 18. Gesenius, W., & Tregelles, S. P. (2003). *Gesenius'*

This "cutting in half" of the sacrificial animal and passing fire between the halves is a clear reference to God's defeat of the dragon with a fiery object (one of Planet X's satellites) and the creation of heaven and the Earth from the two pieces of her body. It also clearly supports the idea of the creation of heaven and Earth as a covenantal act which formed the template for covenantal ritual throughout the Bible and, indeed, the ancient Near East.

This concept of cutting an object in two as the basis of a covenant can also clearly be seen in the cutting of the Mosaic Covenant upon Mt. Sinai. There, God literally cut a covenant with Israel (Hebrew כָּרַת *carat*, Exodus 34:10) by literally cutting a single stone into two stones, or "tablets", upon which God Himself wrote the Ten Commandments, dividing them in two with a finger of fire just after recalling the creation of heaven and Earth (Exodus 31:17-18). Indeed the two tablets may have been meant to symbolize heaven and Earth, respectively. This concept is supported by the fact that, in Deuteronomy 4:15-25, after reminding Israel of the great importance of the first two commandments that specifically forbid idolatry, in verse 26, Moses then calls heaven and Earth as witnesses against them if they break their covenant with God. It may well be that Moses was holding up the two tablets as he was saying this, in order to emphasize the point. Finally, it is also instructive to note that the Sinai event was clearly linked with the Creation battle between God and the dragon Leviathan in Psalm 74.[5]

In summary, God's cutting of the primordial earth "stone", or planet, into two pieces to create heaven and Earth, appears to have formed the basis of the concept of covenant that can be found throughout the Old Testament. This covenantal destruction and recreation process can be seen both in the beginning of the Bible, where the primordial Earth was cut in half, and heaven and Earth formed from its pieces, and also in the destruction and re-creation of the heavens and Earth that takes place again in Revelation 20:11, 21:1. The appearance of Planet X to herald the advent of Christ at

---

Hebrew and Chaldee Lexicon to the Old Testament Scriptures (416–417). Bellingham, WA: Logos Research Systems, Inc. This practice of forming covenants over the slain bodies of dead foes clearly recalls God's defeating of the dragon and dividing its body into heaven and Earth, a belief that was ubiquitous throughout the ancient Near East, and strongly supports the theory that the dividing of the "dragon's" body into heaven and Earth was the very first covenantal act described in the Bible.

[5] Psalm 74 will be studied in more detail later in this chapter.

Bethlehem was, in this sense, the ultimate affirmation of the first covenant God made in Genesis 1, the same all-encompassing, "outer framework" master covenant that He will affirm at the end of the Book of Revelation with the destruction of this present Earth and the creation of a new, perfected one, over which Jesus will rule forever.

Genesis 1:2: God Creates the Moon and Moves Earth to its Present Orbital Station

✟ Genesis 1:2:
² And the Earth was without form, and void; and darkness was upon the face of the deep. And the Spirit of God moved upon the face of the waters.

Genesis 1:2 also has some interesting linguistic surprises that allow it to be nicely retranslated according to the Planet X/Giant Impact paradigm. First of all is the enigmatic Hebrew term וָבֹהוּ תֹהוּ *tohu wabohu*, typically translated as "without form and void". As we saw in Part I, the terms *tohu* and *bohu* may actually be demythologized versions of the names of the sea dragon "Tiamat" that shows up in *Enuma Elish*, and the earth monster "Behemoth" that shows up in Job 40:15-24 in parallel with Leviathan, who is, as we have discovered, the Hebrew version of the dragon Tiamat. Thus, *tohu* is the short, "theologically safe" demythologized form of the word "Tiamat" and *bohu* is the short form of "Behemoth". And together they form the pair "Tiamat and Behemoth", or "Tohu and Bohu", after the feminine affix "-at" is removed with the purpose to downgrade them from being deities to being mere physical objects.[6]

Now by itself this information may seem inconclusive, but if we review what we discovered in Part IV, where we see in *Enuma Elish* that Tiamat gave birth to the earth monster "Kingu" in order to defend herself against Marduk, combined with what we discovered in Part III about how the Moon was actually brought forth from Earth's mantle as a result of the Giant Impact, we can begin to see the mythological dyad

---

[6] See Chapter I, "Echoes of the Divine Conflict in Genesis" for more information on Moses' removal of the feminine affix "-at" to "demythologize" the Akkadian word *Tiamat* to *tehom*. This was done so that the names of foreign deities would not appear in the text of the Pentateuch, the first five books of the Bible.

of sea monster/earth monster that corresponds with Earth and the Moon. In other words, *tohu wa-bohu* does not mean "without form and void" in this context, but "Earth and Moon".

In sum, what Moses is saying here, in his carefully worded, pithy demythologized prose, is that a second division has taken place in Genesis 1:2. Whereas in Genesis 1:1 God cut and divided the primordial Earth in two, creating the heavens from one piece and the Earth from the other, in Genesis 1:2, God creates another division, cutting off the Moon from Earth, as a result creating a situation of *tohu wa-bohu*, or "Earth and Moon". This allusion to the dragon-goddess Tiamat in *Enuma Elish* is further strengthened by the use of the word תְּהוֹם *tehom* to describe "the deep", or deep sea that was also created as a result of the Giant Impact, a word which, as we also saw in Part I, is nearly identical to the Akkadian word *Tiamat*, both in meaning and pronunciation. This impact had also sent huge amounts of rock and subterranean water into orbit around Earth, blanketing the planet in deep darkness. Thus we see in verse 2 how "darkness" was upon the face of the deep – the entire Earth was covered in a "nuclear winter" type of dust cloud left over from the Giant Impact that over time, scientists believe, resolved itself into a ring system, and then eventually precipitated back down to Earth.

Next, we come to the term "Spirit of the Lord". This term, translated from the Hebrew רוּחַ אֱלֹהִים, *ruaḥ elohim,* is traditionally translated as "the Spirit of the Lord," but it can also be (and occasionally has been) translated as "divine wind" — the same kind of "wind" that Marduk used in *Enuma Elish* to destroy Tiamat. Using this account in *Enuma Elish* as a link between the biblical account and the Planet X/Giant Impact Theory, we can see how the Genesis account is an excellent, concise description of how a satellite of Planet X, the "wind" of God, had smashed into the primordial Earth, dividing it first into the heavens and the Earth (verse 1), then dividing it into the Earth and the Moon, and then moving the newly formed Earth to a new orbit closer to the Sun (verse 2).

Though at first glance it would appear that there is no mention of God moving Earth to a new orbit closer to the Sun as part of His creative activity, a more careful exegesis of the rest of verse 2 will reveal that this indeed the case. We can derive this concept from the text of Genesis 1:2 by carefully analyzing the word translated here as "moves". This term should actually be translated "broods", as the Hebrew word מְרַחֶפֶת *mᵉraḥepheth* is based upon the Hebrew root רָחַף,

raḥaph, the word typically used of a mother bird brooding over her eggs.

One could surmise that this simply meant that God hovered protectively over the re-formed Earth prior to His creative activity, and this would not be unreasonable. However, in the astronomical context, an even more interesting and relevant translation is possible here, which we can determine by studying how mother birds actually "brood" on their eggs. While caring for her eggs, one of the things that a mother bird must do is to regularly turn and move the eggs to make sure they are warmed evenly.[7] This may explain why Moses chose to use the term "brooded" here — Moses meant to communicate the concept that God, after He had created the new Earth from the "body" of the planet that previously orbited between Mars and Jupiter[8] very carefully "rolled" Earth to its new orbit closer to the Sun, where it would be more evenly warmed. Thus we see that Moses' use of the term "brooded" here was so very insightful. Like a mother bird caring for an egg, God "rolled" Earth to a place nearer to the Sun where it could be warmer. This then explains how Earth came to be in its present orbit, moved from its former position where the asteroid belt now lies, to a place amongst the inner planets where there was adequate sunlight to sustain life.

In sum, Genesis 1:2 could be better translated thusly: "And then God used a satellite of Planet X to split off the Moon from Earth, and as a result, a great cloud of dust and ashes obscured the face of Earth. The impact between the satellite of the divine planet and the Earth also caused Earth to move to a new orbit closer to the Sun."

Genesis 1:3-5: God Unveils Earth from Its Dusty Shroud and Determines Earth's Rotation Rate

✥ Genesis 1:3-5:
[3] And God said, Let there be light: and there was light.
[4] And God saw the light, that it was good: and God divided the light from the darkness.

---

[7] See http://dogbert.gi.alaska.edu/ScienceForum/ASF14/1488.html for more information on how mother birds care for their young. Interestingly, the generic Hebrew word for star or planet, כּוֹכָב *kowkav*, means literally "rolling ball".

[8] For sake of argument, let us call that planet "Planet Tiamat" after Sitchin.

⁵ And God called the light Day, and the darkness he called Night. And the evening and the morning were the first day.

Next, verse 3 describes how God had, over time, gradually unveiled Earth from a veil of deep darkness that had kept out all light. This again corresponds with the Planet X/Giant Impact Theory, which posits that the dust and rocky materials that had been thrown up into Earth's atmosphere by the Giant Impact had eventually migrated to the equator due to the centrifugal force created by Earth's rotation, leaving the skies clear save a large ring around the equator which, in time, also precipitated back to Earth.⁹

"The Creation of Light"
by Gustave Doré.

In verses 4-5, Moses describes how God then divided the light that now hit Earth's surface into periods of light and darkness. We know now that these periods of light and darkness, day and night, are caused by Earth's rotation. However, Earth has not always rotated at the relatively rapid rate of 24 hours per day. Interestingly, the same men who have deduced that the Moon must have been created by a Giant Impact have also deduced that Earth's relatively rapid rotation rate must have been caused by that same impact. Besides shifting Earth into its current orbit at 1 A.U., the Giant Impact had also significantly increased Earth's rotation rate, making our days twenty-four hours long, by modern reckoning. Whereas Earth may have once had a relatively slow rotation rate, like Mercury and Venus, after the impact Earth days were rapidly accelerated and, of course, divided into periods of light and darkness. Thus, God said, "let there be light," meaning that the veil of deep darkness had been lifted from Earth, once again allowing the light of

---

⁹ Fraser Cain, "Does Earth Have Rings? *Universe Today:* http://www.universetoday.com/guide-to-space/earth/does-earth-have-rings /

the Sun to strike Earth's surface. Then, "God divided the light from the darkness" by rapidly increasing Earth's rotation rate, creating "days" and "nights" in relatively rapid succession.[10] And for those who cling to the dated, and scientifically incorrect, belief that verses 3-5 describe the Creation of the Sun and Moon, they must explain why the Sun and Moon are not actually described as being created until verse 16. Clearly they already existed — the text here and in verse 16 does not describe their creation, but their new positions in the sky relative to the newly formed Earth in its new position, closer to the Sun.

Genesis 1:6-8: God Creates Earth's Atmosphere and the Asteroid Belt

✢ Genesis 1:6-8:
[6] And God said, Let there be a firmament in the midst of the waters, and let it divide the waters from the waters.
[7] And God made the firmament, and divided the waters which were under the firmament from the waters which were above the firmament: and it was so.
[8] And God called the firmament Heaven. And the evening and the morning were the second day.

Moses next describes in verses 6-8 how God had created a "firmament," which he used to divide the waters of Earth into two distinct portions: waters "under the firmament" and waters "above the firmament." Traditionally this has been interpreted as God dividing the waters in the sky, clouds and rain, from the waters in the oceans, lakes and rivers. This is based, as we discussed previously, upon the modern belief that the Hebrews conceived of Earth as an unmoving, flat circle, and the sky as a hardened dome on which the Sun, Moon and stars moved. Modern translators arrived at this conclusion based upon the assumptions that (1) the Hebrews were scientifically

---

[10]Earth's rotation rate before the Giant Impact was probably similar to that of Venus'. If so, Earth's days would have been hundreds of times longer than they are today, making conditions unsuitable to support life. Thus, without the Giant Impact to accelerate Earth's rotation rate to its current 24-hour period, God could not have created life on Earth as it is today. Since the Giant Impact is the only way to explain Earth's rapid rotation rate, and a rapid rotation rate is necessary to support life, then God must have initiated the impact Himself to make Earth suitable for supporting life. Thus, the Genesis narrative *must* include a reference to the Giant Impact, or we must remove science from the equation altogether. Fortunately, it clearly does.

ignorant, and (2) God's revelations to the Prophets concerning the Creation were scientifically inaccurate.[11] However, one of the basic premises of this book is that God's word to His Prophets must be scientifically accurate, meaning that the biblical Creation material must be interpreted in the light of established fact (the sphericity of Earth, the fact that Earth orbits around the Sun, etc.) Therefore, we can discard the flat-Earth model and strive to reach an interpretation of the Creation passages in Genesis that is at once both scientifically, contextually, and exegetically sound.

First of all, the word translated "firmament," רָקִיעַ *raqiya'*, speaks not of an airy space such as our atmosphere, but of a place that had been beaten and spread out by a powerful force. *Raqiya'* comes from the root רָקַע *raqa'*, which means to expand by hammering, beat, make broad, spread abroad, stamp, and/or stretch. As we saw in chapter III, the result of the Giant Impact had been the ejection of large amounts of rock and water from Earth's mantle into space. Some of this material had escaped Earth's gravitational pull, remaining in Earth's original orbit at 2.8 A.U. to become the asteroid belt, which we now know to be a collection of icy rocks floating in orbit around the Sun. Thus the "firmament" can be easily identified with the asteroid belt, a band of (frozen) waters and rock which had been *hammered* out of Earth and *stretched* out into an independent orbit around the Sun. This "waters above" was then effectively divided from the "waters below," the Earth's seas and atmosphere, by millions of miles of space when the Earth was moved to its new orbit at 1 A.U.

Genesis 1:14-18: God Sets the Apparent Motions of the Sun, Moon, Stars and Planets Relative to Earth's New Orbital Position

☥ Genesis 1:14-18:
[14] And God said, Let there be lights in the firmament of the heaven to divide the day from the night; and let them be for signs, and for seasons, and for days, and years:
[15] And let them be for lights in the firmament of the heaven to give light upon the earth: and it was so.

---

[11]Liberal scholars, of course, deny the existence of God and therefore the divine inspiration of the words of the Prophets, making the scientific inaccuracy of the Creation material in the Old Testament, in their minds, a foregone conclusion.

> ¹⁶ And God made two great lights; the greater light to rule the day, and the lesser light to rule the night: he made the stars also.
> ¹⁷ And God set them in the firmament of the heaven to give light upon the earth,
> ¹⁸ And to rule over the day and over the night, and to divide the light from the darkness: and God saw that it was good.

In verses 14-18 Moses then explains how God set the motions of the Sun, Moon and stars in the heavens. As we now know, the Sun and stars only *appear* to move; their apparent movement is relative to Earth's motion through space (the Moon's apparent motion is a combination of Earth's and the Moon's orbital characteristics). However, as we saw in Chapter III, Earth did not always move through space the same way it does now. The Giant Impact had had a dramatic effect upon not only Earth's orbit, but its rotation period and axial tilt as well, and it is these three factors that primarily determine the apparent motion of the Sun and stars in the heavens. Therefore, Moses' description of how God set the motions of the Sun, Moon and stars in the heavens must be essentially a description of how Earth's orbit, spin rate, and axial tilt had been suddenly, radically changed. Moses first introduces the Moon, openly describing it for the first time as "the lesser light to rule the night" (v. 16). The Moon does not appear until later in the Genesis account because it took some time for it to form. The majority of the rocky materials that had been thrown up into orbit around the Earth, as we have seen, gradually cooled and accreted into the Moon, so it took some time for it to become "the lesser light".

Scholars have always had trouble understanding why the creation of light is mentioned twice in Genesis 1, once in verses 3-5 and again here in verses 14-18, and this has been a powerful weapon of those who have attempted to undermine the validity of the Genesis account. However, as we saw in chapter III, the Sun had come into being some time before Earth was fully formed, contradicting the traditional interpretation of these verses which insisted that the phrase, "Let there be light," was a description of the creation of the Sun. But I suggest that there is no mention of creation at all here — simply God's command that light, assumably that of the Sun, will now shine upon Earth. Thus I have interpreted the command for light in Genesis 1:3-5 to be not the creation of the Sun, but the unveiling of the Earth from the cloud of dust thrown up by the Giant Impact. This massive dust cloud had enveloped Earth in deep darkness for possibly thousands of years or more, keeping the light of the pre-existent Sun and other astral bodies from reaching Earth's surface. But, as is described in Genesis 1:3-5, this dust cloud eventually settled back down to Earth, letting the light of the Sun, Moon and stars reach Earth's surface once more. The second mention of light in Genesis 1:14-18, that of the Sun and Moon, is thus more of a description of the affect the Giant Impact had had on Earth's orbit, rotation period, and axial tilt, which together determine the apparent motion of the Sun and Moon in the heavens. This not only makes the account align perfectly with modern scientific theory, it also finally shuts the mouths of the critics.

Thus the creation account in Genesis 1, far from being a vague, nonscientific description of the universe, is instead a very concise, scientific description of the creation of Earth. Instead of going into a prolonged narrative about how God set the days and the seasons, the constellations and the cycles of the Sun and Moon, as was done in the Babylonian creation story, Moses used less than ten verses to summarize how Planet X had struck the Earth with one of its satellites, giving Earth a new orbit, rotation period, and axial tilt, the ejecta from the impact forming the asteroids, comets and, eventually, the Moon.

The Book of Genesis is not the only source for Creation material in the Bible, however. References to the Creation are scattered throughout the Psalms, the Prophets, and particularly Job, which may in fact be *the* primary source of Creation material in the Old Testament (as we will see in chapter VI). These references invariably discuss the Creation in terms of a combat with a dragon and/or the sea, and some even mention "helpers" which fought at the dragon's side against God. These helpers, as we shall see, are not simply mythological accretions, but accurate (albeit mythologized) descriptions of the creation of the Moon and the comets that parallel the astronomical translation of *Enuma Elish* with astonishing accuracy.

REFERENCES TO THE CREATION OF THE EARTH REINTERPRETED

Foremost among the references dealing specifically with the creation of the Earth are some of the Psalms and several passages of Isaiah.

The Creation of the Earth: God's Conflict with the Dragon

✢ Isaiah 51:9-10, 13, 15-16:
⁹Awake, awake, put on strength, O arm of the LORD; awake, as in the ancient days, in the generations of old. Art thou not it that hath cut Rahab, and wounded the dragon?
¹⁰Art thou not it which hath dried the sea, the waters of the great deep; that hath made the depths of the sea a way for the ransomed to pass over?
¹³And forgettest the LORD thy maker, that hath stretched forth the heavens, and laid the foundations of the earth....
¹⁵But I am the LORD thy God, that divided the sea, whose waves roared: The LORD of hosts is his name.
¹⁶And I have put my words in thy mouth, and I have covered thee in the shadow of mine hand, that I may plant the heavens, and lay the foundations of the earth, and say unto Zion, Thou art my people. (KJV)

Here in Isaiah 51 is one of the clearest descriptions of God's primordial combat with the dragon, placing it clearly in the context of the Creation. Verse 9 starts by exhorting the "arm of the LORD" to "awake" and fight for Israel once more. The exhortation for this "arm" to "put on strength," is reminiscent of Marduk's arraying himself for battle. לִבְשִׁי־עֹז, *liveshiy-oz*, "clothe with strength," or "wear armor of power," has a clear parallel with Marduk's donning of an "armor of terror" in preparation of the battle with Tiamat in *Enuma Elish*: "For a cloak he was wrapped in an armor of terror; with a fearsome halo his head was turbaned.... Clothed with the halo of ten gods, he was strong to the utmost, as their awesome flashes were heaped upon him."[12] Isaiah is here calling upon this "arm of the LORD", Planet X, to array itself for battle once again and return to fight against the enemies of God as it had done in ancient times — i.e., at the Creation.

The arm of the LORD is then identified as the one who "cut Rahab," and "wounded the dragon." Rahab, as we saw in chapter I, is one of

---

[12] Speiser, "The Creation Epic," 66, 62.

the names scholars typically equate with the ubiquitous "dragon" figure in ancient Near Eastern myth. The word "cut," הַמַּחְצֶבֶת, *hamaḥᵉtsevet*, translated as "cut up into pieces," and מְחוֹלֶלֶת, *meḥolelet*, "pierced," both align perfectly with the *Enuma Elish* account which describes Marduk as having first *pierced* Tiamat with one of his divine "winds" or satellites, and then cut up, or *dividing* her remains into two pieces which he used to create heaven and Earth:

> Then joined issue Tiamat and Marduk, wisest of gods....
> When Tiamat opened her mouth to consume him,
> He *drove in* the evil wind that she close not her lips.
> As the fierce winds charged her belly,
> Her body was distended and her mouth was wide open.
> He released the arrow, it tore her belly,
> It cut through her insides, *splitting* the heart....
> Then the lord paused to view her dead body,
> That he might *divide* the monster and do artful works.
> He *split* her like a shellfish into two parts:
> Half of her he set up and ceiled as sky [the other as Earth].
> (*Enuma Elish* IV:93, 97-102, 135-138)

This also agrees with the Planet X/Giant Impact theory, which posits that the current Earth-Moon system was created when a satellite of Planet X struck and penetrated Earth, throwing large amounts of Earth's crust and mantle into space and propelling Earth into a new orbit closer to the Sun. Part of this ejected material remained at Earth's original orbit, forming the asteroid belt, which the Babylonians refer to as "sky," or heaven. Most of the ejected material remained in orbit around Earth, to form the Moon. The larger, intact portion of Earth was then thrown into a new orbit, forming the Earth-Moon system with which we are familiar.

Interestingly, the word translated here as "pierced," מְחוֹלֶלֶת, *meḥolelet,* is the "polel" verb form[13] of the word חָלַל, *ḥalal,* "to profane." Used as a polel form, it is best translated as "to penetrate sexually." Thus Isaiah's use of the polel form of this verb to describe the penetration of Earth was probably intended to communicate the idea

---

[13] The polel verb form is similar to the Hebrew piel form, except much rarer and more intensive. To learn more about Hebrew verb forms visit http://kukis.org/Languages/HebrewGrammar.htm.

that Earth was penetrated for the purpose of procreation, to give the reader the idea that God had caused Earth to be "impregnated." But what was the result of this impregnation? Even modern astronomers refer to the creation of the Moon as the "birth" of the Moon. Furthermore, the use of the metaphorical imagery in *Enuma Elish* that describes Tiamat's "waters" flowing out of her womb (V:59–65) could be compared to the water flowing out of the broken amniotic sac, an event which occurs immediately before a woman gives birth. Thus Isaiah intended to communicate that the penetration of Earth had resulted in the creation or "birth" of the Moon This might also help explain why the "birthpains" metaphor is so resonant in the prophesies of the Second Coming, a Second Coming which will be similar in scope to the Creation (Isaiah 13:8ff; 26:17ff; 66:8; Jer. 30:5-7; Matt. 24:21; 1 Thess. 4:16--5:3; Rev. 12:2).

☥ Psalm 89:8-11:
⁸ O LORD God of hosts, who is a strong LORD like unto thee? or to thy faithfulness round about thee?
⁹ Thou rulest the raging of the sea: when the waves thereof arise, thou stillest them.
¹⁰ Thou hast broken Rahab in pieces, as one that is slain; thou hast scattered thine enemies with thy strong arm.
¹¹ The heavens are thine, the Earth also is thine: as for the world and the fulness thereof, thou hast founded them. (KJV)

The battle between God and the dragon "Rahab" (רָהַב *rahab*, lit., "arrogant one") is once again recalled in Psalm 89 and, like Isaiah 51, clearly places the divine battle in the context of the creation of Earth. However, Psalm 89 goes one step further and also mentions in verse 10 that the dragon had helpers allied with her in her struggle against God, which God scattered with his "strong arm". As we saw in Chapter IV, in the Babylonian Creation Epic, Tiamat gave birth to 11 "monster serpents" to help her in her fight against Marduk. After defeating Tiamat, Marduk captured these 11 "monster serpents", that Tiamat had filled with her watery "venom", and placed them in eternal prisons, forever:

> After he had slain Tiamat, the leader,
> Her band was shattered, her troupe broken up;
> And the gods, her helpers, who marched at her side,

> trembling with terror, turned their backs about,
> in order to save and preserve their lives.
> Tightly encircled, they could not all escape.
> He made them captives and smashed their weapons.
> Thrown into cells, they found themselves ensnared;
> placed in cells, they were filled with wailing;
> bearing his wrath, they were held imprisoned.
> And the eleven creatures which she had charged with awe,
> The whole band of demons that marched on her right,
> He cast into fetters, their hands he bound.
> For all their resistance, he trampled (them) underfoot.
> (*Enuma Elish* IV:105-120)

As we determined in Chapter IV, these "helpers" of Tiamat are in fact what we know today as the "comets", those parts of the primordial Earth that were thrown clear of Earth's gravity after the Giant Impact and have circled the Sun in independent orbits ever since. Psalm 89 reiterates this fact, but gives the glory not to Marduk, the god of the Babylonians, but to the God of Israel, the one who defeated the allies of the dragon and caused them to be scattered, doomed to circle forever in space as the comets. There they continue to circle to this day as an eternal witness in heaven to God's defeat of the dragon.

⊕ Psalm 74:12-17:
> [12] For God is my King of old, working salvation in the midst of the Earth.
> [13] Thou didst divide the sea by thy strength: thou brakest the heads of the dragons in the waters.
> [14] Thou brakest the heads of leviathan in pieces, and gavest him to be meat to the people inhabiting the wilderness.
> [15] Thou didst cleave the fountain and the flood: thou driedst up mighty rivers.
> [16] The day is thine, the night also is thine: thou hast prepared the light and the Sun.
> [17] Thou hast set all the borders of the Earth: thou hast made summer and winter. (KJV)

We see here again in Psalm 74 a clear reference to the creation of Earth as a result of God's conflict with a "dragon," or in this case, "dragons", this time given the name of "Leviathan". This plurality of dragons probably alludes to the presence of "monster serpents" fighting alongside Leviathan against God, like the lesser dragons which Tiamat brought forth to help her in her fight against Marduk that was also alluded to in Psalm 89.

God is described in verse 12 as "my King of old." The original Hebrew for "of old," מִקֶּדֶם, *mi-kedem,* can be more accurately translated as "of the Creation." This is because *kedem* comes from the root קָדַם *kadam,* "to precede, to lead, be in front." Thus, *kedem* refers not only to an ancient time, but specifically to the first time, the very beginning of time: the Creation. Thus God is the "King of the Beginning" or, better, the "King of the Creation."

The creation of Earth here, oddly enough, is described as being done by God working salvation in the "midst" (בְּקֶרֶב *be-qerev,* literally, "inside") of the Earth-dragon. In other words, at the Creation, God performed an act *inside* of Earth that caused it to be "re-created." This reflects the procreational concept found in Isaiah 51, and in both passages the penetration of the "dragon" had the same effect: the re-creation of Earth, and the "birth" of the Moon.[14] This concept contradicts the idea that Earth was created complete and whole, because it clearly says in both these passages that God acted upon a fully formed Earth — further undermining the traditional interpretation of Genesis 1.

The word translated here as "salvation," יְשׁוּעוֹת *yeshuot,* can also mean "victory," as in "victory in battle."[15] Since the next verses clearly talk about God's conflict with and victory over the dragon, this translation is clearly the correct one. Therefore, in the beginning, according to Psalm 74, God sent something into the midst of Earth that resulted in the creation of what we now know as Earth. The creation of Earth, then, is described as the victorious climax of a struggle between God and a dragon, wherein God is victorious.

Immediately after the description of the defeat of the dragon and her cohorts are references to the feeding of a people "inhabiting the wilderness" — a reference to the Israelites eating manna in the desert —

---

[14] Perhaps the essential concept behind the fall of man in Genesis 3 and the woman being "saved by childbearing" concept in 1 Timothy 2:15 is endemic in the re-creation of Earth itself, the old "wicked" Earth being destroyed, and the new "just" Earth being re-created from the old one, now worthy of hosting the birth of the Messiah.

[15] יְשׁוּעוֹת *yeshoow'owt* has the root יָשַׁע, *yasha'* from which we derive the name "Jesus": literally, "the savior," "the victorious one."

and of the division of waters and drying up of rivers. These references are undoubtedly meant to graphically link the events of the Exodus and Conquest Period with those of the Creation in order to illustrate a pattern of how God works in history. Verse 16 then brings us back to the Creation, recalling Genesis 1 and the division between night and day and of the celestial luminaries which rule over them. Verse 17 then completes the recollection of the Creation by further illustrating how God set the borders or "boundaries" of Earth, boundaries which are linked with the creation of the seasons. This of course refers both to Earth's orbit and its tilted axis, without which there would be no seasons, so it too is yet another recollection of the effects the creation battle had upon Earth.

All together, the passage states that God created Earth by defeating a dragon and its helpers by "dividing" or "cleaving" that dragon into two pieces, assumedly by sending some sort of weapon into its "insides" in order to do so. As an immediate result of this division of the dragon into pieces, the rotation, orbit, and axial tilt of the Earth were set in their current positions in order to create 24-hour days, 365-day years, and 4 seasons. The only logical conclusion one could draw from this is that this passage is describing a conflict between Planet X and Earth early in Earth's history, a conflict that resulted in Earth being given a new rotation rate, axial tilt, and orbit.

✦ Isaiah 40:21-22:
[21] Have ye not known? have ye not heard? hath it not been told you from the beginning? have ye not understood from the foundations of the Earth?
[22] It is he that sitteth upon the *circle* of the Earth, and the inhabitants thereof are as grasshoppers; that stretcheth out the heavens as a *curtain,* and spreadeth them out as a tent to dwell in: (KJV)

Isaiah 40:22 is similarly important to a clear understanding as to exactly how the Earth was created. Here, Isaiah explains that it is God who "sitteth upon the circle of the Earth." This verse has in the past been the basis for the idea that the Hebrews considered Earth to be a flat circle. However, the word used here for circle, חוּג *hoowg* means literally, "to move in a circle." In other words, it is not a description of the shape of Earth, but of the way the Earth moves — in a circle, or what is modernly referred to as an "orbit". Further, the root חוּג is related to חָגַג *ḥagag,* "to move in a circle, to march in a sacred procession." As such, it is clear that the traditional interpretation of this passage is incorrect. The evidence in fact seems to point toward the fact that the Hebrews — or at least Isaiah — were aware that Earth *moved in a circle,* or "orbit," around the Sun, and that God controlled that orbit. Of course God controls everything as He is omnipotent, but Isaiah is pointing out here a specific fact: God "sits upon" or controls the *orbit* of Earth.

Enuma Elish also describes the pagan god Marduk as a "star" that controls or influences the orbits of all the other "gods," the planets, particularly Earth:

> Nebiru shall hold the crossings of heaven and earth,
> So that they [the planets] cannot cross above and below
> They must wait on him
> Nebiru is the star which in the skies is brilliant.
> Verily he holds the central position, they shall bow down to him,
> Saying: "He who the midst of the Sea restlessly crosses,
> Let 'Crossing' be his name, who controls its midst.
> May they uphold the course of the stars of heaven;
> May he shepherd all the gods like sheep.
> (*Enuma Elish* VII:124-131)

If this is correct, then Isaiah is saying that God uses a planet in our solar system to "shepherd" the orbits of the other planets. And since the search for Planet X was originally started in order to explain strange deviations in the predicted orbits of Uranus and Neptune, orbits that were believed to have been affected, or "shepherded" by some unseen planet in deep space, Planet X is most likely what is being described here in Isaiah 40:22.

Another important clue to solving the mystery of the Creation can be found later in verse 22, where the heavens are described as being like a "curtain" that has been "spread out" in space. The word for curtain here is דֹּק *doq.* This word, which appears several other places in the Bible, is only translated as "curtain" in Isaiah 40:22, indicating that it perhaps has been mistranslated here. This is underlined by the fact that the root of the word *doq* is דָּקַק *daqaq,* which refers to something that has been crushed and broken into small pieces, which is not a good description of a curtain.

It is, however, an excellent description of the asteroid belt, which is made of part of the primordial Earth that was crushed and spread out in a circle around the Sun as a result of the Giant Impact. The term "curtain" was likely used here because later, in verse 22, the "heavens" are referred to as a "tent" (אֹהֶל *'ohel*, "tent, tabernacle, dwelling") in which God dwells that He "spreads out" in space. This once again corresponds perfectly to *Enuma Elish*, where the "star" Marduk is described as constantly "crossing" in the midst of the supercaelian sea, in the rocky firmament of the second heaven, the asteroid belt, where the divine planet "dwells" while on the inner part of its orbital journey:

> [Marduk] crossed the heavens and surveyed the regions.
> He squared Apsu's quarter, the abode of Nudimmud,
> As the lord measured the dimensions of Apsu.
> The Great Abode, its likeness, he fixed as Esharra,
> The Great Abode, Esharra, which he made as the firmament.
> (IV:135–45)

Clearly, since the asteroid belt, or "The Great Abode" *Esharra,* the "Gateway of God" is located in the middle of the solar system, between the inner and outer planets, it must be the same place as the second, or "hammered" heaven referred to in both the Bible and *Enuma Elish*. The asteroid belt marks the perihelion of Planet X, the closest part of its orbit around the Sun, where it "dwells" for several decades before it embarks on the outward-bound part of its orbit. In sum, Isaiah 40:22 reveals some important clues regarding the motion of Planet X in the heavens, including clearly identifying its perihelion, or closest approach to the Sun, as being in the asteroid belt. The belt area of our solar system serves as a "tabernacle" where Planet X appears to "dwell" for several decades before it starts again on its long journey back out of our solar system, back into deep space.

REFERENCES TO THE CREATION OF THE HEAVENS REINTERPRETED

As we have seen, the word for heaven in the Bible, שָׁמַיִם *shamayim*, is a plural word which actually refers to two different physical regions: one just above Earth, and another out in space. These two "heavens" should be equated with the "waters above" and the "waters below" described in Genesis 1, where the "waters below" are the Earth's seas and atmosphere, and the "waters above" are the asteroid belt. The second heaven, the asteroid belt, is also closely linked with the Hebrew word translated as "firmament," רָקִיעַ *raqiya'*, in Genesis 1:8, which essentially means something that has been beaten and spread out — a perfect description of the asteroid belt.

In the previous section we found additional clues regarding the true nature of the first and second heavens, and even the possible existence of a third heaven, in various places in the Bible. These clues correlate with not only modern astronomical theories regarding the Creation, but also with other ancient Creation texts, particularly the Babylonian Creation Epic, *Enuma Elish*. All together, this information has not only powerfully corroborated the Planet X/Giant Impact Theory elucidated in Chapter III, it has also provided us with more details regarding how the prophets understood the heavens to be arranged, an understanding which we will further explore in this section.

The Waters of the Firmament

As we discovered in Chapter III, many if not most asteroids are partially made of water, or were at one time exposed to liquid water. As such, the description in Genesis 1 of "waters above" and "waters below" takes on new meaning. When he was describing the firmament of heaven, Moses was not describing a scientifically inaccurate conception of a "hardened dome" sitting over a flat Earth, but was in reality describing, in precise, scientifically accurate detail, how water and other materials left over from the Giant Impact, the "waters above", had remained floating in space as a layer of icy rocks circling the Sun, forming a curtain, or "belt" separating the inner and outer planets. The term "waters below," then, refers to that water that was ejected into space but was captured and retained by Earth's gravity to form Earth's seas and atmosphere.

The *Theological Wordbook of the Old Testament*'s definition of *raqiya,* "the firmament," helps support the argument that the Hebrews conceived of the heavens not as a domed vault, but as a place of rocks and ice:

> In pre-Christian Egypt confusion was introduced into biblical cosmology when the LXX, perhaps under the influence of Alexandrian theories of a "stone vault" of heaven, rendered

raqia' by *stereoma*, suggesting some firm, solid structure. This Greek concept was then reflected by the Latin *firmamentum*, hence KJV "firmament." To this day negative criticism speaks of the "vault, or 'firmament' regarded by Hebrews as solid, and supporting waters above it:" (*BDB*, p.956); cf. the rendering of Job 37:18, "the skies, strong (*hazaqim*) as a molten mirror (cf. Ps. 150:1, their "mighty expanse"), changed by the RSV to read, "the skies, hard." Babylonian mythology recounts how Marduk used half of Tiamat's carcass to form the heavens (*shamamu*).... In the OT, however, Isaiah insists that God "stretches out the heavens [lit.] like gauze (*doq,* Isa. 40:22); and even Ezekiel's limited canopy (*raqia'*) is "as the [lit.] eye of awesome ice" (Eze. 1:22), i.e. transparent, "shining like crystal" (RSV), though so dazzling as to be terrifying."[16]

In Ezekiel, interestingly, the firmament is described as being like "ice" (NIV), which corresponds perfectly with our modern understanding of the asteroid belt: a place of rock and ice, struck hard and spread out into a ring in heaven. Other interesting words closely related to *raqia* are *raqaq,* "spit," and *roq,* "spittle", which nicely correlate with the "spittle" of Tiamat that formed the waters above and below in *Enuma Elish*, and of course with the creation of the waters of the firmament in the Bible.

By itself, this interpretation of the "heaven" and "firmament" references in Genesis 1 might be considered questionable. However, there are a number of passages scattered throughout the Old Testament which clearly describe the heavenly firmament as being made of both rocky and watery materials. One excellent source for this idea is Psalm 33, which mentions not only the creation of the heavens but also explains how, after Earth was created, some the waters of Earth were put into "storehouses" in heaven:

---

[16]R. Liard Harris, Gleason L. Archer, Jr. and Bruce K. Waltke, *Theological Wordbook of the Old Testament* (Chicago: The Moody Bible Institute, 1980), p.862, "*raqia'*." The phrase in Ezekiel 1:22, רָקִיעַ כְּעֵין הַקֶּרַח הַנּוֹרָא *raqiya' ke-ayin ha-qeraḥ hanowra',* translates literally as "a smooth, shield-shaped crystal that looked like a huge, fearsome eye", relates to another deep mystery of the Bible that is only indirectly related to the focus of this book, so it will handled in a separate volume.

- Psalm 33:6-8, 13-14:
  ⁶ By the word of the LORD were the heavens made; and all the host of them by the breath of his mouth.
  ⁷ He gathereth the waters of the sea together as an heap: he layeth up the depth in storehouses.
  ⁸ Let all the Earth fear the LORD: let all the inhabitants of the world stand in awe of him.
  ¹³ The LORD looketh from heaven; he beholdeth all the sons of men.
  ¹⁴ From the place of his habitation he looketh upon all the inhabitants of the Earth.

As we saw in our analysis of Isaiah 40, heaven is the place where God dwells, an idea which Psalm 33 confirms. According to Psalm 33, God's "place of habitation" is in heaven, wherein He had gathered and stored water from Earth's oceans into "storehouses". Whereas it makes perfect sense that God lives in heaven, one wonders why God would want to store large amounts of water in heaven?

Once again, an analysis of the text in the original Hebrew will provide us with the answers. The word translated "breath" in verse 33 is actually the word רוּחַ *roowaḥ*, which we saw earlier in our retranslation of Genesis 1:2 is best translated in the context of the Creation as "divine wind". This best correlates with the description in *Enuma Elish* where Planet "Marduk" sent one of its divine "winds" or satellites into the mouth of Tiamat, piercing her belly and killing her. It was via this "Giant Impact", and from an additional impact from a second "wind" that followed, that the Earth as we understand it today was created. Thus the entire starry array, as we see it from Earth, was set into place by the divine "wind" of God.

As a secondary result of the Giant Impact by this divine "wind", a great deal of pulverized rock and water ice was left floating in space as mute witness to the divine Creation battle. Verse 7 describes the creation of this "asteroid belt", describing it as כַּנֵּס *konais*, literally, "to gather into a heap", which has been translated elsewhere in the Bible as either a heap of rocks (Ecc. 3:5) or as a heap of "peculiar treasures", probably referring to precious stones (Ecc. 2:8, 26). But this heap of rocks also contained water in its hardened form, known to us as "ice", where they appeared to glitter like precious stones. Thus the next part of verse 7, כַּנֵּד מֵי הַיָּם *kanaid may ha-yam*, "like a heap of water of the sea" — i.e., the crest of a wave, which is translated as such in Joshua 3:13, 16 to describe how the waves of the Jordan "heaped up" when the Ark of the Covenant passed through the Jordan. Interestingly, the word use for "sea" here, *yam*, is also one of the names of the dragon as used in the Canaanite myths, as we saw in Chapter I.

And though that is interesting, the remainder of the verse is particularly telling regarding the parallels to be found between these verses and various ancient extrabiblical creation stories, particularly *Enuma Elish*. נֹתֵן בָּאֹצָרוֹת תְּהוֹמוֹת *nathan be-'otsarowt tehomot* literally means "and he set in a storehouse a great quantity of waters". This may seem to merely confirm the watery content of heaven mentioned previously in this verse, until you take a closer look at the last word in the verse: *tehomot*, which is a direct transliteration of the name of the Babylonian goddess Tiamat, whose rocky tail and watery spittle Marduk twisted to form the *Durmah*, the "great band" of heaven in *Enuma Elish*. In this context, with the demythologized appearances of both the dragon-goddesses *Yam* and *Tiamat* in this verse, verse 7 could be retranslated using their names directly this way: "He piled up like a heap of stones the waters of Yam; he stored the waters of Tiamat (in heaven)." Or, instead of using a mythological approach, we could also translate this verse using modern scientific terminology, as follows: "He heaped up stones and water together, storing a large amount of water (in heaven)." Thus, one part of the Hebrew conception of the "firmament" was that it was a collection of rocks and water ice "flowing" somewhere high up in space.

Demythologized references to the Babylonian dragon-goddess Tiamat also occur in the Bible, both in Genesis 1, Psalm 33, and possibly other places.

"The Firmament": A Curtain of Small Rocks

Psalm 33 appears to indicate that the second heaven, the *raqiya*, is composed of a combination of rocks and water ice, but that is only one of many references to heaven in the Old Testament. Do other references to the second heaven, the "firmament" also describe it as a river of rocks flowing in space? Indeed, several do, and perhaps the most crucial passage for understanding the true Hebrew conception of the firmament, or "second heaven", as being a circle of rocks orbiting around the Sun is Isaiah 40:21-22:

✢ Isaiah 40:21-22:
[21] Have ye not known? have ye not heard? hath it not been told you from the beginning? have ye not understood from the foundations of the Earth?
[22] It is he that sitteth upon the circle of the Earth, and the inhabitants thereof are as grasshoppers; that stretcheth out the heavens as a *curtain,* and spreadeth them out as a tent to dwell in: (KJV)

As we saw earlier in this chapter, the Hebrew word here in verse 22, translated in the KJV as "curtain," is דֹּק *doq*. This is an unusual word in context, as it actually refers to a type of material which Strong defines as "something *crumbling.*"[17] *Doq* is taken from the even more interesting root דָּקַק, *daqaq*, which means "to *crush* (or intrans.) *crumble;* beat in pieces (small), bruise, make dust (into), powder, (be very) small, stamp (small)"[18] and דְּקַק, *deqaq*, "corresponding to 1854; to *crumble* or (trans.) *crush* — break in pieces."[19] Therefore, in this verse, Isaiah describes God as one who spreads the "heavens" out like a thin curtain of crushed and crumbling material of some kind, clearly not a reference to any kind of cloth or fabric. In context, we understand this to be a reference to the asteroid belt, which is essentially a "curtain" of crushed rock hanging in space, orbiting the Sun. The Hebrew Bible refers to it as the *raqiya* (lit., the "hammered heaven"), which we now know was created out of the smashed lower half of Earth. In addition, as if to underscore his intention, Isaiah follows up his reference to the heaven as a hammered-out, curtain-like body of small pieces of crushed material with a clear reference to the Creation: "Have ye not understood from the foundations of the Earth?" (v. 22)

---

[17] Strong's #1852.

[18] Strong's #1854.

[19] Strong's #1855. See also R. Liard Harris, Gleason L. Archer, and Bruce K. Waltke, *Theological Wordbook of the Old Testament* (Chicago: Moody Bible Institute, 1980), 444 and Francis Brown, S. R. Driver, and Charles A. Briggs, *The New Brown-Driver-Briggs-Gesenius Hebrew-English Lexicon* (Peabody, MA: Hendrickson, Pub., 1979), 200–201.

Another unexpected but very telling biblical reference supporting the idea that the heavens are made from dust and rocks comes from Proverbs 8:22-30. This passage is rich in creation imagery, including the now-familiar concepts of God's creation of the heavens, which are made of "dust," and the Earth, with its new orbital motion, as well as the declaration of the limits of the heavenly waters:

- Proverbs 8:22-29:
    [22] The LORD possessed me in the beginning of his way, before his works of old.
    [23] I was set up from everlasting, from the beginning, or ever the Earth was.
    [24] When there were no depths, I was brought forth; when there were no fountains abounding with water.
    [25] Before the mountains were settled, before the hills was I brought forth:
    [26] While as yet he had not made the Earth, nor the fields, nor the highest part of the dust of the world.
    [27] When he prepared the heavens, I was there: when he set a compass upon the face of the depth:
    [28] When he established the clouds above: when he strengthened the fountains of the deep:
    [29] When he gave to the sea his decree, that the waters should not pass his commandment: when he appointed the foundations of the Earth: (KJV)

Even in Proverbs, clear references to the divine creation conflict can be seen, along with some excellent insight into the very advanced astronomical understanding that the wise men and prophets of old had been given by God. Moreover, the entire section of Proverbs 8:22-29 appears to parallel certain passages in *Enuma Elish*, specifically V:47-66:

> [Taking] the spittle of Tia[mat]
> Marduk created [...] ...
> He formed the c[louds] and filled (them) with [water].
> The raising of winds, the bringing of rain (and) cold,
> Making the mist smoke, piling up her poison:
> (These) he appointed to himself, took into his own charge.
> Putting her head into position he formed the[reon] the mountai[ns],

"In the Beginning"

> Opening the deep which was in flood,
> He caused to flow from her eyes the Euph[rates (and) T]igris,
> Stopping her nostrils he left...
> He formed at her udder the lofty m[ountain]s,
> (Therein) he drilled springs for the wells to carry off (the water).
> Twisting her tail he bound it to Durmah,
> [...] ... Apsu at his foot,
> [...] ... her crotch, she was fastened to the heavens,
> (Thus) he covered the heavens and established the Earth.
> [...] ... in the midst of Tiamat he made flow,
> [...] ... his net he completely let out,
> (So) he *created* heaven and earth...,
> [...] their bounds...established.
> (V:47-66)

In these parallel passages, both the Bible and *Enuma Elish* describe the creation of the mountains and the rivers specifically, and of both the heavens and Earth generally, Proverbs 8 using simple, straightforward terminology, with *Enuma Elish* relying on colorful symbolic imagery. The most complicated task for both the ancient Hebrews and the ancient Babylonians, however, was to describe the creation of the asteroid belt, which is a much harder concept to communicate than rivers and mountains. Whereas the ancient Babylonians used the symbolic description of Marduk twisting Tiamat's tail to the *Durmah*, a "great band" that circles in heaven, separating her lower, "private" parts from her upper half, the ancient Hebrews used the concept of the asteroid belt as a wall made of dust that had been thrown up high into space as part of the Creation process. The precise interpretation of verse 8 is somewhat difficult, so we will take each word one at a time:

עַד־לֹא	*'ad-lo'* - "(Did He) not in ancient times"
עָשָׂה	*'aseh* - "set, place"
אֶרֶץ	*'eretz* - "Earth"
וְחוּצוֹת	*ve-ḥoowtsowt* - "and surround (with a wall)"
וְרֹאשׁ	*vero'sh* - "with the highest"
עָפְרוֹת	*'aph^{e}rowt* - "(of) her dust"

תֵּבֵל   *taibail* - "the fertile parts of the Earth"; from the root יָבַל *yaval*, "flood, flow", related to תֶּבֶל *tevel*, "polluted, profaned"

In order to come to the best possible interpretation, we must not only rely on modern science, but also upon other, parallel ancient Near Eastern creation stories to fully understand this enigmatic passage. As we saw in *Enuma Elish*, Marduk took the lower half, or "tail" of Tiamat, including her private parts, and set it to form the *Durmah*, a great circle of rocks and ice in space that we now call the asteroid belt. Similarly, in Proverbs 8:26, after Earth was created, God literally set "her highest dust" as a wall in heaven that surrounded Earth, and the rest of the inner solar system, the word for "dust" actually being the feminine form of the noun.

The unusual feminine form of this noun creates a link with *Enuma Elish*, wherein the dragon was portrayed as a female deity that symbolically represented the Earth, but the clearest linkage can be found in the specific use of the final word in this verse: תֵּבֵל *taibail*, which can mean, depending upon the context, "the fertile parts of the Earth", "flood, flow" (from the root יָבַל *yaval*, "flood"), or "polluted, profaned" from the related word תֶּבֶל *tevel*, which is used in the Bible to describe perverted sexual activity. In the context of *Enuma Elish*, this clearly parallels the description of Tiamat's lower half, including her private parts, being used to create the asteroid belt, the term "flood" and "flow" actually being used in *Enuma Elish* to describe the waters flooding forth from her womb as a result of her being divided in half by Marduk. Thus this part of the verse should not be translated, "the highest parts of the dust of the world", but "and He took the dust of her lower parts and threw them up on high to form a wall in heaven". Or, taking into account our modern understanding of astronomy, "and He used the lower part of Earth to create the asteroid belt". All together, this verse should read, "Did He not, in ancient times, set Earth in its place, and use the lower part of Earth to create the asteroid belt?"

The next verse, 27, is also in need some retranslation, specifically, the word translated, "set a compass". The word for compass here is חוּג *hoowg*, "to move in a circle", which we saw previously is best translated in the Creation context as "orbit". The word previous to that in the Hebrew, בְּחֻקוֹ *be-ḥoowq-ow,* currently translated as "set" (KJV) or "marked" (NIV) literally means "to cut" or "to hack into pieces". It can also mean to carve or inscribe something, such as a document, or a covenant, such as a stone tablet, but in this context, cut or hacked is to be preferred, at least in part. This is because prior to setting the orbit of Earth, God used Planet X to cut the primordial Earth into two pieces, "hacking" it apart, after which He determined Earth's new orbit. The use of the word *ḥoowq* also indicates that this "cutting" of the Earth was also covenantal in nature, as we discovered with our analysis of Genesis 1:1 previously. The cutting of Earth into two pieces was the first of many covenants God would create with man, in this case, one made just prior to mankind's creation, to create an Earth that was suitable for mankind to inhabit.

Finally, instead of the typical word for Earth here, *'eretz,* the author of Proverbs chose instead to use תְהוֹם *tehom,* which can mean the deep sea but, as we have seen, *tehom* is also the demythologized Hebrew name of the dragon-goddess Tiamat who represented Earth in the Babylonian Creation Epic. Therefore, *tehom* should be translated as "Earth" here. As such, verse 27 should be translated not, "When he prepared the heavens, I was there: when he set a compass upon the face of the depth", but "When He prepared the heavens, I was there; when He divided Earth and set it in a new orbit."

This new, more accurate translation, set in the context of the rest of the verse, describes not "setting a compass" on the face of the deep sea, which make little sense, but how God set Earth's new orbit after He cut the primordial Earth into two sections, ceiling one part as the asteroid belt, and moving the larger portion into a new orbit to become Planet Earth.

In summary, the biblical view of the heavens, particularly the second "hammered" heaven, or *raqiya,* was that it was a collections of rocks and ice that flowed in a ring around the inner solar system. This ring of rocks and ice served as a division, or "wall" between the inner and outer parts of the solar system, setting the limit of where the "waters" of the dragon would flow. And it is within this asteroid belt that God had created a "tabernacle" within which He, at least on occasion, would dwell.

REFERENCES TO GOD'S "THRONE" IN HEAVEN REINTERPRETED

To this point we have determined that there are three heavens mentioned in the Bible. The first heaven is to be equated with Earth's atmosphere, and the second, "hammered" heaven is to be equated with the asteroid belt. But what of the mysterious "third heaven" mentioned by Paul in 2 Corinthians 12:2, where he describes how one believer actually traveled to the third heaven? Since we have determined that both the first and second heavens are physical locations in space, could it be that the third heaven can also be identified with a physical location in space? Paul's assertion that the believer in question may have traveled there in his or her own body tends to beg the assumption that it may actually be a physical location.

Of the three heavens mentioned in Scripture, the first two are inappropriate locations for the heaven that is reserved for the saints, and the third is mentioned only once, described in vague terms as a "paradise".[20] The Greek word for paradise, παράδεισος *paradeious*, does not lend much insight either, as it is essentially a Persian loan word which refers to a garden or park enclosed by a wall, and can refer to any sort of guarded enclosure. It is used in the Greek Septuagint in Genesis 3 to describe the Garden of Eden, and it is translated as the "Garden of God" in Revelation 2:7, though it is not clear if the latter garden is on Earth, or somewhere in heaven.[21]

The Asteroid Belt: God's Heavenly Tabernacle

Further complicating the issue, the Bible also makes it clear that God's throne is in heaven (Psalm 11:4) — assumedly the third heaven, as the first two heavens would seem to be inappropriate locations for a "throne", as we understand it. Yet, as we have seen, the second heaven, the asteroid belt, is a tabernacle, or "tent" that God's dwells in:

✝ Isaiah 40:21-22:
   ²¹ Have ye not known? have ye not heard? hath it not been told you from the beginning? have ye not understood from the foundations of the Earth?

---

[20] G. Kittel, G. W. Bromiley & G. Friedrich, Editors, *Theological Dictionary of the New Testament, Vol. 5* (Grand Rapids, MI: Eerdmans, 1964), 765–766.

[21] Louw, J. P., & Nida, E. A., *Greek-English Lexicon of the New Testament*, Electronic Edition of the 2nd Edition, (New York: United Bible Societies, 1996), 1.14.

²² It is he that sitteth upon the circle of the Earth, and the inhabitants thereof are as grasshoppers; that stretcheth out the heavens as a curtain, and spreadeth them out *as a tent to dwell in.* (KJV)

Psalm 68 also describes God as one who "rideth upon the heavens" and as one whose "strength is in the clouds" (vv. 4, 34). As we have seen, Planet X's perihelion, or closest approach to the Sun, is in the asteroid belt, a specific region in space where it stays temporarily while on the inner part of its orbital journey around the Sun. A parallel passage in *Enuma Elish* also describes Marduk as having created the firmament as his "abode," a firmament made from the shattered remains of Tiamat (IV:137–38). Marduk, like God, was also described as dwelling in the heavens, in a "great abode," a great circle of crushed rocks like that described in Genesis 1:

> He crossed the heavens and surveyed the regions.
> He squared Apsu's quarter, the abode of Nudimmud,
> As the lord measured the dimension of Apsu.
> The Great Abode, its likeness, he fixed as *Esharra*,
> The Great Abode, *Esharra*, which he made as the firmament.
> Anu, Enlil, and Ea he made occupy their places. (IV:141–46)

In *Enuma Elish,* Marduk is described as moving around in a circle, "crossing the heavens and surveying the regions". Marduk/Planet X then returned to the place of the divine conflict in the asteroid belt, which ever since has been the place of its perihelion, or closest approach, to the Sun. The Babylonians referred to the asteroid belt not only as the *rakkis*, the "hammered heaven", but also as *Esharra*, "The Great Abode," as that is where Planet X returned to "dwell" when it was passing through the inner solar system. The "tent" that God is said to dwell in is also located in this "hammered heaven", the *raqiya*, so apparently God, or at least His throne, is also located in the asteroid belt — or, perhaps more accurately, moves through it, like a gateway.²²

---

²² There is an interesting parallel with *Esharra* in Genesis 28:17, where Jacob, after the Lord appeared to him in a dream at Bethel, described the area as "the gate of heaven". The Hebrew word for gate here being שַׁעַר *sha'ar*, which is cognate to the Akkadian word *esharra*. Thus the concept of the second heaven as being some sort of "gateway" in which God dwells like a tabernacle appears to have parallels in both the Babylonian and Hebrew

"The Circuit of Heaven": The Orbit of Planet X

Though Isaiah 40 says that God dwells in the second heaven, Job 22 describes God as moving in a circle, the "circuit of heaven":

- Job 22:12-14:
  ^{12} Is not God in the height of heaven? and behold the height of the stars, how high they are!
  ^{13} And thou sayest, How doth God know? can he judge through the dark cloud?
  ^{14} Thick clouds are a covering to him, that he seeth not; and he walketh in the circuit of heaven. (KJV)

The word here for "circuit" is חוג *hoowg*, "to move in a circle", the same word used in Isaiah 40:22 that we saw is better translated as "orbit." Here in Job, however, it is used to describe not the way that Earth moves in space, but the way *God* moves in space: in a circle. A circuit is any circle — not just a perfect circle. The term circuit could mean any circular shape, including an ellipse. Thus Planet X, with its elliptical orbit, would fill this role quite well. But why would *God* be described as moving in a circle? Psalm 19 helps shed light on this mystery:

- Psalm 19:1-7:
  ^{1} To the chief Musician, A Psalm of David. The heavens declare the glory of God; and the firmament sheweth his handywork.
  ^{2} Day unto day uttereth speech, and night unto night sheweth knowledge.
  ^{3} There is no speech nor language, where their voice is not heard.
  ^{4} Their line is gone out through all the Earth, and their words to the end of the world. In them hath he set a tabernacle for the Sun,
  ^{5} Which is as a bridegroom coming out of his chamber, and rejoiceth as a strong man to run a race.
  ^{6} His going forth is from the end of the heaven, and his circuit unto the ends of it: and there is nothing hid from the heat thereof.
  ^{7} The law of the LORD is perfect, converting the soul: the testimony of the LORD is sure, making wise the simple. (KJV)

---

cosmologies, and may also have a link to the Tower of Babel incident mentioned in both the Bible and *Enuma Elish*.

Psalm 19 contains some of the most scientifically accurate references to our solar system in the Bible. To begin with, the reference in verse 1 to "the heavens" appears to refer to the starry sky in general — in particular, the Sun, Moon, and planets — all of which "declare the glory of God." This is contrasted with the firmament which, as we have seen, best corresponds with the asteroid belt, which God had made from part of the remains of post-impact Earth. Thus, it is a witness to his "handywork." Verses 2-4 then explain how the Sun, Moon, and planets all have an effect on Earth. "Day after day" refers specifically to the gravitational influence of the Sun, and "night after night" refers specifically to the gravitational influence of the Moon and planets. Together, day and night, their combined gravitational effect "speaks" to Earth, affecting its orbit over time.[23] These gravitational forces "speak" to Earth by causing Earth's tides, influencing plate tectonics, and even causing Earth to "wobble" on its axis, creating the phenomenon of precession.[24] Comins explains, "Ocean tides are largely caused by the Moon [but] the Moon causes only about two-thirds of our tidal effect. The Sun has half as much tidal effect as the Moon, while the planets, especially Jupiter, cause a small fraction more."[25] In fact, according to Jacques Laskar and his colleagues at the Bureau of Longitudes in Paris, were it not for the Moon, Earth would probably be uninhabitable, as the Moon tends to cancel out much of the pernicious effects that the Sun and the planets have on Earth's axial tilt that, unchecked, would cause radical changes in Earth's weather patterns over time.

> Because Earth spins, it bulges at the equator. The Sun and planets exert a gravitational pull on this bulge, causing Earth's axis to rock slowly. As the planets move in their orbits — and as they deform one another's orbits through their gravitational interactions — the overall strength of the various forces acting on Earth's bulge fluctuates erratically. Laskar and his colleagues found that this would cause the spin axis to oscillate in an inherently unpredictable, chaotic way: a small disturbance in the obliquity today would yield a very large change a million years from now. "We found that without the Moon the obliquity [axial tilt] of Earth is unstable and can go anywhere from 0 to 85

---

[23]Comins, "A New Slant on Earth," 46.
[24]Shawna Vogel, "Wobbling World," *Discover*, August 1989, 24.
[25]Comins, "The Earth without the Moon," 50.

degrees," says Laske. With the Moon around, however, it's a different story. The Moon packs enough gravitational pull to effectively cancel most of the other forces on Earth's spin axis. With just a little help from the Sun, it makes the axis settle into a regular motion, causing it to precess in a small circle every 26,000 years. The tilt of the axis does change over time, but only by 1.3 degrees instead of 85.[26]

The Sun, Moon, and planets all orbit together in a giant web of gravitational force, and each body has an effect — however subtle — on all the rest. All together, these effects upon the Earth are the "language" that the other bodies in our solar system have with Earth, a "communication" which causes subtle but significant effects upon our planet. This explains the enigmatic reference in verse 4, "their line is gone out through all the Earth, and their words to the end of the world"; "their line" must be a reference to the collective gravitational influence that the Sun, Moon, and planets have upon Earth. Verse 4 then completes this thought by explaining that "In them hath he set a tabernacle for the Sun," which means that the Sun is set in the middle of the planets, that surround it like a "tabernacle" or a house. The planets are all gravitationally bound to the Sun, orbiting around it, forming a complex gravitational web between the Sun, themselves, and the other planets, making our solar system a closely knit "family" that all live in the same "house."

Thus, David neatly summarizes in verses 1-4 exactly how our solar system works, at least on a macro scale. But what do verses 5-6 speak of, if this summary is complete? The traditional interpretation of verses 5-6 explains that David then goes on to describe the movement of the Sun through the heavens, moving from one end of heaven to the other, as it appears to move from the perspective of an earthbound observer. But since we are interpreting these verses with the assumption that they are a scientifically accurate description of how our solar system works, David would have been in error to describe the Sun as moving in the heavens relative to Earth. To assume so would be to imply that God's revelation to David was scientifically inaccurate, which would make God a liar. Since this is impossible, I am forced to conclude that David had something else in mind here. But what?

---

[26]Robert Naeye, "Moon of Our Delight," *Discover*, January 1994, 72.

There is one key translation error that takes place between verses 4 and 5 which makes a world of difference in the interpretation of verses 5-6. It is the fact that the translators translated the first word in verse 5, הוא, *hoow'*, "He," as "which." This was done to make the pronoun "he" refer back to the Sun, rather than to God, because the translators could not conceive of why God would move around in heaven in a circle.[27] The translators of the King James Version were probably also somewhat ignorant scientifically, as this version was originally published in 1611. Compounding the error, the translators of more recent versions of the Bible were likely not only similarly limited in their understanding of scientific astronomy, they may also have been influenced by liberal critical scholarship, which may have led them to assume that the Hebrews were scientifically ignorant, forgetting that the Bible, as a divinely inspired writing, must be scientifically accurate or else it ceases to be the truth. Thirdly, none of these translators were aware of the possible existence of a tenth planet in our solar system and the ramifications that it has upon many heretofore mysterious references in the Old Testament. As a result, translators have maintained their assumption that the Hebrews believed that the Sun, Moon and stars moved on a hardened dome which arched over a flat, unmoving Earth, in an Earth-centered universe, and translated verses 5-6 based upon this assumption.

However, as we have seen, it is entirely possible that David was in fact referring not to the Sun, but to God Himself. First of all, the pronoun "He" had been used in reference to God once already, in verse 4. Using the same word to refer to the Sun in the next verse would have been confusing. Furthermore, David would not have referred to the Sun as "he," giving it the status of a living god, and he particularly would not have wanted to equate God with the Sun, which would have been a great heresy, making the psalm sound more like Egyptian mythology than Israelites cosmology. Thus the word "he" must actually refer to God, the One who created the heavens, the firmament, and a tabernacle for the Sun. In fact, verse 5 contains a number of interesting little mysteries, so we will retranslate it in its entirety:

---

[27] There is actually at least one other reference to God "moving in a circle" in heaven: Job 22:14: "Thick clouds are a covering to him, that he seeth not; and he walketh in the circuit of heaven."

וְהוּא֙ *ve-hoow'* - "and He"
כְּחָתָ֖ן *ke-ḥatan* - "like a bridegroom"
יֹצֵ֣א *yotsa'* - "coming forth"
מֵחֻפָּת֑וֹ *ma-ḥoophat-ow* - "from his bridal chamber"
יָשִׂ֥ישׂ *yashiysh* - "to leap, to spring, to rejoice"
כְגִבּ֗וֹר *ke-gibowr* - "like a mighty hunter, like Orion"
לָר֥וּץ *laroowtz* - "to run"
אֹֽרַח *'oraḥ* - "a path, a race, a bull-run"

As you recall, in Chapter I, we discussed the possibility that the Behemoth of Job 40 may actually have been inspired by a huge form of extinct cattle known as the "Aurochs". The term "Aurochs" may have originally come from the almost identically pronounced Hebrew word אֹרַח *'oraḥ*, translated here in Psalm 19:5 as "race". However, *'oraḥ*, may actually have a more relevant translation here. The ancient Germanic name "Auroch" may well be a loan word, derived from the Hebrew word *'oraḥ*.[28] But how does *'oraḥ*, relate to a giant, primordial bull? It may well be that this unusual Hebrew word is a construct, a combination of two words: אוֹר *'or*, "light", plus *aḥ*, "och" (ox?). Thus the term *'or-aḥ*, may literally mean "light-ox", another way of describing the constellation of Taurus, the bull. However, *'oraḥ* is most frequently used throughout the Bible in the more generic sense of a physical pathway, such as a road or trail, so a more precise meaning might be "ox trail", or "cattle trail". It is this version that filtered down into general usage in the Hebrew language as "trail".

---

[28] See http://en.wikipedia.org/wiki/Aurochs#Nomenclature for an excellent article on the Aurochs and the root of their name.

"In the Beginning"

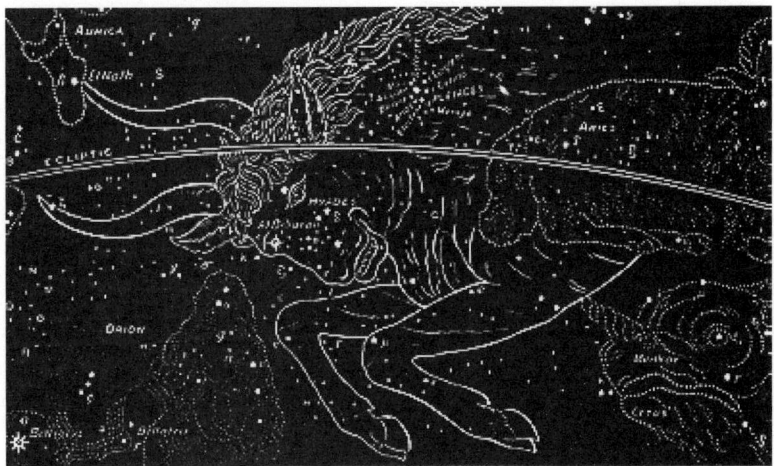

Figure 5.1. The constellation of Taurus, as presented in the classic book on Judeo-Christian astronomy, "The Witness of the Stars" by E.W. Bullinger. The "path" of the ecliptic, shown here passing through the body and between the horns of the bull, was and is where the planets appear to move in the heavens. This heavenly pathway would have been seen by the ancients as a "trail of the gods", and would most likely have had a place of prominence in their rituals. It also would most certainly have found its way into the fundamental linguistic concepts that the various ancient languages, including Hebrew, were based upon, making it so that the "trail" of the gods in heaven, at least that part that passed through the constellation of Taurus, would have been seen as a "heavenly cattle trail", or "the trail of the heavenly bull".

However, in order to achieve the most precise meaning possible for this passage, we must take the other words in the passage into account. Having set the context of the path of the "bridegroom" as being some sort of trail, a trail related to bulls, and possibly even somehow related to the constellation of Taurus, we must then take a look at the concept of why the psalmist chose the word "bridegroom"[29], as well as the rest of the words in this verse. The word-picture that the psalmist is painting here is that of a bridegroom running along a certain path. This bridegroom starts off his journey along the path from some sort of chamber, specifically, a "bridal chamber". However, he does not merely leave the chamber, he "leaps up" from the chamber, "like a mighty warrior" or perhaps "mighty hunter", as גִּבּוֹר *gibowr* is also used in Genesis 10:9 to describe the character of Nimrod, the mighty,

---

[29] Interestingly, the term "bridegroom" can also refer, in more modern times, to one who tends horses, or any sort of valuable cattle or possessions. http://en.wikipedia.org/wiki/Groom_(horses)

arrogant warrior-hunter who set himself against God. It could also refer specifically to the constellation of Orion the Hunter, with which Nimrod was associated, which would fit much better into the astronomical context of this passage. Some of the ancient names of Orion support this position as well: "Other (Arabic) names relate to his person: *Al Giauza, the branch; Al Gebor, the mighty; Al Mirzam, the ruler; Al Nagjed, the prince; Niphla* (Chaldee), *the mighty Nux* (Hebrew), *the strong.*"[30] *Al Gebor* is the Arabic equivalent of the Hebrew word used in this passage to describe the bridegroom: *gibowr*, making a clear linguistic link between the identity of the bridegroom and the constellation of Orion.

Figure 5.2. The constellation of Orion. Orion is most likely cognate to the character of Nimrod in the Bible, a sort of "antichrist of the Old Testament" who set himself against God and His rule over the cosmos. This is why Orion is set as opposing the onrushing bull of Taurus, who represents God swiftly returning from heaven to take the rule of Earth. Based upon the information encoded in Psalm 19, Planet X, God's throne, will most likely reappear in or near this constellation just prior to the Second Coming of Christ.

But this passage has not only an astronomical aspect to it, but also a fertility aspect to it, as the bridegroom is described as coming forth from his bridal chamber, which is where the bridegroom consummates his marriage with his bride. Moreover the concept of a mighty man "leaping" out of his chamber to run down a path, along with the idea of a "heavenly bull" being somehow involved in that process, tends to beg the conclusion that there is something much deeper being communicated here.

The answer to part of the mystery of this passage lies in the ancient practice of bull-leaping, a dangerous sport that has been practiced in various countries in the Mediterranean world from very ancient times, and is still practiced in Spain even to this day. And in ancient times as well as modern, bull-leaping

---

[30] E.W. Bullinger, *The Witness of the Stars*, (Grand Rapids: Kregel Publications, 1967), 127. *Niphla* is also clearly cognate to the Hebrew term *Nephilim*, the name of the giants of the antediluvian world, from whose infernal lineage Nimrod was reborn, being the first, or at least the most prominent, of the giants to be born after the Flood.

was practiced to prove the skill and prowess of the leaper, in order to prove that they were fit and able to sire healthy offspring. So the "race" that the bridegroom/hunter is engaging in this passage is not merely a race around a track, but a brief sprint down a cattle trail towards a mighty bull, over which he leaps to prove his physical prowess.

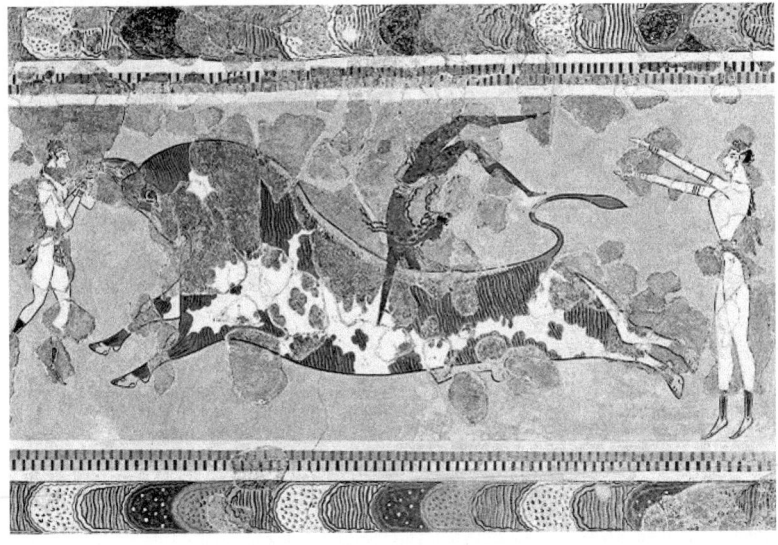

The famous "bull-leaping" fresco found at the Palace of Knossos, in Crete. It shows a scene of a Cretan sport called bull-leaping, which was likely also religious in origin. Here we see a man jumping over the bull as it charges, with female figures on each side. This practice was likely part of a fertility ritual, where the men prove their prowess, and, thus, their viability as a bridegroom. As such, this practice may well have been part of the inspiration for the imagery used in Psalm 19:5.

But since the bridegroom here is not some mere mortal, but God Himself, and the setting is not some dusty cattle trail, but the heavens, the proper translation must take the astronomical context into account. As such, instead of "mighty warrior", we will use "the constellation of Orion", and instead of "race" or even "cattle trail", we will use "a pathway through the constellation of Taurus". This will give us the much more interesting and relevant translation, "And God will first appear in the constellation of Orion, racing down the pathway through the constellation of Taurus." In other words, this passage describes where God will appear in the heavens when He returns.

So, according to this passage, God will appear in the heavens somewhere in or near the constellation of Orion, on a path that will take him through the constellation of Taurus. That is fairly precise, but there is one more important clue in this verse that will give us an even more precise location. The term "bridal chamber" is particularly interesting here, as there is a very large nebula in the constellation of Orion that is modernly called "The Sword of Orion", but it more likely represented, in ancient times his reproductive organs. This is supported by the fact that nebulae are essentially "stellar nurseries", places where new stars are born. As such, "bridal chamber" is a good description of this glorious nebula. If so, then verse 5 could be retranslated most precisely this way:

The "Orion Nebula", located in the "sword" region of the constellation of Orion, like all nebulae is a place where stars are born, and thus the Hebrew term חֻפָּתhoophat — "bridal chamber" is an appropriate description of this region, where God will most likely appear when He returns, according to Psalm 19.

"And God will first appear in the Orion nebula in the constellation of Orion, racing down His orbital pathway through the constellation of Taurus." Verse 6 would then make much more sense: "From the end of the heavens he goes forth, from the gateway of heaven he makes a complete orbit, and nothing is hidden from his jealous eye."

But there is one more thing to consider: what is God riding on when He first appears in the constellation of Orion? On His Imperial throne? On a powerful chariot? On a mighty white horse? Or could it be that He will appear riding something so large, so awesome, that it can be seen from millions of miles away in space? There can be only one thing that God could be riding and be seen from that far away, and that thing, His divine throne-chariot, drawn by a team-of-four, could only be Planet X.

Planet X: God's "Throne" in Heaven

To this point we have reviewed numerous biblical references to God riding through the heavens, moving in a circle, and living in a tabernacle made of rocks and ice that circles somewhere high up in the heavens, and have determined that the only logical explanation for these mysterious attributes of God can be only one thing – that there is another planet somewhere in our solar system that is somehow closely associated with God. This mysterious planet, which orbits in and out of our solar system, occasionally resides in the asteroid belt, and in ancient times came into conflict with the primordial Earth, is a perfect match for the theoretical Planet X that astronomers have been searching for for over a century. However, one question remains. Whereas the volume of evidence appears to point to the fact that God is closely associated with this mysterious planet, is it His place of residence, His "throne", or merely a weapon that He uses, a "battle chariot" that He mounts only on occasion to go to war with His enemies? To determine exactly how God uses Planet X, we will review the numerous, mysterious references to God's "throne" in heaven, and see whether or not Planet X is merely a tool in the LORD's heavenly arsenal, or if He also lives there, in an ancient civilization, with the rest of the saints, in a glorious paradise.

⚜ Isaiah 66:1:
Thus saith the LORD, The heaven is my throne, and the Earth is my footstool: where is the house that ye build unto me? and where is the place of my rest? (KJV)

⚜ Psalm 11:4:
The LORD is in his holy temple,
The LORD's throne is in heaven:
His eyes behold,
His eyelids try, the children of men. (KJV)

Whenever God's throne is described in the Bible, it is invariably said to be in "heaven". Now whereas this is not conclusive in and of itself, what it interesting is the etymology of the word "throne". In the Hebrew, the word for "throne" used in both of the above verses is כִּסֵּא *kisai'*, "high, lofty seat". The idea that this seat is high and lofty, i.e., some sort of "heavenly throne" is interesting, but inconclusive. But what is more interesting is the meaning a close variant of the word *kisai'*: כֶּסֶא *kese'*, "the full Moon". *Kese'* is identical to the word *kisai'*, except for a slight difference in pronunciation, and both derive from the root word, which is unknown to us as it is not used in the Bible. However, we can backwards extrapolate the meaning of the root word for both *kisai'* and *kese'* (which Gesenius theorizes to be spelled כָּסָא *kasa'*)³¹ as being some sort of lofty, royal throne that is round in shape, looking like the full Moon in appearance. In other words, the word *kasa'* is the Hebrew word for "planet", a planet that is bright and white in appearance, that also serves as God's lofty, royal throne in heaven.³²

♀ Isaiah 33:16-17:
¹⁶ He shall dwell on high: his place of defence shall be the munitions of rocks.
¹⁷ Thine eyes shall see the king in his beauty: they shall behold the land that is very far off. (KJV)

Now that we have determined the identity of God's heavenly throne as a planet that is white in color, in appearance something like the Moon, we can examine some of the more enigmatic references to God's lofty royal throne in heaven to verify that this translation fits well with other descriptions of God's throne in heaven. One of the more interesting passages dealing with God's throne in heaven appears in Isaiah 33, where the place that God lives in heaven is described as being like a castle that is in a land (Heb., אֶרֶץ *eretz*) very far away, a place where the believer will be taken to be safe from evil. Verse 16 is somewhat difficult to translate, so we will approach it one word at a time:

הוּא	*hoow'* - "he"
מְרוֹמִים	*merowmiym* - "high, lofty, high fortified places"
יִשְׁכֹּן	*yishcon* - "settle down, dwell, abide"
מְצָדוֹת	*metsadowt* - "high place of refuge, castle on a hill"
סְלָעִים	*sela'iym* - "rocks, rocks of refuge, Petra"
מִשְׂגַּבּוֹ	*misgabow* - "high, lofty place"

---

³¹ Gesenius, W., & Tregelles, S. P. (2003). *Gesenius' Hebrew and Chaldee Lexicon to the Old Testament Scriptures* (כָּסָא). Bellingham, WA: Logos Research Systems, Inc. Could this possibly the root of the Spanish word *casa*, "house", i.e., the "house" of God in heaven?

³² Interestingly, כֶּסֶא *kese'* also shows up in Proverbs 7:20 as "the time appointed" when the master of the house will return. In other words, the return of Planet X, which is at a set time appointed in the future, will be a time of judgment for those who tarried with the harlot while the master was away. Cf. also The Parable of the Wicked Tenants in Matthew 21:33-45.

"In the Beginning"

לַחְמוֹ   *lahmow* - "his bread"
נִתָּן   *nitan* - "he will be given"
מֵימָיו   *maymayv* - "his waters"
נֶאֱמָנִים   *ne'emaniym* - "will be sure"

Rather than the rather strange "munitions of rocks" translation, the actual meaning of this verse is that the believer can look forward to be taken to a place in heaven that is like a fortress, where they will be safe from the snares of Satan. This fortress is in a "land" that is very far away, which we have seen from other verses is in heaven. Psalm 33 echoes this concept, that God lives in a particular location in heaven, from whence He carefully watches, like a great eye, over mankind:

✣ Psalm 33:13-14:
[13] The LORD looketh from heaven; he beholdeth all the sons of men.
[14] From the place of his habitation he looketh upon all the inhabitants of the Earth.

Isaiah 33:16-17 also contains an interesting reference that implies that God lives in a "land" that is very far away. This land, or "far country", is described by Isaiah as being at the "end of heaven":

✣ Isaiah 13:3-5:
[3] I have commanded my sanctified ones, I have also called my mighty ones for mine anger, even them that rejoice in my highness.
[4] The noise of a multitude in the mountains, like as of a great people; a tumultuous noise of the kingdoms of nations gathered together: the LORD of hosts mustereth the host of the battle.
[5] They come from a far country, from the end of heaven, even the LORD, and the weapons of his indignation, to destroy the whole land. (KJV)

God is seen here as coming toward Earth from a specific place, from a "far country." This is no ordinary, earthly country, however; it is located in space, at "the end of heaven." The use of the term "far country", literally, אֶרֶץ מֶרְחָק *'eretz merhaq* in this context, however, indicates that God is coming from a physical location in space, as *'eretz* literally means "Earth". Moreover, מֶרְחָק *merḥaq* is based upon the root רָחַק *raḥaq*, which may be related to רָקִיעַ *raqiya'*, "firmament", so *'eretz merḥaq* could literally mean, "a land that is far away in heaven" — specifically, a land that is located in, or passes through, the asteroid belt, a place where stones are "gathered together" (Ecc. 3:5). So Isaiah is essentially saying that the LORD and his כְּלֵי זַעְמוֹ *celay za'mow*, literally, "vessels of indignation" will be coming to judge Earth from another "Earth" or habitable planet, that orbits at "the end of heaven". This could only refer to Planet X.

✞ Psalm 93:1-2:
> ¹ The LORD reigneth, he is clothed with majesty; the LORD is clothed with strength, wherewith he hath girded himself: the world also is stablished, that it cannot be moved.
> ² Thy throne is established of old: thou art from everlasting. (KJV)

Note here that the establishment of God's "throne" is closely linked with the establishment of Earth. God's throne, which is actually a moveable "throne-chariot," according to Psalm 104, is a bright object that travels through the heavens:

✞ Psalm 104:1-5:
> ¹ Bless the LORD, O my soul. O LORD my God, thou art very great; thou art clothed with honour and majesty.
> ² Who coverest thyself with light as with a garment: who stretchest out the heavens like a curtain:
> ³ Who layeth the beams of his chambers in the waters: who maketh the clouds his chariot: who walketh upon the wings of the wind:
> ⁴ Who maketh his angels spirits; his ministers a flaming fire:
>
> ⁵ Who laid the foundations of the earth, that it should not be removed for ever.

Not only is God's throne-chariot a bright object that travels through the heavens, it "stretches out" the "waters" of the heavens "like a tent"; i.e., a place to dwell. Verse 3 also contains an enigmatic reference to God as one who "lays the beams of his upper chambers" upon these heavenly waters. Based upon our discoveries to this point, the original Hebrew of this passage can now be translated more accurately. Starting with verse 3, הַמְקָרֶה, *ham^ekareh,* has the literal meaning of "build with beams." This translation is taken from the two of the other instances where this word was used, where it was used to describe the setting up of wooden beams for the building of a gate. Thus it could also mean "to build a gate" or, more simply, "to set up," or "to build." This "gate", as we have seen in other verses, is located in the "waters above", i.e., in the asteroid belt, which is the "gateway" that Planet X passes through, the actual gateway probably being Planet X's perihelion, or closest approach to the sun. עֲלִיּוֹתָיו, *'aliyotayv,* is even more enigmatic. It refers to a king's "upper chamber," a special place on one of the upper floors in a palace, a place set on high, above the fray, and could be better translated, based upon Isaiah 33 and 66, as "lofty throne." Or, in light of the previous word, "gate", *'aliyotayv* may be better translated as "ladder", i.e., that which is used to climb up to the lofty gate of heaven.

הַשָׂם־עָבִים, *ha-sham-'aviym,* is only partially translated in the KJV. *'Aviym,* "thick, dark clouds," is translated correctly, but *ha-sham* seems to have been left out entirely. *Ha-* is what is called a "hay directive," a usage of the Hebrew letter ה where it indicates movement in a direction *toward* something. *Sham* means "there," and combined, *ha-sham* means, simply, "to there." All together they mean "to there the dark clouds." רְכוּבוֹ, *r^ecoowv-ow,* is correctly translated "his chariot," but should probably be more closely connected with *'aviym,* "dark clouds" to arrive at "cloudy chariot" or "storm-chariot", meaning "To there the storm-chariot." הַמְהַלֵּךְ, *ha-me-halak,* also remains untranslated in the KJV, strangely. It is a participial form of הָלַךְ, *halak,* "to go, walk," which indicates that an ongoing movement is intended: "moving" or "walking." It is prefixed by הַ, "the," which gives us "the walking one" or "the moving one," apparently referring to God's storm-chariot, the "Sky-Walker".

All together, a better translation for this verse is, "He built a way to climb up to the gateway in the heavenly waters; to there his storm chariot moves on the wings of the wind." In other words, the inner part of Planet X's orbit lies within the asteroid belt, which it "climbs up" to, apparently from beneath. Planet X then moves through the asteroid belt during its orbit through our solar system, and then above it, its perihelion actually being above the plane of the ecliptic, as viewed from the side. The idea of God's heavenly chariot "climbing up" to its perihelion in the asteroid belt makes sense, as modern astronomers believe that Planet X may have an orbit that is out of line with the plane of the ecliptic, so that it actually first approaches the plane of the ecliptic from the south, from beneath the plane of the ecliptic, and its perihelion is actually somewhere above the plane of the ecliptic. Thus the asteroid belt is a "gateway" through which Planet X "climbs" as it makes its way to its perihelion above the plane of the ecliptic where it sits above all the other planets as the "king of the gods".

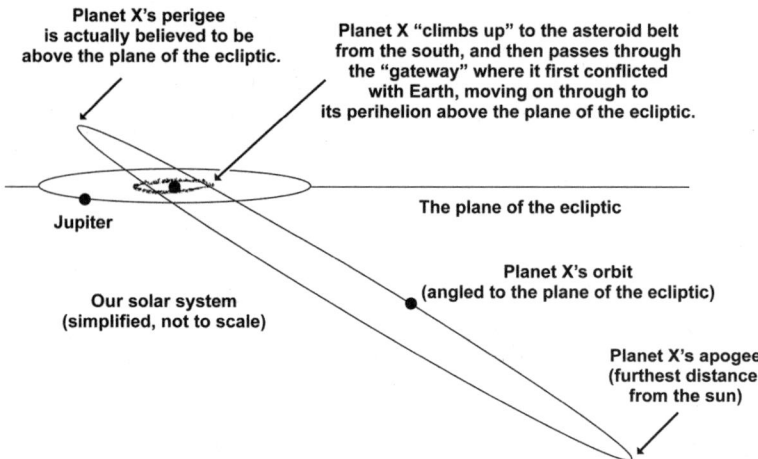

Figure 5.3: According to Psalm 104, Planet X approaches from the south and "climbs up" to its "gateway" in the asteroid belt, where it first conflicted with the primordial Earth. To this day it passes through this gateway on its way to its perihelion above the plane of the ecliptic.

God's throne-chariot is also surrounded with fire and "winds," which draw his chariot like "horses." As Isaiah explains, "Behold, the LORD will come with fire, and with his chariots like a whirlwind, to render his anger with fury, and his rebuke with flames of fire" (Isa. 66:18). Interestingly, this description matches the description of Marduk's "storm-chariot" almost exactly:

> *[Marduk's] destiny thus fixed, the gods, his fathers,*
> *Caused him to go the way of success and attainment....*

The four winds he stationed that nothing of her might escape,
The South Wind, the North Wind, the East Wind,
the West Wind.
Close to his side he held the net, the gift of his father, Anu.
He brought forth Imhullu "the Evil Wind," the Whirlwind,
the Hurricane,
The Fourfold Wind, the Sevenfold Wind, the Cyclone,
the Matchless Wind;
Then he sent forth the winds he had brought forth,
the seven of them.
To stir up the inside of Tiamat they rose up behind him.
Then the lord raised up the flood-storm, his mighty weapon.
He mounted the storm chariot irresistible [and] terrifying.
He harnessed (and) yoked it to a team-of-four...
The lord went forth and followed his course,
Towards the raging Tiamat he set his face. (IV:33-45)

Therefore, both God and "Marduk" display the following characteristics: (1) both wear light as a garment, i.e., appear as a bright object in the heavens; (2) both are surrounded by "winds" and "fire,", i.e., both have satellites; (3) both ride a "storm-chariot" drawn by these winds, i.e., have a cometlike tail; (4) both breathe fire, (5) both fought and defeated a "dragon" and its helpers, and created heaven and Earth from its remains, (6) both confined the defeated dragon's "waters" within certain boundaries, and (7) both still move through the heavens in a circle, returning periodically to the place where the combat had originally taken place, passing through a "gateway" to their location above the plane of the ecliptic where they sit enthroned as "king of the gods".

✤ Isaiah 26:20-27:1
[20] Come, my people, enter thou into thy chambers, and shut thy doors about thee: hide thyself as it were for a little moment, until the indignation be overpast.
[21] For, behold, the LORD cometh out of his place to punish the inhabitants of the Earth for their iniquity: the Earth also shall disclose her blood, and shall no more cover her slain.
[1] In that day the LORD with his sore and great and strong sword shall punish leviathan the piercing serpent, even leviathan that

crooked serpent; and he shall slay the dragon that is in the sea. (KJV)

Finally, Isaiah clearly identifies the LORD as coming "out of His place" to render judgment on Earth in the end times. In that day the LORD will again come into conflict with the dragon Leviathan who, despite having been defeated at the Creation, will awake and reassert herself, giving birth to another evil brood and spreading corruption all over the face of the Earth once more. At that time the LORD will return from His place at "the end of heaven" to once again do combat with the dragon and save His chosen people from certain destruction. The LORD, riding in His "vessels of indignation" from the third heaven, Planet X, will once again make war with Earth and defeat the dragon and her evil cohorts once more.

VI

JOB: THE HEBREW CREATION EPIC

Canst thou draw out leviathan with a hook? or his tongue with a cord which thou lettest down? Canst thou put an hook into his nose? or bore his jaw through with a thorn? Canst thou fill his skin with barbed irons? or his head with fish spears? Lay thine hand upon him, remember the battle, do no more! (Job 41:1-2, 7-8)

To this point we have focused our analysis of the biblical Creation material primarily on Genesis, Isaiah and the Psalms which, as we have seen, contain a create deal of advanced scientific information regarding the Creation that, until now, had remained hidden away in the subtle matrices of the Hebrew language. However, in all that analysis, we have only made occasional references to the Book of Job, and then only if it was directly relevant to the line of argument. This is not due to the fact that the Creation material inside The Book of Job does not contain any data that may shed light on the Planet X/Giant Impact theory that we proposed in Chapter III. On the contrary, my analysis of The Book of Job prior to the writing of this book had revealed such an enormous amount of scientifically advanced information regarding the Creation that supported the Planet X/Giant Impact Theory that I decided that it deserved an entire chapter of its own.

"Job and His Friends" by Gustave Doré. The Book of Job may actually contain many long-hidden secrets regarding the Creation, containing so much Creation information that it could actually be reclassified as the Hebrew Creation Epic.

Reading through the commentaries on Job, I found that the learned scholars, so expert with other books of the Bible, were often baffled by Job's combination of vague imagery and words that were difficult — even impossible — to translate with even moderate certainty. More times than I would care to admit, scholars came right out and said that much of their translations were conjectural, even bordering on speculative — this from some of the most gifted men in the field. Much of the descriptive imagery that dominates The Book of Job so defies clear translation, in fact, that some words have had to be glossed over by translators in order to arrive at "theologically correct" translations. When analyzing the original Hebrew of these enigmatic texts, I realized that the translators of the KJV, and even more modern translators of newer versions of the Bible, stood little chance of deriving accurate translations of the Creation material, as they had not been properly equipped with either an understanding of parallel ancient Near Eastern Creation stories, or a thorough understanding of astronomy. As such, I determined that The Book of Job was likely so badly mistranslated, at least in those sections that dealt with the Creation, that it would require not only a complete retranslation, but a complete recategorization. I believe that The Book of Job should no longer be considered to be merely "wisdom literature", quietly tucked away between Esther and the Psalms as a mere curiosity. The Book of Job should be given its proper place as nothing less than the Hebrew Creation Epic, in some ways, arguably, the most important book in the Old Testament due to the gravity of the subject matter locked within its archaic Hebrew poetic verse.

My first attempts to retranslate Job were limited to those passages that were either creation oriented, and/or contained imagery similar to that found in *Enuma Elish*. However, it occurred to me that since the translators of the KJV and NIV texts of The Book of Job had not taken *Enuma Elish* parallels into account when they did their translations (or purposely ignored them), it could be that more parallel imagery could be locked away under poor and/or biased translation. After a brief survey of creation and creation-related passages in Job, using subject and keyword searches, I found that Job contained as much *Enuma Elish*-related material as all the other books in the Bible *combined*. Unfortunately, I soon discovered, some of the passages, particularly Job 41, were buried under literally centuries of speculative translations that rendered these crucial passages almost incomprehensible. Thus, whereas some passages required only limited retranslation to uncover the "treasures of darkness" contained therein, others required many hours of Hebrew exegesis, using multiple lexicons and commentaries, to glean only a few ounces of precious truth. Thus we will focus in this chapter on those parts of Job that contain the largest amount of relevant Creation material, and save a comprehensive retranslation, including the "gleanings" for a future book.

THE RETURN OF PLANET X: 2000 B.C.
Though there is clear evidence that Earth was dramatically affected by a near fly-by of Planet X some time in Earth's primordial past, we have not yet discussed the possibility that Planet X may have come close enough to Earth at a time within recorded history to cause devastation significant enough to be remembered in the myths and histories of the ancient peoples who were affected by it. It is my belief that we have, in the Book of Job, such a recollection that, in parallel with other ancient histories from the same period, make it clear that Planet X once again came near enough to Earth to cause great destruction. It is my theory that, around 2000 B.C., Planet X came close enough to Earth to destroy the ancient empire of Sumer, including the Tower of Babel, forcing Abram to emigrate to Canaan where the history of the Hebrew nation would begin.

Job 1: The Return of Planet X

In the beginning of the Book of Job, the character of Job is introduced as a man who was "perfect and upright", and "the greatest of all the men of the east". He had 1 wife, 7 sons, and 3 daughters, for a total of 11 family members, he being the 12th. As the greatest of all the men of the east, Job's great wealth was built on cattle, a total of 11,000 of various types. Thus both cattle, and the number 11, were prominent features of Job's life.

Job also regularly sacrificed to the LORD to make sure that God had no reason to attack him, his children or his possessions. And it was because of Job's success in both heavenly and earthly things that Job was accounted to be perfect before the LORD, or at least as perfect as a mere mortal can be, and the LORD boasted of Job's excellence before the divine assembly in heaven:

✞ Job 1:6-22:
⁶ Now there was a day when the sons of God came to present themselves before the LORD, and Satan came also among them.

⁷ And the LORD said unto Satan, Whence comest thou? Then Satan answered the LORD, and said, From going to and fro in the Earth, and from walking up and down in it.

⁸ And the LORD said unto Satan, Hast thou considered my servant Job, that there is none like him in the Earth, a perfect and an upright man, one that feareth God, and escheweth evil?

⁹ Then Satan answered the LORD, and said, Doth Job fear God for nought?

¹⁰ Hast not thou made an hedge about him, and about his house, and about all that he hath on every side? thou hast blessed the work of his hands, and his substance is increased in the land.

¹¹ But put forth thine hand now, and touch all that he hath, and he will curse thee to thy face.

¹² And the LORD said unto Satan, Behold, all that he hath is in thy power; only upon himself put not forth thine hand. So Satan went forth from the presence of the LORD.

¹³ And there was a day when his sons and his daughters were eating and drinking wine in their eldest brother's house:

¹⁴ And there came a messenger unto Job, and said, The oxen were plowing, and the asses feeding beside them:

¹⁵ And the Sabeans fell upon them, and took them away; yea, they have slain the servants with the edge of the sword; and I only am escaped alone to tell thee.

¹⁶ While he was yet speaking, there came also another, and said, The fire of God is fallen from heaven, and hath burned up the sheep, and the servants, and consumed them; and I only am escaped alone to tell thee.

¹⁷ While he was yet speaking, there came also another, and said, The Chaldeans made out three bands, and fell upon the camels, and have carried them away, yea, and slain the servants with the edge of the sword; and I only am escaped alone to tell thee.

¹⁸ While he was yet speaking, there came also another, and said, Thy sons and thy daughters were eating and drinking wine in their eldest brother's house:

¹⁹ And, behold, there came a great wind from the wilderness, and smote the four corners of the house, and it fell upon the young men, and they are dead; and I only am escaped alone to tell thee.

²⁰ Then Job arose, and rent his mantle, and shaved his head, and fell down upon the ground, and worshipped. (KJV)

Job: The Hebrew Creation Epic

Despite Job's near-perfect walk before God, God decided to allow Satan to test him, to see if his righteousness was true, or merely skin-deep. In order to test his devotion, he first allowed Satan to destroy all of Job's great wealth, via three vectors of attack:

🕆 He sent the Sabeans to plunder all of Job's oxen and asses and kill all the servants who managed them.

🕆 He destroyed all of Job's sheep by sending "fire from heaven" against them to destroy both them and the servants who shepherded them.

🕆 He sent the Chaldeans to plunder all of Job's camels, and slew all but one of the servants who tended them.

He then sent a רוּחַ גְּדוֹלָה *roowaḥ gedowlah,* "a mighty wind" to strike the four corners of the house where all of his children were making merry, and they were also all killed. So, God basically destroyed Job's life, using bands of warriors, fire from heaven, and "a mighty wind" to do the job, yet He did not actually kill Job, saving him for another purpose.

Interestingly, around 2000 B.C., the Sumerian Empire was also destroyed by a great wind and "fire from heaven", as recorded in the Sumerian lamentations, "Lamentation over the Destruction of Ur" and "Lamentation over the Destruction of Sumer and Ur".[1] These histories describe how an "evil wind", which had been sent by the god Enlil (the Sumerian predecessor of Marduk) to destroy Sumer for its sins against the divine realm, had swept over the entire region and utterly destroyed the once-mighty empire of Sumer:

> *Enlil called the storm; the people groan.*
> *The storm of overflow he carried off from the land; the people groan.*
> *The good storm he carried off from Sumer; the people groan.*
> *To the evil storm he issued directions; the people groan.*
> *To Kingaluda, the tender of the storm, he entrusted it.*

---

[1] Samuel Noah Kramer, trans., "Lamentation over the Destruction of Ur" and "Lamentation over the Destruction of Sumer and Ur", in James B. Pritchard, ed., *Ancient Near Eastern Texts related to the Old Testament*, (Princeton, N.J.: Princeton University Press, 1974), 455-463, 611-619.

The storm that annihilates the land, he called; the people groan.
The evil winds he called; the people groan.
Enlil brings Gibil [the fire god] to his aid.
The great storm of heaven he called; the people groan....
At the base of heaven it made the ... whirl [wind]; the people groan.
In front of the storm fires burned; the people groan....
Sumer is broken up by the gishburru [a hunting weapon];
the people groan....
The destructive storm makes the land tremble and quake....
The lofty unapproachable mountain, the Ekishnugal —
Its righteous house by large axes is devoured.
The Subarians and the Elamites, the destroyers,
made of it thirty shekels....
Verily Enlil has turned inimical to my house,
by the pickaxe verily it has been torn up.
Upon him who comes from below verily he hurled fire —
alas my city verily has been destroyed;
Enlil upon him who comes from above verily hurled the flame.
"Lamentation over the Destruction of Ur",
Lines 173-181, 186-187, 195, 198, 242-244, 258-260

A parallel account of the destruction of the Sumerian Empire called "The Lamentation of the Destruction of Sumer and Ur" actually places a special emphasis on all of the cattle being destroyed by the mysterious "fire from heaven" that had been sent by the god Enlil to destroy Sumer:

That the day be overturned, that "law and order" cease to exist —
The storm is all devouring like the Flood —
That the me[2] of Sumer be overturned ,
That a favorable reign be withheld,
That cities be destroyed, that houses be destroyed,
That stalls be destroyed, that sheepfolds be wiped out,
That its (Sumer's) oxen no longer stand in their stalls,

---

[2] The Sumerian *me* (pronounced "meh") were "universal decrees of divine authority, the invocations that spread arts, crafts, and civilization.(http://home.comcast.net/ ~chris.s/sumer-faq.html#A1.5). It is unclear what they looked like, but the *me*'s were essentially what we would call "ideas" or "concepts", some of which can be represented in physical form as a sort of "idol", the rest too abstract to represent easily. http://en.wikipedia.org/wiki/Me_(mythology)

Job: The Hebrew Creation Epic

> *That its sheep no longer spread out in their sheepfold.*
> "Lamentation over the Destruction of Sumer and Ur", Lines 1-8

No known natural phenomena, such as a powerful thunderstorm, tornado, or even a hurricane, could account for this level of destruction, even if these phenomena occurred in Mesopotamia, which they do not. Moreover, no known natural phenomena anywhere on Earth would match the characteristics of this storm, which included not only a great wind, but also "fire from heaven" which burned up the entire region. The only possible conclusion that one could draw is that a massive meteorite or comet hit the region, which are the only things that could have created a "mighty wind" with sufficient fiery heat and force to devastate an entire region. And in fact, that is exactly what happened:

> Studies of satellite images of southern Iraq have revealed a two-mile-wide circular depression which scientists say bears all the hallmarks of an impact crater. If confirmed, it would point to the Middle East being struck by a meteor with the violence equivalent to hundreds of nuclear bombs. Today's crater lies on what would have been shallow sea 4,000 years ago, and any impact would have caused devastating fires and flooding. The catastrophic effect of these could explain the mystery of why so many early cultures went into sudden decline around 2300 B.C.... A date of around 2300 B.C. for the impact may also cast new light on the legend of Gilgamesh, dating from the same period. The legend talks of "the Seven Judges of Hell", who raised their torches, lighting the land with flame, and a storm that turned day into night, "smashed the land like a cup", and flooded the area.[3]

A similar epic from that period called "The Erra Epic" also describes a Mesopotamian fire deity named "Erra" who was accompanied by a group of seven lesser deities known as "The Divine Seven", who appeared in the sky and destroyed the land with fire around the same

---

[3] Robert Matthews, "Meteor Clue to End of Middle East Civilizations", *Telegraph.co.uk*, 4/11/2001. No longer available on Telegraph.co.uk, but a similar story is available on Rense.com (http://www.rense.com/general16/mete.htm) and other places online. This is a good source also: http://www.domainofman.com/forum/index.cgi?noframes;read=1229. I am dating the strike at around 2000 B.C.

time.[4] It would appear, then, that the Sumerian Empire was indeed destroyed by the impact of a meteorite, which apparently landed just north of the confluence of the Tigris and Euphrates rivers in what is now southeastern Iraq. This meteorite was believed to have been sent by the gods, specifically, Enlil, whom they believed had literally thrown it down to Earth like a heavenly spear. Enlil, interestingly, was the deity who preceded Marduk as the hero in the Sumerian version of *Enuma Elish*, wherein Marduk, like Erra, was accompanied by seven great "winds" that he used to defeat Tiamat (*Enuma Elish* IV:47).

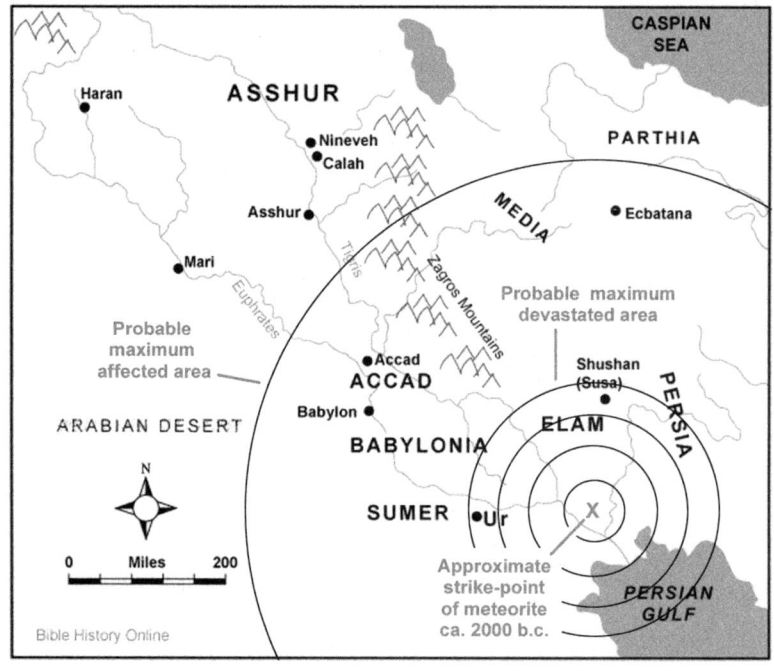

Scientists now believe that a large meteorite struck the Al'amarah region of southern Iraq, north of the confluence of the Tigris and Euphrates rivers sometime around 2000 b.c. The result would have been a "mighty wind" followed by fiery devastation and flooding all around the region, which fits the devastation described in the Sumerian accounts and The Book of Job perfectly. Base image courtesy Bible History Online.

The parallel with *Enuma Elish* is even closer, because of the seven winds that Marduk deployed against Tiamat, the wind that Marduk

---

[4] J.J.M. Roberts, "Erra — Scorched Earth", *Journal of Cuneiform Studies*, Vol. 24, 1971, 16.

used to defeat Tiamat was called "the evil wind". This is the same name as that given to the windstorm that destroyed Sumer in the Sumerian histories. The parallels to the events in Job 1 are also fairly obvious. Just as with the Sumerians, there was a "mighty wind" that swept across the land, killing many in their houses including, apparently, all of Job's children. Also like the Sumerians, Job's flocks and herds were either destroyed outright by the meteoric blast, or were pillaged by bands of marauders. Thus Job's homeland, the land of Uz, though typically thought to be somewhere in the region of Palestine, is probably much closer to southeastern Iraq, where the meteorite fell, or possibly southwestern Iran, eastern Saudi Arabia, or Kuwait.[5] Otherwise, the blast would have had little impact upon his children and his flocks, let alone totally destroy them, and the Chaldeans and Sabeans would have been too far away to carry out raids effectively.

Job 2: A Second Flyby of Planet X

Not satisfied with merely ruining Job's life, the Satan was bent upon destroying Job personally. So, when the assembly of "the sons of God" met again in heaven, Satan once again challenged the LORD that, without his protection, Job would surely curse God and die:

> [1] On another day the angels came to present themselves before the LORD, and Satan also came with them to present himself before him.
> [2] And the LORD said to Satan, "Where have you come from?" Satan answered the LORD, "From roaming through the Earth and going back and forth in it."
> [3] Then the LORD said to Satan, "Have you considered my servant Job? There is no one on Earth like him; he is blameless and upright, a man who fears God and shuns evil. And he still maintains his integrity, though you incited me against him to ruin him without any reason."
> [4] "Skin for skin!" Satan replied. "A man will give all he has for his own life.
> [5] But stretch out your hand and strike his flesh and bones, and he will surely curse you to your face."

---

[5] It is possible, either by scribal error or purposeful subterfuge, that the land of Uz that Job lived in was actually the land, or city, of Ur, the capitol city of the Sumerian Empire.

⁶ The LORD said to Satan, "Very well, then, he is in your hands; but you must spare his life."
⁷ So Satan went out from the presence of the LORD and afflicted Job with painful sores from the soles of his feet to the top of his head.
⁸ Then Job took a piece of broken pottery and scraped himself with it as he sat among the ashes.
⁹ His wife said to him, "Are you still holding on to your integrity? Curse God and die!"
¹⁰ He replied, "You are talking like a foolish woman. Shall we accept good from God, and not trouble?" In all this, Job did not sin in what he said.
¹¹ When Job's three friends, Eliphaz the Temanite, Bildad the Shuhite and Zophar the Naamathite, heard about all the troubles that had come upon him, they set out from their homes and met together by agreement to go and sympathize with him and comfort him.
¹² When they saw him from a distance, they could hardly recognize him; they began to weep aloud, and they tore their robes and sprinkled dust on their heads. (KJV)

The opening scene where these "sons of God" present themselves may actually describe a gathering of the planets Jupiter, Saturn, Uranus, Neptune and Pluto in the same general area of the night sky, an event which actually did occur in both 1955 and 1915 B.C. when many of the planets gathered within a 45 degree arc in the sky. This event would have been perceived as a sort of "congregation of the gods", the planets, and probably formed the basis of the "divine council" concept reflected in both Job 1–2

King Shamshi-Adad of Assyria, pointing to a congregation of the "gods", the planets, in the heavens. The ancients used the stars and planets not only as objects of worship, but as a means of dating key events. The event commemorated by this relief indicates that the moon and several of the planets were in close proximity in the sky, a rough conjunction that can be used to this day to date the relief precisely.

and *Enuma Elish* tablets II–III. This would have been an effective way of dating The Book of Job precisely, as there had been a similar gathering of the planets in the heavens in 1955 B.C., which would account for why The Book of Job begins with not one, but two assemblies of the "sons of God" in heaven — one some time in 1955 B.C., previous to the destruction, and one on or just after the destruction. So, in order to clarify which gathering of the planets marked the occasion of the meteoric impact that destroyed Sumer and ruined Job, it would have been necessary to have not one, but two assemblies of the sons of God, one in chapter 1 and one in chapter 2, to verify that it was the second assembly of the planets, not the first, that marked the occasion of the destruction. It is in this way that the events described in The Book of Job can be dated to some time around 1915 B.C.

But there is more to the story than simply a meteoric impact. Both the ancient Sumerian accounts and The Book of Job both make it clear that this judgment from heaven was purposely caused by the divine council in heaven in order to chastise mankind — either for disrespecting the gods, as was the case with the Sumerians, or to test that respect, as was the case with Job. This judgment was purposely caused by God in the Book of Job, and by Enlil in the Sumerian accounts. Similar accounts, such as Gilgamesh and The Erra Epic, state that the divine being who appeared in heaven and cast the "heavenly spear" that destroyed Sumer was accompanied by seven great warriors. This of course corresponds well with the description of Marduk in *Enuma Elish*, who attacked the primordial Earth with the help of seven "winds". Clearly, then, both the author of Job and of the various Mesopotamian accounts of the disaster that befell Sumer around 2000 B.C. wanted to communicate the idea that this disaster was no accident, that it occurred as the result of the appearance of some sort of heavenly body in the sky that caused a meteorite to be cast down to Earth. This heavenly body, which apparently had seven satellites, could only have been a planet, and that planet could only have been Planet X.

Job: The Hebrew Creation Epic

So we see that The Book of Job was not created merely to describe one man's misfortune. The implications of the situation extended far beyond one man, even if that one man was one of the richest men in the world. Clearly, there are much larger questions in play in the Book of Job. Not only is the scope of The Book of Job greater than Job's predicament, or even that of the once-mighty empire of Sumer. Indeed, the true scope of The Book of Job is about the creation of the entire world, of which Job's situation is merely a microcosm.

The Book of Job is in fact a true story, with real people, but it is designed in such a way so as to showcase Job's life as symbolic of the Creation of Earth. In this "Hebrew Creation Epic", Job plays the role of Kingu, the chief of Tiamat's helpers, and Job's eleven family members play the part of the eleven lesser helpers of Tiamat. The role of Tiamat, as we have seen, is played by Sumer itself, which was utterly destroyed by the "heavenly spear" or "evil wind" that God threw down from heaven. Job's 11 family members were either killed or scattered, just as the eleven lesser helpers were defeated and scattered by Marduk. Job, like Kingu, however, was not immediately killed by the divine conflict, but was instead preserved for another purpose.

There are a number of reasons to believe that The Book of Job is the Hebrew equivalent of the Babylonian Creation Epic, which we will review in the rest of this chapter. They are as follows:

- ✡ Job's name, אִיּוֹב, *'iyowv*, has the literal meaning of "hated one" (from the root אָיַב, *'ayav*, "enemy"). Thus, Job is, literally, the "hated enemy" of God. Since Job was clearly considered to be righteous, as is confirmed by Ezekiel 14:14, this makes little sense, unless there is some sort of hidden subtext, where Job was actually playing the role of God's enemy in the cosmic drama.

- ✡ Job, the "hated enemy," was the patriarch of a family with 11 members. God allowed Satan to attack Job's 11 family members with a "great wind," but only allowed him to subdue Job. Similarly, in *Enuma Elish*, Kingu is the head of an army of 11 "monster serpents". Marduk used his "winds" to defeat and imprison the 11, and then subdue Kingu. In the Book of Job, Job takes the place of Kingu, and his 11 family members take the place of the 11 "monster serpents". The fact that he had a total count of 11,000 head of cattle and animals of various types re-emphasizes the importance of the number 11 in his life, that he is the chief of an army of 11.

✧ Job, as a "cattle baron" whose great wealth was based upon cattle, would have been seen as a sort of "great bull" that led his herd. As we saw in previous chapters, Kingu, the chief helper of Tiamat, was turned into the Moon, which was thought of as the "great bull of heaven" by the ancients. For example, "the Sumerian Moon-god Sin was depicted in the form of bull horns, leading the 'cattle of the stars' in the sky as a bull does when leading cattle on Earth."[6] So, the fact that Job's great wealth was based upon cattle was likely included to emphasize the fact that he was thought of as a "great bull" that led many cattle. As such, he was set in The Book of Job as the earthly equivalent of the Moon, and of Kingu, the consort of Tiamat and the leader of her heavenly army.

✧ There are several direct and indirect references in The Book of Job relating Job, and men in general, with the Moon. These references tend to occur in the context of birth, and many are not recognizable without retranslating the passages in the context of the Planet X/Giant Impact Theory (Job 3; 10:7-10; 16:11-19 [compare Ps.89:37]; 18:13-18; 25:1-6. These references correspond with the description of the creation of man in *Enuma Elish*, where man is described as having been made from the blood of Kingu, whom we now know to be a personification of the Moon. Thus, man was made from the Moon, making Job as "The Man in the Moon" the dominant theme of the Book of Job.

✧ If Job represents Kingu/the Moon in the Hebrew Creation Epic, then Sumer, the land he lived in, surely represents Tiamat. This is supported by the fact that the wind that struck Sumer was referred to as the "evil wind" in the Sumerian histories, the same name that was later given to the "wind" that Marduk used to defeat Tiamat in *Enuma Elish* — the "evil wind" (IV:96-100). Most likely the Babylonians, who superseded the fallen Sumerian Empire as rulers of Mesopotamia, wanted to paint their predecessor as wicked in

---

[6] Abdel-Jalil 'Amr, "A Nude Female Statue with Astral Emblems", *Palestine Exploration Quarterly* 117 (July-Dec. 1985): 106.

order to legitimize their own succession as the ruler of the region formerly controlled by the Sumerians. So, in their updated version of *Enuma Elish*, the chief deity of the Sumerians, Enlil, was superseded by the Babylonian high god Marduk, and the Sumerians themselves were degraded to the role of the evil Tiamat, whom their god, Marduk, was portrayed as destroying with the "evil wind". So the destruction of Sumer was seen by the ancient Babylonians as a microcosm of the destruction of the dragon, and the rise of Babylon was seen as a microcosm of the creation of the Earth from the "dragon's" dead body, both of which were accomplished by the use of an "evil wind" from heaven.

✢ Finally, and perhaps most importantly to our present discussion, The Book of Job is filled throughout with divine conflict imagery. Throughout his laments, Job is constantly invoking Creation imagery, depicting the creation of Earth as the result of a conflict between God and a dragon. As such, clearly both the writer of Job and the ancient Babylonians saw the destruction of the Sumerian Empire as a watershed event in human history that had such import, that it triggered the decision to create Creation Epics to memorialize the event. And though both the Hebrew and Babylonian accounts of the Creation differed in their methods, both clearly recalled the creation of Earth as the result of a conflict between the supreme deity of their respective pantheons and a dragon.

✢ Most important of all, the decision to commemorate the destruction of Sumer with the rewriting of the ancient Creation Epic was triggered by the fact that the heavenly object that had created the Earth, Planet X, had returned.

JOB: THE MAN IN THE MOON
The return of Planet X in the heavens was the prime motivation for the writing of the Book of Job. The Book of Job was written so that this major historical milestone would be preserved for generations to come, so that they would understand the times when Planet X would return and once again judge mankind.

Job: The Hebrew Creation Epic

But how to go about doing it without using the same format of the Babylonians, who deified the Sun, Moon and planets, and were thus able to more easily set them into a dramatic storyline? Since Hebrew theology forbade the use or even mention of deities other than the LORD God in the text, and the use of drama was either unknown or unused by the Hebrews, another method had to be developed.

The Moon's surface is pockmarked with massive craters and maria, or "seas" of molten lava that have long since cooled to form the dark patches that make up the "[Man in the Moon](#)" design of popular mythology. These craters and maria were created early in the Moon's history as it gathered up much of the loose material still floating in space from the Giant Impact via gravitational attraction. Job frequently relates himself to the Moon, leading to the conclusion that he is playing the role of the defeated Moon in a Hebrew version of the ancient creation epic.

Instead, the story of a man named Job, who lived at the time of the Tower of Babel ("Jobab", Genesis 10:29), was taken and used as the basis of a storyline in which to incorporate all of the oral traditions regarding the Creation into one cohesive storyline. Sumer, which controlled the city of Babylon at that time and thus also the Tower, was removed from The Book of Job altogether, mentioned only briefly in the text of Genesis 11:2 as "Shinar" שִׁנְעָר *shin'ar*, literally, עִיר + שֵׁן *shain*, "tooth" + *'iyr* "city" = "city of the tooth", possibly referring to the tower, which may have been a tall, white structure similar in appearance to a canine tooth, or possibly incorporated an object that was similar in appearance. Thus, Ur of the Chaldees may have been remembered as Shin-Ur, or "City of the White Tower"[7]

---

[7] Though the terms "Sumer" or "Shinar" do not appear in the English translation of Job, the capitol city of Ur may have been alluded to in the Hebrew text. When Satan said "skin for skin" the word for skin is עוֹר *'owr*, "skin", which is very similar to the word for city, עִיר *'iyr*, "city". This generic Hebrew word for city was probably derived from the name of the greatest city of the land of their origin, Ur, capitol of the land of Sumer. This is the same "Ur of the Chaldees" from which Abram was called out (Genesis 11:28, 31). Thus "Ur" literally means "The City", sort of an ancient version of Washington D.C. or New York City, i.e., the greatest city of the ancient world. The use of the term *'owr* by the Satan may have been

This tower, and Sumer itself, had been destroyed by the meteorite that struck southern Iraq, forcing Job to start afresh.

Drawing upon the same creation source material as the Babylonians, the author of Job decided to make Job the "enemy" of God, playing the same role that Kingu played in the Babylonian version of the creation story. His 11 family members were then set to play the role of the 11 "monster serpents", and he was also given a total of 11,000 cattle to make his association with the number 11 complete. Thus Job was set in the story as the enemy of God, the chief of the 11 who rebelled against God, the leader of the army of the dragon. In one sense this was a fitting role, as he was the greatest of the men of the east, i.e., Sumer, and was therefore one of the preeminent men of that land. Moreover, as he had made his wealth in cattle, Job was set as the earthly counterpart of the Moon, the great Behemoth or "bull of heaven" that was killed by God, its dead body turned into the Moon. Thus Job, the "child of dust and ashes", was set to play the role in the cosmic drama of the dust-covered Moon as the enemy of God. And as all men, according to the Babylonian Creation Epic, were made from the blood of Kingu, i.e., made from that part of the Moon that fell back to Earth after the Giant Impact, Job was quite literally, "the man in the Moon".

The Birth of the Moon and the Birth of Job

Sitting in a pile of ashes, and covered in dust, ashes and running sores from head to toe, Job looked very much like the newly born Moon which, early in its formation, had its entire face pockmarked with *maria*, or "seas" that were once made of molten lava. Just as Job's sores "oozed", so too did these *maria* once ooze with lava, created by huge asteroids impacting into its surface, creating what appeared to be "oozing sores". These asteroids are probably represented in the story by the potsherd that Job used to scrape the sores, representing the asteroids that orbited Earth for a long time before being assimilated with the Moon, or crashing back down to Earth. Finally, the emphasis on Job sitting on a pile of ashes and also covered with ashes — as it was the custom to throw dust and ashes on one's head when calamity strikes — ably describes the Moon, the entire surface of which is covered in a layer of fine dust.

---

intended, at least in part to say, "take Job out of the safety of the city of Ur (*'owr 'iyr*, literally, "protection of the city"), and then we'll see how loyal he remains".

Job: The Hebrew Creation Epic

It is in this context that the rest of The Book of Job is set, with Job, playing the role of the Moon, discussing the Creation of the heavens, the Earth, and of course, the birth of the Moon:

❖ Job 3:1-10:
¹After this opened Job his mouth, and cursed his day.
²And Job spake, and said,
³Let the day perish wherein I was born, and the night in which it was said, There is a man child conceived.
⁴Let that day be darkness; let not God regard it from above, neither let the light shine upon it.
⁵Let darkness and the shadow of death stain it; let a cloud dwell upon it; let the blackness of the day terrify it.
⁶As for that night, let darkness seize upon it; let it not be joined unto the days of the year, let it not come into the number of the months.
⁷Lo, let that night be solitary, let no joyful voice come therein.
⁸Let them curse it that curse the day, who are ready to raise up [Leviathan].
⁹Let the stars of the twilight thereof be dark; let it look for light, but have none; neither let it see the dawning of the day:
¹⁰Because it shut not up the doors of my mother's womb, nor hid sorrow from mine eyes. (KJV)

In the very next chapter, Job then begins, as if he understands his role as the Moon in this unfolding drama, to curse the very day that he was born. By itself this would be unspectacular, but his use of the name of the dragon Leviathan in verse 8 in the Hebrew text clearly sets this verse in the context of the Creation. The birth imagery, along with the mention of Leviathan, who "gave birth" to the Moon in order to defend herself against God, makes it clear that The Book of Job is telling essentially the same story as *Enuma Elish*. But The Book of Job actually reaches a bit deeper here, as it describes the condition of the Earth when the Moon was born as a day of darkness, where the light is not shining upon the Earth. Neither the stars at night, nor even the Sun during the day, could be seen from Earth's surface due to the massive cloud of dust and ashes that was thrown up into the atmosphere due to the Giant Impact.

The Moon and the Birth of Man

✝ Job 25:1-6:
¹Then answered Bildad the Shuhite, and said,
²Dominion and fear are with him, he maketh peace in his high places.
³Is there any number of his armies? and upon whom doth not his light arise?
⁴How then can man be justified with God? or how can he be clean that is born of a woman?
⁵Behold even to the Moon, and it shineth not; yea, the stars are not pure in his sight.
⁶How much less man, that is a worm? and the son of man, which is a worm?

✝ Job 15:7-8, 14-16:
⁷ Art thou the first man that was born? or wast thou made before the hills?
⁸ Hast thou heard the secret of God? and dost thou restrain wisdom to thyself?
¹⁴ What is man, that he should be clean? and he which is born of a woman, that he should be righteous?

Having established the birth of Job as being equivalent to the birth of the Moon, the birth of mankind in general is then also associated with the Moon. Sandwiched in between two references to the birth of mankind in Job 25, verses 4 and 6, is a reference to the Moon (25:5). Indirectly, subtly, the text of The Book of Job insinuates the information that *Enuma Elish* states clearly, as this text means to equate the birth of the Moon with the birth of man, the dust of which man was created from. In *Enuma Elish*, man is said to have been created from the blood of Kingu, (VI:31-33), who was saved and sacrificed specifically for that purpose. From this information, we may possibly glean a scientific fact that the "dust of the Earth", perhaps the entire continent of Pangaea, was made of that part of Earth's mantle that was thrown into space by the Giant Impact, but separated from the mass that would become the Moon and fell back to Earth. And it was from that part of the Moon, the part that fell to Earth, from which man was made. Thus man was not made "before the hills", he was made from them.

… *Job: The Hebrew Creation Epic*

The Moon Formed from Molten Materials and Its Orbit Set

✦ Job 10:8-10, 18-22:
⁸ Thine hands have made me and fashioned me together round about; yet thou dost destroy me.
⁹ Remember, I beseech thee, that thou hast made me as the clay; and wilt thou bring me into dust again?
¹⁰ Hast thou not poured me out as milk, and curdled me like cheese?
¹⁸ Wherefore then hast thou brought me forth out of the womb? Oh that I had given up the ghost, and no eye had seen me!
¹⁹ I should have been as though I had not been; I should have been carried from the womb to the grave.
²⁰ Are not my days few? cease then, and let me alone, that I may take comfort a little,
²¹ Before I go whence I shall not return, even to the land of darkness and the shadow of death;
²² A land of darkness, as darkness itself; and of the shadow of death, without any order, and where the light is as darkness.
(KJV)

Job 10 focuses on that aspect of the Moon's creation that has to do with its initial formation. The setting of the Moon's rotation period begins first in verse 8, where the verse literally says, וַיַּעֲשׂוּנִי יַחַד סָבִיב *va-ya'soowniy yaḥad saviyv*, "And he set me to move in a circular path", or "and he set me into a circular orbit", the word *saviyv* literally meaning "motion in a circle" or, more properly, orbit.⁸ Applied to the Moon, then, this means that Job was describing that the first thing that God did with the Moon after it had been "born" from the Earth as the result of the Giant Impact (the birth metaphor again appearing here in verses 18-19), was that He set it in a new orbit around Earth.

Verses 9 and 10 also contain some interesting surprises. Job says, כִּי־כַחֹמֶר עֲשִׂיתָנִי *kiy-kaḥomer 'ashiyta-niy*, literally, "like a boiling pot of clay you made me", which ably describes the initial molten mass of boiling magma from Earth's mantle that was thrown up into space. This makes also makes verse 10 make much more sense, which

---

⁸ Gesenius, W., & Tregelles, S. P. (2003). *Gesenius' Hebrew and Chaldee Lexicon to the Old Testament Scriptures* (577). Bellingham, WA: Logos Research Systems, Inc.

describes Job/The Moon as being initially poured out like milk, which later hardened into cheese.⁹ Next, Job says וְאֶל־עָפָר תְּשִׁיבֵנִי *ve-'el-'aphar te-shiyvai-niy*, literally, "then to dust you turned me". This of course is a perfect description of how the lunar mass, at first molten, then cooled into the dry, dusty sphere we know today.¹⁰

The Newly-Formed Moon Massively Impacted by Asteroids

✝ Job 16:12-16, 18-19:
¹²I was at ease, but he hath broken me asunder: he hath also taken me by my neck, and shaken me to pieces, and set me up for his mark.
¹³ His archers compass me round about, he cleaveth my reins asunder, and doth not spare; he poureth out my gall upon the ground.
¹⁴ He breaketh me with breach upon breach, he runneth upon me like a giant.
¹⁵ I have sewed sackcloth upon my skin, and defiled my horn in the dust.
¹⁶ My face is foul with weeping, and on my eyelids is the shadow of death;
¹⁸ O Earth, cover not thou my blood, and let my cry have no place.
¹⁹Also now, behold, my witness is in heaven, and my record is on high. (KJV)

It is an established fact that the Moon was massively impacted by numerous asteroids sometime early in its formative period. What is not so well known is that that event has been clearly described here in Job 16 for literally thousands of years. Some time after Job/Moon had cooled and accreted into a solid form and settled into its orbit, God's "archers" then pierced Job and poured out his blood and bodily fluids onto the ground, much like the blood of Kingu was poured onto Earth, from which man was made. The same occurred after the Giant Impact, when numerous asteroids left in orbit from the same impact that created the Moon crashed into the

---

⁹ This ancient Hebrew hidden wisdom in Job may have been the basis of the legend of the moon being made of cheese.

¹⁰ Though it would require some more extensive translation, I am fairly certain that verses 19-22 have to do with the rising and the setting of the moon, where the "land of darkness" refers to those periods where the Moon is totally invible, being on the other side of the Earth from the observer.

Job: The Hebrew Creation Epic

Moon's surface, creating the massive, dark *maria*, literally "seas" of lava, that later cooled to form the dark patches on the Moon's "face" that we see today. The term יִפְרְצֵנִי פֶרֶץ עַל־פְּנֵי־פָרֶץ *yiperetsai-niy perets 'al-penay-parets*, "he breaks me with break upon the face of a break", or "he breaks me with break upon break", utilizes the word פֶּרֶץ *parats* "break" three times in the same phrase, indicating an unusually intense, repeated action of, in this case, causing great gashes in the surface of the moon. This once again could only have been caused by wave after wave of massive asteroids impacting the Moon's face again and again, which we know today is exactly what happened. These massive open wounds on the face of the Moon were symbolized in the Book of Job as eruptions of the "sores" on the face of Job.

The next verses add additional detail to what happened to the Moon as a result of the impact of massive amounts of asteroids. In verse 15, Job describes sewing "sackcloth" upon his skin, which is a dark, rough fabric, and defiling his "horn" in the dust. This must refer to the dark clouds of dust that were thrown up by the asteroidal impacts with the Moon, the "horn" referring to the horn of the crescent moon itself, the great "bull" of heaven. The sackcloth could also refer to the dark *maria* that were left over as a result of the impacts.

Verse 16 adds some additional details regarding what happened as a result of the Moon's collision with numerous asteroids. The symbolism in Job describes the Moon's "face" as being covered with "tears," which probably refers to lava boiling out of the impact holes. The word here for "foul," חֲמַרְמְרָה *hamaremerah* is an unusual root that means "to boil up" or "become reddened" referring to his face, meaning the face of the Moon was becoming red and swollen with lava flows. Basically what Job is saying is that the Moon turned red as blood when it was hit by asteroids, due to the "boiling up" of the red-hot lava released by the impacts. The reference to Job's eyelids being covered in darkness refers to the lunar dust thrown up by the impacts, causing the Moon to become darkened. This is because the word for eyelids, עַפְעַפָּי *'aph'apay,* can also mean "sunrise," or "dawn," and is usually used to indicate the sunrise. Thus, since the Moon reflects sunlight, covering the "dawn" of the Moon will result in its darkness.

Finally, in verse 19 Job states that his "record", i.e., something that can corroborate his story, is up in the sky, looking down at them. The word for "record" here is שָׂהֵד *sahad*, "eyewitness", literally, something that looks like an eye and is in the sky, which is a good description of the Moon. And though Job does not explicitly state that he is referring to the Moon, *sahad* is an interesting choice of words, as the very next word in Gesenius' Hebrew lexicon is the very similar word שָׂהַר *sahar*, "to be round", which can also be translated as "The Moon".

JOB'S COMPANIONS, THE COMETS

In the previous section we saw how Job plays the role of the Moon in the Hebrew Creation Epic. But there are other players in the cosmic drama, including Job's family of 11, which we have seen, represent the 11 "monster serpents", or comets, that were created at the same time as the Moon. Clear allusion to the creation of the comets appear in a few places in Job, the most prominent being chapters 6, 9, and 27.

The Comets and Their Orbits

☥ Job 6:14-18:
> [14] To him that is afflicted pity should be shewed from his friend; but he forsaketh the fear of the Almighty.
> [15] My brethren have dealt deceitfully as a brook, and as the stream of brooks they pass away;
> [16] Which are blackish by reason of the ice, and wherein the snow is hid:
> [17] What time they wax warm, they vanish: when it is hot, they are consumed out of their place.
> [18] The paths of their way are turned aside; they go to nothing, and perish. (KJV)

One of the ways that one can determine whether a passage in Job contains cryptically concealed information regarding the Creation is when the passage is translated in a way that seems to be contradictory, confusing, or even nonsensical. This often happened in Job because many Creation passages contain information that can only be fully understood in the context of the divine conflict Creation scenario. And since the translators lacked an awareness of the information regarding what really happened at the Creation, they instead translated according to their own limited understanding, creating translations that are somewhat lacking. Job 6:14-18 is a classic example of one of these.

לָמַס   *lamas* - "To melt away"
מֵרֵעֵהוּ   *mairai'aihoow* – "from his companions, allies"
חָסֶד   *ḥased* - "reproach"
וְיִרְאַת   *ve-yire'at* - "and terror"
שַׁדַּי   *shaday* - "God Almighty"
יַעֲזוֹב   *ya'azowv* - "He forsakes [them]"

Verse 14, which makes little sense in the KJV, is actually describing the creation of the comets. First we start with *lamas*, which literally means "to melt away", like ice. The identity of these "melting ones" is then given as "his friends", apparently someone who is a friend or companion to them one of their group. These "melting friends" are apparently the enemies of God whom He casts aside. This is a good description of the comets, which were "cast aside" by God and set in eternal orbits around the Sun, eternally "melting away" every time they approach the heat of the sun. In sum, God is described in this verse as someone who aggressively defeated and terrorized the comets, leaving them to orbit around the Sun forever. Thus this verse could be more accurately translated, "His allies melt away in terror from God Almighty, who banished them".

הַקֹּדְרִים   *ha-qoderiym* - "The black ones"
מִנִּי־קָרַח   *miniy-qaraḥ* - "from ice"
עָלֵימוֹ   *'alaymow* - "upon them"
יִתְעַלֶּם־שָׁלֶג   *yit'alem-shaleg* - "snow is hidden"

Verse 16 then goes into more detail into Job's "melting friends", the verse essentially giving a perfect description of the comets, which are essentially "dirty snowballs" or, perhaps more accurately, "snowy dirtballs", because they are essentially dry, rocky bodies with patches of ice just under their coal-black crusts. And contrary to the belief that comets are bright bodies, the nuclei of comets, when their tails have not been ignited by the solar wind, are typically very dark in color to the point of being almost black, actually being the darkest objects in the solar system, literally darker than coal.[11] Thus the description in verse 16 here of Job's "friends" as being black in color, with ice and snow hidden upon them – i.e., under the blackened crusts, is actually a very accurate description of the comets. This now makes much more sense with verse 14, where Job's friends, the enemies of God, are seen as melted away. Moreover, verse 15, which describes Job's friends as being like deceitful stream of water, must mean that there is water hidden under their surfaces, in the form of ice. Thus though they deceptively look dry, in actuality they have large sources of water ice under the surface, which is once again a scientifically accurate description of the comets.

And it gets even better. Verse 17 describes the comets as "vanishing" when they get warmer, which is an excellent description of the process of sublimation that takes place when the solar wind hits patches of exposed ice on the surface of a comet. When this happens, ice is literally "consumed" away, being converted almost immediately from water ice to water vapor, which then streams behind the comet, forming the comet's tail.

יְלָפְתוּ   *yilaphet-ow* - "They are bent"
אָרְחוֹת   *'arehowt* - "the paths"
דַּרְכָּם   *darkam* - "of their ways"
יַעֲלוּ   *ya'aloow* - "they go up"
בַתֹּהוּ   *va-tohoow* - "to the void, to deep space"
וְיֹאבֵדוּ   *ve-yo'vaid-oow* - "they wander"

Finally, after verses 14-17 describe the origin and composition of the comets, verse 18 describes their orbits. The original Hebrew says, literally that "The paths of their ways are bent". In other words, their ways are not in a straight line, but in a circle. Any path that is bent in a certain direction, unless a turn in made in the opposite direction, will eventually result in a circular path, so "orbit" is clearly intended here.

---

[11] The typical albeido, or percentage of light reflected from the surface of a comet whose "tail" has not been triggered by the solar wind, is only .04, or only about 4%. Earth, by comparison, has an albeido of 0.31, or 31%. http://en.wikipedia.org/wiki/Comet_nucleus#Albedo. Comets are actually the darkest bodies in the solar system when their tails have not been kindled, literally blacker than coal, their surfaces covered in a substance similar in appearance to ink toner. http://www.space.com/scienceastronomy/solarsystem/borrelly_dark_011129.html

The location of these orbits are also accurately described as "going up to the void" or to deep space, outside of our solar system, where they do not perish, but "wander" until the Sun's relentless gravitational pull brings them back into our solar system again. The word used here to describe their wandering, *yo'vaid*, is particularly relevant, because our modern word "planet" comes from the Greek word πλανήτης *planetes,* which literally means, "wanderers".

All together, verses 14-18 should read thusly: "My allies, the comets, melted away at God's reproach. They had deceitfully hidden water under their blackened crusts in the form of ice, but when they approach the sun, the ice is consumed away. Their orbits then take them away from the sun, into deep space, where they wander until they return again." Interestingly, Job refers to the comets as "my allies", indicating that they and Job formed a group that was somehow in opposition to God. Just as Kingu led the army of "monster serpents" in *Enuma Elish*, so too did Job, the Moon, lead the "army" of comets that were created at the same time as the Moon, from the same Giant Impact.

The Comets Created from Earth's Mantle

Whereas Job 6 describes the composition and orbit of the comets, Job 28 discusses their creation. As we saw in the analysis of Job 6 above, the comets are actually "snowy dirtballs", essentially the same as a typical asteroid in composition, except for two major differences: 1) they are covered in a thick, black, tarlike organic substance which is literally blacker than coal, and 2) underneath that jet-black crust are patches of water ice which, when exposed to the solar wind, sublimate into clouds of water vapor that reflect the sunlight, creating the glorious comet tail.[12] This information will help us better understand the enigmatic phraseology used in Job 28 used to describe the creation of the comets:

✣ Job 28:1-5:
¹ Surely there is a vein for the silver, and a place for gold where they fine it.
² Iron is taken out of the earth, and brass is molten out of the stone.

---

[12] Indeed, the modern word "comet" comes from the Greek word *kometes*, "long hair", referring to the comet's tail which, to the Greeks, looked like long, flowing hair.

³ He setteth an end to darkness, and searcheth out all perfection: the stones of darkness, and the shadow of death.
⁴ The flood breaketh out from the inhabitant; even the waters forgotten of the foot: they are dried up, they are gone away from men.
⁵ As for the earth, out of it cometh bread: and under it is turned up as it were fire.

Job 28 begins, speaking about how precious things are dug out of the Earth, but then goes on to talk about seemingly unrelated things, such as "the stones of darkness" and "the shadow of death". On the face of it, it would appear that these things are unrelated, but they are quite closely related, as we shall see.

As we saw in Chapter III, Earth was impacted by an object approximately the size of Mars sometime in its ancient past. This impactor penetrated all the way to Earth's core, where it remains to this day, in the process ejecting a large part of Earth's mantle into space, where it cooled and solidified into the Moon. However, much of this material was blown clear of Earth's gravity altogether, forming the asteroid belt and the comets. So, not only the Moon, but also the asteroids and the comets, originated from within Earth's mantle.

This is why the setting for the creation of the comets in Job 28 is set amidst descriptions of places deep within Earth itself, literally, of things that have been dug out of Earth, such as silver, gold, iron and brass. This implies that these "stones of darkness" from which water "breaks out" were also dug out from beneath the earth. But what are these "stones of darkness", upon whom is "the shadow of death"? Let us look at them in more detail:

קֵץ	qaits - "the end, the edge (of space)"
שָׂם	sam - "put, placed, set"
לַחֹשֶׁךְ	la-ḥoshek - "to darkness"
וּלְכָל־תַּכְלִית	oow-lehal-tahliyt - "and to the entire end"
הוּא	hoow' - "he"
חוֹקֵר	hoowqair - "he searches, he is a secret"
אֶבֶן	'even - "stone"
אֹפֶל	'ophel - "darkness"
וְצַלְמָוֶת	ve-tsalmavet - "and the shadow of death"

Whereas verses 1-2 speak about things that come from within the Earth, verse 3 is speaking more about things that are in heavens, specifically, those things that were taken out of the Earth, and placed in the heavens, where they orbited as far as the outer edge of our solar system, and into the darkness beyond. These "secret stones" that are hidden by a thick, black covering that makes them invisible to the naked eye until they come close to the sun could only be the comets. Covered by a thick, dark crust that conceals them, they travel around the Sun like thieves in the night until they return to their place of origin.

פָּרַץ	*parats* - "it breaks forth"
נַחַל	*nahal* - "streams"
מֵעִם־גָּר	*mai'im-gar* - "from all of the wandering"
הַנִּשְׁכָּחִים	*ha-nishkahiym* - "wanderers"
מִנִּי־רָגֶל	*miniy-ragel* - "from the foot"
דַּלּוּ	*daloow* - "they weaken, they dim"
מֵאֱנוֹשׁ	*mai'enowsh* - "from mankind"
נָעוּ	*na'oow* - "they move to and fro, wander back and forth"

Verse 4 adds additional meaning to these mysterious "stones of darkness" that God dug out of the Earth in verse 3. Verse 4 describes them as "wanderers" from whom streams of water "break forth." These wanderers are described as those who were "left behind from the foot," recalling the helpers of Tiamat whom Marduk had first "tied to his foot" (V:74) and then later "left behind" with his father Ea at the gate of Apsu, where they would serve as permanent monuments to his victory over Tiamat (V:75-76). This of course parallels the divine conflict theory perfectly, even describing in scientific detail how water "breaks forth" from the inside of the "wanderers," the comets, which we now know is due to the solar wind heating and sublimating the frozen water just beneath their surfaces, causing their tails to form. It is these "wanderers" which still wander "back and forth" toward and away from mankind's view, in eternal orbits around the Sun, brightening as they approach, ,and dimming as they recede.

Verse 5 then strongly implies that the comets came from beneath Earth's surface, saying that, though Earth's surface brings forth bread, deep beneath the surface burns very hot fire in the form of molten magma. The word translated in the KJV as "turned up" is הָפַךְ *haphak*, which literally means, "to flip a cake". So these "stones of darkness" were created from Earth's fiery interior when much of Earth's surface was temporarily removed, flipped like a pancake as a result of the Giant Impact, releasing them into space where they wander to this day.

ECHOES OF THE DIVINE CONFLICT IN JOB

Job talks not only about the Moon and the comets, his brethren, as part of his dialogues, but also about the process of the Creation in its totality. It is these Creation passages that are most similar to *Enuma Elish*, describing God's conflict with the dragon and her helpers, and the resultant creation of heaven and Earth. They are also the most scientific, citing numerous events in the Creation process including not only the creation of the moon and comets, but also the moving of Earth to a new orbit, the creation of the asteroid belt, and more.

Job Recalls the Divine Conflict at the Creation

✟ Job 9:1-9, 13, 17:
¹ Then Job answered and said,
² I know it is so of a truth: but how should man be just with God?
³ If he will contend with him, he cannot answer him one of a thousand.
⁴ He is wise in heart, and mighty in strength: who hath hardened himself against him, and hath prospered?
⁵ Which removeth the mountains, and they know not: which overturneth them in his anger.
⁶ Which shaketh the Earth out of her place, and the pillars thereof tremble.
⁷ Which commandeth the Sun, and it riseth not; and sealeth up the stars.
⁸ Which alone spreadeth out the heavens, and treadeth upon the waves of the sea.

⁹ Which maketh Arcturus, Orion, and Pleiades, and the chambers of the south.
¹³ If God will not withdraw his anger, the proud helpers do stoop under him.
¹⁷ For he breaketh me with a tempest, and multiplieth my wounds without cause. (KJV)

According to Job, during the process of the Creation, Earth was "shaken from its place," i.e., moved to a different orbit, and its "pillars trembled," i.e., its axial tilt was altered. Next, as was also recorded in Genesis 1, Earth was covered by a thick, black cloud of dust as a result of the Giant Impact, dust which may have kept out the light of the Sun, Moon, and stars for a thousand years or more. Ever since that conflict, Planet X's elliptical orbit has regularly returned it to the "heavens," the asteroid belt, which Planet X had stretched out into a ring around the Sun. These asteroids were made of both rock and water, thus the metaphor of Planet X "treading on," or orbiting through, "the waves of the sea", which Genesis 1 refers to as 'the waters above". The tilting of Earth's axis to an angle of 23.5° also changed the view of the starry heavens from the perspective of Earth, so that the constellations of the zodiac now appeared to rise and set farther south than they would have previously — thus the term, "the constellations of the south".¹³

Next, verse 13 discusses the "proud helpers" of the dragon which, as we saw in previous chapters and in our analysis of Job 6 and 28, were actually the comets. These comets, like the asteroids, were carved out of Earth's mantle by the Giant Impact. However, these asteroids were particularly large and did not stay in the main belt area, instead taking on long, elliptical orbits that took them in and out of the solar system. Moreover, their composition included a substantial amount of water, so they stood out from the rest of the asteroids by their substantial size, erratic orbits, and glorious comas. Not surprisingly, a few verses later, Job describes himself as being part of the cosmic Creation drama as well, saying that God had broken him with a mighty "tempest", or wind, and continued to beat him until he was totally subdued. Clearly this is a reference to the Moon, which was carved out by a great "wind", or satellite of Planet X, and then later struck with many

---

¹³ The constellation named כִּימָה *kiymah*, may actually be akin to the Greek word *koma*, "hair", which is the root of our modern word "comet".

additional wounds given to it, as we have seen, by multiple asteroid strikes. All together, we have in Job 9 a complete overview of the Creation process, as seen from the perspective of the Divine Conflict Creation scenario.

Planet X Divides Earth, Forms the Asteroid Belt

Another "general overview" Creation passage can be found in Job 26 which, like Job 9, puts a number of Creation events together into a single, contiguous narrative that follows the events of the Creation, based upon the Planet X/Giant Impact Theory, in near-perfect order:

✞ Job 26:6-14:
> ⁶ Hell is naked before him, and destruction hath no covering.
> ⁷ He stretcheth out the north over the empty place, and hangeth the Earth upon nothing.
> ⁸ He bindeth up the waters in his thick clouds; and the cloud is not rent under them.
> ⁹ He holdeth back the face of his throne, and spreadeth his cloud upon it.
> ¹⁰ He hath compassed the waters with bounds, until the day and night come to an end.
> ¹¹ The pillars of heaven tremble and are astonished at his reproof.
> ¹² He divideth the sea with his power, and by his understanding he smiteth through the proud [Rahab].
> ¹³ By his spirit he hath garnished the heavens; his hand hath formed the crooked serpent.
> ¹⁴ Lo, these are parts of his ways: but how little a portion is heard of him? but the thunder of his power who can understand? (KJV)

Like Isaiah and the Psalms, Job also describes the creation of Earth in the context of a battle between God and a dragon, in this case named "Rahab", mistranslated in the KJV simply as "the proud". The Creation-oriented part of the narrative in Job 26 begins in verse 6 with a description of "hell" being "naked", i.e., without a covering, completely open to the air, for all to see. Normally this would not be seen as a Creation passage *per se*, except in the context of the Planet X/Giant Impact theory, where we now understand that much of Earth's crust and mantle was ripped away by the Giant Impact, sending a large amount of the crust and mantle into space and leaving a gaping wound on Earth's surface that would have allowed an observer to, for a time, see right to Earth's molten core. Thus, hell was

Job: The Hebrew Creation Epic

"naked" and destruction (literally, "Abaddon", the ruler of hell) were both clearly visible from space.

Verse 7, as we saw in our analysis in Chapter I, contains some very interesting Creation information. In our analysis in Chapter I of the various appearances of mythological creatures in relation to the Creation material in the Bible, specifically the dragon Leviathan and her companion, the earth monster Behemoth, we concluded that these two mythological creatures symbolically represented the Earth and Moon, respectively. As such, we were able to determine that Job 26:7 actually refers to the creation of the Moon. This is due to the fact that the word *Tsaphon*, translated here as "north", has its linguistic roots as a mythological earth-beast named "Typhon" that is similar in aspect to Behemoth. The word *Eretz*, translated here as "Earth", also has its linguistic roots in a Canaanite earth monster known as *'Arts* that is also very similar to Behemoth. In all of the creation stories, this primordial "earth monster" was "born" out of the Earth, just as Tiamat gave birth to Kingu in the Babylonian version of the old creation epic.

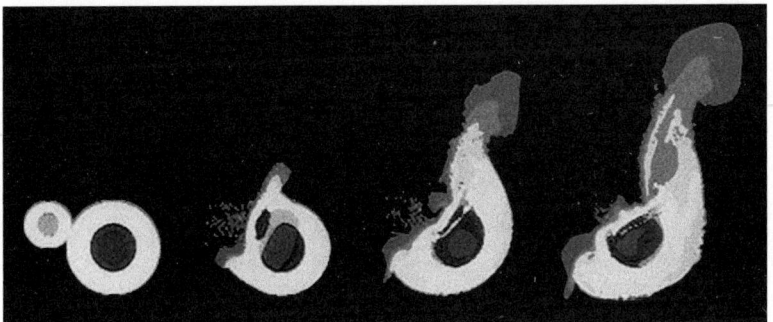

Figure 6.1: The classic Cray supercomputer model showing what would happen if an impactor slightly larger than the size of Mars struck Earth. As a result of the impact, the Moon is not ejected, but "stretched" out of Earth's mantle, just as Job described.

In verse 7, this earth monster is described as being "stretched out" from Earth and hung in space over Earth's surface, where it hung in a gravitational balance, which is of course a perfect description of the Moon. Verse 9 appears to support the idea that the Moon is being spoken of here, as it literally says, מְאַחֵז פְּנֵי־כִסֵּה *me-a'ḥaiz penay-kisaih*, "To seize the face of the Moon", as *kisaih* can mean either "throne" or "Moon", and Moon clearly makes more sense here. God is then described as "spreading His cloud" over the face of the Moon, a cloud that was no doubt filled with asteroids and other debris from the Giant Impact, resulting in the creation of huge *maria*, or dark spots, on the Moon's face.

Generally speaking, the "clouds" and "waters" in verses 8-10 refer to the clouds of dust, rocks and water that were thrown clear of Earth's gravity to form the asteroid belt. Verses 9-10, however, appear to primarily describe Planet X itself. Verse 9 may describe how God "hides" Planet X behind a cloud of deep darkness, just like the comets are covered with dark, black organic materials. This dark black substance was probably left on the comets, and ostensibly Planet X, as a result of flying through the dust and debris left hanging in space from the Giant Impact. Verse 10 may actually be a description of the orbit of Planet X, which has its perihelion in the "waters above" of the asteroid belt, and its aphelion well outside our solar system. Verse 10 describes it as the place "where day and night come to an end", i.e., the very edge of the sun's area of influence. This area is known to scientists today as the "heliopause", where the solar wind is in balance with radiation emitted from other objects in our galaxy.[14] Thus, Planet X's aphelion is well beyond the orbit of Neptune. The "pillars of heaven" in verse 11 of course refer to Earth's axis which, when Earth was struck and moved to a new orbit closer to the Sun, were dramatically affected, just as described in Job 9:6, above.

Verses 12 and 13 then return to a description of the defeat of the dragon and the creation of heaven and Earth. Verse 12 actually uses the name "Rahab", incorrectly translated as "the proud" in the KJV. Translating this word as a personal name makes much more sense in parallel with verse 13, which mentions the "crooked serpent", variously named Tiamat, Leviathan, Rahab, or simply "the dragon" throughout the Old Testament.[15] These Creation passages, along with the many other references to be found throughout Job, make it clear that though Job is poetic in format, it is clearly a Creation story in content.

---

[14] Though the exact location of the heliopause is yet unknown, it has been confirmed as being well beyond Neptune. http://en.wikipedia.org/wiki/Heliopause#Heliopause

[15] The Hebrew word חֹלְלָה *ḥolalah* here is interesting. It is taken from the root חָלַל *halal*, which can mean to pierce with a weapon, but has its roots in the sense of penetrating sexually. The symbolism, that we have seen in other Old Testament Creation passages, is that God is "impregnating" the Earth, which then gives birth to the Moon.

✤ Job 37:15-18:
> ¹⁵ Do you know how God controls the clouds and makes his lightning flash?
> ¹⁶ Do you know how the clouds hang poised, those wonders of him who is perfect in knowledge?
> ¹⁷ You who swelter in your clothes when the land lies hushed under the south wind,
> ¹⁸ can you join him in spreading out the skies, hard as a mirror of cast bronze?

Job 37 adds a familiar description of the heavens as being a place that has been beaten and stretched out, using terminology similar to that used in Proverbs 8:22-29 which, as we saw, described the "second heaven" as being much like what is modernly called the "asteroid belt". And here in Job 37, there are two key words that support the argument that the heaven/firmament described in the Bible is what we now call the asteroid belt. The first is תַּרְקִיעַ, *ta-reqiya'* (which is the Hebrew word for "firmament," *raqiya'*, used as a verb), literally, "Can you hammer (or 'spread') out?" The second important word here, translated erroneously as "skies," is the word לִשְׁחָקִים, *li-sheḥaqiym*, literally, "to clouds of dust." The usual use of *sheḥaqiym* is to simply translate it as "skies." This is inaccurate, however, because the literal definition is "clouds of dust." Together, they form the literal translation of, "can you join him in hammering (the firmament) into clouds of dust," or, "can you join him in spreading out the clouds of dust." Verse 18b is even more interesting, as it too is rather badly translated. The word translated "hard" is actually חֲזָקִים, *hazaqim*, literally, "the mighty ones," as if Job were speaking of some sort of ancient heroes or mythical deities, reminiscent of *Enuma Elish* and Marduk's defeat of the allies of Tiamat.

The word translated "molten" in verse 18 is מוּצָק, *moowtsaq*, literally, "clods of dust" in the sense of dust combining with water and forming clods of earth, or being compacted into rocks.¹⁶ The translator of this passage unfortunately failed to take into account that this was a noun, and not a verb, yet he translated the same word, מוּצָק *moowtsaq* (in Job 38:38), as "hard dust," which is used in 38:38 in a parallel

---
¹⁶*BDB*, 427.

construction with רְגָבִים *regavim,* "clods (of earth)." Thus *moowtsaq* means not "molten", i.e., something that is melted prior to casting in a mold, it means the casting itself. Thus here is should be translated as "clods of compacted dust", or "rocks". All rock is is dust compacted into a solid form through pressure over time, so this translation is best.

Finally, the word translated "mirror," כִּרְאִי, *ki-re'iy,* "like a mirror," is a plausible translation of the word, but it makes little sense in context. רְאִי, *re'iy,* is what exegetes call a *hapax legomenon*—a word that is used only once in the Bible. This means that the translator is not sure of the exact meaning, so he was forced to make an educated guess based on similar words because one or more extra usages of the same word were not available in the text for comparison.

For some reason Gesenius bases his translation of רְאִי on the word מַרְאָה, *ma-re'ah,* which is translated as "appearance" in Job 33:21. However, it is more likely that *re'iy* is more closely related to רֹאִי *ro'i,* "vision" which, unfortunately, also does not fit the context. I suggest that *re'iy* is best translated as "reflection", in the sense of "memory" i.e., the constant, visible appearance of an object in the heavens that causes one to reflect on some past event, and remember it forever. Job does in fact mention that he has a "witness" in heaven in 16:19, "Also now, behold, my witness is in heaven, and my record is on high" (KJV). This witness appears, in context, to be the Moon.

THE THEOPHANY OF GOD: THE DIVINE CONFLICT REMEMBERED

Job 38–41 contains a theophany of God which, when translated properly, is perhaps the clearest evidence in support of the divine conflict Creation motif in the Old Testament. Not only does it prove that the Hebrew concept of the Creation included a conflict between God and a dragon, but the descriptions strongly support both the Planet X/Giant Impact theory and the astronomical interpretation based on *Enuma Elish.* We start our analysis with the classic exposition between God and Job, where God appears to Job מִן הַסְּעָרָה *min ha-se'arah,* "from the whirlwind":

Job 38: God Explains how He Created the Earth

✟ Job 38:1-6:
¹Then the LORD answered Job out of the whirlwind, and said,
² Who is this that darkeneth counsel by words without knowledge?
³ Gird up now thy loins like a man; for I will demand of thee, and answer thou me.
⁴ Where wast thou when I laid the foundations of the Earth? declare, if thou hast understanding.
⁵ Who hath laid the measures thereof, if thou knowest? or who hath stretched the line upon it?
⁶ Whereupon are the foundations thereof fastened? or who laid the corner stone thereof; (KJV)

Verse 1 describes God as answering Job out of "the whirlwind," possibly the same "great wind from the wilderness" that had destroyed Job's family and property. This "divine wind", most likely the same heavenly wind that the Sumerians believed had been sent by their chief deity Enlil to destroy them, was also believed by the Hebrews to have been sent by God to test Job. And now this same heavenly wind was now being used by God as a means of communication with Job.

In rebuke of Job, who has spent much time questioning the justice of God's actions against him, God, interestingly, places his counter-argument squarely in the context of the Creation. *In fact, Job 38, the very first time God speaks in the Book of Job, talks about nothing else but the Creation.* This critical chapter in The Book of Job is concerned primarily with Creation because, as we have seen, The Book of Job is the Hebrew Creation Epic. Unlike *Enuma Elish,* which uses mythical gods and monsters as symbols to communicate what happened at the Creation, The Book of Job uses as its *modus operandi* a real situation, with real people engaging in a theological debate as a format for communicating what occurred at the Creation.

This is not to say that The Book of Job eschews the use of mythical monsters in order to help communicate the ancient Creation story, as does the Book of Genesis. In fact, The Book of Job contains by far the most material involving God battling a dragon at the Creation than any other single book in the canon. References to the divine conflict occur in Job 3:8 (NIV), 9:13 (NIV), 26:12-13, and especially chapters

38 and 41 which are, as we shall see, the best examples of the Hebrew Creation story in the entire Bible.

Though the first five verses of chapter 38 do not contain any information that can support the divine conflict theme directly, references to the divine conflict begin in earnest in verse 6, where the primary meaning of the word for "laid" in verse 6, יָרָה *yarah*, can also mean, "thrown" or "shot" as in shooting an arrow. Job may be trying to convey here the meaning of the "cornerstone" as literally a giant "stone" that God "shot" at Earth, which resulted in the creation of Earth as we know it. Of course this, as we now know from the perspective of modern science, must be a reference to the giant impactor that had struck and shattered early Earth, a stone that God had literally "shot " at Earth in order to create Earth as it is in its present form. This also mightily confirms our conclusion in Chapter V that Genesis 1:1 describes God using a huge stone, a satellite of Planet X, to divide Earth into the asteroid belt and a new Earth.

But whereas the first five verses make no reference to the divine conflict, and verse 6 makes only an oblique reference, from verse 7 onward Job 38 becomes one of the clearest passages in the Bible in support of the divine conflict Creation theme.

⁷ בְּרָן־יַחַד כּוֹכְבֵי בֹקֶר וַיָּרִיעוּ כָּל־בְּנֵי אֱלֹהִים	⁷ When the morning stars sang together, and all the sons of God shouted for joy?

Verse 7 makes a reference to the Creation where the "morning stars" sang and shouted for joy when God created Earth.[17] However, though the word וַיָּרִיעוּ *va-yariy'oow* can mean, "shout for joy," the translators of the KJV left out a critical word in their translation of this verse which gives the meaning of the verse a slightly different shade of meaning. The word *va-yariy'oow* "and they shouted in triumph," which appears to have been glossed over in modern translations, means not joy in general, but a shout of triumphal joy *after an enemy*

---

[17] The word translated as "sang" is actually רָנַן *ranan*, which literally means "make a trilling sound". The technical term in the west is "ululation," and examples can be found on the web: http://en.wikipedia.org/wiki/Ululation, and http://www.freesound.org/samplesViewSingle.php?id=62894. This noise is not unlike the ululating noises emitted by the planets: http://www.bing.com/videos/watch/video/the-eerie-sounds-of-saturn/17wfyluwb?q=sound%20of%20the%20planets indicating perhaps that the joyful ululation sound made by Middle Eastern women has a very ancient pedigree.

Job: The Hebrew Creation Epic

has been conquered. In other words, it was a shout of victory after winning a battle, a shout of joyful praise that God had defeated something *in combat*. This, of course, as we have seen, must refer to the divine conflict at the Creation, and explains the fuller meaning of the cornerstone that had been "shot" at Earth by God in verse 6: that cornerstone was apparently a very real, very large stone that God used as a weapon against Earth to defeat Earth and to create a new Earth from the shattered husk of the old, the planets then singing in triumph for God's victory over the primordial Earth.

Another important fact to consider is that the word for "morning stars," כּוֹכָב *cowhav,* is not limited to stars that appear in the morning, but is used throughout the Bible to denote astral bodies in general. It is taken from the Hebrew verb כָּבַב *cavav,* "to roll," and is related to כַּבְכָּב *cavcav,* "globe," or "ball" and כָּוָה *cavah,* "to burn". Thus *cowhav* literally means a burning globe that rolls through the heavens. *Cowhav* also has numerous cognates throughout the languages of the ancient Near East, particularly the Akkadian (Babylonian) *kakkabu,* "star." As such, it can refer to any nighttime object save the Moon, and is often used to denote the planets, which do indeed literally "roll" across the heavenly sphere.

As we discovered in Chapter II, the "gods" of the ancient Near East were, in fact, the planets. However, Job is not about to give glory to the pagan gods of the nations, so he refers to the planets instead as "the sons of God". If this is true, it makes it clear that the assembly of the "sons of God" in Job 1 and 2 was indeed actually meant to describe two conjunctions of the planets in heaven. It also allows us to draw a close parallel between Job 38 and *Enuma Elish* — specifically, the description of "the gods" in *Enuma Elish,* the planets, who were "joyful and jubilant" immediately after Marduk had defeated Tiamat.

בְּרָן־יַחַד *baran-yahar* - "when they sang joyously"
כּוֹכְבֵי *cowhav* - "the planets"
בֹקֶר *voqer* - "morning, dawn"
וַיָּרִיעוּ *va-yoriy'oow* - "when they give a shout of victory"
כָּל־בְּנֵי *kal-benay* - "all the sons"
אֱלֹהִים *'elohiym* - "God, gods, elohim"

For the rest of this chapter, because Job chapters 38-41 so closely parallel *Enuma Elish*, we will be providing, along with a parallel retranslation of selected verses in the original Hebrew into an "astronomical interpretation" of the biblical Creation material to be found in Job, the parallel text in *Enuma Elish:*

Hebrew Text:	The Astronomical Interpretation	Enuma Elish
⁷ בְּרָן־יַחַד כּוֹכְבֵי בֹקֶר וַיָּרִיעוּ כָּל־בְּנֵי אֱלֹהִים	⁷ When the planets sang joyously, when all the sons of God shouted in triumph together.	The lord trod on the legs of Tiamat, with his unsparing mace he crushed her skull. *On seeing this, his fathers were joyful and jubilant, they brought gifts of homage, they to him.* (IV:129-130, 133-134)

וַיָּסֶךְ בִּדְלָתַיִם יָם בְּגִיחוֹ מֵרֶחֶם יֵצֵא ⁸	⁸ Or who shut up the sea with doors, when it brake forth, as if it had issued out of the womb?

וַיָּסֶךְ	va-yasek - "and he covered"
בִּדְלָתַיִם	bidlatayim - "with doors"
יָם	yam - "the sea"
בְּגִיחוֹ	be-giyh-oow - "to keep it from breaking out"
מֵרֶחֶם	mai-rehem - "from the womb"
יֵצֵא	yaitsai' - "going forth"

Verse 8 goes on to describe how God "covered the sea with doors" to keep it breaking out from "the womb". Outside of the context of the divine conflict Creation scenario we have been discussing, this text would make little sense. However, when one takes into account that this exact terminology is used in *Enuma Elish*, where Marduk is also described as setting a limit to the waters that flowed forth from

Tiamat's "womb" after he had defeated and divided her, then it makes perfect sense. As we shall see, The Book of Job, particularly chapters 38-41, parallel *Enuma Elish* almost point for point, even using some of the same terminology.

Hebrew Text:	The Astronomical Interpretation	Enuma Elish
⁷ בְּרָן־יַחַד כּוֹכְבֵי בֹקֶר וַיָּרִיעוּ כָּל־בְּנֵי אֱלֹהִים	⁷ And he covered the sea with doors to keep it from breaking out of Earth's womb.	Opening the deep, which was in flood ... her crotch, she was fastened to the heavens. (V:54,61)

---

⁹ בְּשׂוּמִי עָנָן לְבֻשׁוֹ וַעֲרָפֶל חֲתֻלָּתוֹ	⁹ When I made the cloud the garment thereof, and thick darkness a swaddling-band for it

- בְּשׂוּמִי — *be-soowmiy* - "when I set"
- עָנָן — *'anan* - "the cloud"
- לְבֻשׁוֹ — *levoosh-ow* - "as a garment upon it"
- וַעֲרָפֶל — *va-'araphel* - "and the dark clouds"
- חֲתֻלָּתוֹ — *hatoolat-ow* - "as a swaddling band on it; to conceal it; as a band surrounding its equator"

Verse 9 contains some very interesting additional material that gives specifics about the massive cloud of dust that was thrown up into Earth's atmosphere as a result of the Giant Impact. Not only was a great deal of water thrown up into space and into Earth's atmosphere, as we saw in verse 8, but also a great deal of dust and pulverized rock remained circulating in Earth's atmosphere for hundreds, possibly thousands of years. And this is what is described in verse 9, where God describes how he set a deep, dark cloud of dust over the entire Earth, wrapping and concealing it completely. The term "conceal" here is appropriate, because the word usually interpreted as "swaddlingband" חֲתֻלָּתוֹ *ḥatoolat,* basically means "to conceal", i.e., to cover and protect the newborn and keep it from harm. Thus God "concealed" Earth completely with this dark cloud of dust. The "band" part of swaddlingband refers specifically to the part of the swaddling cloth that surrounds the baby's waist, which is interesting because astronomers believe that much of the dust that had been thrown up into orbit around Earth gradually migrated to Earth's equator, where it became a series of rings, or "bands", around Earth's equator. Thus the use here of the term "swaddlingband" is particularly astute, as it encapsulates the concepts of not only Earth being covered by thick, dark clouds of dust, but also the fact that Earth, for a time, had a ring around its equator.[18]

Hebrew Text:	The Astronomical Interpretation	Enuma Elish
⁹ בְּשׂוּמִי עָנָן לְבֻשׁוֹ וַעֲרָפֶל חֲתֻלָּתוֹ	⁹ When I made a cloud of dust cover Earth, which later formed a ring around Earth's equator.	(No parallel)

Many astronomers believe that Earth, not long after the Giant Impact, formed rings around its equator from the massive amount of dust that had been thrown up into orbit. That part of the rings that did not eventually precipitate back down to Earth was swept up by the Moon, explaining perhaps the large amount of dust on the Moon's surface.

---

[18] The use of the term "swaddlingband" also supports the birth metaphor so routinely associated with the Creation, where the Moon was "born" from the womb of Earth.

Job: The Hebrew Creation Epic

וָאֶשְׁבֹּר עָלָיו חֻקִּי וָאָשִׂים בְּרִיחַ וּדְלָתָיִם | [10] And brake up for it my decreed place, and set bars and doors,

וָאֶשְׁבֹּר	va-'eshbor - "and I broke into pieces"
עָלָיו	'alayv - "upon it"
חֻקִּי	ḥooqiy - "appointed limit"
וָאָשִׂים	va-'asiym - "and I set"
בְּרִיחַ	beriyaḥ - "the bar, fleeing fugitive"
וּדְלָתָיִם	oow-delatayim - "and doors"

God next describes how He broke up the vast cloud of dust, water ice and pulverized rock that was in orbit around Earth, dividing it into two sections. Whereas much of the loose material orbiting Earth gradually formed a ring, much of it was left in Earth's original orbital station between Mars and Jupiter, where it also formed a ring — the asteroid belt. God then moved Earth far away to a new orbital path much closer to the Sun, effectively creating a "bar", that clearly divided the ring of rocks above, the asteroid belt, from the ring of rocks below, Earth's newly formed ring system and hydrosphere. Interesting linguistic parallels also exist in verse 10, where the word *beriyaḥ*, translated here as "bar", is the same word translated as "fleeing" in Job 26:13. So the water that gushed forth from the "fleeing" serpent was divided by a "bar", that divided the waters and rocks that flooded forth from the womb of the dragon into waters above, and waters below. *Delatayim*, "doors", the doors of the dragon's womb that were shut in order to cease the water from flowing, is also the same word used for "doors" in Job 38:8. Thus the concept of the dragon's womb being shut, and the corrupt waters that flowed forth being imprisoned in a frozen ring in space set far, far away from Earth, should be considered to be one of the core concepts of the Creation event.

Hebrew Text:	The Astronomical Interpretation	Enuma Elish
וָאֶשְׁבֹּר עָלָיו חֻקִּי ¹⁰ וָאָשִׂים בְּרִיחַ וּדְלָתָיִם	¹⁰ And I divided the waters above from the waters below, and created a vast gulf of space as a barrier between them to make sure they remained separate, each in their appointed places.	He split her like a shellfish into two parts: Half of her he set up and ceiled it as sky, pulled down the bar and posted guards. He bade them to allow not her waters to escape. (IV: 137-140)

וַיֹּאמֶר עַד־פֹּה תָבוֹא וְלֹא תֹסִיף ¹¹ וּפֹא־יָשִׁית בִּגְאוֹן גַּלֶּיךָ

¹¹ And said, Hitherto shalt thou come, but no further: and here shall thy proud waves be stayed?

וַיֹּאמֶר   va-'omar - "and He said"

עַד־פֹּה   ad-poh - "until here"

תָבוֹא   tavow' - "you go"

וְלֹא תֹסִיף   ve-lo' tosiyph - "and no more"

וּפֹא־יָשִׁית   oow-po'-yashiyt - "and here He placed"

בִּגְאוֹן   big'own - "like ornaments on high"

גַּלֶּיךָ   galey-ka - "your pile of rocks; your spring of water; your round container"

The interpretation of verse 10 as the "waters above" being the asteroid belt is strongly supported by verse 11, which clearly states that these "waters above" are essentially a ring of rocks and water that is arranged like a great "bowl" in space. This "pile of rocks" is like a group of "ornaments" (*big'own*) which God hung on high in order to commemorate His victory over the dragon. *Galey* is a particularly interesting word, which can mean either "pile of rocks", "spring of water" and or "round container" ("bowl", Zech. 4:2). So, the root concept behind the Hebrew word *galey* is that is something that is made up of rocks, water, and is kept in a circular container. And with the addition of *big'own*, "ornaments on high", clearly what is intended here are rocks and water that are suspended in space, arranged in a circle, and shining like ornaments — a perfect description of the asteroid belt.[19]

Hebrew Text:	The Astronomical Interpretation	Enuma Elish
[11] וָאֶשְׁבֹּר עָלָיו חֻקִּי וָאָשִׂים בְּרִיחַ וּדְלָתָיִם	[11] And He said, "Until here you go, and no more." And He placed there, like ornaments in the sky, a ring of rocks mixed with water ice.	Twisting her tail he bound it to *Durmah*. Her crotch, she was fastened to the heavens. Thus he covered the heavens and established the Earth. (V: 59-62)

[12] הֲמִיָּמֶיךָ צִוִּיתָ בֹּקֶר יִדַּעְתָּה שַׁחַר מְקֹמוֹ	[12] Hast thou commanded the morning since thy days; and caused the dayspring to know his place?

הֲמִיָּמֶיךָ	*he-miyamey-ka* - "Have you from your day"
צִוִּיתָ	*tsyviyta* - "set up, appoint"
בֹּקֶר	*boqer* – "dawn, morning"
יִדַּעְתָּה	*yida'tah* - "you understand, know"
שַׁחַר	*shahar* - "the morning, the dawn"
מְקֹמוֹ	*meqomow* - "from its place"

This verse is a little more straightforward, describing how, as a result of the Giant Impact, Earth's rotation rate and axial tilt were determined, and thereby when and where the Sun rises each morning. The Sun actually rises and sets at a different time and location each morning, the time determined by the rotation rate and axial tilt, and the location determined primarily by the axial tilt.[20] Verse 12 is thus

---

[19] In *Enuma Elish*, Marduk twisted Tiamat's tail into a ring in heaven, fastening it to the *Durmah*, which was seen by the Babylonians as a great "band" in space.

[20] Both are of course also affected by other factors, particularly Earth's location in its orbit relative to the Sun, but for now we will restrict ourselves to the two factors that primarily determine the Sun's apparent motion relative to Earth: Earth's rotation period and axial tilt.

clearly a reference to the Creation, parallel to Genesis 1:14-16: "And God said, Let there be lights in the firmament of the heaven to divide the day from the night ... And God made two great lights; the greater light to rule the day, and the lesser light to rule the night." (KJV) In the context of the divine conflict theory of the Creation, we understand this to be a reference to how the Earth's axial tilt and rotation period were set, which in turn determine how the Sun, Moon and stars appear to move in the heavens. We also now know that the axial tilt and orbit were set as the result of a Giant Impact between Earth and a Mars-sized body.

Hebrew Text:	The Astronomical Interpretation	Enuma Elish
הַֽמִיָּמֶיךָ צִוִּיתָ בֹּקֶר יִדַּעְתָּה שַׁחַר מְקֹמוֹ ¹²	¹² Were you the one who determined the rotation rate and axial tilt of Earth? Do you determine where and when the sun will rise every morning?	He appointed the days to Shamash [the Sun] and established the precincts of night and day. (V: 45-46)

לֶאֱחֹז בְּכַנְפוֹת הָאָרֶץ וְיִנָּעֲרוּ רְשָׁעִים מִמֶּנָּה ¹³	¹³ That it might take hold of the ends of the earth, that the wicked might be shaken out of it?

לֶאֱחֹז	*le'eḥoz* - "to seize, to take, to hold"
בְּכַנְפוֹת	*beḥanephowt* - "by the edge, of the covering"
הָאָרֶץ	*ha-'aretz* – "the Earth"
וְיִנָּעֲרוּ	*ve-yina'ar-oow* - "and shake out"
רְשָׁעִים	*resha'iym* - "the wicked ones"
מִמֶּנָּה	*mi-menah-oow* - "from out of her"

Verse 13 then goes on to describe how God "seized" the edge of Earth and shook His enemies, "the wicked ones", out of "her". The use of the feminine pronoun here is interesting, as it identifies Earth as a "her", just as Tiamat was portrayed as a god*dess* in *Enuma Elish*. These

Job: The Hebrew Creation Epic

enemies must therefore refer to the army of "monster serpents" led by Kingu that Tiamat "gave birth" to to defend herself. But how the Moon and comets were created from the body of Earth is given in a much clearer and more scientifically accurate way here in Job than in *Enuma Elish*. Instead of the dragon "giving birth" to the Moon and comets without any outside help, Job explains that what actually happened is that the same Giant Impact that set Earth's axial tilt and rotation rate in verse 12 also dug out a large amount of rock and water from Earth's mantle and threw it into space. Thus the "wicked ones" that God "shook out" from Earth were, in fact, the Moon and comets. And we shall see in the next few verses how accurate this retranslation is.

Hebrew Text:	The Astronomical Interpretation	Enuma Elish
לֶאֱחֹז בְּכַנְפוֹת הָאָרֶץ וְיִנָּעֲרוּ רְשָׁעִים מִמֶּנָּה	[13] Were you the one who seized Earth's crust, and shook the Moon and comets out of her mantle?	[Tiamat] has added matchless weapons, has borne monster serpents. Sharp of tooth, unsparing of fang, with venom for blood she has filled their bodies. Roaring dragons she has clothed with terror, has crowned them with haloes [comet tails], making them like gods. (III: 81-86)

תִּתְהַפֵּךְ כְּחֹמֶר חוֹתָם וְיִתְיַצְּבוּ כְּמוֹ לְבוּשׁ [14]	[14] It is turned as clay to the seal; and they stand as a garment.

תִּתְהַפֵּךְ	*tith'hapaiq* - "It transformed itself"
כְּחֹמֶר	*kehomer* - "into a heap of boiling hot clay"
חוֹתָם	*howtam* – "a clay seal, a ring used to set a seal in clay"
וְיִתְיַצְּבוּ	*ve-yitaytsevo-oow* - "and placed upon them"
כְּמוֹ	*kemow* - "like"
לְבוּשׁ	*levoosh* - "garment, covering, protective screen"

These two verses, 13-14, should be considered an explanation of how the Moon and the comets were formed. Just as Tiamat brought forth the Moon and comets from her body to help her fight against Marduk, as described in the astronomical interpretation of *Enuma Elish,* in Job we find a similar description of God's enemies being "shaken out" of Earth's "side" or mantle. This description of the enemies of God being shaken out of Earth's mantle turns out to be exactly how scientists now believe the Moon (and, I argue, the comets and asteroids as well) had been created. As we saw in Chapter III, the Moon, asteroids, and comets were created when a Mars-sized body struck Earth. The impact of this body was so great that it ejected a massive amount of Earth's mantle into space, where it gradually cooled and solidified, forming the Moon. In other words, modern scientists now generally agree that the Moon (and the asteroids and comets) had been literally "shaken" out of the side of Earth, shaken out by a large body that had struck Earth in the primeval past.

The material that formed the Moon had been so superheated by the force of the Giant Impact that nearly all the volatile materials in it, such as water, iron, and so forth, had been boiled out and left floating in space. Much of the secondary ejecta from this impact, along with some of the material that had been heated out of the Moon, then settled back down to Earth, covering Earth with a thick, dark cloud of dust and ashes. Due to the centrifugal force created by Earth's spin, this cloud of dust migrated to Earth's equator, where it formed a ring. Over time, the material in this ring gradually lost momentum and precipitated back down to Earth's surface to form Earth's continents and oceans. The material that had remained floating in space, instead of settling back down to Earth, became what we now know as the asteroids and comets. The lion's share of the material ejected from Earth's mantle by the Giant Impact, now bereft of water and other volatiles, then settled into orbit around Earth, over time gradually cooling and solidifying into a large sphere — transforming itself into our Moon.

In this context, תִתְהַפֵּךְ *tith'hapaiq,* "it is turned," is better translated as "it transformed itself." This is a better translation for two reasons: (1) it supports and is supported by the Giant Impact Theory, and (2) since *tith'hapaiq* is actually set in the reflexive *hithpael* tense, and not in the passive *niphal* tense, then the subject of the sentence, "It," is not being acted upon but is, in fact, acting upon itself. There is a subtle, but important, difference. For example, a passive use of the verb "to feed" would mean, "to be fed," whereas a reflexive use of the verb "to feed" would mean, "to feed oneself." Therefore, in verse 14, God's enemies should not be seen as having been passively "turned," but as having actively "transformed themselves" into something. And since this passage is set in the context of the creation of Earth, the only plausible explanation is that this verse describes the creation of things that had transformed themselves after they had been cut out of the side of Earth. This, of course, describes the formation of the Moon, asteroids, and comets perfectly. After having been ejected from Earth's mantle, they had gradually transformed themselves over time, by cooling and accretion, into their present form. In short, the wicked enemies that God had "shaken" out of the side of Earth (v. 13) then transformed themselves (v. 14) into the Moon, comets, and asteroids.

כְּחֹמֶר *kehomer,* translated here as "like clay," can also mean "either "like a boiling pot of clay", "like a heap of earth", or both. The Giant Impact Theory points out that a collision between Earth and another large body would have instantly liquefied the area of impact and jetted the superheated impact area into space, where it would have later cooled and solidified into a sphere, forming our Moon. If this is indeed the message that the author intended to convey, then the best translation of this phrase is "like molten magma."

According to the astronomical interpretation of *Enuma Elish,* Earth had brought forth the Moon and comets as a "defense" against Planet X. Tiamat had given Kingu leadership over the "council" of eleven "monsters," and then had given him a "Tablet of Destiny" which she had sealed with a "seal" onto his breast as a symbol of his status. Thus חוֹתָם *howtam,* "seal," is another excellent link with *Enuma Elish.* The possession of a "destiny" indicated that Kingu was now a god. In other words, he was like the gods, the planets, in that he had a specific orbital path, a "destiny"; i.e., a way that he was destined to travel forever.

Verse 14 next speaks of the eleven other members of the dragon's army. But in order to fit in to this context, the plural verb וְיִתְיַצְּבוּ *ve-yitaytsevo-oow,* translated in the present tense "and they stand," needs to be switched to the past tense, "and they stood," or "and they presented themselves" in order to fit into the divine conflict model. To add to the meaning, לְבוּשׁ *levoosh,* translated here as "garment, clothing," might be translated as "covering" or "armor" in the sense of being protective — i.e., brought forth from the dragon in order to protect herself. All together these words, translated literally and in context, provide a much more accurate translation that agrees perfectly with modern theories on how the Moon — and probably also the comets and asteroids — were formed:

Hebrew Text:	The Astronomical Interpretation	Enuma Elish
14 תִּתְהַפֵּךְ כְּחֹמֶר חוֹתָם וְיִתְיַצְּבוּ כְּמוֹ לְבוּשׁ	[14] A large section of Earth's mantle was thrown into orbit around Earth, from which was formed the Moon, comets, and asteroids, which acted as a protective screen for Earth.	Withal eleven of this kind [Tiamat] brought forth. She elevated Kingu, made him chief among them. She gave him the Tablet of Destinies, [sealed] on his breast. (II:145, 147, 156, [VI:122])

---

15 וַיִּמָּנַע מֵרְשָׁעִים אוֹרָם וּזְרוֹעַ רָמָה תִּשָּׁבֵר

[15] And from the wicked their light is withholden, and the high arm shall be broken.

וַיִּמָּנַע	ve-yimana' - "but they were held back"
מֵרְשָׁעִים	mai-resh'iym - "the wicked ones"
אוֹרָם	'owram – "lights"
וּזְרוֹעַ	oow-zerow'a - "and the arm, and the army"
רָמָה	ramah - "high, high place"
תִּשָּׁבֵר	tishavair - "broken into pieces, shattered"

In the context of the Planet X/Giant Impact theory, verse 15 yields a much more interesting translation. The *resh'iym*, the "wicked ones" appear once again, as if they were part of a narrative. Whereas they were described in verse 13 as having been shaken out of Earth, here in verse 15 they are described as "lights", that were "held back", and that were part of an "army on high" that was "shattered". This clearly refers to the comets, which were dug out of Earth's mantle, thrown into space into orbit around Earth where they became great and glorious lights that rivaled the planets in brilliance. Surrounding Earth like a protective screen, they were then shattered and scattered into independent orbits of their own by Planet X.

Hebrew Text:	The Astronomical Interpretation	Enuma Elish
וַיִּמָּנַע מֵרְשָׁעִים אוֹרָם ¹⁵ וּזְרוֹעַ רָמָה תִּשָּׁבֵר	¹⁵ But the wicked comets were stopped; the army on high was broken and scattered.	After he had slain Tiamat, the leader, her band was shattered, her troupe broken up; (IV:105-106)

In sum, we may derive from verses 12-15 a much more interesting and scientifically accurate description of the creation of the Moon and comets:

✤ Job 38:12-15:
¹² Were you the one who determined the rotation rate and axial tilt of Earth? Do you determine where and when the sun will rise every morning?
¹³ Were you the one who seized Earth's crust, and shook the Moon and comets out of her mantle?
¹⁴ A large section of Earth's mantle was thrown into orbit around Earth, from which was formed the Moon, comets, and asteroids, which acted as a protective screen for Earth.
¹⁵ But the wicked comets were stopped; the army on high was broken and scattered. (Retranslated)

Because the Creation material in Job utilizes a combination of scientific and mythological imagery, our retranslation was only possible because of our understanding of modern astronomy and parallel ancient Near Eastern creation texts such as *Enuma Elish*. All in all, the Job material appears to be a compromise between true science and anthropomorphic imagery reminiscent of *Enuma Elish*.

הֲבָאתָ אֶל־אֹצְרוֹת שָׁלֶג וְאֹצְרוֹת בָּרָד תִּרְאֶה ²²	²² Hast thou entered into the treasures of the snow? or hast thou seen the treasures of the hail?

    הֲבָאתָ   ha-va'ta - "have you entered"
    אֶל־אֹצְרוֹת   'el-'otserowt - "into the treasuries, storehouses"

שֶׁלֶג   shaleg – "snow"
וְאֹצְרוֹת   ve-'otserowt - "and the storehouses"
בָּרָד   barad - "hailstones, scattered stones, asteroids"
תִרְאֶה   tir'eh - "have you seen?"

The Creation paradigm retreats into some more pedestrian descriptions of the huge size of Earth and of the depth of the sea in verses 16-21, but returns in force in verse 22. שֶׁלֶג, shaleg, "snow," is pretty straightforward, and אֹצְרוֹת otseroth, "treasuries," is also a good translation, particularly in the context of Job 38:11, where God describes the asteroids in the asteroid belt as בְּגָאוֹן big'own, "like ornaments on high".

The second use of 'otserowt reinforces the idea that the asteroid belt is being described here. Here it should probably be translated as "munitions," paralleling Isaiah's mention of the "munitions of rocks" as the place of God's dwelling (Isa. 33:16-17). בָּרָד barad can mean hailstones, rocky stones, or anything that is hard and scattered, like hailstones are when they fall. This is because the root of barad is בָּרָד barad, "to scatter", which creates the idea of barad as "stones that are scattered" — yet another excellent description of the asteroid belt. Thus, this verse in context should be translated, "Have you entered into the treasuries of the snow? Have you seen the asteroid belt?"

Hebrew Text:	The Astronomical Interpretation	Enuma Elish
וְיִמָּנַע מֵרְשָׁעִים אוֹרָם ²² וּזְרוֹעַ רָמָה תִּשָּׁבֵר	²² Have you entered into the treasuries of the snow? Have you seen the asteroid belt?	He formed at her udder… wells to carry off (the water). Twisting her tail he bound it to Durmah, her crotch, she was fastened to the heavens. (V:57-61)

אֲשֶׁר־חָשַׂכְתִּי לְעֶת־צָר לְיוֹם קְרָב ²³ וּמִלְחָמָה	²³ Which I have reserved against the time of trouble, against the day of battle and war?

אֲשֶׁר־	*'asher* - "which"
חָשַׂכְתִּי	*ḥasaḥtiy* - "I have reserved"
לְעֶת־צָר	*le'et* – "until the foreordained time"
לְיוֹם	*leyowm* - "in the day"
קְרָב	*qerov* - "approaching battle"
וּמִלְחָמָה	*oow-milḥamah* – "as instruments of war"

Verse 23 concludes the description of the asteroid belt with God explaining that He has kept these huge, icy rocks in store specifically for use against His enemies in some foreordained, approaching battle as instruments of war. This is particularly appropriate for The Book of Job, as it was probably one of these asteroids, dislodged from its orbit around the Sun while Planet X passed through its "tabernacle", on its way to perihelion, that destroyed Sumer and ruined Job, giving occasion to the writing of The Book of Job. The "foreordained, approaching battle" is probably the battle of Armageddon, of which God's destruction of Sumer was merely a preview of coming events.

Hebrew Text:	The Astronomical Interpretation	Enuma Elish
²³ וְיִמָּנַע מֵרְשָׁעִים אוֹרָם וּזְרוֹעַ רָמָה תִּשָּׁבֵר	²³ Which I have reserved until the appointed time, until the day of the approaching battle, as instruments of war.	He formed at her udder... wells to carry off (the water). Twisting her tail he bound it to Durmah, her crotch, she was fastened to the heavens. (V:57-61)

We will discuss Planet X's role in the End Times, particularly its role in the Battle of Armageddon, at length in Chapter VII.

✢ Job 38:24-28:
²⁴ By what way is the light parted, which scattereth the east wind upon the earth?
²⁵ Who hath divided a watercourse for the overflowing of waters, or a way for the lightning of thunder;
²⁶ To cause it to rain on the earth, where no man is; on the wilderness, wherein there is no man;

²⁷ To satisfy the desolate and waste ground; and to cause the bud of the tender herb to spring forth?
²⁸ Hath the rain a father? or who hath begotten the drops of dew? (KJV)

Verses 24 through 28 speak of normal meteorological phenomena such as the sunrise, clouds, and rain, the basic hydrological cycle of Earth. However, as we saw in chapter III, both the asteroid belt, the comets, and Earth's water supply were all released from Earth's mantle by the same Giant Impact. Thus, the inclusion of a description of normal meteorological phenomenon is not only appropriate here, but necessary for a full understanding of God's creative activity. Verse 29, however, jumps right back into description of the asteroid belt:

| מִבֶּטֶן מִי יָצָא הַקָּרַח וּכְפֹר שָׁמַיִם מִי יְלָדוֹ ²⁹ | ²⁹ Out of whose womb came the ice? and the hoary frost of heaven, who hath gendered it? |

מִבֶּטֶן	*mibeten* - "from womb"
מִי	*miy* - "whose"
יָצָא	*yatsa'* – "came forth"
הַקָּרַח	*ha-qaraḥ* - "the ice, the crystal, the icy stone"
וּכְפֹר	*oow-ḥephor* - "and frost, and the cup"
שָׁמַיִם	*shamayim* – "heavens"
מִי	*miy* – "from"
יְלָדוֹ	*yelad-ow* – "gave birth to it"

The description of the asteroid belt, which briefly ended in verse 23, picks up again here, in verse 29, bracketing the description of Earth's atmosphere. This makes sense because, as we saw in Chapter V, the Bible mentions not one but three heavens: 1) Earth's atmosphere, 2) the asteroid belt, and 3) possibly Planet X. Thus it would make sense that a description of the first heaven would appear in relation to a description of the second heaven, as both were created by the same Creation event.

Verse 29 picks up with the divine conflict Creation motif once more, precisely paralleling *Enuma Elish* as close as they can get without actually mentioning Tiamat's name. In this verse, God literally asks from whose "womb" הַקֶּרַח *ha-qarah*, literally, "the stone that looks like ice", came from. This reference to the "icy stones" of heaven is once again clearly an allusion to *Enuma Elish*, where the *Durmah*, the great band in heaven composed of rocks and water ice, the asteroid belt, was seen as having come forth from the womb of Tiamat. God then used Planet X to spread the rocks and water that burst forth from the "womb" of Earth into a ring around heaven, which remains frozen in place to this day. This concept of the "ring of stones" is further supported by the fact that the word "frost" in the second half of the verse comes from the word כְּפֹר *hephor*, "frost", which in turn comes from the root כְּפוֹר *cephowr*, "cup". Thus the "frost of heaven" should be seen as being like the frost on the rim of a cup, i.e., in a ring.

Hebrew Text:	The Astronomical Interpretation	Enuma Elish
²⁹ וַיִּמָּנַע מֵרְשָׁעִים אוֹרָם וּזְרוֹעַ רָמָה תִּשָּׁבֵר	²⁹ From whose womb came forth the icy stones? And the ring of frost in heaven— who gave birth to it?	He formed at her udder... wells to carry off (the water). Twisting her tail he bound it to Durmah, her crotch, she was fastened to the heavens. (V:57-61)

כָּאֶבֶן מַיִם יִתְחַבָּאוּ וּפְנֵי תְהוֹם יִתְלַכָּדוּ ³⁰ | ³⁰ The waters are hid as with a stone, and the face of the deep is frozen.

כָּאֶבֶן	*ka-'even* - "like a stone"
מַיִם	*mayim* - "waters"
יִתְחַבָּאוּ	*yithaba'v* – "they are hidden"
וּפְנֵי	*oow-phenay* - "and the face"
תְהוֹם	*tehowm* - "the deep, the deep sea, Tiamat"
יִתְלַכָּדוּ	*yitelakad-oow* – "they are frozen together"

Whereas the previous verses only indirectly allude to the idea of there being a river of stones in heaven mixed with water ice, verse 30 finally directly states it, saying literally that the "waters above" are hidden in heaven, frozen directly onto the surface of stones in heaven. Frankly, a clearer description of the asteroid belt could not be given without resorting to a much more lengthy and elaborate description.

Hebrew Text:	The Astronomical Interpretation	Enuma Elish
³⁰ וַיִּמְנַע מֵרְשָׁעִים אוֹרָם וּזְרוֹעַ רָמָה תִּשָּׁבֵר	³⁰ The waters are hidden in the stones; they are frozen on the surfaces of the asteroids.	He formed at her udder... wells to carry off (the water). Twisting her tail he bound it to Durmah, her crotch, she was fastened to the heavens. (V:57-61)

✦ Job 38:31-32:
³¹ Canst thou bind the sweet influences of Pleiades, or loose the bands of Orion?
³² Canst thou bring forth Mazzaroth in his season? or canst thou guide Arcturus with his sons?

Verses 31 and 32 take a slightly different look at the Creation event, looking not at the individual objects, such as the Earth, the Moon, the asteroids and the comets, but instead looking at the starry background against which the divine Creation drama played out. In verse 31, the Pleiades, which is a cluster of stars in the shoulders of the constellation of Taurus, is given the name *Kiymah*, and the constellation of Orion, a decan of the constellation of Taurus, is also named as *Kesiyl*, "the fool". Though it is not explicitly stated, it location in the midst of all of this Creation material was likely intentional, in order to give the location where the original Creation event took place — where Planet X and Earth first came into conflict, and to where Planet X regularly returns on its inward voyage from deep space to its perihelion in the asteroid belt.

Verse 32 then further expands to ask Job if he can bring forth *Mazzaroth*, the constellations, as God is able to do. "Arcturus" is then incorrectly cited by the English translation. עָיִשׁ *'Ayish*, is actually not Arcturus, but is generally considered by scholars to be the constellation of Ursa Major, the "Great Bear", which is a much more prominent and important constellation in the night sky than the relatively unimportant Arcturus. Ursa Major, or *'Ayish*, was seen in ancient times by the Arabs as a "bier", or funeral cart accompanied by the deceased's three daughters, which are the three bright stars *Al Caid*, *Mizar* and *Alioth* in the Great Bear's "tail".

Ursa Major, the "Great Bear" constellation in the northern heavens relative to Earth. The "Big Dipper" is comprised of seven major stars in the hindquarters of the bear, with the handle of the dipper comprising the bear's tail, and the cup of the dipper located in its lower back. In ancient times, the dipper was thought of as a bier, or funeral casket, that was followed in procession by the three daughters of the deceased, who were the three stars in the tail. Perhaps these are represented as Job's three daughters, or the three friends who consoled Job in his time of trouble?

Verse 32 may also give details regarding the orbit of Planet X. Whereas verse 31 describes where Planet X will first appear in the heavens, in the constellation of Orion, and then pass through the Pleiades, the constellation of Ursa Major, "on the sides of the north", or northern sky, may mark its perihelion, or closest approach to the sun. If, as astronomers now believe, Planet X's orbit is at an angle to the ecliptic, approaching from the south, passing through the ecliptic plane where the other planets appear, and then moving above the ecliptic to its perihelion somewhere in the northern skies, it may well be that Planet X will be at its most brilliant when it passes through its perihelion in the constellation of Ursa Major. Thus verse 31 gives us the location where Planet X will first appear, in the region of Taurus and Orion, and verse 32 tells us that it will move above the constellations that ring the ecliptic and move into the northern skies, where it will reach its perihelion in or near the constellation of Ursa Major.

הֲיָדַעְתָּ חֻקּוֹת שָׁמָיִם אִם־תָּשִׂים ³³ | ³³ Knowest thou the ordinances of heaven? canst thou set the dominion thereof in the Earth?
מִשְׁטָרוֹ בָאָרֶץ |

הֲיָדַעְתָּ	ha-yada'ta - "do you know"
חֻקּוֹת	ḥooqowt - "the universal laws"
שָׁמָיִם	shamayim - "heavens"
אִם־תָּשִׂים	'im-tasiym - "can you set them"
מִשְׁטָרוֹ	mishtarow - "inscribe on it, the side of it"
בָאָרֶץ	va-'aretz - "in/upon the Earth"

Verse 33 takes an interesting angle, describing how God literally "inscribed" the universal laws upon Earth. As we saw in our analysis of Genesis 1:1, and reiterated in our analysis of Job 38:6, where we saw how God literally "shot" a stone into the primordial Earth, the Creation event should be seen as ultimately covenantal in nature, where God literally "wrote" His covenant upon the Earth, using a huge stone as a writing utensil. The Earth was divided into two pieces by this action, heaven and Earth, two great stones upon which God wrote the very first covenant in the Bible. These two pieces of the primordial Earth that had been divided were remembered in the two tablets of the Ten Commandments, upon which the universal laws of God were written. They were in remembrance of the Creation event, when God used a great stone to divide heaven and Earth, the act of which is once again remembered here, in Job 38:33.

Hebrew Text:	The Astronomical Interpretation	Enuma Elish
וַיִּמָּנַע מֵרְשָׁעִים אוֹרָם וּזְרוֹעַ רָמָה תִּשָּׁבֵר ³³	³³ Do you know the universal laws of the heavens? Can you inscribe them upon the surface of the Earth?	So he created heaven and Earth, their bounds established, when he had designed his rules (and) fashioned [his] ordinances. (V:65-67)

Job: The Hebrew Creation Epic

הֲתָרִים לָעָב קוֹלֶךָ וְשִׁפְעַת־מַיִם תְּכַסֶּךָּ ³⁴	³⁴ Canst thou lift up thy voice to the clouds, that abundance of waters may cover thee?

הֲתָרִים	ha-tariym - "Can you lift up"
לָעָב	la'av - "to, into darkness, dark clouds"
קוֹלֶךָ	qowle-ka - "your voice"
וְשִׁפְעַת־	ve-shiph'at - "great multitude, abundance"
מַיִם	mayim - "waters"
תְּכַסֶּךָּ	tehase-ka - "she must cover you"

Verse 34 is also a parallel construction, the second part of the sentence adding further detail to the first so as to help avoid confusion. Thus the "dark clouds" should be considered the same thing as the "abundant waters," which in context probably refers to the waters loosed out of the womb of Earth/Tiamat at the creation. Planet X probably flew through this cloud of debris, which apparently included a black, tarlike organic mixture and large quantities of water, and was probably covered by it in the same way the comets were. Thus, Planet X is probably much like a comet in appearance: almost completely black, except when it passes near the Sun, when the increased heat causes it to suddenly flare up, forming a massive tail like that of a comet (except much, much larger). This would explain the references to a "bright cloud" and "white hair" that accompanies God in heaven: the cometlike tail of Planet X, and why the Babylonian astronomical symbol for planet "Marduk" is shown with "wings" and a "tail." However, for most of its orbit, Planet X remains almost completely black, with an albeido of only around 4 percent (or less). In effect, it is "hidden" within the "dark clouds" and the "abundant waters", and cannot be seen, like a thief in the night, until it is too late.

Hebrew Text:	The Astronomical Interpretation	Enuma Elish
וַיָּמְנַע מֵרְשָׁעִים אוֹרָם וּזְרוֹעַ רָמָה תִּשָּׁבֵר ³⁴	³⁴ Did you raise your voice to the dark clouds? Did you conceal yourself in the abundant waters?	(No parallel)

| הִתְשַׁלַּח בְּרָקִים וְיֵלְכוּ וְיֹאמְרוּ לְךָ הִנֵּנוּ ³⁵ | ³⁵ Canst thou send lightnings, that they may go, and say unto thee, Here we are? |

הֲתְשַׁלַּח	*ha-teshalaḥ* - "Can you send forth"
בְּרָקִים	*beraqiym* - "lightnings"
וְיֵלֵכוּ	*ve-yailaiḥ-oow* - "and go forth to it"
וְיֹאמְרוּ	*ve-yo'mer-oow* - "and say to it"
לְךָ	*le-ka* - "to you"
הִנֵּנוּ	*hi-nainoow* - "behold, here we are"

Verse 35 has an interesting parallel with *Enuma Elish*, where Marduk used "lightning" as one of the weapons that he used to defeat Tiamat. Though it is not explicitly stated in the text of *Enuma Elish*, it appears to be elucidated in the text of this verse, which literally says that God sent forth lightnings to illuminate some sort of target which, we will see in the next verse, is planet Earth.

Hebrew Text:	The Astronomical Interpretation	Enuma Elish
³⁵ וַיְמַגֵּן מֵרְשָׁעִים אוֹרָם וּזְרוֹעַ רָמָה תִּשָּׁבֵר	³⁵ Did you shoot out lightning bolts that said to you, "here is the target"?	Bel's destiny thus fixed … he constructed a bow, marked it as his weapon … in front of him he set the lightning, with a blazing flame he filled his body. (IV:33, 35, 39-40)

| מִי־שָׁת בַּטֻּחוֹת חָכְמָה אוֹ מִי־נָתַן לַשֶּׂכְוִי בִינָה ³⁶ | ³⁶ Who hath put wisdom in the inward parts? or who hath given understanding to the heart? |

מִי־שָׁת	*miy-shat* - "who put"
בַּטֻּחוֹת	*batoohowt* – "in the inner parts; by a bowshot"[21]
חָכְמָה	*ḥaḥemah* – "wisdom; skill in battle"

---

[21]BDB, 376–77.

Job: The Hebrew Creation Epic

אוֹ	*'ow* - "or"
מִי־נָתַן	*miy-natan* - "who gave"
לַשֶּׂכְוִי	*lasehviy* - "to the meteor"
בִינָה	*viynah* - "intelligence, guidance"

Verse 36 is a particularly interesting verse, which contains some very unusual words that can vary dramatically in meaning, depending upon the context. בַּטֻּחוֹת *batoohowt* is an unusual word, which typically means "in the inner parts", but can also mean, "by a bowshot", based upon the variant root טָחָה, *tahah*, "to stretch a bow". This close similarity is probably because in primitive cultures, an animal's intestines are used to create bowstrings. Thus the concept of "intestines" and "to stretch a bow" are closely connected here. חָכְמָה *hahemah* can mean, simply, "wisdom", or it can mean "skill in battle", which would make more sense in the context of stretching a bow. So, the first half should be translated to mean, "Who skillfully shot an arrow into the vitals?"

The second half of the verse is particularly interesting, particularly in the astronomical context of the Creation. שֶׂכְוִי *sehviy*, typically translated "intellect" or "understanding", can also be translated as "meteor". The root of this word is שָׂכָּה *sookah*, "a sharp weapon", indicating that the root concept is indeed that of a weapon, like an arrow. Thus, in context, *sehviy* should probably be translated as "heavenly arrow," i.e., some sort of object that fell from outer space and crashed into the Earth; a meteorite or, in this case, one of the satellites of Planet X. Thus the second half of this verse should be translated, "Who guided the satellite?" This translation also fits well with the context of the writing of The Book of Job, where a meteorite, or "heavenly arrow" shot by "the gods" struck the ancient empire of Sumer, destroying the empire and ruining Job.

Hebrew Text:	The Astronomical Interpretation	Enuma Elish
וַיִּמָּנַע מֵרְשָׁעִים אוֹרָם [36] וּזְרוֹעַ רָמָה תִּשָּׁבֵר	[36] Who skillfully shot an arrow into the vitals? Who guided the satellite?	He released the arrow, it tore her belly. It cut through her insides, splitting the heart. Having thus subdued her, he extinguished her life. (IV:101–103)

מִי־יְסַפֵּר שְׁחָקִים בְּחָכְמָה וְנִבְלֵי ³⁷ | ³⁷ Who can number the clouds in wisdom?
שָׁמַיִם מִי יַשְׁכִּיב | or who can stay the bottles of heaven?

מִי־יְסַפֵּר	*miy-yesapair* - "Who can number"
שְׁחָקִים	*sheḥaqiym* – "clouds, dust, crushed rocks, asteroids"
בְּחָכְמָה	*behaḥmah* – "with wisdom, with accuracy"
וְנִבְלֵי	*ve-nibelay* - "or the bottles (of water), comets"
שָׁמַיִם	*shamayim* - "heaven"
מִי	*miy* - "who"
יַשְׁכִּיב	*yashciyv* - "who can stop"

Verse 37 is another interesting verse that once again contains some relevant references that significantly support the divine conflict Creation model. The first half of the verse refers to the *sheḥaqiym*, which is based upon the root שָׁחַק *shaḥaq*, "to beat into pieces", and is typically translated as either "clouds" or "dust". It can, however, also be translated as "crushed rocks", which in this context, is a good description of the asteroid belt. The asteroids are then paired in the second half of the verse with a mysterious heavenly phenomenon described as "the bottles of heaven", which apparently move around in heaven. But if the "crushed rocks" are the asteroids, then the "bottles of water" probably refers to the comets, which are asteroids with large amounts of water on their surfaces that move around in heaven, seemingly unstoppable. Thus this verse should be retranslated, "Who can accurately number the asteroids? Or the comets in heaven, who can stop them?"

Hebrew Text:	The Astronomical Interpretation	Enuma Elish
וַיִּמָּנַע מֵרְשָׁעִים אוֹרָם ³⁷ וּזְרוֹעַ רָמָה תִּשָּׁבֵר	³⁷ Who can accurately number the asteroids? Or the comets in heaven, who can stop them?	Her band was shattered, her troupe was broken up....Placed in cells they were filled with wailing; bearing his wrath, they were held imprisoned. (IV:106, 113–114)

Job: The Hebrew Creation Epic

בְּצֶקֶת עָפָר לַמּוּצָק וּרְגָבִים יְדֻבָּקוּ׃ ³⁸ | ³⁸ When the dust groweth into hardness, and the clods cleave fast together?

בְּצֶקֶת	*be-tseqet* - "when poured out, formed, molded"
עָפָר	*'aphar* - "dust"
לַמּוּצָק	*la-moowtsaq* - "cast, hardened"
וּרְגָבִים	*oow-regaviym* - "and the heaps of stones"
יְדֻבָּקוּ	*yedoobaq-oow* - "they freeze, cluster together"

Verse 38 is the last of the divine conflict-oriented Creation verses in Job 38, which finishes the discussion begun in verse 37 of the asteroids and comets. Verse 38 is very similar to Job 37:18, which we discovered in our retranslation was actually referring to the "hammered" heaven", the asteroid belt, which was hammered and spread out from the lower half of the primordial Earth. Here, in verse 38, one of the same words appears, *moowtsaq*, which literally means something that was molten, but then hardened into a solid form. Clearly once again, this is a reference to the asteroids, which were superheated fragments of rock jettisoned from Earth's mantle that quickly cooled and solidified in the absolute zero temperature of space. Thus they were "poured out" of Earth's mantle in molten form, then cooled and hardened into fragments of rock, heaps of stone that were "frozen" in space, where they continue to flow to this day.

Hebrew Text:	The Astronomical Interpretation	Enuma Elish
וַיִּמָּנַע מֵרְשָׁעִים אוֹרָם ³⁸ וּזְרוֹעַ רָמָה תִּשָּׁבֵר	³⁸ Where the molten rocks poured out of Earth's mantle hardened and clustered together.	(No parallel)

CONCLUSIONS

The Book of Job contains the largest amount of Creation-oriented material of all of the books of the Bible. More important to our present study, the Book of Job adheres closely to the Planet X/Giant Impact theory put forward in Chapter III. Moreover, there are verses that describe the Hebrew conception of the asteroid belt and the comets in ways that are scientifically advanced even by modern standards. But by far the greatest discovery in our analysis of Job is the fact that the Book of Job appears to be the Hebrew Creation Epic, with Job playing the role of the Moon, and his 11 family members playing the 11 comets. Sumer, the land of Job's nativity, plays the role of Tiamat which, like Tiamat, was destroyed by a great rock thrown down from heaven. The parallels with the related Sumerian lamentation texts over the destruction of the ancient empire of Sumer and its grand capitol city, Ur, along with the astronomical dating information found in chapters 1 and 2, make it clear that the disaster that led to the destruction of Sumer and ruin of Job occurred sometime between 1900 and 2000 b.c., possibly around 1915 B.C. Thus we may date one of the more recent appearances in human history of Planet X in the heavens to around 1915 B.C. — the time of Abraham and the beginnings of the nation of Israel, the tribe that would in time produce the Messiah.

Next, in the final chapter, we will continue to discuss the role of the great Star of heaven in the destiny of Israel, particularly the greatest Son of Israel, Jesus of Nazareth, where we will discover that it was not only the Star that heralded His birth, but also the Sign that will signal His imminent return.

VII

PLANET X, THE SIGN OF THE SON OF MAN, AND THE END OF THE AGE

> *Immediately after the tribulation of those days shall the Sun be darkened, and the Moon shall not give her light, and the stars shall fall from heaven, and the powers of the heavens shall be shaken: And then shall appear the sign of the Son of man in heaven: and then shall all the tribes of the earth mourn, and they shall see the Son of man coming in the clouds of heaven with power and great glory.*
> *(Matt. 24:29-30)*

"X marks the spot!" a jubilant Indiana Jones exclaimed, realizing he had found his first clue in his search for the holy grail.[1] Infinitely more important than the grail of myth and legend, however, Planet X is the true holy grail of archaeology, of mythology, of astronomy, of ancient Near Eastern history and, most important, of biblical studies. It is the key that unlocks all the mysteries of the Creation, the Nativity, and the Second Coming, and the blessed tie that binds them.

We have come full circle in our study of Planet X and its relationship with both the Creation and Nativity, ending here, in this final chapter, with a thorough analysis of Planet X's role in perhaps the greatest event in history — the Second Coming of Christ. To my surprise, none have considered the possibility that another planet in our solar system might fulfill all the criteria of not only the tool that God used to create Earth, and the Bethlehem star that heralded the birth of Christ, but also the great, heavenly Sign that will herald His

---

[1] *Indiana Jones and the Holy Grail* (Hollywood, CA: Paramount, 1989).

Second Coming. The knowledge of the return of the great star of God has been my pleasant burden for over 22 years, but now is the time to reveal the great secret of secrets — the return of Planet X, the throne of God.

THE "STAR" OF THE MESSIAH: THE BIBLICAL EVIDENCE
Though Jesus describes in Matthew 24:30 how a great, heavenly Sign will precede His Second Coming, its precise character is not explicitly stated. Is it a star, a planet, a "heavenly chariot", a great white horse, or something completely different that appears in the heavens? References to stars related to the Day of the Lord are surprisingly limited, however, and clear references to planets, nonexistent. However, the references to stars related to the history and final destiny of the children of Israel are telling indeed, as we shall see.

Old Testament References

✟ Genesis 15:5:
> ⁵ And he brought him forth abroad, and said, Look now toward heaven, and tell the stars, if thou be able to number them: and he said unto him, So shall thy seed be. (KJV)

The first mention of a "star" related to the children of God in the Old Testament has to do with God's promise to Abraham that He would multiply Abraham's seed as the stars of heaven. Abraham, as we saw in Chapter VI, was ordered by God to leave Ur of the Chaldees not long before it was destroyed by a meteorite sent by God from heaven. And while he sojourned in the land of Canaan, God gave him this promise in a vision, closely comparing the number of the descendants that would come from Abraham with the stars in heaven. Soon afterwards, God actually came down to Earth, appearing as a man in Genesis 18, visiting Abraham in his own tent. Most likely, Planet X was at its peak in the sky at that time, around 2000 B.C., hurling down meteorites upon God's earthly enemies, and marking the time of the coming of the preincarnate Christ, who would return to be born of the flesh 2,000 years later. Thus, by comparing Abraham's descendants to the stars in the sky, while Planet X sat high above the heavenly assembly, God's promise to Abraham made it clear that the destiny of the children of Israel would be to live among the stars — a destiny that would be tied to the occasional reappearance of Planet X in the heavens.

⚚ Genesis 37:9:
> [9] And he dreamed yet another dream, and told it his brethren, and said, Behold, I have dreamed a dream more; and, behold, the sun and the moon and the eleven stars made obeisance to me. (KJV)

The next mention of a "star" related to the destiny of the children of God in the Old Testament occurs in the story of Joseph. Joseph had a dream while wearing his "coat of many colors", wherein his father, mother and 11 brothers, in the form of the Sun, Moon, and "eleven stars" bowed down to him. As we discovered in Chapter VI, the number 11 appears prominently in The Book of Job as the number of family members that Job had, and also shows up in *Enuma Elish* as the number of "monster serpents" that Tiamat created from her body to defend herself from Marduk. We deduced from that, based upon the astronomical interpretation of the Creation material to be found in the Bible, that what was being referred to here, symbolically, was the comets, 11 of which were apparently considered major enough to be classified as "the 11". Furthermore, his father Jacob was described as being like the Sun, and his mother, like the Moon, all of whom, as the dream indicated, would bow down to Him. If so, if his father represented the Sun, and his mother, the Moon, and his brothers, the comets, then Joseph must have represented Planet X, which had conquered Tiamat's "heavenly army", the Moon and the comets, and for a brief time even outshone his father, the Sun. Thus we have in view here, in Genesis 37:9, a reference to the children of Israel being once again equated with the stars, and the leader of the children of Israel being equated with the King Star: Planet X.

⚚ Numbers 24:17:
> [17] I shall see him, but not now: I shall behold him, but not nigh: there shall come a Star out of Jacob, and a Sceptre shall rise out of Israel, and shall smite the corners of Moab, and destroy all the children of Sheth. (KJV)

Later in the history of Israel, early in the Conquest Period when they were migrating north into the lands of Moab, another important reference to a great Star appears in the destiny of the children of Israel. As we discussed in Chapter I, this mention was during the prophecy of Balaam, a magus not unlike the magi of Jesus' time, who also saw a Star that figured prominently in the history of Israel. Balaam had been sent by King Balak of the Moabites, upon whose territory Israel was encroaching, to curse them and drive them away. However, God took over this man Balaam and gave him a vision of Israel that was blessed and eternal, and which involved a great Star — which he compared to a Sceptre — that would actually destroy the Moabites.

This Sceptre is believed by most scholars to refer to Jesus, and the Star prophecy of course refers to the Star of Bethlehem. So the birth of Christ was prophesied not only by the magi of Jesus' time, but also by a magus who live during the time of Moses, ca. 1200-1440 B.C.

It is important to note that the "Star" that is mentioned here will not simply appear, but will appear and *attack* the enemies of Israel. Much like the "Sign of the Son of Man" that Jesus mentions in Matthew 24:30, this "Sceptre Star" is at once both a Sign of God's royal authority and a weapon, a "heavenly mace" that he uses to smite His enemies.

This idea of God using a mace to smash his enemies like a clay pot hearkens back to the old Sumerian myth, "The Feats and Exploits of Ninurta" that we analyzed in Chapter I, wherein the Sumerian deity Ninurta uses a great mace called the *Sharur* to smash the demon Asag like a clay pot, releasing the waters trapped therein. In this context, we can now more easily understand Jesus' enigmatic statement in Revelation 1:26-28: "And he shall rule them with a rod of iron; as the vessels of a potter shall they be broken to shivers: even as I received of my Father. And I will give him the morning star." Thus the destruction of God's enemies in the End Times will have to do with the destruction of Earth, like a clay pot, by a great Star in heaven — just as Balaam had predicted.[2]

---

[2] For an excellent analysis on Balaam, visit http://www.cgg.org/index.cfm/fuseaction/Library.sr/CT/PW/k/790/Prophecies-Balaam.htm, or go to http://www.cgg.org and search for "Balaam".

New Testament References

✟ Matthew 2:1-11:

The Star of Bethlehem has been a celebrated symbol of the birth of Christ since the advent of Christendom, to this day.

¹ Now when Jesus was born in Bethlehem of Judaea in the days of Herod the king, behold, there came wise men from the east to Jerusalem,
² Saying, Where is he that is born King of the Jews? For we have seen his star in the east, and are come to worship him.
³ When Herod the king had heard these things, he was troubled, and all Jerusalem with him.
⁴ And when he had gathered all the chief priests and scribes of the people together, he demanded of them where Christ should be born.
⁵ And they said unto him, In Bethlehem of Judaea: for thus it is written by the prophet,
⁶ And thou Bethlehem, in the land of Juda, art not the least among the princes of Juda: for out of thee shall come a Governor, that shall rule my people Israel.
⁷ Then Herod, when he had privily called the wise men, enquired of them diligently what time the star appeared.
⁸ And he sent them to Bethlehem, and said, Go and search diligently for the young child; and when ye have found him, bring me word again, that I may come and worship him also.
⁹ When they had heard the king, they departed; and, lo, the star, which they saw in the east, went before them, till it came and stood over where the young child was.
¹⁰ When they saw the star, they rejoiced with exceeding great joy.
¹¹ And when they were come into the house, they saw the young child with Mary his mother, and fell down, and worshipped him: and when they had opened their treasures, they presented unto him gifts; gold, and frankincense, and myrrh. (KJV)

As we saw with the prophecy of Balaam, the birth of the leader of Israel was indeed indicated by the appearance of a special Star, rising like a Sceptre to smash the enemies of God. Also like the prophecy of Balaam, Christ's advent was met by a delegation of Magi of a similar order who, like Balaam, knew that the reappearance of the sacred Star, Planet X, meant that God Himself had returned to visit Earth once more — this time, in the form of a babe wrapped in swaddling clothes, lying in a manger.

✠ 2 Peter 1:19:
[19] We have also a more sure word of prophecy; whereunto ye do well that ye take heed, as unto a light that shineth in a dark place, until the day dawn, and the day star arise in your hearts.

✠ Revelation 2:26-28:
[26] And he that overcometh, and keepeth my works unto the end, to him will I give power over the nations:
[27] And he shall rule them with a rod of iron; as the vessels of a potter shall they be broken to shivers: even as I received of my Father.
[28] And I will give him the morning star.

✠ Revelation 22:16:
[16] I Jesus have sent mine angel to testify unto you these things in the churches. I am the root and the offspring of David, and the bright and morning star.

As we saw previously in our analysis of Numbers 24:17, the Star that would accompany the advent of the King of Israel would also be a weapon that that King would use to smite His enemies. We get further clarification from 2 Peter 1:19 and Revelation 2:26-28 and 22:16 that this Star would rise like the Sun, described as a "day star" in 2 Peter, and a "morning star" in Revelation 2 and 22. Perhaps this means that Planet X will be so bright upon its appearance that it will rival the Sun in brightness. However, whereas the Sun rises on both the righteous and the wicked, this "day star" will rise to benefit the righteous, but destroy the wicked. Perhaps it is this same "day star" that Malachi described as the "Sun of Righteousness" that will rise with healing in its wings in Malachi 4:2. Thus Planet X should be understood to be a "Sun of Righteousness", a special Sun that God created for His Son, a Sun that rises only for God's chosen.

The Planet of Bethlehem
The existence of numerous references to a "star" closely associated with Jesus indicates that the Star of Bethlehem was apparently still being used to symbolize Jesus even after his ascension. In Rev. 22:16 Jesus actually refers to Himself as "the morning star." Though the planet Venus was and is still considered to be the "morning star", due to the fact that it is usually the first "star" seen in the morning due to its exceptional brightness, this cannot be a reference to Planet Venus, since Venus continued to be worshiped as a symbol of the goddess Venus well after Christ's death. Even in the unlikely event that Christ would associate Himself with this planet, its pagan connotations would have been confusing to young Christians newly converted from their astrological beliefs, wherein Venus was actually worshiped as a goddess. Therefore, this must refer to some other heavenly body which served as a symbol for Christ, most likely the body with which Christ had been associated all along: the Star of Bethlehem.

But exactly how long Planet X would have remained visible from Earth depends upon the how long it takes to orbit the Sun. Fortunately, in the book of 2 Peter, chapter 3, we have the answer:

☧   2 Peter 3:7-8:
   ⁷ But the heavens and the earth, which are now, by the same word are kept in store, reserved unto fire against the day of judgment and perdition of ungodly men.
   ⁸ But, beloved, be not ignorant of this one thing, that one day is with the Lord as a thousand years, and a thousand years as one day.(KJV)

Second Peter 3 contains some of the most crucial evidence in the Bible supporting the existence of Planet X. Not only does it describe *the* Day of the LORD as a time of judgment by fire from heaven, but it actually defines *a* "day of the LORD" as a period of 1,000 years. This could be interpreted many ways, but in the context of the Planet X/Giant Impact Theory it is best interpreted as a description of the orbital period of Planet X. In this sense, verse 8 is essentially saying that one orbital period for "God" is 1,000 years, where Planet X, God's heavenly throne, returns every 1,000 years to rule the night sky.[3] As we saw in chapter III, most astronomers who have studied Planet X agree that its orbital period is indeed somewhere between 800 and 1,200 years, so Peter's description of the length of *a* "Day of the Lord" makes perfect sense, in context. This is to be distinguished from *the* Day of the Lord, which specifically refers to the Apocalypse, when God will allow Planet X to pass close enough to Earth to cause massive destruction that would have been similar in scale to that of the Creation if God Himself had not cut it short (Matthew 24:22).

If Planet X's orbital period is indeed 1,000 years, even at maximum speed, Planet X only travels between 9,000 and 10,000 miles per hour, similar to the speed of Earth, and it attains this speed only at perihelion:

Velocity (v) at perihelion (closest approach to the Sun):
v = velocity
a = distance from the sun in Astronomical Units (100 A.U. est.)
P = orbital period (1,000 years)
e = orbital eccentricity (1.9, estimated)
$v = (2\pi a / P) \times (1 + e / 1 - e)^{1/2}$
   $= .628 \times 1.79$
   $= 1.12$ A.U./year
   $= \underline{9,847 \text{ miles per hour}}$

Since the inner part of Planet X's orbit lies in the asteroid belt, we can use the size of the asteroid belt to help calculate approximately how long Planet X remains within the inner solar system. Assuming that, according to Figure 7.1, Planet X moves through roughly half of the asteroid belt before it leaves the inner solar system, then we may use this as an approximate figure on which to calculate how long Planet X remains in the inner solar system:

Half the circumference of the asteroid belt:
$\pi = 3.1416$
r = radius (= distance from the Sun)

---

[3] Cf also Job 9:3. The problem with a 1,000 year orbit is that Planet X was not seen around A.D. 1000. Thus it could be that Planet X's orbit is actually 2,000 years long, comprised of one thousand-year "night", where it is heading out of the solar system to its aphelion, and one thousand-year "day" where it returns to its perihelion.

1 A.U. (Astronomical Unit) = 93,000,000 miles
2.8 A.U. = distance of the asteroid belt from the sun
(= radius of the circle of the asteroid belt)

2πr/2
= π * r
= 3.1416 x 2.8 A.U.
= 8.8 A.U.

In miles:
8.8 A.U. x 93,000,000 miles
= 818,400,000 miles

Time Planet X spends in the asteroid belt (perihelion):
818,400,000 miles / 9,847 miles per hour
= 83,111 hours
= 3,462 days
= 9.48 years

Planet X, with its highly elliptical orbit, will dramatically speed up when on the inner part of its orbit around the Sun, explaining why, in Psalm 19:5, God is described as a "strong man to run a race". Accelerating up to around 9,000-10,000 miles per hour through the asteroid belt, Planet X will remain visible for up to 10 years. Before and after that period it will probably be invisible to the naked eye, just as the comets become invisible once they move a certain distance away from the Sun. Thus Planet X, like the comets, probably does not form its "tail" and thereby become visible from Earth, until it passes the orbit of Jupiter on its way to the inner solar system. Otherwise, the near-black (albeido: ~4%)[4] surface of Planet X, without the cometlike tail to reflect the light of the Sun, makes Planet X undetectable by even the most advanced optical telescopes. If Planet X is indeed a black

---

[4]"Albeido" is a measure of the reflectivity of a given body; i.e., how much light that hits it is reflected back. Albeido is measured as a percentage of reflected light, where an albeido of 100% means all light that hits an object is reflected back. For comparison, Earth has an albeido of 0.39, or 39%, whereas comets, before the sublimation process occurs (forming their highly reflective "tail"), actually have albeidos of only around 4% or less. See chapter III for a more detailed discussion of the comets.

body like the comets — in effect, a "stealth planet" — it probably also absorbs energy at all wavelengths and emits little or none, making detection by even infrared telescopes extremely difficult. In effect, God "hides" Himself in clouds and thick darkness (Job 22:10-14; Ps.18:91; 97:2).

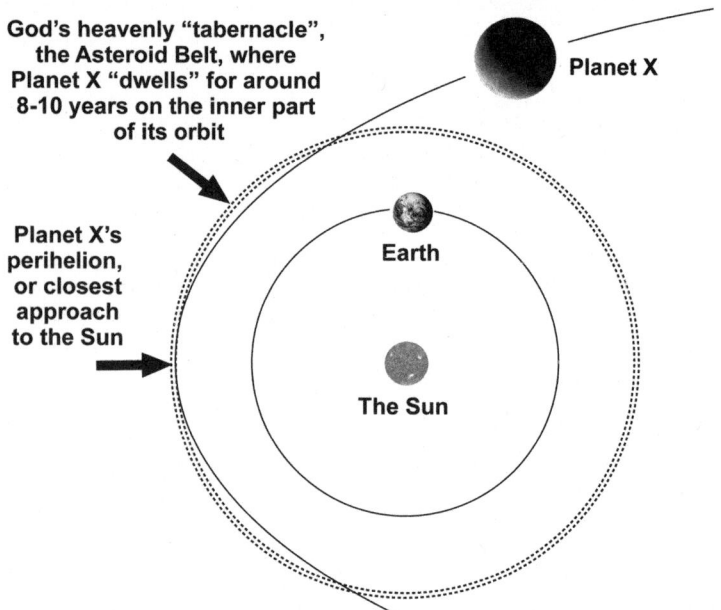

Figure 7.1: Based upon a 1,000-year orbital period, Planet X would take roughly 8-10 years to pass through the inner part of its orbit through the asteroid belt. Since this calculation is based upon only an estimated orbital eccentricity and distance from the Sun, it may well be that Planet X's inner orbit will last 7 years, and thus may actually serve as the "clock" by which the events of the Tribulation Period are set.

Behold, I Come as a Thief in the Night

The evidence for the Second Coming seems to point to the fact that God's coming will not be something that can be predicted, but something that happens suddenly and unexpectedly, something that not even man's advanced technology can predict. On the surface, this would seem to go against the idea of the Sign of the Son of Man being a planet. However, if Planet X is in fact something like a giant comet, then it would, like all comets, only become visible to Earth when it comes close enough to the Sun for its *coma*, or "tail," to form. Though up to that time it should be invisible to all but the most sophisticated telescopes, as soon as the coma forms, it will immediately become the brightest object in the night sky, and be clearly visible to everyone on Earth (Matt. 24:30). Thus, the concept of the Lord as a "thief in the night" is an apt metaphor for Planet X, as it is essentially clothed in deep black, hidden from observation and, like a thief, it approaches Earth stealthily, from beneath. With this in mind, the heretofore mysterious references to the Lord's return being like "a thief in the night" become clear:

☥ 1 Thessalonians 5:1-4:
^{1} But of the times and the seasons, brethren, ye have no need that I write unto you.
^{2} For yourselves know perfectly that the day of the Lord so cometh as a thief in the night.
^{3} For when they shall say, Peace and safety; then sudden destruction cometh upon them, as travail upon a woman with child; and they shall not escape.
^{4} But ye, brethren, are not in darkness, that that day should overtake you as a thief. (KJV)

☥ 2 Peter 3:10:
^{10} But the day of the Lord will come as a thief in the night; in which the heavens shall pass away with a great noise, and the elements shall melt with fervent heat, the earth also and the works that are therein shall be burned up. (KJV)

☥ Rev. 3.3:
^{10} Remember therefore how thou hast received and heard, and hold fast, and repent. If therefore thou shalt not watch, I will come on thee as a thief, and thou shalt not know what hour I will come upon thee. (KJV)

☥ Rev. 16:15:
^{10} Behold, I come as a thief. Blessed is he that watcheth, and keepeth his garments, lest he walk naked, and they see his shame. (KJV)

In 1 Thessalonians and 2 Peter, the "Day of the Lord" is described as a time when God will suddenly and destructively attack Earth. The reference to Jesus returning as "a thief in the night" in Revelation 16:15 actually takes place just before the seventh bowl judgment is poured out upon the Earth. Instead of being seen from afar off as a conquering king, these verses portray God as first "sneaking up" on Earth just before He attacks. It seems that God would have no need to do this if it were just He who was returning in bodily form. In fact, the very idea of "sneaking up" seems to be totally contrary to God's character. The LORD's coming is shown throughout the Bible to be a time of great distress, with lightning and thunder and earthquakes, with the LORD appearing very suddenly and very visibly to judge Earth. The description here of God approaching Earth stealthily is therefore yet more evidence that His return involves something more than His personal, sudden, visible, bodily appearance in heaven. The evidence also indicates that He will return riding some sort of vehicle, in use like a chariot, as it is also a weapon, an instrument of divine judgment that He will use to judge Earth. This "chariot" is capable of approaching Earth stealthily, suddenly appearing as a glorious apparition in the heavens, and wreaking terrible devastation upon Earth. And Planet X, as we have seen, is the only object capable of doing all three of these things, and more.

✦ Matthew 24:29-30, 36, 42-44:
[29] Immediately after the tribulation of those days shall the Sun be darkened, and the Moon shall not give her light, and the stars shall fall from heaven, and the powers of the heavens shall be shaken:
[30] And then shall appear the sign of the Son of man in heaven: and then shall all the tribes of the earth mourn, and they shall see the Son of man coming in the clouds of heaven with power and great glory.
[36] But of that day and hour knoweth no man, no, not the angels of heaven, but my Father only.
[42] Watch therefore: for ye know not what hour your Lord doth come.
[43] But know this, that if the goodman of the house had known in what watch the thief would come, he would have watched, and would not have suffered his house to be broken up.

⁴⁴ Therefore be ye also ready: for in such an hour as ye think not the Son of man cometh. (KJV)

Jesus, right after mentioning the appearance of His Sign in heaven to herald His return, describes that return as being sudden and unexpected, like a "thief." Apparently this "Sign" will appear in heaven rather suddenly, immediately preceded by shifts in the orbits of the planets (the "powers of the heavens") and a massive meteor shower ("stars" falling from heaven). Obviously, if a purely supernatural sign were intended here, there would be no need for God to alter the orbits of the planets or send down massive amounts of meteorites. Instead, God Himself could simply appear, snap His fingers, and His enemies would cease to exist. However, since these things are predicted to happen, surely there must be some reason for God to do them besides dramatic effect.

Some sort of natural object must be in mind here, an object that is capable of affecting the orbits of the planets and launching showers of meteorites at Earth. Clearly, once again, Planet X is in view here. Approaching unseen, Planet X will subtly but noticeably alter the orbits of the outer planets, as it has been doing to the orbits of Uranus and Neptune for over a century. The deviations in the orbits of the outer planets will become more and more pronounced as Planet X moves through our solar system until it reaches the inner solar system, where its massive tail will suddenly flare to life, heralding the glorious Second Coming of Christ.

The Day of the Lord

The Day of the LORD, which occurs every 1,000 years, is measured by each appearance of Planet X in the heavens. Sometimes, apparently, Planet X does not appear at all, as was apparently the case around 1000 A.D. However, it appeared at the birth of Christ, and apparently also during the time of Abraham whose birth around 2000 B.C., according to Jewish legends, was also foretold by a star.[5] Thus it is possible that Planet X's orbital period is actually 2,000 years, 1,000 years outbound, and 1,000 years inbound, which would explain why it makes prominent appearances only every 2,000 years: 1) During the

---

[5] Louis Ginzberg, *The Legends of the Jews Vol. I: From the Creation to Jacob* (New York: Jewish Publication Society of America, 1909). Available online at http://classiclit.about.com/library/bl-etexts/lginzberg/bl-lginzberg-legends-1-5h.htm

time of Abraham, 2) at the birth of Jesus, and 3) almost certainly in our near future. However, for sake of argument, we will assume that the period of Planet X is 1,000 years.

The "Day of the LORD", which appears to be a special day that occurs every 1,000 (or 2,000) years, has its beginning and end defined by the "Planet X Clock", which begins and ends when Planet X reaches its perihelion. However, in the Bible, *the* "Day of the LORD" appears to refer to a specific day yet future when God will return to Earth, smite His enemies, and take over the rulership of Earth. But because He returns not as a suffering Servant, but as a conquering King, He will be met by fierce opposition from the remaining inhabitants of Earth. Thus all direct and indirect references to the Day of the LORD in the Bible make much of the awful carnage that will take place when the LORD destroys those who dare to oppose His coming.

Isaiah 33:16-17 contains an interesting reference to the Day of the LORD that implies that God lives in a "land" that is very distant. This "land," or "far country" (Isa. 13:5), lies at the "end of heaven" (v. 5). According to Isaiah, God will travel from this far country which lies at the end of heaven in order to return to Earth and destroy those who oppose His rule:

✢ Isaiah 13:1-13:
¹ The burden of Babylon, which Isaiah the son of Amoz did see.
² Lift ye up a banner upon the high mountain, exalt the voice unto them, shake the hand, that they may go into the gates of the nobles.
³ I have commanded my sanctified ones, I have also called my mighty ones for mine anger, even them that rejoice in my highness.
⁴ The noise of a multitude in the mountains, like as of a great people; a tumultuous noise of the kingdoms of nations gathered together: the LORD of hosts mustereth the host of the battle.
⁵ They come from a far country, from the end of heaven, even the LORD, and the weapons of his indignation, to destroy the whole land.
⁶ Howl ye; for the day of the LORD is at hand; it shall come as a destruction from the Almighty.
⁷ Therefore shall all hands be faint, and every man's heart shall melt:

⁸ And they shall be afraid: pangs and sorrows shall take hold of them; they shall be in pain as a woman that travaileth: they shall be amazed one at another; their faces shall be as flames.
⁹ Behold, the day of the LORD cometh, cruel both with wrath and fierce anger, to lay the land desolate: and he shall destroy the sinners thereof out of it.
¹⁰ For the stars of heaven and the constellations thereof shall not give their light: the Sun shall be darkened in his going forth, and the Moon shall not cause her light to shine.
¹¹ And I will punish the world for their evil, and the wicked for their iniquity; and I will cause the arrogancy of the proud to cease, and will lay low the haughtiness of the terrible.
¹² I will make a man more precious than fine gold; even a man than the golden wedge of Ophir.
¹³ Therefore I will shake the heavens, and the earth shall remove out of her place, in the wrath of the LORD of hosts, and in the day of his fierce anger. (KJV)

As we saw in our analysis of this passage in Chapter V, the "far country" that is at "the end of heaven", actually appears in the Hebrew text to be describing another planet in our solar system. This is supported by the fact that Earth will actually be moved out of it current orbital station, "out of *her* place", as a result of God's wrath. This would require a planet-sized object to accomplish. Once again, as it was "in the beginning", in the End Times, God will use Planet X to attack Earth and move it to a new orbital station.[6]

✝ Isaiah 26:20-27:1
²⁰ Come, my people, enter thou into thy chambers, and shut thy doors about thee: hide thyself as it were for a little moment, until the indignation be overpast.
²¹ For, behold, *the LORD cometh out of his place* to punish the inhabitants of the Earth for their iniquity: the Earth also shall disclose her blood, and shall no more cover her slain.

---

[6] This may result in a perfect 360-day year as part of the setup for Messiah's reign. Likewise the Moon's orbit may equate to exactly 30 days, instead of the current 29.5.

¹ In that day the LORD with his sore and great and strong sword shall punish leviathan the piercing serpent, even leviathan that crooked serpent; and he shall slay the dragon that is in the sea.

The classic reference in Isaiah 27:1 to God's end-time battle with Leviathan is, interestingly, immediately after a reference to God "coming out of His place" to punish the inhabitants of Earth. The parallels with the Planet X/Giant Impact Theory and *Enuma Elish* are obvious. This reference, along with Isaiah 13:5, make it clear that God revealed to Isaiah that the instrument of his revenge was a physical object in heaven. This object would move toward Earth and wreak havoc upon it in one specific day which had been designated since the beginning of time. With clockwork precision, God knew from the beginning exactly what would happen and when. No wonder the Psalmist says,

> Why do the heathen rage, and the people imagine a vain thing? The kings of the earth set themselves, and the rulers take counsel together, against the LORD, and against his anointed, saying, "Let us break their bands asunder, and cast away their cords from us." He that sitteth in the heavens shall laugh: the LORD shall have them in derision. (Ps. 2:1-4, KJV)

In chapter 29, Isaiah further describes the end-times, when the nations of the Earth are arrayed against Jerusalem, or "Ariel." Even though at that time Jerusalem will be in a state of apostasy, God will judge and purify her through war, and then utterly destroy those who made war against Jerusalem with fire.

✟ Isaiah 29:1-7:
> ¹ Woe to Ariel, to Ariel, the city where David dwelt! add ye year to year; let them kill sacrifices.
> ² Yet I will distress Ariel, and there shall be heaviness and sorrow: and it shall be unto me as Ariel.
> ³ And I will camp against thee round about, and will lay siege against thee with a mount, and I will raise forts against thee.
> ⁴ And thou shalt be brought down, and shalt speak out of the ground, and thy speech shall be low out of the dust, and thy voice shall be, as of one that hath a familiar spirit, out of the ground, and thy speech shall whisper out of the dust.

⁵ Moreover the multitude of thy strangers shall be like small dust, and the multitude of the terrible ones shall be as chaff that passeth away: yea, it shall be at an instant suddenly.
⁶ Thou shalt be visited of the LORD of hosts with thunder, and with earthquake, and great noise, with storm and tempest, and the flame of devouring fire.
⁷ And the multitude of all the nations that fight against Ariel, even all that fight against her and her munition, and that distress her, shall be as a dream of a night vision. (KJV)

Not only will God destroy the nations that will array themselves against Jerusalem, he will destroy them so quickly and so completely that it will be as if their vast armies never existed in the first place. The fire from heaven will be so intense that they and their equipment will be turned to dust instantly, leaving little or no evidence that they had ever been there at all. It is unlikely that nuclear weapons are being referred to here, as all the armies of Earth will have, by this time, dropped their mutual animosity toward each other and united to resist Christ at His Second Coming (Ps. 2:1-4; Zech. 14:1-4; Rev. 16:13-14; 19:19-21). Thus, barring some sort of supernatural force, this fire could only come from Planet X, the only other physical object capable of generating such awesome destructive power.

Isaiah's description of the end-times continues in chapter 30, where he describes in detail the conditions that will accompany the return of Planet X:

✡ Isaiah 30:26-33:
²⁶ Moreover the light of the Moon shall be as the light of the Sun, and the light of the Sun shall be sevenfold, as the light of seven days, in the day that the LORD bindeth up the breach of his people, and healeth the stroke of their wound.
²⁷ Behold, the name of the LORD cometh from far, burning with his anger, and the burden thereof is heavy: his lips are full of indignation, and his tongue as a devouring fire:
²⁸ And his breath, as an overflowing stream, shall reach to the midst of the neck, to sift the nations with the sieve of vanity: and there shall be a bridle in the jaws of the people, causing them to err.

²⁹ Ye shall have a song, as in the night when a holy solemnity is kept; and gladness of heart, as when one goeth with a pipe to come into the mountain of the LORD, to the mighty One of Israel.
³⁰ And the LORD shall cause his glorious voice to be heard, and shall shew the lighting down of his arm, with the indignation of his anger, and with the flame of a devouring fire, with scattering, and tempest, and hailstones.
³¹ For through the voice of the LORD shall the Assyrian be beaten down, which smote with a rod.
³² And in every place where the grounded staff shall pass, which the LORD shall lay upon him, it shall be with tabrets and harps: and in battles of shaking will he fight with it.
³³ For Tophet is ordained of old; yea, for the king it is prepared; he hath made it deep and large: the pile thereof is fire and much wood; the breath of the LORD, like a stream of brimstone, doth kindle it. (KJV)

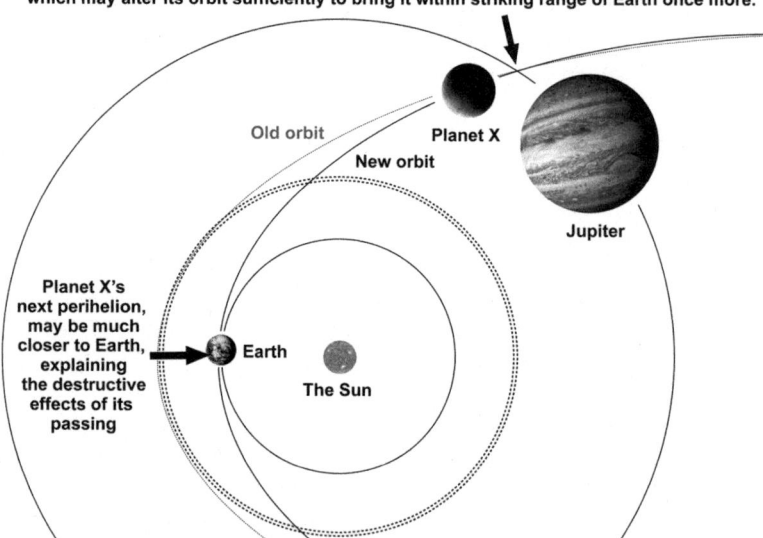

Figure 7.2: The events of the Tribulation appear to describe Planet X passing near enough to Earth so that an electrical discharge, "the grounded staff", will pass between the two planets. If so, then the words of Jesus "And except those days should be shortened, there should no flesh be saved: but for the elect's sake those days shall be shortened." (Matthew 24:22) should be taken literally. Thus shortened, Planet X's time within the inner solar system may be reduced from 9-10 years to 7 years.

The End of the Age

This time, Isaiah adds much more detail to the conditions that will prevail in the end-times, when Planet X returns. Isaiah first refers to Planet X as "the Name of the Lord," His throne-chariot that He uses when He goes to war against His enemies. Planet X is described as "returning from afar," after having spent many centuries orbiting outside of the solar system, the "end of heaven." Planet X's massive, cometlike coma will reflect a great deal of sunlight back onto Earth, seven times as much as normal. Much of this light will also reflect off of the Moon, making it appear much brighter. Naturally this 700 percent increase in ambient light will make temperatures soar on Earth, as is prophesied in the Book of Revelation. "And the fourth angel poured out his vial upon the Sun; and power was given unto him to scorch men with fire. And men were scorched with great heat, and blasphemed the name of God, which hath power over these plagues: and they repented not to give him glory" (Rev. 16:8-9, KJV). Furthermore, when Planet X reaches its closest approach to Earth, an electrical discharge will pass between the two planets, described here as "devouring fire" that comes out of God's mouth. This has parallels in both *Enuma Elish* and the Book of Revelation. In *Enuma Elish,* "Marduk," or Planet X, was also described as having the ability to breathe fire: "Perfect were his members beyond comprehension, unsuited for understanding, difficult to perceive. Four were his eyes, four were his ears; When he moved his lips, fire blazed forth (I:93-96).

The Book of Revelation also describes Christ as having a flaming sword coming out of His mouth, which He also uses to destroy His enemies (Rev. 19:15-21). The sword of God's mouth is further described as "lightning" and as a "flame of devouring fire" and, interestingly, as "the grounded staff", which is reminiscent of an electrical charge like lightning that must find "ground" in order to equalize the disparity between earth and sky.

This staff, "the breath of the LORD," is prepared for "the king," most likely a reference to the Antichrist, the king of this world (cf. Rev. 9:11; 13:11-18). It is notable that the Antichrist, along with the Beast, is to be thrown directly into the "lake of fire" at the Second Coming of Christ. (Rev. 19:20) The reference to "Tophet" in verse 33 refers to the place in the valley of Gehenna where idolatrous Israelites once burned their children alive as a sacrifice to Molech — a practice so evil that it warranted instant execution (Lev. 18:21; 20:2-5; 1 Kings 11:7; 2

Kings 23:10; Jer. 23:25; see also Jer. 7:31-32; 19:6, 11-14).[7] Thus, by associating end-time Earth with the utter abomination of the Tophet, God is saying that not only will Earth practice mass infanticide in the end times (as it does now, in the form of so-called "abortion"), but the people of end-time Earth will be destroyed by fire just as they destroyed their innocent unborn.

Isaiah continues his prophecies of the end times in chapter 34. The references to Armageddon, along with the description of intense meteoric activity and shifts in the orbits of the planets, align perfectly with Jesus' description of the end times in Matthew 24. However, Isaiah adds along with this description a mysterious reference to a "heavenly sword" that finds an easy parallel in the other flaming swords so common to references to the Second Coming.

⚛ Isaiah 34:1-5:

¹ Come near, ye nations, to hear; and hearken, ye people: let the Earth hear, and all that is therein; the world, and all things that come forth of it.

² For the indignation of the LORD is upon all nations, and his fury upon all their armies: he hath utterly destroyed them, he hath delivered them to the slaughter.

³ Their slain also shall be cast out, and their stink shall come up out of their carcases, and the mountains shall be melted with their blood.

⁴ And all the host of heaven shall be dissolved, and the heavens shall be rolled together as a scroll: and all their host shall fall down, as the leaf falleth off from the vine, and as a falling fig from the fig tree.

⁵ For my sword shall be bathed in heaven: behold, it shall come down upon Idumea, and upon the people of my curse, to judgment.

This is another clear reference to the End Times when the armies of Earth will make a desperate and foolish attempt to stop Christ from returning to Earth. The Book of Revelation also speaks of this time, when the assembled armies of Earth will be literally annihilated by the fiery sword that proceeds from the mouth of Christ (Rev. 19:11-21). Interestingly, the word used here in verse 2 for "utterly destroyed" is

---

[7] "Tophet" may be related to טַף, *taph*, "children."

הֶחֱרִימָם *he-ḥariym-am*, from the verb חָרַם *ḥaram*, "to ban, make illegal, wipe out completely, exterminate." This word is only used in one other situation in the Bible — during the Exodus period, when the Israelites were ordered to literally erase the Canaanites from the face of the Earth: "And when the LORD thy God shall deliver them before thee; thou shalt smite them, and *utterly destroy* them; thou shalt make no covenant with them, nor shew mercy unto them (Deut. 7:2, KJV). In other words, the people of Earth at the end time will have become so irretrievably corrupt that God will declare the death penalty for all mankind, just as He had with the Flood. However this time, instead of coming by water, judgment will come by fire, a judgment that will leave only a small percentage of humanity alive (Matt. 24:21-22). Those who live in the End Times will be as evil as those of Noah's day (Matt. 24:37-39; cf. also 2 Peter 3), and as evil as those of Sodom, who were also destroyed by "fire from heaven" (Gen. 19:24-25) around 2000 B.C. — a previous time when Planet X passed near Earth, causing the destruction of Sumer and the ruin of Job.

Verse 4, which appears to have been paraphrased by John the Revelator in Revelation 6:13-14, describes what could only be a massive meteor shower. Since all of the asteroids and asteroid clusters of any significance have been cataloged and are being closely monitored, and since none of these asteroids poses any significant threat to Earth in the near future, this apocalyptic meteor shower must have some other source. I suggest that, since Planet X passes through the asteroid belt on the inner leg of its orbit, this verse may be saying that Planet X will, in effect, end up launching many of the asteroids out of the belt area toward Earth. Planet X would most likely capture many asteroids in its orbit as it passes through the Belt, many of which would strike Earth if Planet X were heading in that direction. This would explain the many references to stars "falling from heaven" so common to end-time prophecies (Isa. 13:10; Ezek. 32:7; Dan. 8:10; Matt. 24:29; Mark 13:25; Rev. 6:13; 12:4). More importantly, it explains some of the more enigmatic references to heaven as a "munition of rocks" (Isa. 33:16-17), a place where rocks are stored which God uses as weapons of judgment against His enemies (Ex. 9:18-24; Josh. 10:8-14; Ps. 18:12-13; Job 38:22-23; Isa. 30:30; Ezek. 13:11, 13; 38:22; Nahum 1:6; cf. also Matt. 24:29; Mark 13:25; Rev. 6:13; 12:4). And if Planet X's orbit is indeed sufficiently altered by the gravitic pull of one or more of the outer planets as it returns to the inner solar system, it could well be that Earth will be showered with one of the many asteroids that Planet X no doubt carries in its train during its grand orbit around the Sun — remnants of the primordial Earth, ironically, used to attack Earth once more.

REVELATION: THE RETURN OF THE DRAGON

As it was in the beginning times, so it will be in the end times, when the dragon rises again, along with her companion, the beast. The same characters we saw emerge as the enemies of God in the great Creation battle, the sea dragon and the earth-beast, will emerge again in the End Times, ready to fight against God once more.

After several appearances in the Old Testament, "the dragon" does not appear again in the New Testament until the very last book: the Book of Revelation. The dragon is first mentioned in Revelation 12, where it is described as having been thrown down from heaven to Earth as the result of a losing battle against Michael and his angels:

✟ Revelation 12:3-4, 7-9:
[3] And there appeared another wonder in heaven; and behold a great red dragon, having seven heads and ten horns, and seven crowns upon his heads.
[4] And his tail drew the third part of the stars of heaven, and did cast them to the earth: and the dragon stood before the woman which was ready to be delivered, for to devour her child as soon as it was born.
[7] And there was war in heaven: Michael and his angels fought against the dragon; and the dragon fought and his angels,
[8] And prevailed not; neither was their place found any more in heaven.
[9] And the great dragon was cast out, that old serpent, called the Devil, and Satan, which deceiveth the whole world: he was cast out into the earth, and his angels were cast out with him.

Unlike the dragon of the Old Testament, the dragon of the New Testament does not appear to symbolize the Earth, however, which it did in the ancient Creation battle. Instead, it is portrayed as the evil spirit that is within the Earth, that is the primary motivator behind the current world system. However, like the dragon of the Old Testament, this dragon also has seven heads, just as Leviathan is described in Psalm 74 and in the Canaanite myths, so John the Revelator appears to be drawing upon the old dragon myth of the Old Testament to revive her as the primary antagonist of God in the End Times. Thus we see in the next chapter, chapter 13, a mysterious "beast" rising out of the sea....

The Beast from the Sea — The Return of Leviathan

☧ Revelation 13:1:
   [1] And I stood upon the sand of the sea, and saw a beast rise up out of the sea, having seven heads and ten horns, and upon his horns ten crowns, and upon his heads the name of blasphemy.

Just after we are told that the dragon who was cast down to Earth has determined to persecute the people of God, in the next chapter a mysterious "beast" rises, Tiamat-like, out of the sea to take the rulership of the Earth. While this beast is dragonlike, with its bestial character and seven heads, it is not the dragon, but the dragon's puppet, most likely symbolic of the governmental system that rules the world at the time of the Second Coming. Perhaps what is intended here is to clarify that "the dragon" is not the Earth itself, but the evil spirit that is bound within it and empowers the wicked world system which, if left to its own devices, will inevitably rise up to rebel against God.

The Beast from the Earth — The Return of Behemoth

☧ Revelation 13:11:
   [11] And I beheld another beast coming up out of the earth; and he had two horns like a lamb, and he spake as a dragon.

Just as in *Enuma Elish* and The Book of Job, the sea dragon is also accompanied by an earth-beast in The Book of Revelation. John the Revelator clearly understood that the sea dragon and the earth-beast were a pair, so he reused them to symbolize the leader of the End-Times world system, who was "born" from the dragon, and is crowned by her as the leader of her armies. Also like the earth beast, which was symbolic of the great "bull of heaven", the Moon, the End-Time earth beast will also be uniquely identifiable by his horns. And these horns will make it look like he is of heavenly origin, but his diabolic character will show through in his words and actions as the wicked son of the dragon, whose destiny is not heaven, but destruction.

THE SIGN OF THE SON OF MAN AND THE END OF THE AGE

☥ Matthew 24:3, 26-31:
³ And as he sat upon the mount of Olives, the disciples came unto him privately, saying, Tell us, when shall these things be? and what shall be the sign of thy coming, and of the end of the world?
²⁶ Wherefore if they shall say unto you, Behold, he is in the desert; go not forth: behold, he is in the secret chambers; believe it not.
²⁷ For as the lightning cometh out of the east, and shineth even unto the west; so shall also the coming of the Son of man be.
²⁸ For wheresoever the carcase is, there will the eagles be gathered together.
²⁹ Immediately after the tribulation of those days shall the Sun be darkened, and the Moon shall not give her light, and the stars shall fall from heaven, and the powers of the heavens shall be shaken:
³⁰ And then shall appear the Sign of the Son of Man in heaven: and then shall all the tribes of the earth mourn, and they shall see the Son of man coming in the clouds of heaven with power and great glory.
³¹ And he shall send his angels with a great sound of a trumpet, and they shall gather together his elect from the four winds, from one end of heaven to the other. (KJV)

Here again, in Matthew 24, we have a reference to lightning accompanying the return of Planet X, the "Sign of the Son of Man". Having snuck in unnoticed, Planet X will then flare into glorious brilliance to herald Christ's Second Coming. The next reference to the "carcass" in verse 28 is also very interesting, as there is a close parallel with a passage in Job 39, which takes place between the major Creation passage of Job 38, and the description of Behemoth, the beast from the Earth and Leviathan, the beast from the sea in Job 40-41:

> Doth the eagle mount up at thy command, and make her nest on high? She dwelleth and abideth on the rock, upon the crag of the rock, and the strong place. From thence she seeketh the prey, and her eyes behold afar off. Her young ones also suck up blood: and where the slain are, there is she. (Job 39:27-30, KJV)

This passage, particularly verse 30, seems to have been the basis for Jesus' mysterious prophecy in Matthew 24:28, where He described His Second Coming as a time when eagles would gather together at a "carcass." This description was given immediately before a more detailed description of His Second Coming as a time when there would be signs in heaven, falling stars, and shifts in the movements of the planets (the "powers of heaven"). Even more importantly, notice that Jesus automatically associates the tribulation that will accompany His Second Coming with the tribulation that accompanied the creation of the world — "such as was not since the beginning of the world" (Matt. 24:21). Clearly, Jesus was aware that Earth had been created not peacefully, but as the result of some sort of heavenly disaster. Further, He knew that this disaster would reoccur again at His Second Coming, *the same kind of disaster that had also occurred in Job's time* (ca. 2000 B.C.). Thus he paraphrases Job 39:29-30 in his description of the end-time:

> For then shall be great tribulation, *such as was not since the beginning of the world* to this time, no, nor ever shall be. For as the lightning cometh out of the east, and shineth even unto the west; so shall also the coming of the Son of man be. *For wheresoever the carcase is, there will the eagles be gathered together.* (Matt. 24:21, 27-28)

This carcass is that of the defeated dragon — specifically, the bodies of the dragon's armies who will be empowered by her in the End Times to fight against God once more. This "carrion" metaphor is further verified by John's description of the Battle of Armageddon, in Revelation 19:17-19, where the armies of Earth that are slain by God are described as carrion that is devoured by birds:[8]

---

[8]Eagles are actually closely related to vultures, and have many of their habits, including eating carrion.

And I saw an angel standing in the Sun; and he cried with a loud voice, saying to all the fowls that fly in the midst of heaven, Come and gather yourselves together unto the supper of the great God; That ye may eat the flesh of kings, and the flesh of captains, and the flesh of mighty men, and the flesh of horses, and of them that sit on them, and the flesh of all men, both free and bond, both small and great. And I saw the beast, and the kings of the earth, and their armies, gathered together to make war against him that sat on the horse, and against his army. And the beast was taken, and with him the false prophet that wrought miracles before him, with which he deceived them that had received the mark of the beast, and them that worshipped his image. These both were cast alive into a lake of fire burning with brimstone. And the remnant were slain with the sword of him that sat upon the horse, which sword proceeded out of his mouth: and all the fowls were filled with their flesh. (Rev. 19:17-21, KJV)

The close similarity between the eagle references in Job and Matthew makes it likely that Jesus had Job 38–41 in mind when He was describing the conditions that would accompany His return. Matthew 24:21 also provides evidence that not only was the creation of Earth one of the primary themes of Job, but also that this Creation was not a peaceful birth at all but a time of great tribulation, a tribulation that also included signs and wonders in the heavens. It further supports the idea that the End Times will include disasters that are comparable in scope to the sort of disasters that Earth endured during the Creation.

Next, in verse 29, the signs immediately preceding the Second Coming of Christ begin to make themselves manifest. Massive amounts of meteorites that precede Planet X in its orbit begin to bombard the Earth, sending up huge amounts of dust and ashes into the atmosphere which blanket Earth like a swaddlingband and cover it in deep darkness — so deep, that the Sun turns into a dim, deep red, and the Moon is not visible at all. The fact that the "powers of heaven", which in ancient times would have referred to the "gods", the planets, are shaken, means that something really, really big is moving through our solar system — so big, that even the orbits of the planets are affected by it. Approaching in stealth mode, Planet X will still be unable to completely mask its presence, as it will definitely have an effect on the orbits of the outer, and inner, planets on its way to its fateful rendezvous with Earth.

The End of the Age

Finally, at the climax of the Olivet Discourse, Jesus describes the appearance of the heavenly throne: Planet X, the Sign of the Son of Man, and the End of the Age. At last, the answer to all the riddles makes itself manifest. At last, the great mystery of mysteries is revealed.

The Seven Stars: The Return of Planet X

☥ Revelation 1:9-20:
[9] I John, who also am your brother, and companion in tribulation, and in the kingdom and patience of Jesus Christ, was in the isle that is called Patmos, for the word of God, and for the testimony of Jesus Christ.
[10] I was in the Spirit on the Lord's day, and heard behind me a great voice, as of a trumpet,
[11] Saying, I am Alpha and Omega, the first and the last: and, What thou seest, write in a book, and send it unto the seven churches which are in Asia; unto Ephesus, and unto Smyrna, and unto Pergamos, and unto Thyatira, and unto Sardis, and unto Philadelphia, and unto Laodicea.
[12] And I turned to see the voice that spake with me. And being turned, I saw seven golden candlesticks;
[13] And in the midst of the seven candlesticks one like unto the Son of man, clothed with a garment down to the foot, and girt about the paps with a golden girdle.
[14] His head and his hairs were white like wool, as white as snow; and his eyes were as a flame of fire;
[15] And his feet like unto fine brass, as if they burned in a furnace; and his voice as the sound of many waters.
[16] And he had in his right hand seven stars: and out of his mouth went a sharp twoedged sword: and his countenance was as the sun shineth in his strength.
[17] And when I saw him, I fell at his feet as dead. And he laid his right hand upon me, saying unto me, Fear not; I am the first and the last:
[18] I am he that liveth, and was dead; and, behold, I am alive for evermore, Amen; and have the keys of hell and of death.
[19] Write the things which thou hast seen, and the things which are, and the things which shall be hereafter;

[20]The mystery of the seven stars which thou sawest in my right hand, and the seven golden candlesticks. The seven stars are the angels of the seven churches: and the seven candlesticks which thou sawest are the seven churches.

The Book of Revelation opens with John being visited by Jesus on the isle of Patmos, a small island in the Aegean Sea between Greece and Asia Minor. Jesus then dictates to John, bidding him to write seven letters to the seven churches of Asia Minor. In these letters, he promises one of the seven churches, Thyatira, that if they remain faithful to Him, they would join Him in shattering the nations "with a rod of iron", and He would also give them "the morning star". In other words, they would be a part of the winning army at the final battle, the army led by the "heavenly mace", Planet X.

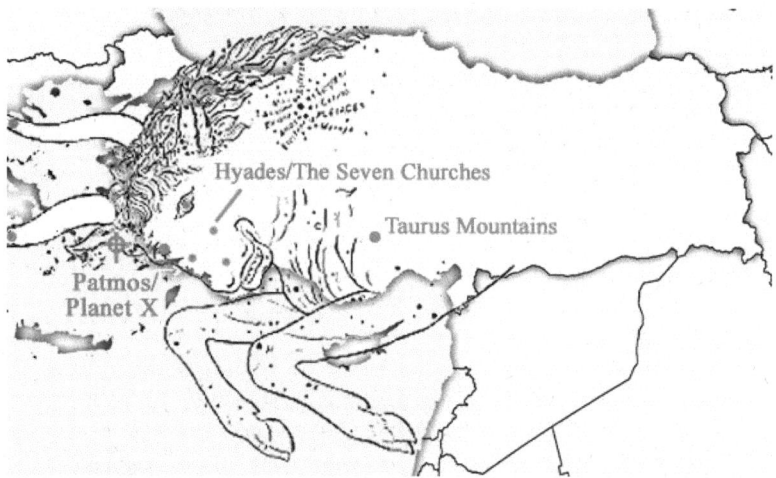

Figure 7.3. The constellation of Taurus mapped over Asia Minor (modern Turkey). In ancient times, this minor continent was associated with the constellation of Taurus, as evidenced by the mountains that still bear its name. The seven churches mentioned in Revelation 1-3 roughly correspond with the Hyades, an asterism in the face of the bull. Patmos most likely corresponds with the place that Planet X will reappear in the face of Taurus, explaining why Jesus appeared there to John.

The seven churches were arranged in a rough "V" formation, all clustered in southwestern Asia Minor, modern Turkey (see Figure 7.3). In ancient times, Asia Minor was associated with the constellation of Taurus, and a major mountain chain, the Taurus

Mountains, still bears that ancient name. The seven churches appear to correspond with an asterism in the face of Taurus called the Hyades which, including the stars in the horns, make up seven stars. This is probably why Jesus referred to the seven churches as "seven stars", and why He stood "in the midst" of them — this is the place in the sky where Planet X will reappear, from which Jesus and His army of saints will conquer Earth.

The Heavenly Throne: The Revelation of Planet X

☥ Revelation 4:1-6:
¹After this I looked, and, behold, a door was opened in heaven: and the first voice which I heard was as it were of a trumpet talking with me; which said, Come up hither, and I will shew thee things which must be hereafter.
²And immediately I was in the spirit: and, behold, a throne was set in heaven, and one sat on the throne.
³And he that sat was to look upon like a jasper and a sardine stone: and there was a rainbow round about the throne, in sight like unto an emerald.
⁴And round about the throne were four and twenty seats: and upon the seats I saw four and twenty elders sitting, clothed in white raiment; and they had on their heads crowns of gold.
⁵And out of the throne proceeded lightnings and thunderings and voices: and there were seven lamps of fire burning before the throne, which are the seven Spirits of God.
⁶And before the throne there was a sea of glass like unto crystal: and in the midst of the throne, and round about the throne, were four beasts full of eyes before and behind.

The description of Jesus having hair "white like wool" in Revelation 1:14 was purposeful, as John was describing how Jesus would appear in the heavens when He returns from His long journey. Planet X, when it suddenly becomes visible, will do so because of its brilliant, cometlike tail that will flare into life as soon as it comes close enough to the Sun for the sublimation process to begin. The description

An example of a sardine stone, which is in appearance blood red.

of Jesus having white hair is perfect, as the word "comet", as we have seen, comes from the Greek word *kometes*, "hair". Thus John saw Jesus as returning on a bright, cometlike planet that first appears among the seven stars in the head of the constellation of Taurus. This location makes perfect sense, as the first word in the Bible, בְּרֵאשִׁית *be-ra'shiyth*, "in the beginning", can also be translated as "in the head".

Naturally, after John finished describing Jesus as "the morning star" that will appear in the midst of seven other stars, he was taken up into heaven, where he was given a tour of this "morning star". This morning star, which is also the throne of God, is described as being like a jasper stone that is similar to a sardine stone. Sardine is a dark, reddish-brown stone, so Planet X, when heated by the sun, is apparently red in color, its cometlike tail of course appearing as pure white in the heavens. This corresponds perfectly with the description in the ancient Sumerian texts that describe the planet "Marduk" as a "red star":

> The red star, that, when stars of the night have finished,
> stays where the south wind comes from,
> halves the sky and stays there,
> is the god *nibiru, Marduk.*

The rest of the description of the throne of God in Revelation 4 details the other characteristics of Planet X. Here they are, in total, as taken from our analysis of Revelation 1-4 in light of the Planet X theory:

- First appearance in the head of the constellation of Taurus
- Bright, white cometlike tail (Rev. 1:14)
- Dark red in color (v. 3)
- Green-colored ring comprised of ice crystals (vv. 3, 6)
- 24 "Elder" satellites (v. 4)
- 7 "Archangel" satellites (v. 5)
- 4 "Living Creature" satellites (v. 6)

Thus in chapters 1-4 the hero of the story, Jesus, the returning King, has been properly introduced, or "revealed", and the weapons of His righteous might, Planet X, its great comet tail, and its many satellites, described in great detail. As if purposely to reassert Jesus as the true Master of the heavenly throne, Planet X, John uses imagery that is strikingly reminiscent of that used to describe the weaponry of Marduk in *Enuma Elish*:

> [Marduk's] destiny thus fixed, the gods, his fathers,
> Caused him to go the way of success and attainment.
> He constructed a bow, marked it as his weapon,
> Attached thereto the arrow, fixed its bow-cord.
> He raised the mace, made his right hand grasp it;
> Bow and quiver he hung at his side.
> In front of him he set the lightning,
> With a blazing flame he filled his body.
> He then made a net to enfold Tiamat therein.
> The four winds he stationed that nothing of her might escape,
> The South Wind, the North Wind, the East Wind, the West Wind.
> Close to his side he held the net, the gift of his father, Anu.
> He brought forth Imhullu "the Evil Wind,"
> the Whirlwind, the Hurricane,
> The Fourfold Wind, the Sevenfold Wind, the Cyclone,
> the Matchless Wind;
> Then he sent forth the winds he had brought forth, the seven of them.
> To stir up the inside of Tiamat they rose up behind him.
> Then the lord raised up the flood-storm, his mighty weapon.
> He mounted the storm chariot irresistible [and] terrifying.
> He harnessed (and) yoked it to a team-of-four,
> (Their) lips were parted, their teeth bore poison.
> They were tireless and skilled in destruction.
> On his right he posted the Smiter, fearsome in battle,
> On the left the Combat, which repels all the zealous.
> For a cloak he was wrapped in an armor of terror;
> With his fearsome halo his head was turbaned.
> The lord went forth and followed his course,
> Towards the raging Tiamat he set his face.
> (IV:1-4, 29-60)

The imagery, though described using a different style, is very similar to the description of God's throne in heaven in Revelation 4. Both Marduk and Jesus are said to have a set of four and a set of seven satellites moving around them (for a total of 11), both shine brightly, both shoot forth lightning, and both have several other common attributes, as described in the following table:

Table 7.1: Comparison of the "Throne-Chariots" of Jesus and Marduk

Attributes of Marduk and His Throne-Chariot	Attributes of Jesus and His Throne-Chariot	Modern Scientific Term
Main weapon a "mace"	Star of Jesus described as a "sceptre" (mace)	Planet
The "flood-storm"	Hair as white as wool and snow (i.e., ice)	Cometlike tail
Marduk described as a "red star"	Color of throne described as like a sardine stone (red)	Red in color
Head turbaned with "fearsome halo"	Throne surrounded by a sea of glass/crystal	Ring system
The four winds	The four "beasts"	Four primary satellites
The seven winds	The seven lamps of fire	Seven secondary satellites
Body filled with a "blazing flame"	Shines like the sun in its strength	Very high albeido, particularly with the tail
Set lightning in front of him.	Preceded by lightning, thunder and voices.	Powerful electric exchange when passing near other planets.

The similarities are so close as to be almost exact, almost to the point where one could easily argue that John the Revelator was writing a polemic against the Babylonians, whom he probably (and correctly) felt had usurped the God of the Hebrews in the old Creation story, placing Marduk in the role rightly reserved to God and His Son, Jesus. Thus Revelation chapters 1-4 have their primary role as setting Jesus up as the true Master of the Heavenly throne, and giving praise to Him — and no other god — as the true Master of the Highest Heaven: Planet X.

The Seven Seals: Planet X Prepares for War

✡ Revelation 5:1-7:
¹And I saw in the right hand of him that sat on the throne a book written within and on the backside, sealed with seven seals.
²And I saw a strong angel proclaiming with a loud voice, Who is worthy to open the book, and to loose the seals thereof?
³And no man in heaven, nor in earth, neither under the earth, was able to open the book, neither to look thereon.
⁴And I wept much, because no man was found worthy to open and to read the book, neither to look thereon.
⁵And one of the elders saith unto me, Weep not: behold, the Lion of the tribe of Judah, the Root of David, hath prevailed to open the book, and to loose the seven seals thereof.
⁶And I beheld, and, lo, in the midst of the throne and of the four beasts, and in the midst of the elders, stood a Lamb as it had been slain, having seven horns and seven eyes, which are the seven Spirits of God sent forth into all the earth.
⁷And he came and took the book out of the right hand of him that sat upon the throne.

With Jesus now properly introduced as the Hero of the story, the next phase of the Book of Revelation discusses how the Hero is made the King of the Universe, by having the "keys to the Throne-Chariot" handed to Him by His Father. Having overcome sin and death, Jesus has earned the right to rule the universe, and His first duty is to take the reins of the mighty Throne-Chariot of God, and use it to defeat His Father's enemies on Earth. Taking the scroll from His Father's hands and then ascending to the throne, Planet X, Jesus is now officially God, and ready to crush all those who lay claim to the throne. Thus the stage is set for the great End-Time battle, when

God's Son will once again defeat the dragon that His Father had defeated "in the beginning", confirming His supremacy before the heavenly assembly that He is now King of the Universe. And the scroll, with its seven seals, holds the key to that victory.

☥ *The First Seal: Western Crusader War*
Year 1 of the 7-year Tribulation Period will be initiated by an attack by the West upon the East, most likely an attack of the United States against Iran. Though Jesus is portrayed in the Book of Revelation as the first mover in the great End-Time battle, the dragon's preparations for this battle have also been underway for thousands of years. After having been thrown down to Earth in ancient times, the dragon has been diligently working to raise an army in an attempt to storm heaven and take the throne of God for herself. Working covertly through various secret societies in the ancient Near East, and later in the countries of Europe, the Americas and eventually worldwide, the dragon has also been rebuilding her forces in secret, ready to make total war and bring the entire world under her dominion so as to raise an army against heaven itself. In order to accomplish this, she must create a world war to end all world wars, a war so chaotic and destructive that one-world rule will be necessary for mankind's survival. This situation will of course have been contrived, as mankind, had they followed the teachings of Jesus, would be living in a paradise. But with the dragon cast down from heaven to Earth and now ruling this prison planet, there will be no hope of ever achieving true freedom without the aid of a more powerful outside force that is stronger than the strong man armed.

The dragon's plan, which is now nearly complete, is to pit East against West in a winner-take-all fight for survival. Having raised up the Western powers and given them mighty gifts of technology, giving them her power and great authority by giving them the secrets locked within the riches of the Earth, she also created powerful and challenging opponents in the East, whom she also gave skills and powerful motivations that are able to undermine and undo the skills that she gave to the West. East and West, the two will wear down and cancel the other out, leaving the way open for a powerful third party to rise up and take control of the Earth after the old order is destroyed. One man, given power by the dragon, through secret societies working behind the scenes, will rise spectrally from the chaos, and the throne of the Earth will be given to this son of the dragon — one man to oppose the Son of God on His heavenly throne, to lead the armies of the Earth in their final battle against God's chosen.

✞ *The Second Seal: Eastern Counteroffensive*
By the end of year 1 of the 7-year Tribulation Period, there will be a general uprising of subversives and insurgents around the world, particularly in the West. After having raised up the right hand to strike the East, the left hand of the dragon will counterstrike against the West. The forces of Western order will be met by the forces of Eastern chaos, and while the serpent's head is crushed, it will also bite the heel, causing the rider to fall backwards, and anarchy to reign worldwide. Groups of insurgents that have been slithering into Western countries for decades will all revolt as one against the Western powers, massively disrupting the supply chain, bringing down governments, and ushering in an era of civil unrest in the West.

✞ *The Third Seal: Worldwide Economic Collapse*
Year 2 of the 7-year Tribulation Period will be characterized by a worldwide economic collapse. The result of this anarchic situation in the West will lead to a collapse of the worldwide financial system, which even now is on the brink. As a result, a Weimar Republic-like situation will arise, where it may once again require a wheelbarrow full of money to buy a loaf of bread. Systems will begin to critically degrade as what remains of the supply chain finally breaks down, and panic begins to set in as those who lived carelessly in the isles realize that the party's over.

✞ *The Fourth Seal: Global Anarchy*
Year 2 of the 7-year Tribulation Period will be completed by a period of general collapse of religious, social, economic and political order. After the supply chain coming from the West,

which feeds and supplies much of the rest of the world, breaks down, anarchy will spread all across the globe as millions of people, starving, begin to fight for their very survival. Local, regional and national wars will explode as peoples and nations wrestle each other for the precious few remaining resources left over from the former golden age of Western supremacy. Law and order will break down as the law of the jungle literally overrides civil order, with even the animals eating away at the fringes of failing civilization.

☥ *The Fifth Seal: The Downfall of Christendom*
Year 3 of the 7-year Tribulation Period will begin with the destruction of organized Christianity. With law and order completely broken down around the world, the forces of the dragon will then be able to act with impunity. Taking revenge against being destroyed and driven out of Europe by Christian monarchs, the secret societies will follow Order 666 and wipe out organized Christendom. Many if not most Christians who had been sadly deluded into believing the pretribulational rapture myth will find themselves completely unprepared for this chaos. Most of them will be executed by the rising New World Order of the Dragon, and those who survive will remain imprisoned in labor camps, or forced into hiding as organized Christendom ceases to exist.

☥ *The Sixth Seal: Planet X Returns*
Midway through the third year of the 7-year Tribulation Period, when the forces of the dragon have risen to completely take over the West and are poised to conquer the rest of the world, the LORD will begin his attack on the forces of the dragon by softening them up with a preliminary bombardment of asteroids. This bombardment will be so powerful that every land mass will move, meaning that Earth's crust will actually be temporarily slowed down in its turning — or possibly reversed, as it was in Joshua's day, when the sun and moon briefly stood still, and the LORD rained down rocks upon his enemies. (Joshua 10:10-14) Not only would this result in massive destruction from earthquakes, tidal waves and of course meteor strikes all over Earth, it would also result in time needing to bet reset on all of Earth's clocks —

possibly by several hours, depending on how far Earth's crust was displaced, and for how long.[9] Interestingly, it appears that the existence and rapid approach of Planet X is already generally known at that time, probably around the middle of the Tribulation Period, as the text says that everyone, from kings down to slaves, is scrambling to hide "from the face of him that sitteth on the throne." (Rev. 6:16) It is also interesting to note that God's throne has something to do with asteroids being hurled down from heaven to Earth, as only a planet-sized body could do that. So, based upon this fact, it may be that Planet X's cometlike tail has ignited by this time, and it is now visible to the entire world. Or, if it is not yet actually visible, it may have been discovered by advanced technology by this time, and its pending attack on Earth widely communicated in order to warn the people who remain alive and loyal to Earth to prepare to defend it from the Second Coming of Christ.

✝ *The Seventh Seal: Planet X Attacks*
Around the beginning of the fourth year of the 7-year Tribulation Period, the Lord will begin to attack Earth with a series of asteroidal and comet bombardments which will continue and increase until the end of the Tribulation Period. The seventh seal is largely a setup for the trumpet judgments, and is characterized by what appears to be a targeted bombardment of Earth by more asteroids based upon the specific prayers of the saints remaining on Earth. Like spotters shining lasers onto a bomb target, the Christians of that period will aid the LORD in targeting and continuing to weaken the forces of the dragon prior to the primary attack.

---

[9] Even normal earthquakes can actually shift Earth's crust a bit: Hector Becerra, "Easter Sunday earthquake shifted Earth's crust nearly 3 feet near Calexico", *Los Angeles Times Online*: http://articles.latimes.com/2010/jun/24/local/la-me-624-mexicali-earthquake-20100624. Though this shift was too small to force clocks to be reset, a much larger earthquake of the type described in Revelation 6:12-14 could.

The Seven Trumpets: Planet X Attacks

Whereas the first five seals had largely to do with the dragon's mobilization of her forces, marshaling and consolidating all of her earthly armies under the banner of her son, the Antichrist, seals 6 and 7 have to do with the reappearance of Planet X in the heavens to oppose the rising of the Antichrist and the utter destruction of his forces. Sneaking in like a thief in the night prior to that time, Planet X must have "ignited" around the middle of the Tribulation Period, coming close enough to the Sun for the process of sublimation to begin and its glorious tail to be unfurled like a banner of war. Midway through the Tribulation Period, then, Planet X must have come within range of Earth, close enough to start hitting Earth with asteroids that its gravitational pull no doubt launched in many directions as it passed through the asteroid belt. Thus the 6th and 7th seals, and all of the trumpets, have to do with increasingly frequent and more powerful attacks on the forces of the dragon with asteroids, and possibly also comets.

⊕ *The First Trumpet: A Massive Meteor Shower*
Probably sometime in the 5th year of the Tribulation Period, the "trumpets" will begin to blow. When the first trumpet sounds, "hail and fire mingled with blood" are cast down upon the entire Earth, burning up 1/3 of the trees and all the green grass. The use of the number 1/3 is interesting here, as 1/3 is also the number of the "stars" or angels that the dragon dragged down with him when he was thrown down to Earth. Thus the "trumpet" attacks appear to be limited in scope, specifically targeting the works of the dragon and its allies for destruction. Thus God's patience is manifest even in the End Times, targeting only those parts of the Earth that he deems unacceptable.[10]

It is important to note that this "hail" most likely refers to asteroids from the asteroid belt, many of which, as we have seen, contain large amounts of water ice. There are also many other accounts in the Bible where God has used "hail," "hailstones" or just "stones" falling from the sky to destroy His enemies (Ex. 9:18-24; Josh. 10:11; Ps. 18:12-13; Job

---

[10] Probably the LORD is targeting areas of forest and grass that has been artificially created by man, and therefore need to be destroyed lest they imbalance the natural order.

38:22-23; Isa. 30:30; Ezek. 13:11, 13; 38:22; Nahum 1:6; Rev. 8:7; cf. also Matt. 24:29; Mark 13:25; Rev. 6:13; 11:19; 12:4; 16:21). I believe that all of these references, of hail, hailstones, and stones in general, all refer to meteorites, containing varying mixtures of rock and water.

For example, in the Exodus reference, the hail was mixed with fire, meaning that the hail was probably actually a meteor shower. This would explain why the "hail" was afire and why it started fires on the ground where it hit. Psalm 18:12-13 describes God's coming as being accompanied by "hailstones and coals of fire," the parallel construction meaning that the hailstones and coals of fire are two different aspects of the same object: a meteor, which is essentially a red-hot, burning rock. Both Isaiah and Ezekiel mention that God's judgment will be by, among other things, fire and hailstones. Nahum also mentions that it is by "fire" and "rocks" that God judges his people. (Nahum 1:6) Last but not least, great Babylon itself will be destroyed by a "stone cut without hands" in Revelation 18:21.

Finally, the strange appearance of blood with the hail appears to indicate that these asteroids were originally created from a planet that once had animal life on it — animal life that had been destroyed and pulverized into basic organic matter, which looks like blood in appearance when mixed with water. This would explain why, as we saw in Chapter III, some asteroids have been found with organic materials on them, including simple proteins. If the primordial Earth had once hosted animal life upon its surface, then all that life would have been annihilated by the Giant Impact with the satellite of Planet X, pulverized and incinerated into a fine, black powder — exactly the sort of powder we find on the asteroids, comets, and, we believe, Planet X itself. Thus it may be that the primordial Earth, which once orbited between Mars and Jupiter, was called Tiamat, the "dragon planet" by the ancients, because this was the version of Earth on which the dinosaurs once lived and thrived. Thus, among many other things, the Giant Impact may have also wiped out the dinosaurs in the process of creating a new Earth whereon God created a brand new natural order that would be dominated not by reptilian, but by mammalian life forms.

All together, it is clear that meteors — not "hail" per se — are one of the primary weapons God uses against his enemies, particularly during the end times, and especially during the last battle at Armageddon. And the asteroid belt is the largest source of meteors in this solar system, so the connection is obvious. Passing through the asteroid belt on the way to Earth, Planet X will snare prodigious amounts of asteroids in its gravitational field, some of which will be hurled toward Earth like weapons.

⚴ *The Second Trumpet: A Huge Asteroid Falls into the Sea*
The second trumpet announces the arrival of a particularly large asteroid striking the sea. Such a large asteroid would cause massive devastation from earthquakes and tidal waves on all the surrounding coastal areas, and would of course wipe out all life in the impact area and for some ways around it. This would explain why 1/3 of the sea is turned to blood as a result of this impact, but it may also be that this asteroid also hosts a significant amount of organic matter from the primordial Earth, which would also make the sea literally turn to blood as the dehydrated blood of the pulverized animals of the primordial Earth rehydrates in the waters of the sea.

This "plague", like the hail of the first trumpet, is also highly reminiscent of the plagues of Egypt that Moses and Aaron witnessed. The fiery hail also happened in Exodus 9:22-26, and was predicted by Isaiah (30:30) and Ezekiel (38:22), who also predicted blood will rain down with the fire and the hail. The waters turning to blood also happened in Exodus 7:17-25, where not only the River Nile, but all the lakes, streams, and even the water kept in pots turned to blood. Thus the trumpet judgments appear to mirror the plagues of Egypt, except the trumpet judgments take place on a global scale.

⚴ *The Third Trumpet: Toxic Comet Syndrome*
Another large object, described as "burning like a torch", then falls upon the rivers and "the fountain of waters". One

single object could not strike every river on Earth, so it is more likely that this object releases some sort of toxin into the air, possibly exploding in mid-air after traveling some time through Earth's atmosphere much like the Tunguska meteor, thereby spreading its poisons far and wide through our atmosphere's wind currents. This poison, which is described as "Wormwood", will then essentially circulate throughout our atmosphere and precipitate out as rain over large parts of the world — effectively poisoning much of the world's water supply. Thus the rain is the "fountains of waters" described in this verse. And the rivers, lakes and streams, which are the first to collect the rain, and are the source of all of our fresh water, will be the first to be poisoned.

The description of the poison as "Wormwood" is interesting, as Wormwood, or *Artemisia absinthium* as it is known in the scientific community, is a bitter herb that is used in a variety of ways, including ridding the body of intestinal parasites (thus the name "worm wood"). It can also be fatal if taken in pure form.[11] However, it is best known as the main ingredient in absinthe, an alcoholic drink that also possesses mild hallucinogenic properties.[12] Wormwood, and its derivative, absinthe, are both known for their bitter taste, so the description of the waters turning "bitter" does seem to indicate that the herb absinthe is somehow involved.

The answer may lie in that same reason that blood is said to rain down along with the hail and the fire — this particular comet is full of plant life from the primordial Earth instead of animal life, so instead of raining down blood, it is instead raining down dehydrated, super-concentrated plant life from primordial times. And apparently these plants were the same or very similar to *Artemisia absinthium*, as the effects appear to be the same. In effect, a massive amount of concentrated absinthe, or possibly something much more potent, will be integrated into 1/3 of the world's fresh water supply, and those who do not die outright from the toxic waters will suffer terrible hallucinations.

---

[11] "Artemisia absinthium", *Wikipedia*: http://en.wikipedia.org/wiki/Absinth_Wormwood.

[12] "Artemisia absinthium", *Wikipedia*: http://en.wikipedia.org/wiki/Absinthe.

It would seem that God, tired of dealing with the drug-obsessed culture of the Earth, and wanting to take away their ability to escape the world's increasing ills through drugs, will give them the sort of drug-induced hallucinations that they crave — so much of it, in fact, that the ultimate "bad trip" that mankind will suffer as a result of the bitter waters will make many turn away from drugs, and those who do not will no longer find it a pleasurable experience. So, not unlike the plagues of Egypt, which served as warning signs for hundreds of generations afterwards, the plagues of the End Times appear to be setting fresh, new examples of what happens when you take drugs and engage in other sinful behaviors forbidden to mankind.

☥ *The Fourth Trumpet: Asteroid Winter*
It would appear that the first four trumpets are a group of events that occur in relatively rapid succession, as the "asteroid winter", or the throwing up of large amounts of dust and ashes into the atmosphere, could only have been caused by the asteroids that struck land masses as described back in Trumpet #1. That, and the fact that "an angel flying through the midst of heaven" warns about the next three trumpets, seems to indicate that the first four trumpets and the last three trumpets form subgroups within the seven trumpets sequence.

This asteroid winter is once again only partial in its application, as only 1/3 of the light of the Sun and 1/3 of the light of the Moon is affected. In other words, most of the dust and ashes thrown up by the asteroidal impacts is circulating nearer to the earth, closer to the horizon, so that that Sun and Moon are not clearly visible until they climb 30 degrees above the eastern horizon. And when setting, they will disappear from view 30 degrees above the western horizon, cutting short the days and making the Earth colder and less hospitable.

☥ *The Fifth Trumpet: Another Large Asteroid Strikes Earth*
Sometime in the 6th or 7th year of the Tribulation Period another large asteroid will strike Earth. This one, however, will strike a particularly sensitive area: the mouth of the Abyss, beneath which lie the legions of hell, which have been

prepared for a day and an hour to be released upon the Earth to torture and enslave those who swore their allegiance to the dragon. As we saw in our analysis of Job 26:6, the Abyss had been opened in a similar fashion at the Creation, when the Giant Impact ripped a gaping hole in Earth's crust and mantle, literally ripping the roof off of the Abyss and exposing it to space. Abaddon, the ruler of hell, according to Job 26:6, "had no covering", which protected him from detection, but also kept him from rising up and causing destruction on Earth's surface. So, this "star" with "the key of the bottomless pit", most likely is yet another asteroid striking the Earth.[13]

✪ The Sixth Trumpet: The Slaughter of the Semites

In the final year of the Tribulation Period, the sixth trumpet will sound, and the dragon's greatest act of villainy will unfold. This trumpet, and the 5^h trumpet that preceded it, appear to have more to do with the final mobilization of the dragon's forces just prior to God's attack on Earth. Just as Hitler ordered the extermination of all of the Semitic peoples in Germany, and wherever the iron boot of German military power reigned, so too will the dragon attempt to wipe out all of the remaining Semitic peoples, from India to Israel. To accomplish this foul deed, the dragon will raise up an army of Asian peoples of the East, 200,000,000 strong, to wage a war of extermination against all the descendants of Shem, from India to Israel, and everywhere in between. This will be done to make absolutely sure that there is no dissent remaining on Earth in order to maximize the efficiency of the dragon's armies when fighting against the Second Coming of Christ.

Yet the dragon and its worshipers do not know that the LORD has placed it in their hearts to gather themselves together against Him, because it is His intention to bring them all together into one place so as to destroy them most efficiently. For the sword of the LORD will be bathed in

---

[13] The smoke from the Abyss, the scorpion centaurs, and the rest will be handled in a separate book. A good reference for this subject is Tom Horn, *Apollyon Rising 2012: The Lost Symbol Found and the Final Mystery of the Great Seal Revealed,* (Crane, MO: Defender, 2010).

heaven, and come down upon His enemies, in judgment, with one swift stroke.

⊕ *The Seventh Trumpet: Planet X Attacks*
So great is the importance of the 7th trumpet, that a substantial amount of parenthetical material exists between it and the description of the 6th trumpet. Immediately after the description of the 6th trumpet, the scene seems so shift away from the armies of the dragon to a "mighty angel" which suddenly appears in heaven: "And I saw another mighty angel come down from heaven, clothed with a cloud: and a rainbow was upon his head, and his face was as it were the sun, and his feet as pillars of fire." (Rev. 10:1) However, though most commentators seem to think that this has nothing to do with the action on the ground, we now know, based upon our analysis to this point, that this is clearly a description of the glorious appearance of Planet X about to attack the forces of the dragon. The description of the object in heaven, surrounded by a cloud, its face bright as the sun, with a rainbow around it, sounds nearly identical to the description of God's heavenly throne in Revelation 4. Thus, the description of the "mighty angel" in Revelation 10 must be a description of Planet X's near fly-by, where it destroys the massed armies of the dragon in one swift stroke.

Then, after the description of the two witnesses, whose ministry no doubt has something to do with the revelation of the secret of Planet X, they are killed by no less a personage than Apollyon himself, the beast from the bottomless pit. Three and a half days later they rise again, however, resurrected along with the living and dead in Christ throughout history, and then, and only then, does Planet X attack.

After additional, important parenthetical material in verses 12, 13 and 14, designed to review the reason why God is judging Earth, including the throwing down of the dragon from heaven to Earth, the rising up of the beast government, and the mobilization of Earth to fight against Christ's Second Coming, what then follows is the resurrection of God's chosen from Earth prior to the attack by Planet X. This resurrection (which clearly happens here, at the seventh trumpet, and not at the beginning of the Tribulation Period) is described as another angel "like unto the Son of man" coming down from the heavenly throne with a sickle in his hand to reap the harvest of the Earth. This harvest, of course, is of all the saints since the beginning of human history, some of whom have been waiting for this moment for literally thousands of years.

Figure 7.4: A representation of the Jupiter-Io plasma torus (not to scale). The Io plasma torus is "a ring-shaped cloud of ions and electrons surrounding the planet Jupiter"[14] that passes between the poles of Jupiter and its nearest moon, Io. This sort of torus forms when planetary bodies with sufficient electrical charges pass near one another, the plasma showing the lines of electrical force between the poles of the two planets. When Planet X passes near Earth, a similar torus will be created, which is described in the Book of Revelation as two "sickles".

---

[14] "What Is the Io Plasma Torus?" *The University of Arizone Online:* http://vega.lpl.arizona.edu/iotorus/

This "sickle" in the hand of the angel who is "like unto the Son of man", is probably descriptive of the plasma torus that forms between the north and south poles of two planets as they pass near each other. As can be seen in figure 7.4 above, there is already a similar torus in our solar system, between Jupiter and its moon Io, and a similar torus will likely form as Planet X passes near Earth. This is what John the Revelator probably saw in his vision, and he described the torii as "angels" that reached out with "sickles" from the throne of God, Planet X. One of these torii, apparently the first to touch earth, apparently forms a sort of "rainbow bridge" that the redeemed from the Earth will use to cross over from Earth to Planet X.

This bridge may have been remembered in Norse mythology as the rainbow bridge "Bifrost" that connects Earth with the Norse heaven, "Asgard", which is a common theme in ancient mythology.[15] Thus, when Planet X passes near, that may be the mechanism God uses to resurrect and transport the righteous to heaven — via this "rainbow bridge". However, when the second "sickle" passes, instead of power being taken from Earth, the righteous along with it, power will be passed into Earth, and anyone who gets in the way, such as the armies of the dragon, will be utterly destroyed — which is exactly what happens next. The Sword of the LORD, the "grounded staff" passes near to Jerusalem and totally destroys the armies of the dragon, the blood reaching up to a horse's bridle up to 200 miles away. Needless to say, only the power of a planet could cause that much destruction so quickly.

The Seven Bowls: Planet X Victorious

And that is not all — there are still seven "bowl" judgments that need to occur. As Planet X passes by, probably only over a course of a few days, the most intense destructive power of the passing planet will come to bear on Earth and its remaining inhabitants:

✿ *The First Bowl:*
  Electromagnetic Pulse Burns out the Beast's Control System
  The first bowl appears to be targeting the beast kingdom's method of controlling its subjects. Without getting into too much detail, the "mark of the beast" is most likely an

---

[15] "Rainbows in Mythology", *Wikipedia*: http://en.wikipedia.org/wiki/Rainbows_in_mythology#Norse_mythology.

implanted microchip in the hand and/or forehead which, connected through a nanotechnology-created internal network inside the human body, connects those who have accepted the mark of the beast to a central computer, which literally controls their actions and, to some extent, their thoughts. In this way, Satan will control humanity in the End Times, by literally turning them into cyborgs — part man, part machine, and completely under his control.

However, the system is vulnerable to electromagnetic attack, so the first of the bowl judgments is to send out an electromagnetic pulse which will literally burn out the chips and internal networks that had been placed inside humanity by nefarious means, freeing them from the iron grip of the beast, but also making them much less coordinated and more easily conquered. Thus the "grievous sore" has to do with the chips and related technology being literally burned out from inside their bodies by an electromagnetic pulse, causing terrible burns to those who have the mark. This electromagnetic pulse could probably be caused by the airburst of a large asteroid, particularly one that had a large percentage of magnetic iron.

☥ *The Second Bowl: The Oceans of Earth Poisoned*

Much like the second trumpet judgment, the second bowl judgment will attack the seas, except this time, instead of 1/3 of all life dying, everything in the oceans will die. Without the restraining influence of the Holy Spirit keeping God's judgment in check, God is now able to freely attack His enemies with maximum force. In the process He destroys all of the dragon's maritime forces, but also, unfortunately, all life in the seas. It is interesting to note that the seas became like the blood of a dead man — if indeed the dehydrated blood of ancient life forms on the primordial Earth is responsible for the seas turning to blood, then the description of them being like "the blood of a dead man" is not so much a metaphor, but more like a statement of fact.

✟ **The Third Bowl: Rivers and Lakes Poisoned**
Much like the third trumpet judgment, the third bowl judgment will once again attack the rain cycle and the rivers and lakes, poisoning the fresh water supply for those who are left alive on Earth. However this time, instead of being poisoned by an absinthe-like substance, the rain and the waters they replenish will literally turn to blood, most likely due to another comet, this one filled with pulverized animal matter passing through the atmosphere instead of plant matter. Thus all the water on Earth will turn to blood, and all marine life will be destroyed.

✟ **The Fourth Bowl:**
Intense Light and Heat Reflected from Planet X
As Planet X passes by, its enormous cometlike tail with its high albeido will reflect back a great deal of sunlight onto Earth — seven times as much, according to Isaiah 30:26: "the light of the Moon shall be as the light of the Sun, and the light of the Sun shall be sevenfold, as the light of seven days, in the day that the LORD bindeth up the breach of his people, and healeth the stroke of their wound." This would literally happen if a large planet with a huge, cometlike coma passed by Earth, and the reflected light, both day and night, would make temperatures on Earth soar well past the ability for most life to endure.

✟ **The Fifth Bowl:**
Another Electromagnetic Pulse Takes out the Electrical Grid
And for those who have sufficient resources to be able to still afford air conditioning, God then turns out the lights, destroying the power grid with another massive electromagnetic pulse. With no lights, no air conditioning, no TV, Internet or any other creature comforts, there will be very few men left alive to oppose Christ's Second Coming. And those who are, will probably wish they were dead.

✟ **The Sixth Bowl: The Armies of Earth Led to their Doom**
The 6th bowl then sets up the remaining forces of the dragon for total destruction. The headwaters of the Euphrates River starts in the lakes of the Taurus Mountains in Asia Minor. By

drying up the Euphrates, the angel must be cutting off the headwaters of the Euphrates in the Taurus Mountains. Interestingly, as we saw previously in this chapter, the constellation of Taurus corresponds with the minor continent of Asia Minor. And beneath the constellation of Taurus is the constellation of Eridanus, the river of judgment. It could well be that this "river of judgment" in heaven prefigures the cutting off of the Euphrates River just prior to the judgment of mankind, just as Taurus prefigures the return of Planet X.

⊕ *The Seventh Bowl:*
One Last Massive Asteroid Finishes off the Beast
Finally, the 7th angel pours the 7th bowl into the air, which completes the judgment on Earth decreed by God. Though it is not explicitly stated, this last judgment is probably one last massive asteroid. This is because it is followed by the greatest earthquake since the Creation, and because Babylon is mentioned in this passage, and Babylon, according to Revelation 18:21, is destroyed by a great stone thrown down from heaven. Thus the Empire of the Beast will be finished off with one last, massive asteroid.

FINAL CONCLUSIONS

The rest of the Book of Revelation then describes Jesus returning on His white horse, most likely another metaphor for Planet X. He then finishes off the armies of the Antichrist with a "sharp sword" that goes forth from His mouth, and takes the throne of Earth away from the dragon, who is imprisoned for 1,000 years. Interestingly, after this 1,000 years is over, the dragon is once again loosed, the armies he raises to conquer Jerusalem once again destroyed by fire from heaven, after which time he is thrown into the lake of fire along with the beast and the false prophet. And then, the great white throne of God appears in heaven, heaven and Earth appear to be destroyed and, apparently, replaced by a new heaven and Earth. Could it be that this "great white throne" is once again Planet X, returning after 1,000 years? Could it be that Planet X is also being prepared to become the new Earth, replacing the old?

Upon reviewing the massive amount of evidence for the existence of another, "hidden" planet in our solar system, the conclusion is inevitable. Planet X has been searched for by mainstream astronomers for over a century, and is still sought after to this day. Ancient astronomers recorded the movements of this planet in the heavens, records which we still have, to this day. This planet was remembered in the ancient texts of the Hebrews, Sumerians, and many other peoples as the great throne-chariot of God in heaven, being known for going away for long periods of time and then suddenly returning, wreaking great destruction on Earth in the process. Moreover, many of the events described in the Book of Revelation, and other apocalyptic writings in the Bible, could only occur if caused by another planet passing near Earth. Lightning that destroys entire armies, wave after wave of asteroids and comets, a heavenly Sign that portends both the birth and the Second Coming of the Messiah, all point inevitably towards the existence of another planet in our solar system that moves in and out of our solar system "like a thief in the night". Conclusively, decisively, inevitably, the only logical conclusion that one can draw to answer all of these questions is that X marks the spot.

In that day the LORD with his sore and great and strong sword shall punish leviathan the piercing serpent, even leviathan that crooked serpent; and he shall slay the dragon that is in the sea.